TALKING BLUES

TALKING BLUES

The Police in their Own Words

ROGER GRAEF

RESEARCH BY MARC GILTROW

Collins Harvill
8 Grafton Street, London W1
1989

Collins Harvill
William Collins Sons and Co Ltd
London Glasgow Sydney Auckland Toronto Johannesburg

British Library Cataloguing in Publication Data

Graef, Roger
    Talking blues: the police in their own words.
    1. Great Britain. Police
    I. Title
    363.2'0941

ISBN 0–00–272436–7

First published by Collins Harvill 1989
© Roger Graef 1989
Reprinted 1989

Photoset in Monophoto Sabon by
Butler & Tanner Ltd, Frome and London
Printed and bound in Great Britain by
Butler & Tanner Ltd, Frome and London

To the families of police officers. I hope they will learn something useful about why their husband or wife, Mum or Dad is away for so long. I hope my family will understand as well.

Acknowledgements

I am deeply grateful to the hundreds of police officers who so willingly cooperated with the making of this book, and to the Chief Constables who gave me their blessing to work in their areas, especially my friend, Sir Peter Imbert, Commissioner of the Metropolitan Police, and Sir John Hermon of the RUC, among others I cannot name without disclosing their areas. Without the permissions granted by the various police forces who feature in the following pages this book would not have been possible, let alone published. I must particularly thank those who guided me through the shoals of police procedure as the book was being assembled. I cannot name the serving officers, but I can thank various representatives of the Police Federation and Brian Hilliard of *Police Review*, Barry Irving and Molly Wetheritt of the Police Foundation, and Professor Robert Reiner of Brunel University for their limitless support and attention to detail.

The patience of Laura House, Lucy Cohen, Anne O'Brien, Rachelle Gryn, Bonella Ramsay, Kylie Ferguson and the many others who transcribed the interviews was remarkable. The skill of the editors, Annabel Edwards and Mark Crean, and their dedication to the book was inspiring. It was like trying to put a large octopus into a small box and I learned a great deal from them. I am also grateful to Bill Swainson for seeing the book through its final stages with such care. But this book would not have happened without the commitment of the researcher, Marc Giltrow, who joined me several years ago in hopes of a job in television, and instead found himself deep in the world of police officers. He showed great resourcefulness throughout both the interviews and the compilation. Now his television career is launched, I hope his exceptional skills will be recognized.

Contents

Introduction

The British police are going through an extraordinary period of change, not apparent to the general public. The police have always taken the line that their affairs are well in hand, so their recent efforts to deal with internal problems have been underrated, if noticed at all.

It was the sheer implausibility of their public front during the 1970s that first led me to study the police. It was a difficult period. Experienced men were leaving for better-paid jobs. Recruiting was so poor that, as one Superintendent put it, "If you had two of everything – arms, legs, and eyes, and could read and write your name, you were in. They were dragging them in off the streets." The CID in both the Metropolitan and City of London police were badly compromised by corruption. The racist behaviour of some officers in areas with large black populations was laying the groundwork for the inner-city riots of the 1980s. Nevertheless, senior policemen dismissed their critics as politically motivated. But I also doubted whether the sweeping anti-police indictments were wholly accurate either.

I was given the chance to find out for myself when the BBC asked me to produce a lengthy television series from inside the police, in the so-called "fly on the wall" mode, observing and filming the police in their normal work over the best part of a year.

Making the two television series *Police* and *Operation Carter* with the Thames Valley Constabulary and Regional Crime Squad No.5 took three years. We came to see the police neither as thugs and villains nor as morally perfect heroes, but as a group of ordinary people asked to do extraordinary things. The pressures of police work are usually invisible to the public, who expect them to behave with equanimity in the face of all provocation. Some officers have only two O-levels as formal education, yet do more writing than most of us, and may be cross-examined on every word in court by highly-trained specialists. Entering the force as early as their teens, they may face domestic emotional crises with people many years senior to them, meet danger from much stronger adversaries, or enter physical, psychological and legal predicaments that require skill and finesse to defuse. Yet their training is far shorter than for the other professions who deal with those situations, such as social workers, nurses, doctors, and lawyers. Even with recent extensions, British police receive less training than most other forces in Europe.

The *Police* series challenged the official version of police perfectability by showing their mortality on television. It was criticized from within some police circles for presenting an unfair picture which undermined their standing with the public. I disagree. I do not believe that public support depends on the illusion that policemen seldom make mistakes or misbehave like the rest of the society from which they are drawn. In my view, the Thames Valley officers who allowed themselves to be filmed "warts and all" helped people understand the police predicament at least as much as the attacks on the times we live in by various Chief Constables on the warpath against their critics. An NOP poll taken after the series ended showed that most people's perception of the police was either unchanged or positively improved by what they saw.

I suspect this book may produce similar reactions inside and outside the police. It arose from the recognition that the inner-city riots and the miners' strike had changed policing dramatically in the six years since the *Police* series was shown.

The police have been at violent odds with a certain section of society for the past one hundred and fifty years, but until recently their encounters were rarely seen by the rest of the public. In one of what I found to be several parallels to the Vietnam war, the television presentation of the urban riots and miners' strike made an important difference to the public's perception of the police. Although each side complained that the media were biased against them, the wide coverage – largely edited highlights of the violence – showed policemen in such adversarial roles that their whole relationship to the public seemed to shift. Their newly acquired protective armour rendered them anonymous and frightening.

To go behind the riot shield, my researcher, Marc Giltrow, and I interviewed some five hundred officers from twelve different forces, including the RUC. We spoke to people of every age and rank from Chief Constable to beat PC, to old hands and new recruits, including some from ethnic minorities and some who had recently left the force. Our method was to record anonymously, so that the people talking could express themselves without fear of recriminations from senior officers. To protect their identities in the book, key details have been changed. The accuracy of the interviews in such books is always open to question, as subjects may well be giving highly coloured or selective accounts of events that happened under circumstances impossible to confirm. However, in sensitive areas such as corruption and marital problems, officers and their wives have little to gain by fabricating stories.

Nor is it possible to include all that people said. Our interviews probably contain some fifty times as much material as is published in this book. Nevertheless, there was remarkable consistency across the country on many subjects, particularly among lower ranks.

I have tried to present *Talking Blues* as an emotional mosaic, hoping to convey the essence of what it is like to police Britain today, particularly for those in uniform serving in larger towns and cities. This is a book of voices, organized to reflect what the officers we spoke to feel the public do not understand about their job.

Much as I admire them, I have not tried to use the pure form of Studs Terkel and Tony Parker because the complexities of current policing need too much explanation to serve just as a slice of social realism. There may well be another side to each of the accounts we were given, but that does not mean they can be dismissed. They are the distillation of a lot of strong feeling. Of course, not all police officers and their wives feel this way, but three years of interviewing has shown that many do.

The interviews took place at all hours of the day and night, in cars, in every part of stations from the cells to the canteen, in pubs and private houses, off and on duty. Some were done while delivering parking tickets in armoured cars in the most dangerous parts of West Belfast, or dodging bottles and stones in the middle of the night at the Notting Hill Carnival. Many more were carried out during the stupefying limbo that is standard policing, walking up and down the same streets, or standing around for hours at demonstrations in Trafalgar Square and Wapping.

Virtually all the interviewees were chosen at random from officers likely to be exposed to the pressures of modern policing. On the whole we avoided the specialist squads, and the CID, on the grounds that it was the uniform branch, the ordinary beat officers in particular, who have borne the brunt of the criticism and violence during and after the riots and the miners' strike. The CID were seldom involved in either. At the same time the ordinary bobby on the beat is now expected to rebuild the links to the public, and restore confidence in police ability to win what is known as the War Against Crime.

We asked those bobbies and their supervising officers to describe what it feels like to be on the receiving end of such violence and criticism. The police officers we spoke to were unanimous that the media was against them, and that no one put their point of view. As one Scottish Inspector put it, "It's bloody unfair that if a cameraman catches an officer in what may be an isolated moment of violence, if the news editor decides to show it – out of context, without showing the patience or the provocation that led up to it – those ten seconds can blight that officer's career."

That police are by far the most widely covered profession on television through fact and fiction makes no difference to their sense of isolation from the public. They also feel cut off from their senior officers, whom they believe left the beat too long ago to know what it is like out there now.

The lack of a shared history is a major problem in the police today. The gap is not just between the perceptions at the top and the bottom normal to any organization, but also in the middle: and the differences do not simply correspond to rank. The force is split between the Old Guard and New Guard, the "hard" and "soft" policemen, those who admit there are things that need changing, and those who prefer things as they were done in the past.

The most important division is over the issues at the heart of the Scarman Report on the causes of the Brixton Riots of 1981, which figure large in police thinking, especially in urban forces. Lord Scarman's call for more community policing, for more formal liaison with the public, for improved training and better handling of complaints, and for a greater sensitivity towards racial differences have all been taken seriously at the top. Many changes have been made to implement them. How much they affect the day to day behaviour of officers recruited and trained before this change of heart is a deeply intractable matter.

The mounting concern about assaults on and by policemen suggests, yet again, there is a gap between the theory professed by senior officers and the practice on the streets and in the privacy of police vans. It spreads confusion and mistrust both within police circles and among the public whose renewed trust is a major aim of all the changes.

This struggle between old and new, hard and soft, liberal and autocratic styles of policing and management is being fought in earnest. In this book, I have taken the key issues one by one and where possible present both sides. A brief summary suggests the level of change involved:

1. After several disastrous mistakes, the number of officers eligible to carry firearms has been cut. Many handed in their authorizations and the procedures for issuing them have been tightened up.

2. The training of recruits has been transformed from rote learning and square bashing to an open-ended liberal style of teaching that encourages individual development. It has been extended by six weeks to deal with ethnic differences and what they call "human awareness".

3. In some forces, control has been decentralized to area level wherever possible, and consultation of all ranks, though far from effective yet, is now encouraged as standard management practice.

4. To combat corruption, senior uniform officers at area head-quarters now oversee much of the CID. Promotion within the CID requires a return to uniform at each rank.

5. The lack of trained leadership and proper equipment caused

chaos during the inner-city riots. Both have been provided in recent years. Since 1986, public disorder has changed from large to small-scale disturbances. The level of public order training may now be too intense for current needs.

6. Stress and welfare are no longer taboo words: provision for stress counselling of some sort has been established in some forces and is growing in acceptance as a necessary support.

7. New training and facilities have been established – albeit on a modest scale – for the handling of rape, child abuse and domestic violence, which are now acknowledged as having been badly handled in the past.

These are encouraging signs for those of us who wish the police to build a relationship with the public that allows them to do their job, while we carry on about our business, exercising our rights within the law. In many parts of Britain that is what happens. But in the cities, many officers are worried by the grey areas in which mistrust on both sides can so easily lead to trouble. The confusion in their job description between enforcing the law and keeping the peace confronts them daily in what they call "sensitive" areas. They are supposed to have discretion. It was "handed to them as they left training school" in the old days, now it is directly encouraged. But they feel second-guessed at every turn by the public, the media, their senior officers and the courts. No one seems aware of what the moment of decision on the streets feels like to the officer involved.

Although the majority of police officers vote Conservative, many officers resent being seen as political pawns, assumed to be siding with the government on any issue which they are called in to police. The police cannot be held responsible for cruise missiles, nuclear dumping, student loans, the closure of pits or printing works, or youth employment. Yet, as the most visible symbols of authority the police are the targets for stones and bottles in situations they are powerless to affect.

In the miners' strike, they complained of the government's decision not to use the courts and the newly passed civil law instead of the police on the ground. Many resented the use of Special Branch to raid the BBC in connection with the Zircon affair. Others objected to being caught between News International and the printers at Wapping.

Many officers feel betrayed by a government which employs the rhetoric of law and order but which has left them for long stretches with police cells full of remand prisoners, and with no new men to deal with the "War on Drugs". The number of police officers has risen by 11 per cent in the decade since 1979, but one per cent per year is not enough to make an impact on the streets. To the police, the reality of government support is tested in such issues as the pressure to civilianize and privatize police jobs, and the threat to rent allowances that nearly brought the lower ranks out on strike last year. Spending on the police has gone up 52 per cent since 1979, yet enforced local authority cuts hit overtime bills and squeeze resource budgets that directly affect policing strategies. The Drugs Squad in at least one major city cannot afford the overtime for the long-term surveillance needed to secure convictions. They cannot even buy their own binoculars. The Chief Constable of the Royal Ulster Constabulary recently announced that there were insufficient funds to tackle both terrorism and community policing. The long-term benefits of community policing have gone to the wall in favour of "hard" short-term fire fighting strategies which do nothing to solve fundamental problems in Northern Ireland. Similar decisions have been taken in the other trouble spots around Britain. Those same community police officers saw no expense spared on overtime during the miners' strike or at Wapping.

This engenders cynicism both among the officers charged with reaching out to the public, and among those members of the public whose trust is essential for the police to do their job. This is not a glib notion. The police on their own can only affect a small proportion of crime – that committed in public, like pub fights. The rest, from drug dealing, rape and murder to burglary and fraud take place in private. In the vast majority of cases it takes members of the public to report and provide the evidence for crimes to be solved.

How is this public trust to be won? Saatchi & Saatchi are currently engaged in trying to win it through advertising. Wolff Olins, corporate image specialists, have done a useful report for the Metropolitan Police. Amongst their suggestions are new and better fitting uniforms bearing the officer's name (as is customary in the United States), police cars bearing their local station name, and improvements to police stations both for the public and the police. These are more than cosmetic changes and should be implemented.

But it is the conduct of the police which must make the strongest impression on public trust. Recently, tens of thousands of students protested against the abolition of student grants by blocking Westminster Bridge. The majority of the students were peaceful, but a small minority threw missiles at the police. After enduring the barrage for a time, the police used mounted officers riding at a gallop to clear the bridge. Horses charging youths evoked images of Wapping, Orgreave, and Red Lion Square – where a student was killed – at a time when such memories were beginning to fade. The police believed they had good reason to charge, but that must be set against the long-term cost – a negative memory for those students, their friends and families, and the millions who saw it on television.

The violent minority, or "Rent-a-Mob", as the police call them, are not just creations of right-wing paranoia. Many of the same people are a regular source of provocation at most demonstrations. At Wapping, they joined the pickets after the pubs closed and then the violence would start. Taking their taunts and missiles wears the patience of PCs standing in the cold. But responding to them reverses what Robert Mark described as the police secret: "Winning while appearing to lose." Charging crowds at the gallop is losing while appearing to win.

Although the police see themselves as "piggy in the middle", to their critics they are also one side of a vice in which the state on the other squeezes whoever is caught in between. In January 1989, Viraj Mendis, a Sri Lankan student, was seized forcibly from sanctuary in a church by more than fifty Greater Manchester police officers. However firm the legal basis for their action, such hard tactics hand police critics their next issue on a plate, and alienate the Asian community from whom recruits are being sought. What is worse, it confirms stereotypes on all sides.

Yet the policemen who perform such duties, like those who came back from Brixton, Toxteth, Tottenham and Orgreave, the Falls Road and Londonderry, cannot understand why they are not thanked for defending our democracy. It is another echo of the Vietnam war, when returning GIs encountered the same hurtful hostility. I use the Vietnam parallel because I can find no other recent event which adequately describes the shock which the riots and miners' strike delivered to the police in general, and many officers as individuals. The degree of violence was so extreme and unexpected, like lightning it cracked the foundations of police confidence about their place in society. The long-term effects are still emerging. In Northern Ireland two decades of terrorism have produced battle fatigue in the RUC, especially since the Anglo-Irish Agreement has provoked Protestant hatred against the police as well.

This is the essence of the current confusion now facing our police. They are deemed to act for the public against the public. In public order situations, neutrality is impossible, yet the next day they are back on the beat maintaining good community relations with the same students, miners, lager louts and black youths they were confronting the day before. The fiction is unconvincing to all parties. But under orders and force policy, the PCs involved must go along with it. The aggression and mistrust is often real and mutual – the phrase "army of occupation" was used often by the police – but soft policing strategies in the worst areas of tension stop PCs from arresting people and doing their job as they see it. If they do act, they risk a complaint that stays on their record, even if it is unproven. When combined with the public pressure on the police to produce results, this predicament is what psychologists call a double bind. And it drives people mad.

Glossary

AA Alcoholics Anonymous. Support group run by and for ex-drinkers.

ABH Aggravated Bodily Harm. Minor cuts, bruising around the eye, or shock caused by an assault. (See also GBH.) Defined in Section 47 of the Offences Against the Person Act 1861.

AFO Authorized Firearms Officer.

All Saints Road Short street in West London near Portobello Road, central to local West Indian community. Until recent crackdown, scene of regular drug traffic. Locals organize the annual Notting Hill Carnival, the largest event of its kind in Europe.

Area Beat Specific area for patrol. Often officers are given the same beat so they become familiar with its community. (Also known as Home Beat and Community Beat.)

Area Car Police vehicle assigned to back up a large number of foot beats. With current manpower shortages, it is often the only cover for large stretches of territory.

ACC Assistant Chief Constable. Responsibilities cover (1) Territorial operations (general police work) (2) Specialist operations (inc. Special Branch, Central Crime Squads, etc), (3) Personnel and training (4) Management support (inc. complaints).

Beanfield, Battle of the Nickname for a violent confrontation between police and hippies en route to Stonehenge in 1985.

Beat Crimes Minor crimes reported locally.

Bird, Doing Serving a prison sentence.

Brief Lawyer in East London slang.

Brixton Area in South London with large black community. Scene of major riots against the police in 1981 and 1985.

Broadwater Farm Modern council estate in Tottenham, northeast London. Scene of major riot in 1985.

Bizzy (Busy) Police officer (Merseyside term).

Cadet Sixteen to eighteen-year-old trainee police officers. Few in number, due to scarce resources.

Canteen Cowboy Macho officer who sets the tone in the canteen culture. The term is always used derogatorily.

Canteen Culture Informal ethos of the lower ranks at the sharp end: often cynical, racist, sexist and aggressive in words, but not always in deeds.

Carrier Transit van used for patrolling and transporting prisoners back to the station. Scene of most complaints of police violence.

Car Squad Officers assigned to solve and prevent car thefts.

Castlereagh Belfast holding centre used to question suspected terrorists.

CC Chief Constable. The most senior officer in each police force with the exception of the Met. (See Commissioner.)

Charge Room The room to which all arrested prisoners are brought first, to be charged, searched and registered, before being put into a cell.

CI Chief Inspector. In charge of men, operations or administration.

CID Criminal Investigation Department.

CLO Community Liaison Officer.
CPO Community Police Officer.
CRO Community Relations Officer. Officers with special local responsibility for liaison with public, via schools, council committees, Neighbourhood Watch schemes, ethnic groups, etc. Often work in plain clothes. Not part of shift system.

Code of Practice Guidelines for the implementation of PACE.

Collator Local intelligence officer who pools and circulates data about local criminal fraternity and any other useful news. (Members of the public may ask to see what is held about them.)

Commander Met only. Rank above Chief Superintendant.

Commissioner The most senior officer in the Metropolitan Police.

Community Beat (see Area Beat.)

Criminal Injuries Compensation Board provides compensation to individuals (now including police officers) injured by a criminal act.

Customs and Excise Department of the Treasury which deals, amongst other things, with VAT offences and drugs at the point of entry into the UK.

Custody Sergeant Created by the Police and Criminal Evidence Act (PACE) to ensure the proper handling of prisoners. Is held responsible for all that happens in the cells and charge room.

D and D Drunk and disorderly. Each area has its own wording or favourite bylaw for arresting people causing a local nuisance.

Deputy Assistant Commissioner Met only. (See Assistant Chief Constable).

DCC Deputy Chief Constable. Amongst other duties, responsible for discipline.

Deputy Commissioner Met only. Shares responsibility with Commissioner for force policy, also annual force inspection.

DSU District Support Unit. Some ten PCs and a Sergeant who patrol the area waiting to be called as backup. Often said to be looking for trouble. In London, now replaced by more tightly supervised Territorial Support Group (TSG).

Duty Officer/Sergeant Operational responsibility for the shift.

Fatal Incident in which someone has died. Usually associated with traffic.

Fit Up To frame someone by planting, adding to or tampering with evidence.

Flying Squad Elite group of top Scotland Yard detectives. Alleged to be heavily masonic, and corrupt in 1970s, but also very good at their job.

GBH Grievous Bodily Harm. Under the Offences Against the Person Act 1861, Section 18, even a minor injury is GBH if there is intent to harm. Section 20 makes any serious injury GBH with or without intent. (See also ABH.)

Handsworth Area of Birmingham with large ethnic minority and long-standing reputation for good community relations, which was shattered in the rioting of 1985.

Hendon Metropolitan Police training school.

Home Beat Officer often live on beat and work their own hours rather than the shift system.

Hytner Report Inquiry headed by Benet Hytner, QC, appointed to investigate causes of Moss Side riots in 1981.

Inspector Responsible for relief/section/shift.

Met Metropolitan Police. Force of 27,000 officers, the largest in Britain. Responsible for Greater London except for the City.

M.O. Modus operandi, used to identify criminals through their distinctive method of operation in a burglary or fraud, etc.

Moss Side Area in Manchester with large West Indian community. Poor police–public relations. Scene of riots in 1981 and 1985.

Observation (also **obbo**, **obs**) Hidden surveillance of a suspect.

OTS Over the side. Married officer being unfaithful.

PACE Police and Criminal Evidence Act 1984. Major new law codifying hundreds of earlier Acts, codes and powers guiding police on the street and in the station (e.g. Judges' Rules).

Peach, Blair A London teacher killed during the Southall riot of 1979. Although the finger pointed at the Special Patrol Group (SPG), the inquest returned a verdict of Death by Misadventure.

Plod A derogatory name for a PC.

Plonk A derogatory term for a WPC.

Previous Previous convictions.

PSU Police Support Unit. Group of ordinary PCs, Sergeant and Inspector who are riot-trained. Sent to help other forces.

PT 17 Full-time Met firearms squad. (Level 2 does most sieges and CID raids, etc. Level 1 are also firearms instructors.)

Racial Awareness Course Explores racism. Informs officers of the customs of ethnic groups (e.g. purdah, turbans and ceremonial knives).

Rape Suite Special rooms decorated in a homely way to help reassure rape victims.

RCS Regional Crime Squad. Teams of detectives seconded from neighbouring forces to deal with major crime. There are nine in England and Wales.

Relief In London and some forces, the basic group of PCs, Sergeants and Inspector on normal 8 hour duties together. In most forces called a section.

Relief Bicycle Derogatory term referring to the sexual availability of certain women police officers.

Royal Commission on Criminal Procedure (1979) Codified the hundreds of common law powers under which the police previously operated. Prompted by concern at the Maxwell Confait case.

RUC Royal Ulster Constabulary. 10,000 officers plus 2000 Reserve officers who police Northern Ireland. All male officers trained to bear firearms.

SAO Serious Arrestable Offence. Any crime for which the penalty is more than five years in prison.

SAS Special Air Service.

SB Special Branch. Responsible for political aspects of police work, involving watching and assessing any activity which may threaten the stability of the state. Originally founded to fight the Fenians, forerunners of the IRA.

Scarman Report (1981) Influential study of the causes of the 1981 Brixton riots. It proposed major changes to urban policing.

Section 38 (Offences Against the Person Act 1861). Covers assault with intention to resist arrest.

Section 47 (Offences Against the Person Act 1861). Defines categories of assault against the person. (See also ABH, and GBH.)

Section One (of PACE) Removed the "SUS" Law (see SUS) and redefined police powers of stopping and searching.

Section House Subsidized accommodation for police officers, similar to army barracks, but with private rooms and amenities.

Section Sergeant Assigns PCs to beats. All sergeants also called "skippers".

Serious Crime Squad Team of detectives assigned to major crimes.

Shift/Section (See Relief).

Situation book Daily record of CID office work in hand.

Skipper Sergeant.

SPG Special Patrol Group. Metropolitan Police version of the Support Group. Disbanded in 1986 and replaced by the TSG after much controversy at their role in riots and strikes.

Square Box (... into the square box) Reference to the witness box in court.

Station Officer/Sergeant Responsible for station. First line of contact with the police.

Street Duties Sergeant A Sergeant who makes up weekly and monthly notes.

Superintendent In charge of a sub-division at a large station.

SUS Nickname for a section of the Vagrancy Act 1824, which gave the police powers to stop and search on *suspicion* of a person being about to commit a crime.

TA Traffic accident.

Taking and Driving Away Theft of a motor vehicle.

TIC Taken into consideration. Reference to other crimes which a prisoner may take responsibility for.

Tom Prostitute.

Toxteth Triangle Area in Liverpool 8 where the highest proportion of ethnic minorities live. Long record of poor police/public relations. Scene of riots during the 1980s.

TSG Territorial Support Group. Specially trained unit of the Met deployed as mobile reserve in sensitive and often potentially violent police operations. (See SPG.)

Verbal Unofficial practice of saying that a suspect said something when the suspect claims he didn't.

Vice Squad Officers who deal with prostitution and pornography.

Welfare Department that deals with widows and pensions. Now linked to a counselling service in some forces for police officers.

RANK AND SALARY STRUCTURE*

METROPOLITAN POLICE

Commissioner
£68,500

Deputy Commissioner
£54,231

Deputy Assistant Commissioner
£38,277

Commander
£33,591

Chief Superintendent
£28,000–£30,000

Superintendent
£25,629–£27,831

Chief Inspector
£18,840–£20,958

Inspector
£16,593–£18,840

Sergeant
£14,466–£16,593

Police Constable
£8,352–£15,123

Special Constable
unpaid

OTHER FORCES

Chief Constable
£40,000–£50,000†

Deputy Chief Constable
£35,000–£40,700†

Assistant Chief Constable
£33,591

Chief Superintendent
£28,000–£30,000

Superintendent
£25,629–£27,831

Chief Inspector
£18,840–£20,958

Inspector
£16,593–£18,840

Sergeant
£14,466–£16,593

Police Constable
£8,352–£15,128

Special Constable
unpaid

* as at 1 September 1988 (source: *Police Review*).
† salary linked to size of population and force area.

A Decade of Trouble

1980

JAN Supt. John Keane, ex-Met Flying Squad detective, jailed for three years for trying to bribe a fellow officer with £10,000 to let a man go free.

APR Drugs raid on the only black café still open in St Paul's area of Bristol leads to riot that leaves 19 officers wounded. At one point police withdraw altogether. Subsequent court cases fail to secure convictions.

APR Gunmen occupy the Iranian Embassy in London, holding a PC among the hostages. After six days of police siege, the SAS storm the building.

APR A London coroner's court holds that Blair Peach, a teacher, died by misadventure during clashes between the local Asian community and the police following an anti-National Front demonstration in Southall in 1978. Recommends that the Met's Special Patrol Group (SPG), accused of causing Peach's death, be more tightly controlled. Also disapproves of police use of unauthorized weapons.

JUNE In Birmingham, a West Midlands officer shoots pregnant Gail Pinchin dead when her boyfriend uses her as a shield in the dark.

JUNE Law Lords rule "with regret" it is unlawful to seize assets of drug smugglers in Operation Julie. Their appeal against seizure is allowed, but assets are kept by Inland Revenue as tax arrears.

JULY After investigating 274 deaths in police custody 1970–80, the Commons Home Affairs Committee finds no evidence to support allegations of police brutality in police stations.

SEPT Four City of London officers jailed for stealing £2700-worth of clothing while investigating a burglary at Austin Reed. Two other officers are convicted later.

DEC In 1980, ten officers are killed (nine are RUC).

1981

JAN Royal Commission on Criminal Procedure reports, "balancing" the needs of the police with rights of the accused. Critics attack proposals for detailed powers for police against vague protection for individuals.

JAN A fire at a home in Deptford in South London kills thirteen black people. Arson suspected. Conflicting evidence in heavily criticized coroner's court leads to open verdict. Black community accuses police of ignoring possible racial motive.

JAN West Yorkshire police arrest Peter Sutcliffe for "Ripper" murders. He is later jailed for life, with a minimum of thirty years. Police criticized for having interviewed him early in the inquiry and let him go.

FEB Home Secretary announces a joint inquiry by Home Office and police into extreme right-wing organizations and racial violence.

FEB Errol Madden, a black youth who confessed during detention in Battersea Police station to stealing two toy cars, is freed. Charges are withdrawn when evidence is produced that he had a receipt.

MARCH March in support of Deptford fire victims breaks into rioting and looting as it passes through Fleet Street.

MARCH Met bans marches in London to prevent a National Front march in Lewisham, South London. Similar bans are imposed in Barnsley, Leicester, Rotherham, Sheffield and Wolverhampton.

MARCH In Brixton, South London, the SPG begin Operation Swamp '81, saturation policing to combat street crime. At the end of three weeks, 1000 stops lead to 100 arrests, and high tension on the streets.

APRIL Following a disputed stabbing incident in Brixton, hundreds of white and black youths embark on three days of looting and rioting. Government announces urgent inquiry headed by Lord Scarman.

MAY IRA hunger striker Bobby Sands dies in prison, after being elected Sinn Fein MP for West Belfast. Home Office admits two prisoners in solitary confinement for two years.

MAY Labour wins control of many Police Authorities in local authority elections, and aims to make Chief Constables more accountable. In Thames Valley, new leadership tries to block £1.5 m investment in computer system for local intelligence. In Merseyside, the Labour manifesto involves detailed changes including dismantling Special Branch. The GLC tries to establish itself as the Met Police Authority to replace direct control by the Home Secretary. All such changes are resisted on the grounds of "keeping politics out of policing".

MAY 10,000 Asian and white people march through Coventry demanding protection from racist attacks.

JUNE Stuart Blackstock given life for shooting of PC Philip Olds in December 1980, leaving him paralysed. Olds later commits suicide.

JUNE Operation Countryman, Dorset Police investigation into corruption in the Met and City of London police, is aborted. A second trial ends with acquittal of two detectives accused of stealing £18,000 from the proceeds of a £500,000 robbery.

JUNE Met Commissioner Sir David McNee announces robberies and muggings risen by 20 per cent since 1980. 60 per cent of those arrested for such crimes are under twenty-one.

JUNE Lord Scarman's inquiry into the Brixton riots opens.

JUNE Police confront a violent mob in Peckham, South London.

JUNE Asians and skinheads clash in Southall. Police accused of allowing racist provocations.

JULY Police in Toxteth, Liverpool 8, attempt to arrest a black youth for stealing his own motorbike. Angry mob of white and black youths go on rampage, and serious riot ensues. Hospital looted and doctors attacked.

Reinforcements summoned from neighbouring forces. Rioting lasts for three days.

JULY In Manchester, Moss Side police station besieged by crowd throwing petrol bombs after racist taunts to black youths. Also disturbances in London, Reading, Hull, Preston, Sheffield, Wolverhampton, Bradford, Leeds, Halifax, Huddersfield, Cirencester, Blackpool and Birmingham. "Copycat rioting" blamed by Mary Whitehouse and others on wide television coverage; later disproved by British Film Institute research.

JULY Later in month renewed rioting in Toxteth, met by hard police tactics including driving Land Rovers at crowd which leads to death of handicapped bystander, and first use of CS gas on mainland.

JULY Lord Scarman calls Operation Swamp '81 "a serious mistake" and a primary cause of Brixton riots, along with poor inner-city conditions. Chair of Liverpool Police Authority, Councillor Margaret Simey, says conditions are so bad in Toxteth residents "would be apathetic if they didn't riot". Mrs Thatcher rejects unemployment or poor housing as cause of violence, ascribing it to "criminal greed". Government approves use of water cannon, CS gas, plastic bullets. Police Federation spokesman, Eldon Griffiths, MP, demands guns be available as well.

AUG Met announce a special reserve of 500 officers as potential response to public order disturbances. New ban imposed on demonstrations in London.

SEPT Association of Chief Police Officers (ACPO) criticize John Alderson, Chief Constable of Devon and Cornwall for suggesting "the police are in danger of sacrificing a tradition which is the envy of the world because of a few hours of madness on the streets".

SEPT James Anderton, Chief Constable of Greater Manchester, refuses to give evidence to inquiry headed by Benet Hytner, QC, into Moss Side riots. Manchester Police Authority therefore decline to hear Anderton's report on the violence. Greater Manchester police acquire two submachine guns for evaluation but fail to inform the police authority.

DEC In 1981, twenty-three officers are killed (twenty-one are RUC).

1982

FEB BBC *Police* series shown. Outcry over the "Allegation of Rape" episode after judge sentences rapist to two years on grounds that victim "asked for it" by hitchhiking in the late evening. Thames Valley announces all-woman squad to deal with rape cases.

MARCH In last of three Operation Countryman trials, four Scotland Yard detectives acquitted of "fitting up" two known criminals in 1977.

MARCH Met issue statistics which break down offenders by racial group for the first time. They are heavily criticized for reinforcing racial stereotypes, and for exaggerating small increases by showing them in percentage terms.

MAY Home Office Minister arranges for Met to be given three German water cannon for testing. Plans to use them are dropped due to operational problems in London streets.

JUNE Trials of major London bank robbers abandoned after Regional Crime

Squad detective is secretly taped by defence solicitor offering inducement for help catching corrupt Met officers.

JULY Eight die when IRA bomb explodes as Horse Guards ride between Knightsbridge and Whitehall. Three more people killed when another IRA bomb explodes within minutes at a Regents Park bandstand where Royal Greenjackets are playing.

JULY Fourteen people arrested after IRA bombing of Chelsea barracks. Eleven are released after seven days of questioning. Police criticized for allegedly depriving the suspects of basic rights and facilities.

JULY Barry Prudom, wanted by South Yorkshire police for the killing of two police officers, is shot dead by a police marksman after holding a family hostage and shooting at police officers.

JULY Police embarrassed when Michael Fagan is apprehended inside Buckingham Palace. He had entered before, but not been detected. On 9 July, while on remand, he spent some time at the Queen's bedside. Sergeant on duty is later transferred for failing to respond to the Queen's request for assistance. The Queen's Personal Bodyguard, Commander Michael Trestrail, resigns following media coverage of the palace break-in and his homosexuality. Michael Fagan is eventually acquitted of burglary and theft of half a bottle of wine.

NOV Met reserve of specially equipped anti-riot police is used to disperse a crowd of 600 youths, mostly black, in Brixton in South London. No serious injuries occur.

NOV Three RUC officers are killed when a roadside bomb explodes at Craigavon in Northern Ireland.

NOV A special squad of RUC officers shoot dead three unarmed suspected IRA terrorists when their car fails to stop at a police road block.

NOV Members of the same squad shoot two unarmed teenagers, one fatally, in a hayshed previously used as IRA explosives cache. RUC officers later stand trial for murder and are acquitted.

DEC Eleven off-duty soldiers and five civilians are killed by an IRA bomb at a disco in Ballykelly, Northern Ireland.

DEC RUC officers shoot dead two men in County Armagh. The men are later identified as belonging to the Irish National Liberation Army (INLA).

DEC In five separate incidents during November and December, special squad of RUC and Army shoot dead seven unarmed suspected terrorists, prompting accusations of a "shoot to kill" policy. Later to be subject of Stalker inquiry.

DEC In 1982, eighteen officers are killed (twelve are RUC).

1983

JAN Stephen Waldorf shot and pistol-whipped by armed Met detectives in crowded Kensington High Street, London. He was mistaken for David Martin, wanted for armed robbery and attempted murder of a policeman. Two detectives later charged with attempted murder, reduced to wounding with intent. Police severely criticized for poor firearms training.

APR 25,000 women gather at Greenham Common to encircle the airbase and decorate the wire protesting against Cruise missiles. A permanent Peace Camp established which becomes the scene of regular trouble with Thames Valley police.

AUG In Holloway Road, North London, five teenagers (2 white, 1 black, 2 Cypriot) allege that police officers jumped out of a van and assaulted them for no reason. Police investigations fail to identify their assailants for two years.

SEPT Neighbourhood Watch schemes are started in London.

DEC Five Greater Manchester police officers jailed for one year and a third ordered to do community service after a court hears of "shocking and disgraceful attack" on a deaf and disabled man, Bernard Hughes. Mr Hughes later awarded £2000 in damages.

DEC IRA bomb explodes outside Harrods, killing three police officers.

DEC In 1983, twenty-two officers are killed (eighteen are RUC).

1984

FEB Police and Criminal Evidence Act (PACE) passed by Parliament after fierce public debate. Both police and civil libertarians object.

FEB Home Secretary announces fines imposed by magistrates in England and Wales are to be raised and maximum fines are to be doubled.

MARCH Miners' strike begins. Mass picketing arranged by NUM. ACPO establish their own National Reporting Centre (NRC) at Scotland Yard to move police to areas which are undermanned and unable to deal with flying pickets. Critics warn this is start of national police force.

APR High Court finds police have a duty to anticipate a breach of the peace and upholds their right to prevent miners from driving across the country to take part in mass demonstrations.

APR To keep pits open and disperse pickets, police use baton charges, mounted police charges and dogs. Officers issued with riot equipment to protect them from stones, bricks, concrete blocks, etc., during disturbances. Labour MPs accuse police of over-reacting and escalating the violence of the strike. Home Secretary Leon Brittan says "the police have a right to take what action is necessary".

APR Yorkshire picket David Jones dies in a disturbance. Pickets and police observe two minutes' silence.

APR WPC Yvonne Fletcher is shot dead in St James's Square in Central London. Armed police surround Libyan Embassy, from which shots were fired.

MAY Biggest confrontation of miners' strike so far takes place at Orgreave. More than 8000 police face 10,000 miners. Pickets dispersed by mounted police using long batons.

JUNE Month of demonstrations brings 113 arrests at NUM march, 201 arrests at CND rally and 6 arrests at demonstration by Sikhs. Arthur Scargill arrested at Orgreave.

AUG South Yorks village of Amthorpe besieged by police. Hundreds of complaints of police violence. Later, investigators say officers were from diverse forces and cannot be traced. No disciplinary action taken.

SEPT 676 policemen injured so far in miners' strike. Pickets' injuries not known. 6427 arrests for breach of the peace. 300,000 stopped en route.

OCT IRA bomb explodes in Grand Hotel, Brighton, during Conservative Party Conference. Five people killed. Later, Patrick Magee is sentenced to eight life sentences for his part in plot to cause, according to the judge's summing up, "carnage too great to contemplate".

NOV In Wales, two miners charged with murder after dropping concrete block on a taxi, killing the driver as he took a miner to work. Eventually found guilty of manslaughter. Police describe violence at Cortonwood in South Yorkshire as worst yet.

NOV Two men are jailed for their part in the Brinks Mat gold bullion robbery at Heathrow Airport.

DEC Efforts by Liverpool Police Authority to block Merseyside officers going to miners' strike fail.

DEC Arthur Scargill fined £250 with £750 costs for obstruction while picketing.

DEC The cost of policing the miners' strike now exceeds £200 million.

DEC In 1984, twelve officers are killed (nine are RUC).

1985

JAN Thirteen miners are sent to jail for arson attacks on buses being used to take miners to work.

JAN Police Federation express concern at loss of manpower in 1984.

FEB Police road blocks are set up near Molesworth Airforce base in Cambridgeshire where demonstrators protest against American Cruise missiles. Police demand evidence of identity before allowing people into the area. Ratepayers Against Molesworth Settlements (RAMS) petition government to rid area of protesters. Wearing a military flakjacket, the Secretary of State for Defence, Michael Heseltine, arrives to support police tactics in a dawn raid to clear the area.

FEB Nine RUC officers die when Newry police station is mortar-bombed by the IRA.

MARCH Home Secretary, Leon Brittan, visits Manchester University student union to give a speech. A crowd of hostile students gather peacefully outside the hall. Without warning police charge to clear Brittan's exit from front door. The ensuing "Battle of Brittan" leads to 38 arrests and four of the 40 injured being taken to hospital. Students claim that they were not cautioned before being arrested, were asked to give their fingerprints for no apparent reason and that police officers had their insignia blacked out by boot polish. Later, two students report beatings, harassment and burglaries to dissuade them from giving evidence in disciplinary proceedings. No disciplinary action taken.

APR Met publishes *Principles of Policing* laying down ethical standards to deal with sagging morale and poor behaviour. It advises against membership of the Masons. Shortly afterwards St James Lodge opens across from Scotland Yard.

APR Fifty-three people are killed when fire engulfs a stand at Bradford City

Football Ground. Police perform heroically to rescue trapped people. Their emotional upsets last for years afterwards, forcing the police service to recognize post-incident trauma, and the need for counselling.

MAY Four RUC officers are killed when their armoured vehicle passes by a lorry-trailer bomb parked yards from the border in Newry.

JUNE Avon and Somerset, Wiltshire and Hampshire officers confront a convoy of hippies in a field near Stonehenge. After hippies bombard them with ball-bearings, reinforcements in riot gear are called, including Ministry of Defence police. The ensuing "Battle of the Beanfield" shocks the nation who see it on television. A Chief Constable later says his men went "berserk".

AUG In Birmingham, John Shorthouse, aged five, is accidentally shot dead in his bed by West Midlands PC Brian Chester while searching the house for the boy's father, who is wanted for armed robbery.

AUG Home Secretary announces attempts to identify officers responsible for the assault on youths in the Holloway Road in 1983 have failed. *Police Review* publishes editorial critical of "wall of silence" and arranges immunity from prosecution for anyone with information. Two officers break ranks and identify those concerned, who are arrested and charged.

SEPT Rioting erupts in the Handsworth district of Birmingham after a crackdown on drugs and illegal parking. Two Asian shopkeepers are killed. Home Secretary, Douglas Hurd, is himself attacked when he visits the area after police have restored order.

SEPT During a police raid on her home in Brixton, Mrs Cherry Groce is shot and paralysed. Crowd outside police station is aggressively dispersed. Rioting follows and police record 140 serious offences, including two of rape. Press photographer dies when he is struck by masonry.

OCT Toxteth, Liverpool, sealed off after mob of 300 or more people attacks police station. Violence later attributed to arrest of four black youths for affray.

OCT In Tottenham, North London, police raid the home of Mrs Cynthia Jarrett. She is knocked to the ground and suffers a fatal heart attack. After efforts to disperse angry crowds fail, rioting breaks out on the Broadwater Farm Estate. While escorting some firemen, PC Keith Blakelock is hacked to death, shocking police service and public. Home Secretary reveals that permission had been given for the use of CS gas and baton rounds, although they were not used. Several hundred riot-trained men had been on stand-by all day and were sent home just before the rioting began. Councillor Bernie Grant says "The reason why the police are calling for plastic bullets is because they got a bloody good hiding".

NOV Anglo-Irish Agreement signed. Protestant anger aroused at provision giving Eire government a role in Northern affairs. Parades Policy brought in to control marches after severe disturbances in Portadown, including violent attacks on policemen's houses. Many RUC officers feel both measures damage their ability to police the province.

NOV Merseyside Police on threshold of bankruptcy after their local authority ignores central government orders to cut spending. Five Merseyside officers sacked, demoted or fined for "racial abuse or abusive conduct".

NOV Met receive much criticism when national crime figures reveal their average clear-up rate to be only 17 per cent. Critics argue that the force is inefficient at managerial level and undersupervised at junior level, and junior ranks spend too little time actually investigating crime.

NOV Supergrass system falls into disrepute after DPP withdraws immunity from prosecution in cases where information fails to lead to convictions.

DEC In Kent, Kenneth Noye is acquitted of brutal killing of DC John Fordham who was watching Noye's house in an undercover surveillance operation in connection with the Brinks Mat robbery. Police morale damaged by Noye's acquittal and the sense that Fordham should not have been so exposed to danger.

DEC In 1985 twenty-five officers are killed (twenty-three are RUC).

1986

JAN The Police and Criminal Evidence Act (PACE), passed by Parliament in 1984, is implemented throughout England and Wales. Some provincial officers are given week-long residential courses to learn its complexities, Met officers have a one-day seminar.

JAN Police officers armed with Heckler & Koch sub-machine guns patrol Heathrow Airport. Officers at Manchester Airport also issued with firearms. Critics call the weapons "too powerful for the safety of bystanders".

JAN RUC Police Federation officials ordered by Chief Constable, Sir John Hermon, not to comment beyond welfare issues after publishing an editorial calling for disarming of RUC once troubles are over.

JAN Woman Police Sergeant Meynell submits savage report to Police Federation alleging that senior officers failed to act on intelligence that trouble was brewing at Broadwater Farm. Leaked to the *Daily Mail*.

JAN Bristol sociologist Michael Banton publishes *Investigating Robbery* which analyses figures for fifty years and concludes "the police can do little to reduce the incidence of robbery" and that detections are so problematic that "it would be most unwise of the police to allow their effectiveness to be evaluated by the detection rate" (for robberies).

JAN Met Working Party on Domestic Violence reports after two years. Estimates 28,000 domestic calls p.a. in London alone. Acknowledges vast majority of cases not reported. Urges police to take issue more seriously.

JAN Print Unions and News International begin an industrial dispute at Wapping in East London, where News International plant is picketed.

FEB As a result of the coverup when police officers assaulted a group of youths in Holloway Road in 1983, all police carriers will bear identification marks.

FEB Held back by police, more than 3000 pickets fail to prevent newspapers from leaving News International plant at Wapping.

FEB Man suffering from AIDS bites two Nottinghamshire police officers who are subsequently ordered off duty.

FEB Met's SPG replaced by new 900-man mobile reserve called Territorial Support Groups (TSG) with more structured supervision.

MARCH Seven Met officers suspended after second inquest jury rules Hell's

Angel John Mikkelson, was unlawfully killed in July 1985 when denied medical treatment at Hounslow police station for head injuries received during his arrest. DPP decides not to press charges due to lack of evidence.

MARCH *Police,* Journal of the Police Federation, explains why Holloway Road coverup was "no surprise" in "a force which comes to see itself as isolated ... and not properly understood by those whose support was once taken for granted".

MARCH A Sergeant and four PCs are charged with assault and conspiracy arising from Holloway Road incident.

APR A group of policemen say racial discrimination should be scrapped as a police disciplinary offence and threaten to appeal to the European Court of Human Rights if necessary.

APR The independent Crown Prosecution Service (CPS) is implemented throughout England and Wales, removing the decision to prosecute from the police.

APR Some 400 officers disperse a Peace Convoy of hippies near Stonehenge.

APR Home Secretary, Douglas Hurd, promises 3200 more police officers over next four years, an increase of under 3 per cent.

APR Ministry of Defence Police arrest 51 people during anti-nuclear protest at Molesworth Airforce base. Cost of policing Molesworth area is £2.5 million over 18 months, half the sum going in overtime payments.

APR Lord Gifford starts independent inquiry into Broadwater Farm riot. Met Commissioner, Sir Kenneth Newman, says Met will not testify.

APR In Stockport, Police Sergeant Alwyn Sawyer charged with murder after discovery of his boot-print on back of prisoner, Henry Foley.

APR Despite complaints, no disciplinary action is taken following death of Mrs Cynthia Jarrett at Broadwater Farm in 1985, but in future all search warrants must carry time of day as well as date.

APR Police Complaints Authority (PCA) becomes Independent Police Complaints Authority (IPCA). The Authority has new powers to investigate complaints against police, but critics – including the Police Federation – argue that they are still inadequate, and not sufficiently independent.

MAY At Police Federation Conference it is claimed football hooligans and "picket-line subversives" have left police morale "at rock bottom". Other officers highly critical of force training standards and leadership skills.

MAY Met Commissioner's annual report omits any mention of riot at Broadwater Farm in 1985.

MAY Superintendent Rachel James, the only woman of her rank in Devon and Cornwall force, complains of persistent discrimination against women in police. "So much expertise is going to waste."

MAY Deputy Chief Constable of Greater Manchester, John Stalker, is removed from inquiry into allegations RUC had been operated "shoot to kill" policy. Replaced by Colin Sampson, Chief Constable of West Yorkshire, who announces that Stalker is himself under investigation.

JULY West Midlands PC Brian Chester is acquitted of the unlawful killing of five-year-old John Shorthouse during a raid on a Birmingham house in 1985. West Midlands Police establish an elite firearms squad on permanent standby. Members of the squad must pass strict psychological tests.

Notting Hill Carnival, 1976.

Left: Toxteth, 1981.

Below: Brixton, 1981.

Opposite: Greenham Common, 1983. Guard duty (*above*). The perimeter fence under attack (*below*).

The miners' strike, 1984–5. *Above:* Police and strikers playing football. *Below:* Arthur Scargill and audience.

The miners' strike, 1984–5. *Above:* A Special Patrol Group baton charge.
Below: The aftermath of a confrontation with pickets.

The miners' strike 1984–5. The NUM Headquarters, Sheffield.

The problems of community relations.
Above: One of the five Sikh officers
in the Metropolitan police. *Below:* A PC
surrounded by a crowd of angry youths.

Opposite above: Broadwater Farm, 1985.

Opposite below: A few minutes respite,
Tottenham, 1985.

Above and below: Brixton, 1985.

Wapping, 1986. *Above:* A scaffolding pole is
hurled at police. *Below:* A mounted police charge.

Above: Weapons recovered from Arsenal football fans, 1988.

Opposite: A local resident speaking at Hackney Police Consultative Committee, 1987.

Armed police. *Above:* Police wait in an armoured Land Rover at the Notting Hill Carnival, 1987. *Below:* Officers from CID and PT17 after successfully ambushing some armed robbers.

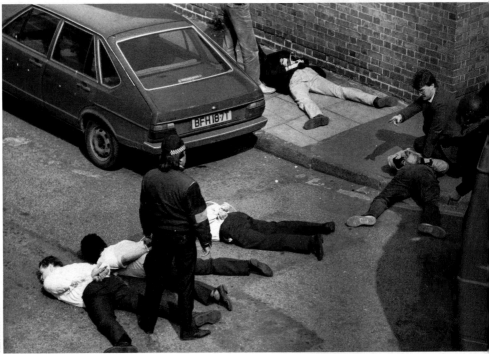

PRESS ASSOCIATION

Above: RUC officers taking cover, Londonderry, 1986.
Below: Teenage petrol bombers in the Ardoyne area of Belfast, 1988.

ANDREW MOORE/REFLEX

Life on the street, 1988.

JULY Kenneth Noye jailed for his part in Brinks Mat gold bullion robbery.

JULY The Met publishes *Public Order Review,* a report on Broadwater Farm and Brixton riots of 1985 critical of senior officers for allowing "no-go" areas. Met launches recruitment drive among ethnic minorities.

JULY Home Office gives police permission to buy 26 bullet-proof vehicles and 80 armoured personnel carriers plus 1500 long truncheons to be used with riot shields in conditions of extreme disorder. Home Secretary rejects creation of separate force of trained riot police on grounds of cost.

JULY Lord Gifford publishes report on Broadwater Farm riot It is highly critical of police handling of local black people in general and the Jarrett family in particular. Criticizes treatment of suspects after riot.

JULY Inspector Keith Fleming loses claim against the Criminal Injuries Compensation Board for injuries received during Toxteth riots of 1981.

JULY PC Ron Walker of Kent Constabulary alleges that false confessions have been extracted from convicted criminals to be "taken into consideration" (TIC) and used to inflate crime clear-up rate. When Met investigating officers raid thirteen Kent stations they find documents have disappeared.

JULY Following an exhaustive investigation, and a fifteen hundred page report, John Stalker is reinstated by Greater Manchester Police Authority. No disciplinary action is taken but he is urged to be "more circumspect" with his personal contacts and police vehicles in future.

AUG Home Secretary announces all 43 British police forces now have stocks of CS gas and that 14 have stocks of baton rounds which have been available to the police since the 1981 riots in Toxteth.

SEPT In a crackdown on drug dealing, 600 officers raid St Paul's district in Bristol. Local community leader describes the operation as using "a sledge hammer to crack a nut". There are street disturbances but police avoid major breakdown of public order. BBC television journalists reject police requests to examine footage of the disturbance.

SEPT RUC Reserve officer acquitted of manslaughter of man killed by baton round when police try to arrest Martin Galvin, American leader of Noraid.

SEPT At the Liberal Party Conference, David Steel calls racism in the police force a major social menace.

OCT Among many forces complaining of similar shortages, Dorset police reveal a manpower crisis: out of 1203 men, only 352 are available per day. Some CID officers have a caseload of more than 400 incidents (the recommended load is 200).

OCT New Criminal Justice Bill giving police powers to seize assets of drug dealers and other major criminals. It also proposes to abolish the right of peremptory challenge of jurors by the defence, extends age of jury eligibility beyond sixty-five, gives Customs officers the right to detain suspected drug carriers and gives anonymity to rape victims.

DEC Chief Constable of Greater Manchester, James Anderton, reveals he was moved by the voice of God after remarking that AIDS was a "self-inflicted scourge" and that those at risk were "swirling around in a cesspit of their own making".

DEC John Stalker announces his retirement eight years prematurely. He later writes *Stalker,* which gives details of his experience, upsetting the government and the police establishment. He accuses RUC of being "amateur at murder investigations or deliberately inept".

DEC In 1986, twelve officers die (all are RUC).

1987

JAN Home Secretary announces that in future police officers will be covered by the provisions of the Criminal Injuries Compensation Scheme.

JAN Home Secretary refers cases of six men convicted of the IRA Birmingham pub bombings to the Court of Appeal after former police officer alleges that their confessions were obtained by force. Appeal is later dismissed.

JAN Huge crowd gathers at anniversary of News International dispute at Wapping. Violent clashes lead to 67 arrests and 163 police officers injured. Many complaints of excessive police violence lead to investigation by Northamptonshire police. Police point to trip wire against horses as proof of premeditated violence.

JAN Following government criticism of forthcoming programme on Zircon Satellite, Special Branch raid BBC's Glasgow offices and seize all available material relating to entire TV series on British Intelligence.

JAN Met Inspector Douglas Lovelock acquitted of unlawfully and maliciously wounding Mrs Cherry Groce during armed raid on her house in Brixton which sparked off rioting in 1985. It is announced that rank and file CID officers will no longer be issued with firearms.

JAN Trial of six people accused of murdering PC Keith Blakelock during Broadwater Farm riot in 1985 begins.

JAN Met Commissioner, Sir Kenneth Newman, announces "It would be self-defeating and irresponsible if we were to devote equal attention to every class of crime regardless of their human and social significance." To make better use of sparse manpower police will now tackle crime on a priority rating.

MARCH Three men convicted of the murder of PC Blakelock and are jailed for life, but case against two juveniles is dismissed because confessions were extracted in interviews which breached the new Police and Criminal Evidence Act and the Young Offenders Act.

MARCH In his annual report, Chairman of the IPCA, Sir Cecil Clothier, calls for new powers to remove unsuitable officers. He states that "a small number of officers are causing a disproportionate damage to the force".

JUNE Officers at Stonehenge solstice celebrations make 43 arrests under new Public Order Act. This gives police powers to disperse gatherings of more than twenty people if they believe gathering may be disruptive. Critics see this law as pushing police further into oppressive role with respect to maintenance of public order.

JULY In his annual report the Commissioner of the Met states new legislation and 6 per cent rise in crime rate leading to critical manpower shortages. He also states that increasingly sophisticated jury nobbling required 18,000 officers to protect juries during 1986.

JULY Record number of remand prisoners being held in police cells across the country (80 per cent of them held in London).

JULY Met Sergeant and four PCs are tried and sent to prison for the Holloway Road incident in 1983, and for conspiring to deceive subsequent investigation. Pleas for mitigation are rejected. Judge says accused men "behaved like vicious hooligans and lied like common criminals".

JULY In Operation Trident hundreds of police officers from all over London provide saturation policing over several weeks to clear drug dealers from "no-go" area in All Saints Road area of Notting Hill. Local residents welcome move but fear retaliation from black youths at next Carnival.

AUG West Midlands police open a five-language hotline and set up liaison clinics for victims of racial abuse.

AUG A new Met computer system, TOPSY, with terminals in all Met stations, gives instant access to all crime reports. Teething problems abound, including shutdown of system around midnight for several hours to load new data, the time when it is most needed to identify suspects picked up when pubs close.

AUG Home Secretary orders new investigation into cases of four people convicted of Guildford and Woolwich IRA pub bombings. New evidence is presented by a delegation including Merlyn Rees, Lord Jenkins of Hillhead, Lord Scarman, Lord Devlin and Cardinal Hume.

AUG New Commissioner of the Met, Sir Peter Imbert, promises to root out corruption in the force, to recruit more officers from ethnic minorities and to devote more resources to the fight against street crime. Police Federation welcome his appointment, hoping he will raise sagging force morale.

AUG At Hungerford in Wiltshire, Michael Ryan, unemployed gun enthusiast, shoots dead 13 people including Thames Valey officers and injures a further sixteen. The worst incident of its kind in British criminal history. Police criticized for delay in responding and for inadvertently directing victims towards Ryan.

AUG At the Notting Hill Carnival one person is murdered, but violence is less organized than feared after Operation Trident. Running fights between gangs of youths and police, some in riot gear, occur only in the evening and last for several hours.

AUG Inquiry into child abuse in Cleveland opens under Justice Butler-Sloss. Report later criticizes police for poor liaison and insensitivity.

SEPT In his last speech as President of ACPO, the Chief Constable of Greater Manchester, James Anderton, suggests that sex offenders should be castrated. He also calls for closer control of nudity and sex on TV.

SEPT Met considers replacing traditional eight-hour shift with more flexible approach, including job sharing and part-time policewomen to encourage female officers to return to work after leaving to have children.

SEPT After a nine-year-old prosecution witness breaks down in court, Police Federation calls for changes in procedure in sex abuse cases and asks that videos be admitted in court as evidence.

OCT Home Secretary announces that unsworn and uncorroborated evidence of children from age of five will be admissible as evidence in court. He also announces police powers to search people suspected of carrying knives, as well as a ban on knuckle-dusters, death stars and hand claws.

NOV Met Chief Inspector Brian Woollard faces disciplinary charges after persistently alleging that Freemasons had him removed from the Fraud Squad and interfered with investigations into local government corruption.

NOV In the first case of its kind, Met PC Grant Prescott wins a private prosecution for assault against an assailant after the case was dropped by the CPS.

NOV At a meeting of Brent Police Consultative Committee in London, Superintendent Ganley attacked after claiming that 99 per cent of street crime in Stonebridge is committed by a hard core of 200 black youths. He says, "I wanted to appeal to the black community to help in tackling this small core of offenders."

DEC Government publishes white paper on proposals to reform 1968 Firearms Act, including ban on pump-action and self-loading weapons and on short-barrelled shotguns. In future, police can refuse a gun licence if the applicant cannot show good reason for possession. Gun lobby criticizes proposals as too hasty and damaging to interests of sportsmen. Police Federation states they are both inadequate and long overdue.

DEC In 1987, seventeen officers are killed (sixteen are RUC).

1988

FEB Under government pressure to produce value for money, Scotland Yard announce plans to privatize a range of inquiries, such as cases of cheque and credit card fraud.

FEB Avon and Somerset Chief Constable calls for privatization of lost property work.

FEB Police worried as private security firms growing apace.

MAR Following their investigation into allegations of violence on the first anniversary of the Wapping dispute, Northamptonshire Constabulary announce some officers are expected to face criminal charges. The Met's TSG is much criticized for using excessive force on picket lines.

MAR Assaults on police officers in Derbyshire running at rate of one for every 2.8 officers. Elsewhere, lager louts seen as disturbing new feature of British rural life.

MAR In Milltown Cemetery, Belfast, 3 people killed, many injured when Michael Stone attacks funeral of three IRA members shot by SAS in Gibraltar. Three days later, two undercover soldiers are dragged from their car and shot dead at funeral of IRA man killed at Milltown Cemetery.

APR Commissioner of the Met, Sir Peter Imbert, meets Home Secretary to discuss allegations that some 5000 Met officers are Freemasons.

APR Two members of the "Bushwackers", a group of Millwall football supporters, sent to prison following police under cover operation, Dirty Den. Officers involved say their work was extremely stressful.

APR In Stockport, a Lancashire PC informs superiors that two colleagues beat a prisoner to death in the cells "to teach him a lesson he would not forget". Later, the two officers are convicted of murder and jailed for life.

APR Parliament told that police officers in England and Wales were issued with firearms on 2185 occasions in 1987, a fall of 11 per cent on 1986. Shots were fired on seven occasions. By the end of 1987, 7349 officers were licensed shots – equivalent to 6 per cent of force membership.

MAY In a London court defendants are acquitted of charges arising from Operation Full Time, an undercover investigation into football hooliganism. After nine months of work by 250 officers, the court hears that police log books were altered and that oral evidence contradicted written evidence provided earlier. Later, defendants are photographed sharing a drink with jurors in a public house.

JUNE Alarm is expressed about juries. Leeds jurors claim to have been intimidated by friends of the accused during a second football trial. Right of defence lawyers to challenge jurors is questioned after two incidents imply the practice can lead to biased juries; it is subsequently withdrawn.

JULY Labour MP, Dale Campbell-Savours, alleges that in 1981 thirty-three out of fifty Chief Constables were Freemasons. Private Member's Bill to ban Freemasonry in the police is introduced but fails to become law.

JULY Following the Stalker-Sampson inquiry into the alleged "shoot-to-kill" policy of the RUC, 20 junior officers are to be disciplined. No measures are to be taken against senior officers.

JULY Parliament learns that 200,000 crimes were cleared up as the result of TICs filed after police prison visits in 1987.

AUG In 1987 the police responded to some 980,000 false alarm calls. It is suggested that in future the public should pay for a police response to security alarm calls, 98 per cent of which are false.

AUG After threats of cancellation, the Notting Hill Carnival passes off without serious incident and with a major reduction in crime. Nearly 10,000 men (more than one third of the Met), together with firearms and rapid-entry squads are deployed for the event.

AUG National Intelligence Football Unit established by Scotland Yard to correlate intelligence from forces around Britain.

SEPT Wolff Olins, management consultants, publish results of an internal survey commissioned by the Met. They find "no evidence that there ever was a time when the police were universally loved and admired". Although they find the Met "basically sound", they find management and communication in poor shape and point out that the absence of clear force goals is damaging morale.

DEC Outgoing President of ACPO, Roger Birch, Chief Constable of Sussex, calls for urgent Royal Commission on role of police.

DEC 10,000 students block Westminster Bridge to protest against the abolition of student grants. London traffic in chaos. Majority are peaceful, but minority throw bottles and stones at police. Bridge is cleared when mounted police gallop into crowd. Student leaders say no warning was given, but police insist there was. Watching MPs criticize police handling of the crowd.

DEC There are over 149,000 police officers and civilian staff in the UK.

DEC In 1988, nine officers are killed (six are RUC).

1989

JAN Magistrates summons 18 Met PCs, 4 Sergeants, 1 WPC and an Inspector and charge them with assault, conspiracy to pervert the course of justice and perjury arising from the violence at Wapping on 24 January 1987. Both the Commissioner and the Police Federation criticize the DPP for the delay in bringing the prosecution.

JAN At least 50 Greater Manchester police officers break into sacristy of a church at dawn, cutting wires and causing damage, to forcibly remove Sri Lankan Viraj Mendis from sanctuary on Home Secretary's orders. Mendis overstayed his entry permit by 2 years, but claimed refugee status fearing his support for the Tamil cause would endanger his life if returned to Sri Lanka. Denied by Home Office and UN High Commission for Refugees. Petition for right to stay signed by 105 MPs. Mendis deported two days later, after fierce Commons debate critical of police tactics.

JAN Guardian Angels, American vigilante group, start training British recruits to help control violence on the London Underground. Police claim they are unnecessary and dangerous. 80 Met and City of London PCs seconded to British Transport Police. Angels warned they risk arrest.

FEB Wandsworth Prison officers go on strike. Met officers sent in to replace them.

CHAPTER ONE

Familiar Laments

*The refrain that runs through virtually all the interviews is the
sense of being underrated by the public. I begin the book with
two extracts which characterize the PCs' predicament. The first
is a conversation between a dozen PCs in the Met who have
just completed their two-year probation. The attitudes they
express are shared by all officers of all ranks in all the forces
we visited.*

**A group of Met PCs and WPCs, average age 23, average service
two years.**

PC1: We get Police Orders twice a week, and usually the front
page on that will be a commendation for a successful trial, or
saving a life, outstanding bravery, dedication to duty. It's not
actually in our job description, you know, we don't come into
the job saying, "I will definitely put my life on the line to save
other people."

WPC1: Three lads on our relief went to a fire. One of them
ended up getting carried out by a fireman because he was
overcome by smoke. They couldn't go in any further. The other
two had gone in and rescued this woman. Actually all three of
them got up to the top floor and threw the woman out of the
window. That was about four floors up. She wasn't that
injured – there was snow underneath. The other two PCs then
jumped and one of them was really quite badly injured. It took
a lot of nerve. It's quite a way up. They jumped from two floors
up and one of them ended up with a shattered leg and a lot of
internal injuries. There was a little bit in the *Standard* the next
day: "Three Paddington officers save woman's life . . ." but that
was it.

PC2: Everybody has this image of the police force and what the force is. They watch television and "that's what it's like". But 95 per cent of our job is nothing like that, 95 per cent of our job can be boring. You can be sitting in the carrier for hours. But nobody would take any interest if a newspaper article said: "95 per cent of the police force sits around doing nothing." It's not interesting. Mr Joe Public outside doesn't really want to understand. He knows his job is fucking boring, and he doesn't want to hear that the police are bored in their job.

WPC2: Something like us having to move prisoners around the country overnight, or the picket at South Africa House – there you've got a situation where we just have to go there and follow orders. We're told beforehand: "You can't arrest anyone. When there's trouble, just look above their heads and ignore them." I've got no qualms – I'm totally anti-apartheid. But I said to my Chief Superintendent, "I never wish to be in that situation again."

One time there was quite a crowd – about sixty – very jumpy. And in there was a five-year-old whose shoe laces were undone. I'm standing there and I said to the little girl, with her mum, "Your shoe laces are undone, darling." She said, "Fuck off, you fascist pig." The five year old! I said, "Fine, fair enough."

What a situation! To me, that five-year-old was in moral danger. She's in the middle of sixty people jumping up and down going crazy. They've got a police helmet on a stick, they're saying, "Kill! Kill! Kill! Blakelock! Blakelock! Blakelock!" And we're all standing there focusing 50 yards behind them at a point in the distance. That child should have come out, because that child's in just as much danger as a child looking in a peep show in Soho. We spoke to the guv'nor and said, "Don't you think that child should come out? This place is going crazy." They were building trestles, they were getting tannoys out, they were just building up and building up until they could go crazy. "Don't you think that child should come out now, before that child gets hurt?" "No, no. Focus above their heads. There's a video camera, remember." That was it. We all stood there and took it for hours and hours and hours.

We didn't have any qualms against most of those people. Like I said, I agree with their protest about apartheid. I suspect many police officers do. But there were just some people who were only there because we were going to be there. It was simple as that. You can't chant "Kill Blakelock!" at people without expecting them to get feelings back. We were stopped from doing our job.

PC3: The video camera is just to monitor the demo – it's on the roof, way away from you. We're on it and they're on it. One woman was arrested and she was going, "Go on – nick me, nick me!" Eventually this PC said, "I'm left with no choice." The Inspector said, "No, you can't. Don't." Eventually they just went crazy. They started screaming, pushing barriers, throwing paint or whatever. The TSG had to come in and eventually the guv'nor finally had to make a decision about arrests. Whoever put the rostrum up and whoever had the tannoys, which weren't allowed, only they were taken away. We had this fake "I'm being beaten up! I'm being beaten up!" screaming and chanting. It was a great big circus. They were there to make a point and we just let them do it. Either you stop them doing it or let them get on with it. No one realizes what it does to us. What a pressure to put normal people under!

WPC3: The trouble is, Joe Public doesn't take us for a person, they take us for a uniform. My answer whenever I get involved with somebody who starts playing up, who wants to pick a fight with you, is: "What have I ever done to you? This is the first time you've ever met me. Just calm down. I don't want to fight you. Just calm down and we'll sort this out. I've never done anything to you. You've never met me before. You don't know who I am."

PC4: I got the impression when people are in the station, when we had our open day, "Yeah, this is nice. But this isn't the real police force. This isn't you arresting me and banging me up in a cell. How do I know you're going to be like this when you are doing that?" So they take their views from what they see in the papers and on the television, which is generally bad news. People obviously don't write in the newspapers: "The other day I was arrested and I was treated really nice."

WPC1: It's crazy. A personal experience for me: myself and a colleague stopped a chap whom we believe had stolen purses on him. We had that information. In the end, yes he did have some and he was arrested, but a fight ensued between him and the other WPC. He started to run away and we grabbed him. We started struggling. He pushed me. My foot was trapped between his feet and I fell to the side. I ended up with a fractured ankle. The other WPC held on to him, was bounced off the road. She ended up with bruised ribs, cut knees, everything. He got nicked. He admitted handling stolen goods, "GBH with intent to resist arrest" on me and "ABH" on the other officer. He went to court and was given eighty hours community service, partly because he'd been held in custody, but that was only four months. That's three offences he admitted freely. The judge said to us that we should consider ourselves lucky we weren't seriously injured. It was as if it was our fault that we were injured! "What were you doing arresting this person?" was the impression I got. I thought, "Well, sod you mate! Why should I get involved in anything if this is how the courts are to behave?"

WPC4: Sergeants will tell you not to charge for assault unless it's really bad – and bruises can't be photographed so they're ignored. So are kicks which you get when they're trying to get away. The Sergeants reckon they're not being punished in court because so many assaults go up that there's a danger of undervaluing the offence. So we just don't bother with a great many of them. They go unpunished.

WPC2: We all moan about all the bad things, but I wouldn't do another job. I doubt if anyone else would. We do enjoy that confrontation because it tests your ability to deal with people.

WPC1: Is it down to us to make people realize the person underneath? We can, but wouldn't it be nice if the media turned round and said: "Hey, people out there, OK you get the bad coppers, but underneath that uniform in a lot of circumstances there is someone who will deal with your problems. Don't look just at the uniform, look at the person and how that person deals with you." Wouldn't it be nice for that to be published?

The other familiar lament is from the PCs caught in the trap of other officers' misbehaviour. The pressure to close ranks is also the source of esprit de corps, of team spirit, but it can turn sour very quickly. Like the sense of being misunderstood, it is the other anxiety common to most constables. Both feelings accompany them on their daily rounds.

Met WPC, age 30, five years service in Central London.

I have known a whole relief of cowboys. I was the driver. Another PC was with me in the front. We're driving along when a shout comes out that there's an incident just round the block. We pile out. It's a cul-de-sac. Myself and another WPC stay in the van because there's loads of people there. We think: "If someone comes out this way and we're mobile we can cut them off."

Over the radio we hear:"OK, we've got them." It's a couple of blokes, one's a bit legless. They're arrested and put in my carrier. This young PC got in through the side door and started winding them up. Neither of them had caused us any problems. The drunk one was perhaps a little bit difficult, but nothing out of order.

The young PC wound him up to such an extent – the drunk went to head butt him. Personally, I thought it bloody well served the PC right because he was saying such stupid things. The first drunk was telling the young PC: "For Christ's sake mate, lay off. You don't have to do it." He was trying to reason with the PC. By this time it was getting a bit rough, so we put cuffs on the drunk. As soon as the cuffs were on, the young PC steps forward, grabs the bloke's head – bangs it down, jamming it between his knee and the seat, and starts smacking him in the face. I count ten. I said very quietly to him: "Look, let's knock it off shall we?" Sometimes fights happen because the adrenalin's going, and just a quiet word like that, no big deal, had made them back off. He turns round and says: "No fucking plonk tells me what to do!" I thought, "Me! Bloody Hell!" I said, "Now knock it off! It's my van. I'm the driver – just shut up and leave him alone!" He just carried on.

It had been radioed that the bloke was getting out of hand and stroppy. Another van turns up, the bloke is taken out of my carrier and put into the van. The last I see of him, his head's going "smack".

It's the first time I have ever seen this happen and it's the point I think which most coppers must hate. "What the hell do I do?" You have seen something that the young PC should be nicked for. After all, the guy hadn't done anything. They would only be done for Drunk and Disorderly. Probably one of them just wanted to have a pee and they would have fallen asleep in the bushes.

We drive back to the station. Later that evening I went to the front office and it goes deathly quiet. You think perhaps you made a smell or something's gone wrong! It really hadn't dawned on me. They said, "You're her, aren't you?" I said "I'm her what?" "You've been talking." "I haven't." A WPC that I know said, "I told you, it wouldn't be her – she doesn't do that sort of thing." I had to walk out. I was a bit peeved, because I hadn't said anything at this point.

Later on, I called up this young PC on the radio to speak to him. He drives up and stays in the car. An older PC gets out and I say: "I don't want to speak to you, it's purely between this fella and me." He says: "It's got everything to do with me." I say, "No, it hasn't. I'm prepared to forget what I saw, but I want an apology from him and I want it now. Otherwise I'm going to the skipper and if he doesn't do anything I'm going to the guv'nor. If the guv'nor doesn't believe me, I'm going further." I say to the young PC, "You were out of order and no one, but no one, criticizes WPCs – let alone me – in front of prisoners, especially after they've done what you'd done. How dare you!" So he says: "No fucking plonk tells me what to do. You go and fuck off!" I said, "I'm no ordinary plonk, I'm a WPC and don't you ever forget it."

We got back into the station and the skipper said: "What the hell has happened to that prisoner?" He had a broken nose or something, blood all over the place, and it's patently obvious that he'd been done over. And this PC I'd been talking to stood up and said: "It was him," and he put the finger on the PC. The blokes on the relief couldn't believe that any PC would shop another one. They thought I'd done it.

The next day I get all the people on the radio saying abusive things. I got hissing. "Is there anyone else you're going to shop?" Every time I try and speak they cut me off. This sort of carrying on hurts. I hadn't said a word, because I knew I didn't have to – it had been brought out into the open.

This goes on for a number of weeks. I had some support from some very good people. About five or six weeks afterwards, the young PC is suspended – but not because of this. He had gone into a Chinese restaurant, waving the old warrant card around, causing aggravation, and he gets done over by the Chinese. He goes into the station and he tells them that he's been mugged. As it happens, the CID were having a meal at the same restaurant. So he's done for wasting police time. He was suspended for many months. Technically he should have been thrown out, but he wasn't. Last I heard, he went to Beat Crimes or something – he got a cushy job out of it.

Towards the end of my posting, two PCs came up from that relief and my name was mentioned and they said: "You're not her are you?" I thought: "Oh God! It's all going to come back again." These two butch lads – not wimps or anything like that. They said: "We know you had nothing to do with any of that. That bloke's a complete nutter and should have been kicked out of the job."

I don't know whether that case ever went through Discipline. I was never spoken to about the incident, so perhaps it was hushed up.

CHAPTER TWO

Public Order

The British tendency to riot as an expression of political dissent has ancient roots: ever since the Peasants' Revolt, "the mob", which could not vote, had only the streets in which to make its presence felt politically. By the nineteenth century, the persistent threat of this kind of social disorder was threatening to impede industrial expansion. In 1819, the nation was shocked by the brutal Peterloo massacre in which some five hundred unarmed protesters were injured and eleven killed by sabre-swinging mounted "yeomen" militia, the equivalent of the Territorial Army. The police were founded ten years later by Sir Robert Peel in 1829 to provide a more reliable means of controlling disorder, crime and what was seen as the decline in moral values. Pointedly limited to working-class men, the police seemed to its many critics to be designed to use one part of the working class to keep the rest of it in place. Ever since, British labour history has been marked by clashes with soldiers or police. From the Luddites and Chartists onwards, riots, strikes and marches throughout the country from Glasgow to Merthyr Tydfil, from Birkenhead to Belfast have been more or less brutally put down. Yorkshire and Welsh families still remember Churchill with loathing for sending troops to deal with the miners.

On the other hand, many thousands of other marches, strikes and demonstrations have passed off peacefully, at least by continental standards. Initial working-class hostility to the "peeler" was moderated by his difference from the Army. Unarmed and moving about on his own, he became accepted over time, by the majority of citizens, as a stabilizing feature of British life. The fictional expressions of this affection for the police spanned the avuncular Dixon of Dock Green and the shrewd latterday

Sherlock Holmes, Fabian of the Yard. Significantly, even today, with television series such as The Bill *and* Juliet Bravo *trying to show the ordinary spectrum of police life, none of the many fictional police heroes is seen dealing with public order. Apart from the cost of filming crowd scenes, rioting is too impersonal for tarnished heroes. When enforced, public order conflicts with such democratic notions as free speech and the right of assembly. When enforced violently, it clashes with the restrained ethos of British policing. And "public order", of course, is far too polite a term to convey the degree of anger and violence often involved in riots and other street disturbances.*

In the past, such encounters happened almost privately, on industrial picket lines in remote places. Although discussed in the press, they made no lasting impact on public perceptions of the police. But scenes of crowd violence make good television. Since the 1960s the likelihood of violence has become a key factor in news coverage of marches, demonstrations, strikes and riots.

The police feel persecuted by the media's obsession with violence, and like most paranoia it is two-thirds true. It is impossible, in a one-minute news clip, to give a balanced account of twelve hours in which nothing has happened compared with the five minutes of violence to which those hours may have led. Thus, a crude, vivid image stands for the more complex reality.

On the one hand, television fiction creates a false impression of how the police actually deal with crime, which in fact is largely a matter of paperwork and precious little detection. Also, crime accounts for only a small portion of real police work. Even those series that concentrate on the uniform branch make no reference to the central role of the police in public order incidents. On the other hand news coverage creates an equally false impression of the degree of violence involved in maintaining public order, through vivid images of officers attacking civilians. For reasons of safety, most television shots are taken from behind police lines and give no balanced idea of the provocation from the other side.

Television coverage in the last ten years has played a major role in the management of public order on both sides. On the mainland, it has restricted police tactics, virtually eliminating the baton charge when cameras are present. It has also had a restraining effect on picket lines, though push and shove exercises are mounted for visiting news teams as a show of strength. Strikers complain equally bitterly and with some justice of media bias that ignores the issues behind the violence.

In Northern Ireland, it is believed that scenes of crowd violence have been staged for visiting news crews short of footage. Coverage of Northern Ireland has left the RUC very bitter. Officers feel that until recently Gerry Adams, MP, the Sinn Fein spokesman, has had television to himself, that no senior officer has put the police position, and that the almost nightly catalogue of deaths presented on the mainland news is a brief insulting gesture that shows how unimportant the Troubles are to the rest of Britain until they happen on the mainland, when they lead the news.

Opinion polls indicate that most people support police tactics in public order incidents, though that support has recently declined, and the police can no longer take it for granted. The cumulative impact of a decade of public disorder – after fifty years of calm – has shaken many officers. And the fact that their homes are not exempt from these scenes of violence replayed on television has made matters worse. As television coverage of the Vietnam war frightened Americans at home so the violence of confrontation frightens their families without adequately explaining why some people should feel such hatred towards them. Some explanations are awkward for policemen to admit even to themselves.

PC in an eastern Home Counties force, age 27, six years service. Now in a coastal town.

I got back from holiday in Spain, picked up a *Daily Telegraph* and saw a picture of a policeman covered in blood. I realized then that the country had been rioting, that policemen who just joined up to be like the blokes in *Z Cars* – catching burglars, helping old ladies – were all of a sudden involved with shields and attack squads.

I never thought I would ever have to hold a shield. I never thought I would see thousands of policemen flying all over the country to keep order. I never thought I would see a policeman killed by a rioting mob.

Met Inspector, age 43, sixteen years experience. Formerly with the Special Patrol Group.

Brixton was a nightmare, an absolutely copper-bottomed fucking nightmare. We zoomed down there with our carrier into what looked like World War III. Cars blazing, people running everywhere. The air was filled with orange smoke. The radios only had two channels and both of them were overloaded with people trying to get through. Then suddenly this hurricane of bricks and bottles and God knows what other shit hits the roof of our van from the flats overhead. We were about to debus and go find the trouble when it found us good and proper. We couldn't get out of the carrier without risking our lives. I said, "Fuck this for a lark," and we got the hell out of there. (*Brixton, 1981*)

PC in a large northern force, age 33, twelve years service. Now in a racially mixed inner-city area.

Out of twelve men I went in with, eleven of us went to hospital. It was like that for everyone. There were policewomen, and even doctors and nurses, crying. Everywhere you looked it was carnage. My Sergeant had a double fracture of the skull, a broken jaw, and his leg was broken. There are fellows who have never worked since. Our Inspector still walks with a permanent limp. He hasn't got a job with the police any more.(*Toxteth, 1981*)

Met Superintendent, age 48, twenty years service. Now in East London.

It was like Beirut, not London. It was like another country. A vanload of youngsters came up as reinforcements – they were petrified. "New at it, are you?" I said. "A couple of years in the job? Ever held a shield before?" "No, sir," they said, "it's not the end of our first two years. It's the end of our first month." (*Brixton, 1981*)

TROUBLE BREWING

Such violence was utterly alien to the style of policing traditionally taught at training school. Despite growing public unease at the number of deaths in police custody, at news pictures of rough handling by officers at strikes and demonstrations, and alleged misuse of the "sus" laws to stop and search black youths, the official police response was one of reassurance. Critics were dismissed as "anti" (police). Senior policemen seemed unaware that, far from quelling public disquiet, their complacency only fuelled it.

While life at the level of public relations seemed under control, on the streets of inner-city areas like Brixton and Toxteth it was not. From the time of the Notting Hill Carnival of 1976 onwards, some black youths were becoming more and more aggressive towards the police. In their turn, young PCs groomed in the era of punks and skinheads were more aggressive too – especially towards blacks and Asians. National Front rallies became the focus of much violent disorder – two protesters were killed, and rumours of police sympathy for the National Front were common in the black community.

As formal complaints of racial harassment seemed fruitless, communication between senior officers and community leaders gave way to hostility. Meanwhile, both were losing touch with their respective younger generations. Urban deprivation and rising unemployment provided the context for trouble on the streets. The police provided the target.

Most police officers never saw it that way. For some, it was a breakdown of parental discipline which, as ever, had landed on their doorstep, yet was beyond their control. Others, such as James Anderton, Chief Constable of Greater Manchester, echoed the Prime Minister's view that the rioting had nothing to do with unemployment: it was just "mindless criminal greed". Most blacks saw the troubles as provoked by the police. All these interpretations allowed each side to avoid responsibility for their own part in what was to come.

BRIXTON 1981

In April 1981, 110 officers of the Special Patrol Group were put on the streets of Brixton in plainclothes to stamp out street crime. Known as SWAMP 81, the operation lasted for three weeks and led to a thousand stops and searches of black youths, a hundred arrests and a massive increase in local tension. Lord Scarman was later to call it "a serious mistake". SWAMP even carried on through the days of rioting.

The first riots were triggered when a crowd of youths attacked detectives questioning a black youth with a stab wound. The detectives claimed to have been protecting him, but the trust that might have allowed the crowd to give the police the benefit of the doubt did not exist. The second wave of rioting was set off by a prolonged and fruitless search of a black minicab driver in front of a hostile crowd. It was a classic instance of police harassment.

BRIXTON 10–12 APRIL 1981

Numbers: hundreds, but no clear figures. Police estimate that at least one third of the rioters were white.

Damage: £4,750,000: 20 buildings destroyed; 30 private cars destroyed and 61 damaged, 4 police cars burnt out. In all, 118 police cars and 4 ambulances were damaged.

Arrests: 779 crimes reported; 257 arrests; 172 cases found guilty; 5 cases bound over; 41 cases withdrawn, dismissed or acquitted; 20 cases in which no further action was taken.

Injuries: 48 civilians, 401 police officers.

Met Inspector, age 34, twelve years service. Now in an inner-city area of London.

I remember that last night in Brixton. I was doing the football. I had an awful hangover. A quick start: turn up at 11.30 and you're off to the ground straight away. Didn't have any breakfast. Turned up for work at half time and they said, "It's your lucky day – you're going to Brixton!" I had planned to see some friends that weekend but I ended up having bricks thrown at me at 1.30 in the morning, when I should have been in Windsor. It was ridiculous.

I had bottles and bricks at the Notting Hill Carnival, but this time it was petrol bombs and everything – a lot more organized. After the first petrol bomb you're less worried, but the first one is a very frightening experience.

I went from that without sleep to a lovely country pub in Windsor for lunch – everybody was sitting there as if the world was still at one, and I'd just come out from this crazy society where there was anarchy. Thirty miles away and you're back in civilization. Going from one to the other – I was in grave difficulty. My friends said they could see I was bubbling out of control.

Met WPC, age 30, ten years service. Now in a South London suburb.

Somebody said to me, "My god, the Blitz must have been like this." At one point, all we could see was orange, everywhere around was smoke. But there wasn't time to stop and think what the hell was going on, because you were so busy. It's only afterwards when you sit down and think about it that you start to shake. "Jesus, that was dreadful." I had nightmares long afterwards.

In his report on the causes of the Brixton riot, Lord Scarman judged that although police harassment was exaggerated by the black community's "rumour factory", black youths had indeed been unfairly singled out under the "sus" laws. Research by the Policy Studies Institute and the British Crime Survey showed that black youths were thirty-five times more likely to be stopped and searched than a white person of the same age.

In effect, black youths were challenged by aggressive younger PCs for control of the streets. Although the legal powers were all on one side, a gang war of attrition was going on. For macho youths on both sides, their pride was at stake. There was more to come.

TOXTETH

As in London, tension had been growing for a decade between the police and the long-established West Indian community living in serious urban decay in Liverpool 8. On 3 July 1981, three months after the Brixton riots, police chased the son of a well-known local West Indian, who was already suing them for harassment. The boy fell off his motorbike, which the police wrongly accused him of stealing. Other black youths then came to his aid, and the rioting began. Many white youths joined in the looting. Whole families came out and filled supermarket trollies while the police stood helplessly behind their shields and watched the area burn.

TOXTETH 3–7 JULY 1981

Numbers:

Damage: £4,676,041.

Arrests: 244, of which 222 (91 per cent) were white; 172 cases found guilty, 6 cases bound over; 58 cases withdrawn, dismissed or acquitted.

Injuries: 132 civilians and 128 police officers.

Two PCs from a large northern urban force: PC1, age 33, nine years service; PC2, age 30, eleven years service. Both now in an inner-city area.

PC1: The whole of the town was boarded up because the rumour had gone round that they were going to come into the city centre that night. It felt like shit or bust. No amount of training can prepare you for that. I hope to God I never see anything like it again.

PC2: I said to my relatives, "Take your kids and get out of town. Not being melodramatic, just go – because if they get a chance, the whole frigging city'll be on fire." They very nearly did it.

PC1: I saw bobbies getting injured with stones, bricks and all that stuff they were dropping out of the flats – coping stones, railings. I honestly thought one or two lads in particular had snuffed it, the way they took the blow. I thought to myself "You must be careful" and then got one full on the head.

PC2: They set light to milk floats, lorries, even a fire engine at one stage. I don't know where the bloody hell they got it from, but they aimed a tractor at us as well.

PC1: I realized, standing there with a shield, that people out there wanted me dead. That's a frightening thought.

PC in a large northern force, age 36, fourteen years service. Now in an inner-city area.

We had fellows coming here that never had a change of socks or a shirt for a week. They dossed on the floor of the police club bar or in local pubs. The fighting used to stop about dawn. Six o'clock in the friggin' morning at our local, the landlord used to open up the back room and the lounge. They were full of bobbies just crashed out because there was nowhere for them to go.

The violence at Toxteth was far worse than at Brixton earlier in the year and rapidly became the worst seen in half a century or more on mainland Britain. After the first two nights, police tactics had failed to control the crowd. Neighbouring forces were asked to help: men came from Cheshire, Lancashire and Greater Manchester, but still the rioting continued. At 2.15 a.m. on 7 July, with the skyline ablaze with more than forty fires, the Chief Constable of Merseyside, Kenneth Oxford, authorized the first use of CS gas on the mainland. It was seen as the only alternative to baton charges which had failed. Against the manufacturer's instructions, canisters were fired directly into the crowds, injuring several people badly. Both Oxford and, in the House of Commons, the Home Secretary William Whitelaw insisted that CS gas was still the minimum force available. On the mainland, it has not been used since.

It had been traditional British policing to "win while appearing to lose". At Toxteth in early July 1981, the police lost. For local police, used to winning, it was a shock. To police officers who had seen service with the Army in Northern Ireland, the handling of the riots was itself a shock.

Inspector in a large northern force, age 35, ten years experience. Now in a racially mixed area.

When I was out in Northern Ireland I was mortared. On two or three occasions I was shot at, but I was more frightened when I was in the front line down at Toxteth than I ever was in Ulster. Not because of what was happening, but because I was stuck there behind a shield with no chance whatsoever of doing anything to the people who were throwing petrol bombs at me, driving cars at us and trying to set fire to us by pouring diesel down the road. We stood there from 1 a.m. to 9 a.m. the next morning, taking that lot, and there wasn't one decision made.

Chief Inspector from a large northern force, age 37, twelve years service. Now in an inner-city area.

When I was in Northern Ireland, a riot like the one we had in Toxteth would have been dealt with by no more than 100 men. On the Sunday night at Toxteth, there were over 4000 police officers deployed and we still lost. Half of the Toxteth area was burnt to the ground. Now we lost, not because of the skill and the courage of the bobbies, but because you just stood there for most of that night and waited your turn to become injured.

On the first night of the riot I stood in the front line for about twelve hours with seven other officers. At the end of that night, one was in hospital with a fractured skull, one was in for about two weeks with complications to his spleen after being hit by a brick, and two other officers were in for two or three days each. It was only myself and two others who returned to duty the next day. It was a bloody disaster.

THE LESSONS

Among the many shocks of the rioting of 1981 was just how unprepared the police were to deal with them. For a force keen to be seen to be professional, the riots showed the police to be ill-equipped, poorly trained and badly led. In addition to physical injuries, for many officers the pride of the police had been badly hurt. Physical injuries could be seen and treated: the psychological damage is still being felt.

Met Chief Inspector, age 46, twenty years service.

We were so basic. We started with the dustbin lids in '76 –
that's all we had for protection when we were attacked. Then
we went to the large plastic shield you see today. That's called
the Metropolitan Police Shield, because we designed it out of
necessity. It was purely defensive so that if people threw things
at you, you had something other than dustbin lids to hide
behind. Then it was realized that when you were behind this
"wall" you were in fact cowering. In psychological terms, the
policeman is adopting a stance which is in fact cowardly – he's
bent down, crouching, and this tends to attract people to throw
missiles at the plastic wall. People would carry on throwing
because they knew they were safe and that we would not come
away from behind those plastic shields. In serious riots of 1981
they started coming closer and closer – I've got shields that have
been split right the way down, attacked by machetes on the
streets of London.

WEAK LEADERS

*No amount of equipment, however, can compensate for poor
leadership. Senior officers had not been trained for such emergencies and their indecision amplified the distress of the events
among the rank and file.*

*A story much repeated at the time was of a young PC who
had "lost his bottle" on the front line, thrown down his shield
and run away. Finally he collapsed in a doorway and wept. A
voice from behind him said, "Come on, son. Get back in there."
"Sorry, Sarge," said the lad, "I just couldn't take it any more."
"I'm not your Sergeant," said the voice. "I'm your Superintendent." "Crikey, sir," said the boy. "I didn't know I'd run
that far."*

**Two PCs from a large northern urban force, average age 30,
average service ten years. Both now in an inner-city area.**

PC1: It was so frustrating. American TV crews were saying:
"One black and white car could handle it" – and they were

right. They'd have gone to the boot and pulled out a grenade launcher. "Pop a bit of tear gas into that, will you? while I fire my shotgun over their heads." I've been training since and we learnt bugger all.

PC2: After all, it's still only training. The minute the real thing happens they'll do exactly the same as they did last time: we'll stand in a big line and get murdered.

PC1: It's a terrible thing to say, but sometimes the more super-vision you have the more unsupervised and the more confused it becomes. It's not a supervisor you want, it's a goddamn leader.

PC2: The highest rank you should have there should be an Inspector. Our bosses are no bloody good in a riot, by their mere age, their size and the fact that they've been drinking twelve pints of bitter a night for the past ten years – they're no bloody use. The man who's there is the man with ultimate responsibility. And the thing is with your bosses, if they make a wrong decision, they bugger their chances of going to the top. They'd sooner make none than make the wrong one. And unfortunately we're getting that lower down now as well.

PC1: When we were in Toxteth, one Inspector had a nervous breakdown. He literally froze. Then he came into the parade room a couple of days later to apologize to our fellows because he'd froze, and he just broke into tears, absolutely cried his eyes out. He couldn't take it, which is understandable really. In the end he resigned.

PC2: You look at some of the shifts and you look at some of the shift Inspectors, and you're thinking: "Oh my God, don't let me draw the short straw."

Policing is all about confidence. It takes courage and confidence to wade into a fight when outnumbered and trust that your uniform, your baton and your common sense will win the day. Toxteth shattered such confidence for the men who were there.

PC in a large northern force, age 33, twelve years service. Now in a racially mixed inner-city area.

I suppose there are some things you should never see. I don't know how you can describe the smoke and the flames and the terror, absolute terror. You're confined to a little space, you're stood behind the shield; there's petrol bombs flying through the air and every now and then someone's on fire who's in the same line as you, or your shield's on fire, or your shoes are on fire. It went on for so long. I was dreaming about it. I had to see a psychiatrist.

I had a dream about all of us, about the Section going round in a car. We were in plain clothes and we were indiscriminately murdering everybody in the daytime that was causing the trouble in the night time. I've never enjoyed a dream so much in my life.

After such experiences, the rank and file had to go back into the streets of Toxteth and Brixton and practise "community policing" with their enemies of the night before.

Three weeks after the first riots, Toxteth erupted again with even greater ferocity: boiling water and old television sets were hurled at policemen. But this second round gave officers the chance to seek the revenge they had dreamt of. The Chief Constable of Merseyside called it "positive policing". This included the Northern Ireland tactic of driving armoured Land Rovers high speed at the crowds – a tactic which, it was alleged, killed one bystander and broke the back of another. Police behaviour on the streets and later in the station was ferocious.

PC in a large northern force, age 32, ten years service. Now in an inner-city area.

When it happened again we were ready for them, at least more so. You have to make the first move, use your vehicles, drive the Land Rovers straight at the bastards. Then they scatter. You deal with the rest with your sticks. No problem. I don't give a fuck about the kids who got hurt. What were they doing on the streets in the first place in the middle of the fucking night?

In Toxteth the police eventually won, but at a price. The tensions there continue to this day. In fact, the local Authority is currently holding an inquiry which covers relations between the black community and the police. For legal reasons the police have decided that they cannot assist the inquiry.

Winning in Toxteth, however, was only the beginning of a sea change in police attitudes towards public order. It was the miners' strike that was to prove the decisive factor.

THE MINERS' STRIKE 1984

The inner-city riots had directly involved relatively few forces, though they shocked everyone in the service. The year of the miners' strike was to affect every officer in mainland Britain, either directly or indirectly through the tangle of moral, political and financial issues that the strike raised. The strike also marked a decisive stage in the gradual politicization of the police during the 1980s. The National Reporting Centre (NCR) at Scotland Yard directed support operations for the small forces in the mining areas. This was seen as the first step towards a national police force. Critics assumed that the NRC was run by the Home Secretary on behalf of the Prime Minister.

In fact, the NRC was first devised in 1973 by the Association of Chief Police Officers (ACPO) in response to the police defeat at Saltley Coke Depot in the Midlands. Arthur Scargill had had too many men for the police to take on without reinforcements, which had been impossible to mobilize in time. The peace was kept by closing the gates and withdrawing the police: "winning while appearing to lose." But ACPO and the government were determined never to let that happen again. A decade later, ACPO ran the NRC, asking its member forces how many men could be spared and moving them around the country as required. The Home Office and the Prime Minister were informed daily. Their financial and political support was essential, especially over controversial matters such as the stopping of pickets at the Dartford Tunnel and on the motorways.

In fact, the government had no need to order the police to act along these lines. Despite the concern for civil liberties expressed in Parliament and in the liberal press, the interviews show that police officers of all ranks supported these moves. Indeed, they failed to understand why anyone should object to actions designed to head off violence.

Despite their largely Conservative inclinations, however, the lower ranks resented being known as "Maggie's boys". Many PCs came from mining families, which was an added source of tension. As with the inner-city riots, they knew that whatever their personal feelings, their duty was to maintain the Queen's Peace. That was sometimes small consolation for the abuse heaped on them on the picket line.

For many officers, memories of violent encounters in Brixton and Toxteth had not yet faded when they found themselves facing hostility from yet another section of the working class – this time often kith and kin. To be treated as class traitors just for doing their job was traumatic and disillusioning for many PCs, and not unlike the frosty reception often afforded to GIs returning from Vietnam.

Sergeant from a large Midlands urban force, age 36, twelve years service. Now in an inner-city area.

I had some sympathy with the miners. I come from a poor working-class family with a mining community background. I know how close-knit they are, and how they must feel when their main source of employment is likely to disappear. It isn't just a job. It's your whole way of life going. You try to put yourself in that situation.

There were a lot of incidents of violence, but it was on both sides. There's no doubt about that. Every time it happened it got nastier and nastier. Now you've got 120,000 anti-police people, just on the mining side. Then you've got their wives and families. We've got enough enemies out there now – political enemies, coloureds, youngsters. We don't need the working man as well.

Met Sergeant, age 30, five years service. Just resigned.

I come from Derbyshire originally and I was going back to be billeted within fifteen miles from my parents' house! The miners then had a march and went up to London, to Downing Street. The police cordon went along the front of Downing Street. I was there. It was a very dumb job. That day the march didn't do anything particularly bad but for some reason a police charge was ordered. I never saw what did it and to this day I don't know why it happened. It really was horrible, I felt sick watching it. Then all the women walking past spat at me and said in Derbyshire accents, just like all my friends at home would say "and you're going to go home to your wives and children" – that kind of abuse. That was the most upset I ever was in the police. I really felt bad. But I went home and sat down in my nice flat in a civilized country town outside London and had a glass of port, and suddenly I was in a different world, I'd escaped. Escape was one of the most important things. Perhaps I was wrong, perhaps I should have stayed there and talked about it and suffered.

Some policemen were itching to get "stuck in", to feel the power and freedom that comes from moving as a forceful group. The miners' strike took them from the restraints of home and local policing to a situation where force would be used with the full backing of the government, if not the local community.

PC in a West Country force, age 27, six years service, and a graduate.

The first couple of times I went to the miners' strike I did not like it at all. This sort of show was almost paramilitary; turning up in bus loads. All of a sudden, you'd find yourself ranked up and marching to places. You wonder what on earth's going to happen and you don't quite believe it. We'd been practising for two years before. We'd march round wet Army camps having people throw squeezy bottles and things. It was a bit of a joke. When you started going to the real thing, using these techniques on real people, it was slightly awesome, but after a while it became easy.

Going up to Yorkshire, for one week in four, living in an Army barracks and working funny hours, wearing riot kit, crash helmets, regularly during the day – it becomes second nature after a while. I think you enjoy the genuine power it gives you. The power to inflict the collective will of the job on to a large crowd of people. It's much easier than walking the street by yourself when you've got to make decisions and take responsibility. You are just part of a vast crowd and if the whole thing is wrong or illegal, it's not you who's going to be picked up for it. It felt quite exciting, which is worrying really. If it's exciting being faced by that sort of violence it becomes quite addictive.

The miners' strike gave the police the first chance to try out the public order tactics, training and equipment with which they had been practising since the riots of 1981. This too is a strange echo of the Vietnam war, which served the Pentagon as a useful proving ground for new hardware.

Critics of the police felt the strikers were immediately subjected to unnecessarily heavy policing which escalated the violence. Within two months, the largest movements of police in British history were taking place across the country. Although much of the contact between pickets and police was peaceful – and unreported – the occasional violent showdowns were often terrifying to both sides. In one instance, when miners attacked unprotected policemen, visiting Home Office observers were so frightened by what they saw that they returned to the safety of their London offices to tighten up the nascent Public Order Act.

Superintendent in a southern Home Counties force, age 49, twenty-four years service. Now in a market town near London.

One time a group of over 3000 pickets had stoned and driven off a team of Yorkshire policemen and smashed two dog vans. It was essential that my officers moved the pickets back. There was a railway bridge which you could defend. Once they got past that, you'd had it.

As we moved our first unit down, we were stoned. So we baton-charged them and moved the crowd back. Then we were stoned from the railway bridge above, so we moved two units up there and took it. We held that for an hour, but at a cost – we had thirty-seven men injured out of eighty.

They didn't stand up to us because of the frightening effect of the way we moved. First of all, you put in a shield wall. Behind it you have spotlights. When a hail of missiles comes at you, immediately you aim the spotlights. They don't like that at all; you've thrown a brick and suddenly a spotlight comes right on you. Then the shield wall breaks in a perfectly disciplined formation and two groups of twenty officers come through that at the double. They have riot helmets on. They have round shields. They have sticks. They go straight at the crowd in a disciplined double march. It's bloody frightening. So the crowd moves. Then your long shield wall moves forward through your men with round shields and takes a new line there.

We moved down the road like that and took the railway bridge without actually coming into hand-to-hand fighting with the crowd, angry as they were.

Chief Inspector in a rural Midlands force, age 39, twenty years service. Now in charge of a large market town.

The token battles were astonishing as expressions of police/miner relationships. At the end of the day, it was so orchestrated that the Superintendent at our pit used to go up to the pickets and say, "Right lads, five minutes. They're on their way." And they'd come out of the warm hut and line up. There was a line marked on the pavement and they stood there. This is absolutely true. The Superintendent would say, "Now, we're going to have a good clean push, no fighting, no rubbing bollocks. I don't want to see anybody hurt." And the policemen would march out about two minutes before the buses came. As soon as they arrived, there was a shout of "Push!" and it was a rugby scrum. It was so orchestrated that if anybody broke through they'd run round and get in the back again. It was absolutely amazing!

PC in a Home Counties force north of London, age 40, nineteen years service. Now a village bobby.

Some bugger at the back of the crowd starts to push and the poor sods at the front meet Mister Wood. They try to escape backwards and it creates panic. It's usually a great barney where we get stuck in. Some people think you use the truncheon on a

man's head – you don't. You'd kill him. Breaking a collar bone
is best, then an elbow or a leg.

They hated the bastards from Thames Valley Police in the
miners' strike. They said we were the hardest force they came
up against. I was a beat bobby back here. When I came back
south, the parishioners didn't know what hit them. If they'd be
even slightly rowdy they'd be up against a wall, getting a good
talking to.

*Aggression was in the air. Everyone knew that violence might
be going on somewhere, and like most policemen they wanted
to be in on the action: it gave them a reason for being there.*

**Two PCs in a northern urban force, average age 28, average
service six years.**

PC1: I had a whole week when I was posted to a junction in
the middle of the Derbyshire countryside, where the flying
pickets was allegedly supposed to have been coming. We was
there for a whole week and there was nothing. Apart from the
sky.

PC2: We had bonfire night, and there was bonfire parties. We
were bored, very bored.

PC1: Everywhere we went there was vans. It was like an army.
When a convoy went past us on the motorway, it took about
five minutes to pass you. You would just stand there counting
police carriers. There were convoys of eighty vans!

PC2: Sometimes we just seemed to miss everything. We'd be
sent off to a holding point, wait there for something to happen,
and then they'd send us on, dispatch us to some sort of picket.
We'd get there, and we'd see a few vans with broken windows
and men with sweaty brows, and they'd say "It's all finished.
Drive to somewhere else." You spent the whole week on motorways – we was always just too late.

PC1: We were disappointed. You build yourself up – especially
as each time you're getting kitted up in riot gear as well. Then
as soon as you get all your kitting done it's back on the transit

and away you go somewhere else. It could be two hours before we got to where we were going next. When you're sat in a van for two hours, you want to get out and do something.

Crowd psychology played an important part throughout the strike. As in Vietnam, the anonymity of one side to the other was an encouragement to violence. Already frustrated by the impotence of their position, miners were enraged by the sheer scale of police tactics often used against them. With riot shields, plastic helmets and cavalry brought into play, an alien army seemed to be tearing up the social contract in which persuasion and consensus are vital tools in keeping the peace.

Met PC, age 29, seven years service. Now in the TSG.

You react to body language. If a person is getting on the offensive, he will lean forward. If the guy is on the defensive, he will start to move back. He's like an ape, he starts to turn his bum on you, he's surrendering. That's what they taught us, anyway. And they talked to us about challenge. If you face a crowd, and take the ground early, and stand and face a miner, and chat to him, the guy on the front row is never your enemy, he is always your friend. The guy on the second row is always pretty friendly; even the guy on the third row is possible – and after that forget it, because then they become a crowd.

Met Chief Inspector, age 48, twenty-seven years service. Now in training.

The mine gate opens at eight o'clock to let the shift in. So we form up at seven o'clock with reserves down the road, because you never knew which mines the pickets would head for; it was all bush telegraph. Suddenly a call comes through: pickets are making for mine X. Now, when the pickets get to mine X, they're going to block that gate, so you have to get your first line of uniform across the road to stop them. Immediately, you get confrontation. If you put barriers up, the buggers smash them up and throw them at you. If you put up a white tape, they just face you and push against you. That's what happened every day at the mines. The miners come up, the police come up, more miners, more police, and you have a shoving match.

Now, if both sides are being pushed from the back, the tonnage in pressure on the front line is incredible. And eventually there's trouble – the majority of miners were ordinary people, but one or two were very evil men. You'd get people holding darts through their fingers. They were normally in the second row of miners – all of a sudden through the line comes pff! and hits one of my officers in the face. Immediately he goes down, and that starts an eruption because his mates straight away go for that miner. The violence is escalated, the officers are now entitled to use minimum force to restore order. But people forget that minimum force is not about just standing there and saying, "I'm going to report you."

Some miners sought to provoke police violence, to solidify support for the strike. Many officers described how a core of militants toured the coalfields, transforming peaceful pickets into an attacking mob.

To the strikers, the police became the symbol of the National Coal Board and the government, much as they had represented the "haves" to those in the inner-city riots who were "have nots". When the militants turned up, the violence could get very nasty indeed.

Ex-Met PC, age 27, eight years service. Just retired.

I was up at South Yorkshire at a place called Gascoigne Wood. We turned up there on the Monday and there were 6000 pickets and not many policemen. We were there to see two people go to "work" – it wasn't even a working pit. By the end of the week there was going to be trouble, you could just sense it. On the Thursday, having got these two people into work all week, the pickets ripped down the farmer's fence, rolled these massive bails of hay into the road, set fire to them, put the fence on top and got a really good bonfire going. They blocked the road. Then the taxi with these two miners started to come down the road and the crowd pushed forward against the one blue line of police officers – who weren't in riot gear. We were pushed across the road and down into a ditch against a barbed wire fence. It was terrifying. You feared for your safety – for your life! Then all the brave people at the back of this crowd started picking up rocks, flints and large stones from the field and started throwing them. So the stuff started coming over and there were police officers dropping all round and pickets as well because they were hitting their own people.

In that situation what do you do? A senior officer from the Greater Manchester Police told us to draw our truncheons and we did. Then you hit the first thing in front of you. But the first person in front of you wasn't doing anything. They haven't thumped you. They were getting hit by the stones as well. It was like doing a baton charge in Palestine or something, you fix your bayonets and run down the road and the road clears like dust. You hit the first person in front of you. All right you are going to hit some innocent people, but in general you are going to stop a riot. And that's what we did.

Legally we didn't have a leg to stand on. When you are sitting in your armchair back in London drinking tea, or having a beer, and you see the television showing something on the miners' strike and you see this policeman running across the road belting someone with his truncheon you think that's a bit out of order. But if you were actually there, you were in fear of your life. That's no exaggeration.

The fundamental split between "hard" and "soft" policing that was raised by the inner-city riots (see "Community Policing") surfaced as an issue in the miners' strike. Smaller provincial forces were staffed largely by local men. Even if they were not themselves from the coalfields, they were more sensitive to community feeling in the pit villages. No such ties restrained officers from further afield, particularly those from cities which had seen rioting. They were contemptuous of the caution exercised by local forces and were determined not to lose face at a public order disturbance again.

Met Sergeant, age 34, sixteen years service. Now in West London.

The Met used to bundle out of the van, putting bits of uniform on. We were the scruffiest cunts up there. But at the end of the day, when it came to actually doing anything, the other forces just waited for orders, whereas we waded in and dealt with it.

Half way through the strike you might go to a pit which hadn't been policed by the Met before. You'd get there 3 or 4 a.m. Monday morning and the pickets all turn up expecting what they had last time. From that morning on there'd be nobody up there for the rest of the week. We liked our reputation – I'm not sure it was 100 per cent justified, but that's what happened.

Met Superintendent, age 43, twenty-seven years service (ex-cadet). Now in an inner-city area of North London.

We were outside a pub in South Yorks which wasn't closing. Quarter past eleven, and the local Superintendent wanted to close it down. But he didn't know how to handle it, either because he had been an Admin man all his life or he was useless. The people outside were from Hampshire Constabulary. They were ultra-smart and they marched about – a Sergeant and ten PCs – "left, right, left, right." They looked bloody silly. All these miners were taking the piss. We had some Met officers there. They looked a right shambles compared to these super-dooper Hampshire blokes, but the Sergeants and Inspectors knew exactly what to do. It's like facing a dog when you are scared, they can sense your fear, but if you are a vet or someone with the ability to handle them, you go straight in and grab it by the scruff of the neck and tell it to shut up. It's the same with people.

Chief Inspector in an eastern Home Counties force, age 33, ten years service, and a graduate.

You saw why the Met is known for its lawlessness, more than any other force. One Met support unit developed a special technique where any picket who was a little troublesome got shoved in at one end of the line. This was in broad daylight, two lines of ten policemen, six feet tall. They'd sort anyone out.

These blokes would stagger out the other end punch drunk, but not a mark on them. They didn't know what had happened to them, and they sure didn't want it again. All the other forces there were talking about it.

When Met support units were about, other people were very, very careful about their equipment, because they would nick it given half the chance – shields, whatever. In Kent once a whole field of potatoes was dug up in the night by the Met. That's a lot of serious work. Perhaps they were desperate for chip butties! When you've got serious public order problems, though, that's when you need the morals of the Met. They don't take any nonsense.

The police expected the miners' strike to end quickly. It was summer and the National Union of Miners (NUM) was split, and a massive show of police strength was calculated to see off further trouble. The sheer scale of police tactics, however, stiffened the resolve of wavering miners and faced the police with a much larger and more prolonged operation. Men were mobilized on a para-military scale, with up to 4000 officers being accommodated in local barracks. At Orgreave, 8000 officers were massed in one place – more men than belonged to any other mainland force except for the Met.

Two Met Sergeants, average age 33, average service nine years. Now in a racially mixed area of North London.

Sgt1: The main problem when we were there was that the shifts were so awful. Getting up at 2 a.m. in the morning and doing fourteen-hour days. Your tempers were on a thin edge anyway. Most of the accommodation was absolutely atrocious. In Derbyshire we were on stretchers which were inches off the floor, living out of a suitcase. You were virtually sleeping on the ground; a piece of string on the wall to hang any clothes on and one chair, one basin with cold water only between forty men. This went on for eight days. When you did sleep it was short naps. So when you are confronted with violence, you don't think straight and you act out of frustration.

Sgt2: You can have all the briefings you like, but the situation changed so quickly that you had got to act independently –

you lost touch with your commanders anyway, they tended to disappear over to the other side. Most of the time you were without radio communication. I couldn't exercise responsibility as a Sergeant, there was just no way. Sometimes the bobbies would find themselves isolated, in threes and fours. Being on your own with 3000 or 4000 miners around, you are just damned bloody scared and you are a liar if you say you're not. You work on the basis that "we should do something before they do", and you haven't got many options. A lot of trouble was going on because there was a lot of short-fuse police around.

Sgt1: I certainly did not agree with all the aggressive police tactics. OK, there was violence from the miners, but sometimes you can see just as much on a Saturday night down here.

For men up from the inner cities of Liverpool, Manchester and London, the strike was a moral no man's land. It was a break from the pressures of urban policing. No one knew them and they knew no one. They had plenty of money, and time: they would finish duty at noon, sleep until six, then drink until the pubs and clubs finally closed. Officers frequently rolled up for duty at 2 or 3 a.m. much the worse for wear. The behaviour of some off-duty PCs in these "foreign parts" was yet another echo of Vietnam.

PC in a Midlands force, age 30, nine years service. Now in a city centre area.

You just had to have a few drinks in the evening. You were working ridiculous shifts. It wasn't how many incidents you went to, it was the expectancy of going to incidents and having your sleep broken. You're not prepared for anything and your mental state is bizarre. Back home you literally took a bloody week to get over it, by which time you had to go back again.

Sergeant in a large northern force, age 36, twelve years service. Now in a working-class city suburb.

A lot of the lads pulled – liked to go for local girls. A lad from the south married one. Most of them, it was just a case of having a couple of drinks and then hitting the sack. But there was mixing, we had good laughs. There was one time, we had a charity football match for a local appeal. We all got dressed up as girls with dresses and everything and we played their girls – real girls. That was a hell of a laugh. And we raised quite a lot of money – about £400. Just on that one night.

Met Sergeant, age 42, twenty years service; Met PC, age 23, three years service. Both now in West London.

Sgt: I knew from the officers involved about a rape by two Met PCs that was covered up during the miners' strike. It was up at Nottingham. We were on duty for eighteen days straight so we all ended up on the piss down the Palais in Notts. They picked up this girl, took her back to her flat. One went upstairs where she performed, while the other waited downstairs pissed out of his brains. Finally he decided he'd have a go too and went upstairs and raped her. Then they caught a cab back to the pit, and the girl complained.

Suddenly they were taken off the picket line by two plain-clothes DCs from the local force and thrown in the cell. They were scared shitless. They sobered up very fast, very very fast.

The blokes just put their hands up and asked if there was anything the Notts lads could do to help them. And there was. It was talked about at high management levels – don't know how high, but pretty high up. In the end the girl agreed that "if he'd asked nicely she might have let him", so it wasn't what I'd call a serious rape. She wasn't hurt or anything. So she withdrew the complaint. They were on the train from Grantham that night back to London, and never went back up there.

PC: There you are. That shows how the police react to rape. I think they should have been slung out.

Deputy Chief Constable from a northern force in a mining area, age 50, twenty-six years service. Recently retired.

We had off-duty police officers, partially dressed in uniform, getting drunk and then being abusive to ordinary people – like anybody who's away from home and living in semi-military conditions. It's not too easy to take for the people who happen to live there and see their husbands, sons or fathers out of work. People refused to serve them, they were an army of occupation. And a lot of places were out of bounds to them. Policemen rolled money down to the pickets, shouting "You're hard up!" Others flashed ten pound notes from the windows of police vans. These miners are proud men, defending what they see as being their right to keep their pit. These outsiders come in – men who were much younger than them – and do these things that were pretty indefensible. It was bound to lead to violence. You could never discipline them because you could never prove there was anyone responsible. We used to send them back to London, Liverpool, Manchester, wherever. We don't want them here again.

Orgreave coking plant near Rotherham in South Yorkshire was the setting for the most violent scenes of the miners' strike. On 28 May 1984, 1500 police faced 1800 pickets. Police used dogs and horses, baton charges and riot shields against missiles of all sorts, iron railings and wire stretched across the road to catch the horses. Sixty-four people were injured and eighty-four arrested, including Arthur Scargill who complained of "scenes of unbelievable brutality ... reminiscent of a Latin American state".

On 18 June, 10,000 pickets faced 8000 police. This time the weapons used against the cavalry included paving stones, bricks, bottles, petrol bombs and sharpened posts. Assistant Chief Constable Clements, from Yorkshire, who was in charge that day, said, "It was a miracle no one was killed."

The nation was split by the scenes of violence on television, reminiscent of wartime. Both sides accused the media of bias: the miners charged ITN with switching shots of stone throwing to before the police mounted charge, in order to help the police justify their actions. The police felt the news played down the provocations. The shot of a bobby hitting a miner with his truncheon became a national image. Phalanxes of police in riot gear were seen attacking apparently unprotected miners who seemed to be trying to escape. Even for viewers with pro-police sympathies, it was a disturbing sight.

Sergeant in a large northern force, age 32, ten years service. Now in an inner-city area.

Before the horses went in up at Orgreave it was bloody chaos. There was smoke bombs, all sorts of missiles. They were up in a field; blokes that had ripped up bloody palings and they were waving them at us. We should have gone in, taken them out, but for some reason we just stood there watching them. I've never seen so many bloody policemen in all my life. On the road we must have been thirty or forty thick.

They had the advantage of higher ground. Like they got this telegraph pole and set it on fire and rolled it down the road at us. Then they set that caravan on fire with all the gas bottles in it. That's when they realized they were going to have to do something to stop the miners being injured. So then the fire brigade came and sorted it out.

There was nothing you could do. There was that many policemen you were hemmed in. Like there were thirty rows in front of me and another ten behind. It was bloody confusing, I can tell you. We'd had so much bloody aggravation. Like the miners were just getting away with murder.

At the trial of those arrested at Orgreave, the judge reminded ACC Clements that the pickets had a legal right to be there. While briefly agreeing, Clements reverted to the view that "he would not be the slightest troubled if they were trampled by police horses." Evidence was also provided of a police film showing horses charging pickets with no apparent provocation. But those officers we interviewed were convinced the cavalry were needed.

PC in a northern force, age 34, ten years service.

It was late in the afternoon the horses went through. And when they came back, we all applauded. I've never been in a situation like it. It was great to see them smashing into all them bastards who'd been giving us grief all day. A lot of bobbies were injured. It was as though somebody thought, "Right. We're not standing for this crap anymore. We'll sort it out." And that's what they did. It was the greatest thing I ever saw.

PC in a northern force, age 27, eight years service. Now in an industrial town.

With all that riot clobber you can't hear what's going on once you've got the bloody helmet on. You can't help feeling vulnerable. It doesn't matter how much gear you've got on. At Orgreave at one point two fellows on either side of me got knocked down. I thought, "Surely I'm knackered", but they moved back the crowd. It all got worse towards the end, when the violent element were using nails to fire at the horses. I mean we just stood there in a bloody line and were gradually removed by ambulance.

A reasonably high-ranking officer got involved regularly. He'd been through five or ten uniforms himself because they'd been covered in bricks, petrol, everything. But the respect he had from the lads was unbelievable. He even had time to come round to our unit, "How are you?" etc. I know it's simple, but it surprised me.

It was only after a couple of days of being home that we realized how dangerous Orgreave had been. I'm surprised it took so long for a bobby to be killed in recent times. It stunned me in the miners' strike that none of us were killed. It's more luck than anything else.

The huge bill for the strike was largely picked up by the government. At a time of cutbacks in police resources at home, this fed police cynicism that they were just pawns in a political game. "It's all politics" is a cry of despair even with a government claiming to be supportive.

PC in an eastern mining area, age 33, seven years service.

The Tories have a reputation for being extremely pro-police. They've been in since I've been a policeman. Quite what another government would do, I don't know. Tories tend to be verbally supportive but I think we are in serious danger of being used as a tool. Like we were during the miners' strike. No question, we were "Maggie's boys". I hated that. I hated the feeling we were being used. But they had us by the short and curlies. We had no choice. No choice at all.

I like to think the Chief Constables do have independence. We're supposed to be fucking impartial. I don't think we are. Not now. That's the unpleasant truth.

MINERS' STRIKE 1984–5

Police deployed: 40 million hours worked by police from 42 forces.

Reinforcements: Average deployment: 3000 a day, rising to 8000 a day at the height of the strike; 12 forces requested aid; 30 forces gave aid.

Cost of policing: £200,000,000.

Police injuries: 1392 (10 per cent needing hospital treatment), 85 serious.

Arrests: 9810 arrests; 5653 cases brought; 4318 convictions.

Charges:

    3 Murder
   39 Assault causing grievous
      bodily harm
  429 Assault causing actual bodily
      harm
  360 Assaulting a police constable
   49 Possessing an offensive
      weapon
  137 Riot
  509 Unlawful assembly
   21 Affray
 4107 Conduct conducive to a
      breach of the peace (Section
      5, Public Order Act 1936)
  207 Breach of the peace
 1019 Criminal damage
    4 Criminal damage with intent
      to endanger life
   15 Arson
   31 Burglary
  352 Theft
    1 Handling stolen property

 1682 Obstruction of a police
      constable
   19 Assault with intent to resist
      arrest
   32 Breach of bail conditions
  640 Obstruction of the highway
   16 Reckless driving
    5 Threats to kill
   13 Threats conspiracy to cause
      damage
   18 Attempt (various offences)
    1 Incitement
  275 Intimidation (Section 7,
      Conspiracy and Protection
      of Property Act 1875)
    2 Unlawful imprisonment
    3 Explosive offences
    1 Drug offences
   20 Railway offences
   66 Drunkenness
  296 Minor and miscellaneous
      offences were also charged

RETURN TO NORMAL

The miners' strike was a victory for the police. After the humiliation of the inner-city riots, they saved face. But some PCs had lost heart and many others had lost their innocence. Some found that the strike had changed them from being friendly local bobbies into hard, suspicious, aggressive men.

The psychological cost of the strike was paid over the following years on the streets of the towns and cities to which the police returned. Morale was low, particularly in inner-city areas. The strike had been a time of action, but the men returned to find their independence now considerably circumscribed: the "sus" laws had gone and racial awareness was the new theme. In the eyes of the rank and file that meant allowing black people to do what they liked. Official policy endorsed community policing. But on the street tension between black youths and the police – now veterans of the strike – was reaching dangerous levels once again.

In the late September of 1985, Handsworth went up. It was a multiracial area of Birmingham, previously noted for its good community relations. Recent "hard" policing against local drug dealers was believed to have motivated the riots, but the trigger was insensitive police handling of a minor traffic offence during a crackdown on illegal parking. Despite the training and equipment introduced since 1981, it still took three days to control the disorder. There was £5 million worth of damage and two Asians died defending their shops.

One week later, in Brixton in South London, armed police raided the home of Mrs Cherry Groce looking for her son. During the search of the house, Inspector Douglas Lovelock, an Authorized Firearms Officer (see Firearms), accidentally shot and paralysed her. An angry crowd then formed outside Brixton police station and serious rioting soon broke out.

BRIXTON 29 SEPTEMBER 1985

Demonstrators: 57 per cent West Indian/African, 39 per cent white, 2 per cent Asian, 1 per cent other.

Damage: 114 buildings damaged; looting; cars set alight.

Arrests: 292, of which 13 people were charged with looting.

Injuries: Civilians 31 (including 2 killed), police 93.

A few days later, the most vivid test of the new police approach to public order came at the Broadwater Farm Estate in North London.

BROADWATER FARM, TOTTENHAM

On 5 October 1985, in Tottenham, in North East London, police raided the home of Mrs Cynthia Jarrett, looking for evidence against her son. She was knocked over in their rush through the house and suffered a fatal heart attack. The next day, a crowd of three hundred marched on the local police station to protest. They were allowed to do so, and dispersed peacefully. Meanwhile, on the nearby Broadwater Farm estate, which the police considered extremely dangerous, officers were attacked by a group of black youths. Riot police were called in to close off the estate. Youths set up burning barricades and began throwing missiles at the police from behind them.

Police units were positioned on the access roads into the estate in such a way as to be vulnerable to the missiles, but they were unable to move in to contain the situation without serious risk of ambush from the maze of walkways above street level. For the most part local policemen were not involved, and communications were poor. Two commanding officers clashed openly on the radio about whether to go into the estate. By 9.15 p.m., the Commissioner of the Met had authorized the deployment of CS gas and plastic bullets if necessary. Up to 1300 police officers were available to control the riot, but only a few hundred were actually used. Many were kept in vans near the estate from which they could hear the fighting on the radio and learned of the death of PC Kenneth Blakelock, stabbed in an ambush on firemen whom he was escorting. Firearms were also reported to have been used.

By 2 a.m. the fighting had died down, and the Special Patrol Group were sent in to clear the area.

BROADWATER FARM, TOTTENHAM 6 OCTOBER 1985

Demonstrators: 71 per cent West Indian/African, 25 per cent white, 2 per cent Asian, 3 per cent other.

Damage: £293,000; 346 crimes reported, including 34 of arson and 53 of criminal damage; one building destroyed and 16 damaged.

Arrests: 319, of which 159 people were eventually charged.

Injuries: 17 Civilians, 163 police (including one killed), one fireman.

Met PC, age 25, four years service; Met Sergeant, age 33, twelve years service. Both now in a West End station.

PC: It was awful. Just fucking awful. It's hard to find the words to describe it. It was much too upsetting to watch on TV after eighteen hours of being there, I can tell you that. It was too much for my wife too. She was in fucking pieces. And so was I.

Sgt: I watched the telly because I learned more from the TV than I did from the guv'nors. I thought "Oh yeah, that's where we were."

PC: We was sitting in the station in the West End just listening to the World Service on the radio about how policemen were under attack in Broadwater Farm in London. And we all just looked at each other and said, "Broadwater Farm? Where the fuck is that?" Then we found out.

Sgt: Yeah, I remember driving up past these nice houses in the carrier and just wondering where it was, what kind of farm we were going to see in the city. And then suddenly you see it behind the nice little houses – really ugly like a grim castle.

PC: They had the local District Support Unit [a riot-trained team of ten PCs, a Sergeant and Inspector] who knew all the fucking walkways and twists and fucking turns, yet they were the ones sent home. They were young and fit, and shield-trained, but they were never used. Instead they put in people who were forty years old, Home Beat officers like Blakelock who had never held a shield. They were the ones put in, and had to figure out how to hold a shield while some fucker's throwing petrol bombs at you. The bastard thing weighs 27 pounds. It's heavy and it's awkward. Then you form up into five-man teams and you look around to see who's with you and they're all fucking strangers! It takes time to learn to move as a group. And you need to trust them. You wouldn't know if they'd bottle out if you went and snatched someone. Lots of them did bottle out that day.

Sgt: Yeah, the telly was very misleading with its images of rows and rows of helmets. Only two hundred police were involved in the fighting. It was very, very scary. I still have nightmares and it's two years later.

Met Superintendent, age 46, twenty-eight years service. Now in a racially mixed area of North London.

I'm not given to fear, but I thought: "We're going to lose this." Bottles of flaming petrol were coming down, they were getting brazen and running up to the shields, and the blokes are standing there, not quite knowing what to do. We were being pushed back. For the first time in my life I'm frightened.

Every entrance to the estate is barricaded, with big fires. Just getting into the place is completely impossible. I was with the commander in Gloucester Road when a call came over, saying these people were trapped in a fire above a shop. The fireman says, "We've got to go in there. My blokes will need some protection." The commander calls for help, but it doesn't come so he sends nine or ten of his own men to cover the firemen.

Whatever you've heard, whatever you believe, the reality is that when the firemen went in there they were all chased out, including the policemen. One man fell over and he was hacked to death. I was actually there when Keith Blakelock was carried out. The firemen were trying to resuscitate him – he was covered in cuts, you couldn't see his face. They turn his head over and there's a knife in his throat. You know he's got to be dead.

I can remember blokes from his unit – one bloke saw it and his legs went from under him, he flaked out. The word went round and about three or four blokes just physically went down in the road like that – just couldn't believe it was one of their own mates.

The tragedy of Broadwater Farm forced a major reconsideration at the highest levels of the service, as well as deep anguish among the lower ranks. The fact that plastic bullets had been available but not used seemed one simple solution.

Scottish Inspector, age 39, thirteen years service.

You can have the best soldiers in the world, but if you haven't got a good general to lead them you end up with a big cock-up. Broadwater Farm showed us a good example of that. For a lot of the time senior police officers have got to be more managers than leaders. But when the muck and bullets start flying they have got to be leaders as well.

I came from the Royal Marines, where the officers were there to look after the welfare of the men. You come to this job and find a lot of senior officers aren't looking after the welfare of the men at all. They are looking after their own welfare to ensure they get to the next rank. That's a sad reflection. It grieves me.

Inspector in a Home Counties force, age 35, ten years service. Now in a port city.

The old hindsight brigade is great. You're stood there on the street with things happening and you make your decision: it's great for some fellow to come in the next morning at 9 a.m. and say, "You made the wrong decision." He hasn't stood there with his arse going and knees knocking, he's sitting in a nice office the next morning when he knows the result. That's when it takes the guts to stand by the decision. There should be officers who will turn around and say: "Well done lad. You made a decision. OK, so you made a cock-up – learn by it." But they don't in this job. They will hang that fellow for it. There is a good chance that will be the end of his career.

Broadwater Farm is a prime example of when no one was willing to make a decision. They were being shot at. They almost certainly knew an officer had been killed, and they didn't have the bottle to give the order to use plastic bullets. They were firing revolvers and shotguns at the police officers there. If police officers had returned fire with plastic bullets, I know what the headlines would have been.

Plastic bullets are a familiar weapon to the RUC, who were astonished at the restraint shown at Tottenham.

RUC Chief Inspector, age 36, sixteen years service; PC, age 32, twelve years service. Both now in West Belfast.

Chief Insp: Seeing a person on fire is a dreadful sight. I always think that if it hadn't been for the advent of the plastic bullet, we'd all be lying dead on the ground. Each baton charge used to lose us a quarter of the men. There's thousands of people in a riot. You are limited in the number of charges you can make and you can't run up and down the streets all night.

PC: Those who criticize us have never been standing in a riot. You ask any policeman who was at Broadwater Farm if they'd have used plastic bullets. But they had their baton guns chained in a Land Rover with the key in the guv'nor's pocket. Nobody could use them. One thing people forget: plastic bullets are an intermediate force. If we wanted to kill people, we'd use guns.

Chief Insp: The protection of life and property is your priority. You don't allow your men to be injured or property to be burned down. Quick firing of a plastic bullet can prevent all that. You can suddenly become surrounded by a crowd, you can be in a vehicle that is going to be turned over and burned with the men in it. As the old saying goes, "To do nothing is to fail."

We've had eighteen years of experience, very hard experience. The public order situations in England are totally new to them. I have a lot of sympathy. The guv'nor's at dinner somewhere and he suddenly gets a telephone call: "There's a riot in your Subdivision." The man hasn't a clue. He gets policemen there to try and settle the situation. He gets a community relations man. What can you do? Really you are grabbing at straws as to what you do, unless you have been trained in it.

RUC Sergeant, age 34, fourteen years service. Now in a border town.

The problem, in England, is with image. The police in England want to project the image that they're still policemen in normal circumstances. They went out there with absolutely no protection apart from shields. They were taking casualties left, right and centre. I've got an awful lot of sympathy. I can remember, as most of us can, the outbreak of the riots in Derry where policemen were on their feet for days with no shields, their handkerchiefs over their faces for the CS gas! It was a ridiculous situation. We learned, I must say that the Police Authority came to our aid with the training and equipment. Maybe it's the kind of thing the English police are reluctant to do – and perhaps rightly so. Perhaps they don't want to be seen to be going this far, if they can settle it with normal policing.

THE PARADOX OF PUBLIC ORDER POLICING

Since 1985, there have been no major riots in mainland Britain, but public order has remained high on the police agenda. "Hard" policing in the St Paul's area of Bristol in 1986 and in All Saints Road in London in 1987 produced drug raids supported by large numbers of men sent in to contain any local reaction. In the Notting Hill Carnival of 1987, youths went in for serious stone and bottle throwing in "revenge" but were put down by hundreds of policemen in riot gear. Some 7000 officers policed the event itself. In 1988, the threat of the cancellation of the whole event, together with elaborate preparations and a heavy police presence, reduced crime to a new low.

The return to normality after the riots of 1985 took another jolt from the year-long strike at Wapping in London, against Rupert Murdoch's News International. It was deeply unwelcome in police circles: quite apart from the sheer unpleasantness of long cold hours standing on the picket line, the police were yet again placed between two unpopular causes.

WAPPING

Wapping was the worst kind of public order policing. Every night for a year, hundreds of officers were bussed across London, disrupting their shift and rest patterns and denuding their local community of cover. Most nights passed uneventfully save for the minutes of excitement after midnight when the newspaper lorries emerged. But the tedium was mixed with the threat of harassment from the pickets, and unpredictable violence from their visiting supporters – some of whom were known as "Rent-a-Mob" from their regular appearances at demonstrations and marches. They would join the crowd when the pub closed and the tension would rise. On Wednesdays and Saturdays large crowds were expected and the whole area was turned into a police camp, with each side street filled with dog handlers, mounted police, and coach loads of reserves with riot gear. On the anniversary of the start of the strike, real violence broke out that was put down with such heavy measures as cavalry charges into the crowd. A huge array of stones and other missiles was revealed when the crowd retreated, but eighteen Met officers now face charges of excessive violence for their actions that night.

This is the paradox of public order policing: strength works in the short term, but may defeat longer-term objectives. Swamping an area with hundreds of policemen may keep the lid on, but the drain on manpower and the damage to community relations is too costly to be sustained. Older members of the community may be reassured, but not the young on whose trust the future of policing by consensus depends. Endorsed at the top in theory, can community policing work in practice, while "slow rioting" is going on?

Superintendent in a northern urban force, age 40, eighteen years service. Now in an industrial suburb.

Truthfully, we haven't yet found an alternative strategy to replace the clip round the earhole. Not that I'm advocating a return to those ways of doing things, we just haven't come up with a replacement. From Grosvenor Square in '68 to the riots to the miners' strike, we've been disastrously wrong and have tried to learn from our mistakes. But really the only thing we've been able to do is to throw more men at the problem.

Met Deputy Assistant Commissioner, age 47, twenty-four years service. Now in Central London.

If the day comes when we have to use plastic bullets, we will have lost. The issue of policing by consent will have disappeared.

Although public order duties have their benefits in terms of overtime and an initial change of scenery, their negative side takes a longer and more damaging toll on the morale and experience of the force. After the riots and the miners' strike, the wastage rate increased. Officers left because they found the reality bore too little resemblance to police fiction, or there was too little future for talent and imagination, or simply too much aggravation for the pay.

The gaps left by the departure of experienced men were not being filled while public order duties like the year-long strike at Wapping absorbed so much police time. Day after day and night after night on the picket line or the demo, young PCs were learning nothing about normal police work, no processing of cases, no court work, no contact with the public out in the community. Instead they found themselves the target of abuse, which is dispiriting at the best of times. It was bad for the public image of the police to be seen so often in a heavy-handed mode. Indeed the experience was bad for the police's image of themselves. Public order duties are the least creative, least rewarding of police tasks, but they dominated policing in the 1980s.

CHAPTER THREE

Community Policing

BUILDING BRIDGES

Community policing has been hailed in some quarters as the antidote to public order problems, as the key to the future, but it is really an echo of the past: Dixon of Dock Green is dead. Long live Dixon of Toxteth or Tottenham or Belfast. From our interviews with Community Liaison Officers, it seems the voice of Dixon is still alive.

Lord Scarman, in 1981, and many others since, have spoken of the need for community policing. It is as if it has magical powers – like the laying on of hands – to restore the trust broken by the inner-city riots and the insensitive policing that helped to cause them. But "community policing" is a vague phrase. It covers the simple provision of more neighbourhood bobbies on the beat. They may be too shy or lazy to do more than show the flag. It also covers old-fashioned beat policing in which constables talk to the public and feed local intelligence back to the station to be dealt with in the usual way.

Community policing at its most elaborate is what John Alderson, former Chief Constable of Devon and Cornwall, called "pro-active policing". It is meant as an alternative to "fire fighting" policing: waiting for things to happen, reacting to them with two-tones blaring like the cavalry in a Western. Instead, "pro-active policing" means taking an active role with other agencies in the area to do something constructive about the causes of public disorder, vandalism and crime, ideally before they happen.

But the very term "community policing" begs the question of how the other agencies and the community feel about the police. If they are seen as hostile, their presence among social workers or in schools is likely to be more a cause for concern than for welcome. This puts the Community Police Officer into a bind. He must act as part of a community that may not want him there.

Research by the Police Foundation and other academics has raised questions about the nature of community policing itself. For example, Community Police Officers who set up formal Neighbourhood Watch schemes may find that they interfere with informal observations that worked well before. Nosy or distrusted neighbours may spoil such schemes for the rest of a street. Police response to their information can undermine the local officer's position. Is community policing really just a way of persuading the public to spy on itself? How much will social workers share with a police officer if they believe it will go straight on to the police computer? Do Neighbourhood Watch schemes prevent crimes or just move them to other areas or on to the streets?

Even if community policing is desirable, it is a specialized area which needs scarce manpower. And what do Community Police Officers actually do much of the time? Because of the nature of their job – away from shifts and normal policing duties – they are not seen as "real coppers". Yet, as the first point of contact between the community and the police, and because they actively seek the community's views, they tend to be blamed both for social problems, such as vandalism, which are beyond their control, and for police misbehaviour, which is also beyond their control.

Community Police Officers are in limbo, caught between the public and the rest of their colleagues, whose actions during a single incident can undo months of reassurance. In the weeks following, it will be up to the Community Police Officer to pick up the pieces.

**Met Superintendent, age 46, twenty-eight years service.
Formerly a Community Relations Officer, now in a racially mixed inner-city area of North London.**

I've had three years as CLO in North London. I'd go to a meeting and they'd be spitting on the floor as I got up. You get talking with these people and you begin to understand their reasons. Stories about people being brought to a station and given a hiding. Once I managed to follow it right the way through and spoke to the guy who said he got a hiding. He admitted to me – a major triumph – that he never got one. He laughed and said it was expected.

I've got a hundred or so Neighbourhood Watches spread around the ground. They're all active and they're eyes and ears in the community, telling me what they're unhappy about. They might complain that their policemen are being taken away too often for demonstrations, or that a policeman who's been promoted has not been replaced. I go along to their meetings. I'm on the spot.

Initially it was very discouraging – I arrived thinking: "Here I am – appreciate me, give me a pat on the head and a sugar lump because I'm doing the best I can for you." What I learnt is that you've got a long long way to go to change attitudes. Too many people kid themselves that the problems are easily solved. At the end of the day all you can do is provide a little nudge and a push. One major disadvantage is that the Met recruits only one in seven from London – if that. How can you implant an outsider and make him instantly in tune with the vibes of the locality? You can't.

As an immigrant myself, with immigrant sensitivities – my mum was Irish and I can remember going down the street with her and someone saying: "You fucking Irish cow!" after a bombing – I know what it can be like. That gives me an edge. But I'm white, I'm protected, it's not until I open my mouth that I'm subject to hostilities.

Some people in the force think that anything to do with the community is not macho. For young men who join to prevent crime and catch criminals, going around and talking to Mrs Jones to find out what her problems are is a long way away from what they wanted to be. They'll think differently ten years on. They'll realize that it is the key to it all, because unless Mrs Jones says: "I saw him do it and I'm coming along to make a statement," it's all for nothing. And when Mrs Jones spots someone and rings the station our new young man will get his chance to catch a criminal.

TALKING TO STRANGERS

Community policing presupposes a certain kind of police officer, whose attitude towards the public is open and constructive. In volatile inner-city areas, the job of Community Police or Home Beat Officers demands exceptional skills, yet we ask ordinary young men and women to achieve them. Talking to strangers is not easy for most people. It is not easy for police officers either. The uniform is an added complication, with its built-in authority and unpleasant associations. Despite more training in what are called communication skills, the aggressive-defensive reactions of young PCs unsure of their authority are still all too common. Some older bobbies are just cynical. Rudeness and assaults by policemen are the major complaints against the force.

Met PC, age 28, six years service. Now in an inner city area in South London.

I was based out in the periphery of London in a slightly more rural setting, yet that area was busier than here. It had its own problems with the Asian community. Their outlook on life and their reaction to law enforcement was totally different. For a start they were used to being bashed senseless by the police back home and they were used to the police making judgements, whereas in this country most laws are about compromise. They could never see it.

The younger ones have been brought up Western but then the family want them to live in the traditional way, arranged marriages and that. If you've looked at the missing persons reports, you'll find that there are an awful lot of Asian girls listed. Seventeen, eighteen-year olds, just been through school, got very good A Levels – and mum and dad are finding some peasant from India to marry her to. You have got to deal with that. How can you talk to these people? You can't learn it, you've just got to find your way.

Now we're under pressure to justify our jobs. There are all these evaluation people who want to see little boxes ticked, "This is what our policemen have done today." You can't. You talk to a bunch of kiddies on the street, and they want to play with your helmet. You can't quantify that as a tangible result. But you've made contact with people. That's what we're here for.

GUESSING IN THE DARK

Since 1981, there has been a general consensus that neighbourhood and community policing and more bobbies out of cars and on to the beat – are a "good thing". But a US study in Kansas City established there is no direct link between crime in a given area and the number of policemen patrolling the streets. It is hard to measure whether the bobby on the beat is doing anything useful or not.

The research carried out in Britain by the Police Foundation and others makes clear community policing cannot be assessed until it has a serious chance of being implemented fully, with enough resources, planning and supervision to see ideas put into practice. It is a point which forcefully emerged from our interviews.

This leaves community policemen in a bind. Pressure is on senior officers from politicians to produce value for money and results in the War Against Crime. Community policemen can only argue for approaches as yet unproven. They are competing against conventional demands for more manpower on the streets which is believed an effective barrier against crime. No research supports either the community police idealists or the cynics. It is hard to know how far the crime rate has to drop before public confidence in the police is restored. The police have made their own job harder by linking public confidence in their whole *function to a narrow though important dimension of their work which they are relatively powerless to affect. Community policing offers an alternative which they have yet to put to the test.*

PC in a Home Counties force west of London, age 37, eighteen years service. Now a beat policeman on a suburban council estate.

My job is Area Beat policeman, which in most forces is Community Beat policing. I see it as front-line contact. Before I started this kind of work I was twelve bloody years on Traffic as a motor-cyclist. If you are flashing past on a motorbike the only contact with the public is at an accident or when you are stopping someone for speeding or breathalyzing them. That was far too narrow a field of work for me, so I wanted to do this. This is all about grassroots. We get to the school children, we get to the little old ladies.

This is quite a rough council area. A lot of the school kids get the wrong idea about policemen, probably from their bloody parents. They are trapped almost. You have to try to break down the barriers. You know the business: "If you do such a thing, I'll call a policeman and he'll lock you up." I use the schools to talk to the kids in the absence of their parents. In these days when you hear so much about child abuse, we don't want kids to be frightened of the uniform. The kids in the primary schools know me by name. They call out to me across the road and tell their mums who I am. I like to think that all my kids, if they were in any trouble, would come and talk to me. The only time some kids see a uniform is when their dad is beating up their mum at 11 o'clock at night.

THE FRIENDLY BOBBY

To the public, a policeman in uniform is an ambiguous signal. It could mean trouble. For community policing to work, each officer must have the wit and patience to turn potentially hostile contacts into positive ones. This is no mean task, day after day, night after night, in all weather. No matter what their mood, police officers are expected to be firm but pleasant.

PC in a West Country force, age 26, four years service, and a graduate. Now in a large city.

Policemen are definitely happier dealing with stereotypes. If they're caught without one, their usual opening gambit is cautiously friendly. If you go in sounding heavy then it's very hard to back out again. You'll always try to get the first line in and make it funny, to set the tone of the conversation. Factors like time of day affect you. You're much more guarded at night.

You only give an appearance of openness, because you don't want to tell them things that would give them some leverage on you. You keep a sort of patois of safe comments. In any domestic disputes you joke about your home environment. The tales you tell may not even be true, it really doesn't matter. The whole point is them telling you something. There's very little reason for you to want to actually tell them anything.

PC in Midlands force, age 27, ten years service. Just resigned.

There was a generation of Panda car drivers after walking policemen went out of vogue and before they came back in again, who did not have imagination and really didn't need it. They went to each call, got out of their car, got on with it, got back in their car and disappeared. They all universally hate walking because it's a stressful business. People come up and talk to you and you probably don't want to hear them because it's bound to be bad news. Although you go to far less real work, you come home feeling much more tired than driving a Panda car. You also end up flat-footed and arthritic.

PC in West County force, age 29, seven years service. Now in a large city.

I was supposed to be a Community Police Officer in a black area, but you find me a community and I'll police it. Community policing in St Paul's – what's that? I went to the schools and youth clubs and I went a few times to an old folks knees-up on a Wednesday night. It's very hard to get to know people in the city because they move around. You only get to know the more colourful characters. At first, I felt positive about it, but as time went on I realized it was a sort of fiction. It did not feel quite like real policing – you have to be effective in detecting crimes, not just shaking hands and smiling.

PC in Midlands force, age 32, eleven years service. Now in an industrial suburb.

There was a wonderful old sergeant who must be about fifty-four now – coming up to retirement. He was born in this area and he's policed it since he was twenty-five. He knows most of the faces and he dislikes them all. He universally dislikes the human race. He's terribly fierce with people. But he does the odd thing and you realize that underneath he does care. All the kids call him "Mister" and if they don't he takes them by the ear and twists. If I did that, I would get a complaint.

There was an old lady who paid £300 to a cowboy to mend her roof and someone down the road told her he hadn't done the work. So this Sergeant put the old lady in the Panda car and went to see the guy who did it. The Sergeant said: "Have you been doing this old lady's roof?"

"Yes."

"What did you charge her?"

"£300."

"Still got the money?"

"Well, no I haven't. I've spent it on this van on the front step."

The Sergeant said. "Right, everyone in the van." So we all piled into the van and went to the two brothers who sold the van to him.

"What did he pay you for the van?"

"About £290."

"Right, well give him £280 and take the van back."

Then, the Sergeant turns and says: "OK, give the old lady her £300."

"But I'm £20 short!"

"Well give her £290, you've got £10 for the work you did, which is about what it was worth." To the garage guy he says, "You've got your van back and have made £10, so we're all happy." And he says to me, "Tear up the form and nobody's the wiser."

I thought, "What a wonderful solution." I'm sure it's not legal, but the old lady got her money back and thinks the Sergeant's marvellous. I'm sure that's how senior policemen have worked for donkey's years.

VILLAGE BOBBIES

As this book is mainly about the problems of policing in the 1980s, the continued success of village bobbies in making contact with their community has been omitted. But it is a feature of policing in many parts of the country that demonstrates a form of trust between the police and the public which is only dreamt of by inner city Home Beat Officers. A static population, not highly stressed, clear loyalties to one's place of residence and a sense of community are all conditions which make the police officer's job easier.

But things have been changing in the country lately, as the current fashion for looking after number one spreads across Britain.

WPC in northern force, age 29, seven years service. Now a village bobby.

It took me ages to get this posting. No one would give me a reason why, but in the end I won, and thought I was into a good, clear-cut community to work with. But it has commuters now, and somehow – I don't know if it's fair – the place isn't like the village I knew as a girl.

Last month we had a chap knocked over on his bike by a lorry that just kept on going. Hit and run. I was down on the ground at the crossroads with him, trying to help until the ambulance came. Can you guess what these villagers did for their own local bobby when I needed them? They just drove around me and kept on going. So much for community spirit.

PC in a West Country force, age 35, thirteen years service. Now a village bobby in a rural area.

I felt like it's a different world when I saw the riots on the telly. Then I found myself dragged into the troubles when they started to spread near us. It's completely the opposite of what policing is like for me out here. I'm not saying it's all lovey-dovey. I've got villains on my patch, poachers and the odd burglar. Usually I'm on to him through my sources. Any lad tries to get off with things he shouldn't from a shop, or the market, or joyriding, I'm pretty sure I'll be on to him within the day, if not the hour, They don't have many places to go.

It is changing, no doubt about it. There are new people moving out from the cities. They see us as the enemy, or at least not as their friend. And there's no denying ever since the miners' strike weekend nights are getting rougher. We've got our own lager louts. We used to go along and break up fights. Now they turn on us. Maybe it's our turn for a rough time. God forbid.

COMMUNITY POLICING IN THE CITY

Community policing presumes there is a community to police. In cities, people form their own little groups, which are usually far less cohesive or accessible than in villages. It is almost cruel to describe the many lonely pockets of alienated, often embittered people with whom the police most often have to deal as "the community". There are many other social groups that overlap to form a city that normally have no contact with the police except through traffic offences, or when they are burgled. It is the task of Community Police Officers to seek out "the community" wherever it can be found.

In rural areas, police officers often live on their patch, and so start off with the advantage of having neighbours – though one village bobby said he was barred from all three pubs in his area because he wouldn't look the other way to after hours drinking. Still that is milder than the majority of pubs in Kentish Town where off-duty PCs are warned they risk their lives if they enter.

Met Chief Inspector, age 43, twenty-one years service. Now a Community Liaison Officer in a racially mixed inner-city area.

I am trying to please everybody. I am very busy. I am on twenty-three main committees, some of them maybe seventy people. The big ones are the Race Relations Committee and the Police Consultative Group – ours is quite successful. I sit on three drugs committees in the borough, plus the Disabled Association, the Victim Support Scheme, Crime Prevention, Licensed Victuallers Association, and so it goes on ... Area Youth Committee – that's child abuse – Physical and Mental Disablement, Street Lighting Committee, Racial Harassment Working Party, Neighbourhood Watch, General Youth Facilities. I'm asked as a policeman for input or advice that may relate to us.

In the borough there are forty-seven different languages spoken. There are also in excess of 750 voluntary organizations. There are the minority fringe groups – the gay groups, the lesbian groups, Women's Aid, many others. They are obviously part of the community but in the past we have been guilty of not bothering about them.

I spent a year and a half trying to go and talk to gay and lesbian groups. I've managed it, I'm giving a talk to the gay community on the police. I've offered myself up if you like, because they are very angry and hurt by police attitudes. I hope that it will bring a closer understanding between them and my younger police officers. Perhaps then they will come back for discussions with my young new probationers. A lot of police officers would laugh and say, "I see, you're one of those yourself, are you?" They may think I'm a bit radical, and also think it's totally a waste of time. I'll still do it, because I believe in it.

My promotional prospects are finished now. I've been put forward on four occasions – by my own Deputy Assistant Commissioner and Commander. It is nice they think I am worthy of it. At Scotland Yard you're interviewed by three complete strangers who don't know anything about you. Before I knew there was no more promotion I had to play the game a little bit. I would like to have said and done things which I didn't – now I can be more honest. I would never be disloyal to the police service or my hierarchy, but I now feel I can say things – sensible, constructive things – without the fear of somebody up there saying, "You shouldn't have done that." I doubt, this time last year, whether I would have openly said at a meeting that I feel the black community are not getting a good deal.

If every police officer could be a Community Liaison Officer for at least six months then the problem would be solved.

THE SOFT OPTION

Many older bobbies see the fuss over community policing as reinventing the wheel. When extended to restraints on enforcing the law as they see it, it hurts their morale as well. That feeds the division between "hard" and "soft" policing inside police culture, which further isolates Community Police Officers from their colleagues.

Met PC, age 34, fifteen years service. Now in a racially mixed area in North London.

Community policing is just another word for Home Beats. What do they think we've been doing? If you walk the streets normally, people will talk to you, and unless you're some kind of maniac, you're going to talk back to them. Community policing is total bullshit. Long before anybody thought of that phrase, I knew loads and loads of shopkeepers around my area. I obviously knew all the publicans. I knew loads of villains. I knew loads of ordinary people. I was there twelve years on foot duty. By the end of it, I couldn't work plainclothes – because I couldn't get far down the road without somebody saying, "Hello officer".

Community policing's a hot-air exercise. Of course the public are losing confidence – because we don't deal with crime. We're too busy fucking about. I had this cabbie who'd been robbed help me chase the villain into a black pub where the guvnor stopped me going in. That cab driver's memory of it won't be that I chased the bloke, it'll be that I was told to give up at a black pub: "Fucking police?" he'll say, "I wouldn't give you ha'pence for 'em." That was community policing in action. I'd been to that club previously on a similar errand. I walked in the door and I knew who ran it and he knew I was a policeman – nobody's going to touch me. He knew that if he didn't walk round me I'd fucking make him suffer for it in the months to come. Now that's community policing!

Chief Inspector in a Home Counties force east of London, age 34. Ten years service and a graduate.

I remember having an amazing conversation with the Community Relations Department. We were sitting there and I said, "Why does the Community Relations Department exist?" They said "Her Majesty's Inspectorate said the force had to have a Community Relations Department." I said, "Doesn't that rather excuse us, all other policemen, from any obligation to work for proper relationships with their communities: they can just blame it on you and say, 'You should have been there, you should have seen what was going to happen.'" Then we talked about their role. That was one of the very few occasions when I had a conversation with other senior managers, and they said, "These are really good issues, let's go away and think about them." That sort of conversation is extremely rare. The prevailing culture clamped down on it fairly soon. Nothing happened.

My point was that if there was a need for a specialist Community Relations Department, it could only be in training police officers how to deal with the public. They tentatively agreed, but they hadn't had time to think about it. An awful lot of the time they spend is on all the nice things: schools, educational programmes, charity, publicity, the sort of stuff that no one could ever complain about. It gets the force some good publicity, but it's not dealing with the issue of community relationships. That's got to be dealt with, not at headquarters, but down on the ground. It's by giving us a new kind of commission for the officers involved: territorial responsibility, not only for PCs but for their managers too.

If I said what I said just then, I'd be written off as a raving lefty. You don't have much debate. You pick and choose, and you're very careful.

COMMUNITY POLICING IN NORTHERN IRELAND

Community policemen in Northern Ireland are in the same bind as their mainland colleagues, but with the extra dimension of danger as they cross between sectarian communities, seeking the confidence of both. They have focused on youth as the most susceptible group. They are the ones out on the street throwing bricks and petrol bombs as young as eight or nine years old. If anything is to change in the future, it must start with them.

It took the bombing of a school bus for children of different faiths on the same bus to begin talking to each other. The RUC community policemen offer school children a series of mixed-faith events: Top of the Form quizzes in more than 450 schools;

over 1400 teenagers of both religions attend their summer adven-
ture camps. They have weekend camps, Blue Lamp discos and
five-a-side championships, swimming, boxing and 8000 young
people taking part in the Rambles walking competitions. Juv-
enile liaison schemes involve cautioning and warning people
under seventeen, turning to custodial sentences only when absol-
utely necessary.

This achievement must be set in context, however: more than
90 per cent of the RUC are Protestant. The police are not yet
trusted by many Catholics – and those that do trust them are
under threat not to show it. Indeed, part of the bind is that the
very success of community policing in achieving normalcy must
go unrecognized, for fear of attracting terrorist efforts to stop
it. And now the Chief Constable has decided he cannot afford
community policing at all because the government has refused
to cover the £1 million he ascribes to the cost of fighting
terrorism. It is a sad decision for Northern Ireland.

**RUC PC, age 38, twelve years service. Now a Community Beat
Officer in a rural area near the border with Eire.**

Nobody wants our end of the work. They think we are silly. A
lot of people have got it into their heads that community
relations in Northern Ireland is a lost cause and the only way
you can police Northern Ireland is by riot squads. My attitude
changed 100 per cent when I switched from car work. I would
have been out on foot in the odd day, but then you had a
different attitude because you were on beat when you could
have been in a nice warm car. Doing the beat on foot constantly
you are meeting the people day in and day out. They chat about
where they are living, about problems they're having, whether
it is rowdy or boys racing about during the night. Whether
strange cars have been left sitting around or anything suspicious
going on. These are all things to follow up and even if it's one
out of ten success rate, it is always worth it. If you save some
old dear from having herself robbed, you have saved her from
total devastation. And even though you'll never know everybody, you are always building up your knowledge.

I see people committing offences day in and day out and I
could bang them into court, no problem. But now I wonder if

it was deliberate, to break the law, or was it an accident? Maybe I have a word in his ear so it doesn't happen again. There are uniformed police who have been here twice as long as me but running around on tyres all day long, and they don't know half the people I know. That is the barrier.

Some of the local uniform boys get my lads for no tax or bald tyres or some minor thing. Instead of telling the fellow to put a new tyre on they drag him into court. He then asks me, "Can you do anything for me?" I speak to the other policeman who says, "No way." Now he is just breaking down what I'm trying to build up. To give that man a chance would mean a chance for us to get in there. We know he's only going to get maybe a £10 fine, but in his head it's very serious, terrible things are going to happen to him and his name will be in all the papers and his neighbours are going to know he went to court. But if you tell him he'll hear no more about it, he thinks you are the greatest fellow in the world and he will come to you and say, "You did me a favour. I'll do you a favour and give you information on such and such." I don't see why you can't pull a few strings.

Because I'm plainclothes, the kids don't look on us as policemen. I took some on an overnight camp once. A few weeks later I was working on a public order squad and a riot broke out between the two sides. We were in the middle. Two of the boys who went on the camp with me were actually on the front line of that riot. And they saw us and it was "Hiya Jimmy, Hiya Joe!" and the whole thing was stopped there and then.

A HIGH RISK JOB BUT NOT REAL POLICING

RUC officers have a particular difficulty as community policemen. They need to be out and about in the community, which puts their lives and their families in greater danger. Despite this, the standing of community policing inside RUC police culture is no greater than on the mainland. Their achievements such as being accepted in Catholic schools may seem modest in the Home Counties, but are major risks for both parties in West Belfast. It makes their abolition all the more poignant.

RUC Superintendent, age 42, twenty-one years service. A former Community Liaison Officer, now in Belfast.

Our people can't turn up at schools on a regular basis, unlike somewhere in Hampshire or Dorset, in case some of the locals catch on they're policemen. We have had two members killed. One was murdered in the transit van, waiting for a group of youngsters taking part in the Top of the Form competition. The other one was murdered when he was out making contact with members of the community. He was a well-known chap and he was a target.

You can get Army cover, police cover, but that defeats the purpose. A Community Relations Sergeant was going into a school one day, dressed in civvies, of course, and there were fellows there repairing the windows. They must have had sympathies in certain directions because they went along to the caretaker and said, "Was that a peeler going in there?" He said, "Oh no, that's our road safety man." Luckily the caretaker was geared to protect him. People in those areas are very sensitive to strange questions. We had a group of school children taken away for a weekend by a policewoman. The headmistress was at the school at about six o'clock the day they were coming back and she noticed people about and thought, "That's odd. I haven't noticed people standing about here before." Of course they were waiting for the transit to come back.

It is very much in the mind of officers, not only for their own personal safety, but also for the children. One unfortunate incident with a couple of children injured would be a terrible blow for us. It is something everyone in the force has to live with, but in community relations maybe even more so. You are in the community and working with so many people – you are taking a lot on trust.

In one camp one of the lads was later discovered to be a young bombardier. When the news came back, the Divisional Commander said, "You can't say we aren't getting the right people on the youth camps!" You can't exclude the youngsters from the juvenile liaison scheme just because their parents are sympathizers to the terrorist scene. At a sixth-form seminar, one of the girls was from a Sinn Fein family. Both her mother and father are involved with the IRA. She had come along, without their knowledge, to meet the police and see what they had to say. It's a big step.

The police, in respect of community relations, have a constant battle with Sinn Fein. We arranged a weekend camp from a local Roman Catholic secondary school, and there were veiled Sinn Fein threats to the teachers. To be fair to them, they had no other choice. They said the weekend camp was off because they were worried for the young people's safety. But the school kids got together themselves and decided they were not having this and they attended the weekend camp.

I went to a Metropolitan Police conference a while back in London, talking about ethnic culture and ethnic groups. Police officers throughout the mainland UK were asking, "Why should we be doing this for their group? Why don't they conform to what's here?" This was at management level! I know it's a reflection of society out there, but as police we should set our own house and our own attitudes in order first. That is the difficult one.

I was walking in Sheffield one time with a constable and six black fellows were coming up, walking close together, wearing fancy hats, and they were shouting to see if they could get any reaction from the policeman. I could feel for that poor constable, because I felt threatened by them. This ethnic group situation is very complex. We can say to ourselves: I am born and bred in Northern Ireland and these are the people in my community. They might not share the same views and their aim in life might be to shoot me – but that's still quite different to what the officer in England is facing. He's feeling, "This guy is a total stranger." You could say it's easy to identify the problem: "He's a different colour." But they don't have a security problem, it's an attitude problem.

NO-GO AREAS

The "attitude" problem on the streets of the inner-cities is shared by the police as well. In the worst areas, the mutual hostility between the police and young people, both black and white, became a difficult security problem for everyone involved to the point where streets like All Saints Road in London's

Notting Hill and Granby Street in Liverpool were for a time effectively no-go areas. Restoring links with local people was a real challenge even for the best Community Police Officers. As an answer to the problems that caused the riots, community policing has several weaknesses when translated into day-to-day policing on the streets.

In areas of high crime there is often no acceptable community, only diverse and sometimes overlapping groups within which different generations may have opposing views. Older residents of Broadwater Farm, All Saints Road or Handsworth want the law enforced, drug pushers driven out and the streets made quiet and safe. Certain gangs of youths do not. They loathe the police. They are ultra-sensitive to moves against any of their number. These days, even fights between white and black youths stop when the vans arrive, as both groups unite against the police.

To satisfy the demands of older people, the police risk provoking the younger ones, with damaging consequences to everyone of more "slow rioting". So in the name of good community relations the police tread carefully in what are known as "sensitive areas". They become sanitized zones – embargoes are placed on conventional arrests, on movements in and out of the area by other police officers and on the handling of controversial figures in the community. But police officers know that whatever they do, or fail to do, they will be criticized by someone somewhere.

To many ordinary bobbies, this is "soft" policing at its worst. It seems like abandoning the job to the tyranny of the "community" – police code for blacks and white militants. They see it as a reverse form of discrimination which does nothing to promote tolerance in the police canteen. It makes them cynical about the whole exercise of community policing.

Met PC, age 31, six years service. Now a Home Beat Officer in an inner-city area of London with a large black population.

Unfortunately, there's a very, very hostile relationship between me and the black activists in the community. There is virtually no relationship other than open hostility. They despise the uniform I wear with a pathological hatred, and I have little or no contact with them. I have personal reasons as well as professional. The personal ones are that, as far as I'm concerned, they are not the legitimate elected representatives of this community, however they describe themselves. I don't feel that I as an individual or as a police officer should have any contact with people who aren't elected representatives, who openly insult me in the street all the time.

It's very difficult. If I happen to rescue people involved with them, there is contact but it's usually abuse. I don't have to put up with that so I ignore it. It's not just swearing and saying that I "shouldn't be in this road". When I arrest somebody I get accused of planting drugs on them, regardless of what the offence is.

I do have a bit of fun occasionally. The "leader" came up to me talking about a skip – some renovations were being done. "I've got no lights for this skip. Are you going to report me?" He said the owners of the skip didn't supply him with any lights. I said, "Normally it is the responsibility of the hirer to see that the skip is properly lit in the hours of darkness. But I see little or no point in reporting you for that offence." He asked me why and I said, "If I did, you'd only allege that I'd planted the skip on you in the first place, so it's a waste of time!" He walked off in a huff. I walked off with a smile on my face.

BROADWATER FARM

Met Superintendent, age 43, twenty-five years service.
Community Liaison Officer at the time of the Broadwater
Farm Riot.

Before the riots in 1985, I thought we were making progress in Broadwater Farm. You get to feel that what happens elsewhere is not going to happen here. Handsworth went, a few copy-cat things around the country. All the alarm bells go. I speak to my contacts, get out and about. Nothing went here. Cherry Groce shot – boom goes Brixton! Dead worried. Nothing went. I thought, "I don't believe it. We've really made progress." Then another West Indian mother, Cynthia Jarrett, was killed – for want of a better word – locally, in her own home. Most of the black community wanted to think that it was a brutal act by a policeman – pushing a sick mother to the floor, rather than her falling over as someone passed by. Such a head had been built up from the other things that it blew its top.

I was devastated because I've put a lot of work into this place. Suddenly everyone that wants us to fail clapped their hands and said, "We were right, you can never live with black people." The media respond to that type of thing. They make it even worse.

Putting your finger on why it happened is very difficult. The black community feel they're stopped and harassed just because they're black, and there's evidence to support this. I've spoken to black magistrates and other middle-class blacks. They say; "My son's got a new car, he's been stopped ten times this week. I tell him to keep his cool, but he's a young man with a responsible job who works hard for his living." On the other hand, you have got policemen who live in an area where a lot of crime is by young blacks. To their mind, a white guy driving a new car is less suspicious. How do you get past that?

The Broadwater Farm itself, geographically and architecturally, stands out in the area. It's self-contained – it's a hothouse. Because of troubles in the past we have given it particular attention. Is it right to put the vast majority of tenants, who are law-abiding, under heavy police pressure? But you've got a young element there who are unemployed, frustrated, unhappy and bored.

Generally I had done as well as anybody, probably a little better than most. Broadwater Farm is only 3 per cent of my division. Thanks to my policemen, it isn't even the worst part. But the riot put community relations back a long way. I can't give you a formula for repairing that. All you can do is recognize that things will get better. People will sort the problems out. They don't like living in fear.

We're just coming through the deepest part of the tunnel. The trials have finished. I suspect that some people wanted to manipulate it. They had a defence campaign to counter even the most obvious cases of crime, and tried to make martyrs of everybody. Broadwater Farm had an identity before. It's got a national and international one now.

The investigation had a major impact. Guns were known to

have been used. One journalist was sprayed with shot. A couple of shields had bullet holes. The firearms were never found. So you end up with a massive investigation involving hundreds of arrests. There was a police army of occupation for a while – armed officers protecting the detectives because they haven't found these guns. More hostility and bitterness built up there.

As a Community Liaison Officer I wanted to minimize the effect of this. We asked the council if we could have the keys to a lot of empty flats, but they refused. They've all got reinforced doors and you have to have a sledgehammer to smash them in. This is great for the media – going in with sledgehammers. And then you are arresting young kids – fourteen-year-olds. Before the riots, the phone would go: "There's a car being done." The PC would go down there and as soon as he got to the car, he'd be bombarded with bricks. All we could do was double the patrols.

With hindsight, people say; "You were wrong. This is what you get for being namby-pamby and soft." There's been a succession of Chief Superintendents that had a problem with Broadwater Farm. What are your options? Do you go down and put a battalion of men in there? It is their community. Just recently there's been evidence of drugs. I went to the community leaders and said, "Let's talk about it. We can either have lots more stops, lots more searches – which was said to trigger events – or you can help us. It's your problem too. I can't deal with it without your support." I had a letter back saying: "You're not going to get our cooperation. It's a major crime, it's your job. You sort it out."

Met PC, age 24, four years service. Now in Central London.

Just walking in pairs, up and down those bloody walkways at Broadwater Farm – it was like a rabbit warren, crawling with policemen. We were scared, I can tell you. It was bloody frightening to be wandering around this fortress knowing they'd just killed a bobby. No one could invite us in because they were too frightened of reprisals, of being seen talking to us. The middle-aged ones used to open their doors as we passed by and say, "We're glad you're here. You're much nicer than our usual lot.

But we can't ask you in. Just daren't, sorry." It was like Northern Ireland.

TOXTETH

Following the riots of 1981, Kenneth Oxford, the Chief Constable of Merseyside, acknowledged that racial harassment had occured in Toxteth and apologized to the black community. In 1985, after black youths had been arrested for affray, rioting broke out again and three hundred youths, both black and white, were arrested. This created yet more community policing problems in the area.

In 1987, a local jeweller sued Kenneth Oxford for not protecting community property, accusing him of allowing villains committing robberies elsewhere in Liverpool to escape safely into Toxteth. He claimed Toxteth was a "No-Go Area" for policemen. He lost.

Superintendent in a large northern urban force, age 41, twenty years service. Now in a "sensitive area" with a large black population.

If a police officer sees someone driving a stolen car who they know, they don't bother to chase them. They come in and make a report. This prevents the chap driving straight off to get friends and causing a confrontation. One time we got a chap in the community to bring someone in and presented him with thirty-two summonses. The man said, "I've never been stopped." We said "Would you have stopped if a policeman tried to stop you?"

"Probably not."

"Well, there you are then."

We don't go trying to arrest people unless it is something bad. If we know who they are we just go round sometime during their night, which is in the morning, having got back at 4 or 5 a.m., and ask them to come with us. His friends are not around so we can avoid disorder. Little techniques like this we use all the time. We are accused of letting people get away, but they seldom hear about the follow-up and subsequent arrest. A riot can develop from something seemingly trivial.

This is a very close-knit area. Large numbers of people can get out on the streets very quickly. The vast majority are just curious passers by, and they aren't going to take any part. It's all a question of judgement.

What our white critics don't realize is that if our back-up support carriers were allowed to attend every incident, what are they going to do when they get there? Probably the offender has gone and the rest are just bystanders. If we go away, then they'll disperse.

If a police officer from outside wants to go into our area he must first contact the police here. We assist people from other areas all the time. They might not be so aware of the "rats being led into a trap" situation, where a car is used to lure police into an area and when they drive around the corner there is a crowd of sixty waiting for them. If a visiting officer needs to be in our area on CID business, we will arrange for a local officer to accompany him. If the locals see a strange bobby, they won't be very happy. One of our men might end up getting assaulted later as a revenge for an outside policeman's poor attitude.

Two PCs from a northern force; PC1 age 29, PC2 age 31, both ten years service.

PC1: Blacks come into the city centre and they generally don't misbehave, but if you speak to the same black in the Toxteth triangle, it's a different ball game because he's on his territory then.

PC2: You can't go down the street at one o'clock in the afternoon. Cars are double parked – blocking the road – there's open drug dealing, a guy walking around with a machete. One street between midday and three o'clock is "downtown drugs", it's unbelievable.

PC1: If we go out somewhere to do a raid, if we want to go through that Subdivision's patch, we have to ask permission first. It's usually denied, so we have to go round it. It's like the Berlin Wall. If we get caught going through in our own car, and an incident happens, we will be nailed to the bloody floor.

We followed four coloured fellows in a stolen car. We were literally right behind it. We chased it right round town, nearly TA'd [crashed] about five times, risking our lives. Immediately they head towards the Toxteth triangle we're told to withdraw. These fellows may have done a bank robbery, may have murdered somebody. We only did a vehicle check because "that's a nice car", and it came back as stolen. The bosses are thinking that if we go in we are going to cause a riot, that we are going to cause a problem for them in their air-conditioned offices.

PC2: There's a student club in town. Full of drugs. The blacks started moving in. Now I have no objection to blacks, decent blacks. But in these clubs, pot is being smoked in the toilets, you can smell it. Black guy walks in, spots me for a "bizzy" and spits on the floor. That's what they do in the triangle all the time to a uniformed bobby on the street, you can't do anything about it. No one does that to me. So I say, "I want a word with you – I'm a police officer." Show him my ID. "You may do that in the triangle, but if you ever do that again, I'll lock you up. Give me any hassle and I'll knock shit out of you. Know what I mean?" This guy's totally shocked. He's obviously so accustomed to spitting at policemen that it's second nature to him. The bosses may have allowed it. I was down here in '81 during the riots and if that had been dealt with properly by the senior officers then we wouldn't have the problem we have now.

PC1: The blacks rule the game now. They want it quiet. They don't want an abundance of police officers. If they started rioting and we saturated the area for a few days, that's their drug dealing gone.

PC2: Baseball bats and shotguns are the normal tools to carry. That's their m.o. for attempting to do a jeweller's. There's maybe two a week up there. You can guarantee the cars will end up in Toxteth. I'm sure white fellows also do jobs and abandon the car in the triangle, simply to make it look as if blacks have done it.

PC1: They are trying to enforce the law at the moment with "community bobbies" on foot. That should be totally scrapped. They should be treated exactly the same as anybody else in this city. If carriers are needed to police the area, then carriers police the area. We police this city, not just bits of this city, and they should be treated just like anybody else.

PC2: The only way for the CC to adopt a new system on the triangle is for a riot to occur and for us to go in with hard-line police tactics, lock as many people up as we can. That will take two or three days. Continually police the area for a month or maybe two with high visibility uniform policemen in vans and carriers, and then not go back to the old way.

Sergeant, age 38, twenty years service; WPC age 22, three years service. Both now in Toxteth.

Sgt: I am proud of the fact that I am based here in Toxteth. You go into the police club and they say: "Where are you posted?" "Toxteth." And they look at you in a different way. You get a lot of people who wouldn't work here: they don't know the area.

   You get little lifts, like the occasion I had last week. The son of one of our local West Indian families came in and told us that as long as he passes his fitness test, then he's in the police force. And we'd like to think that all of us have had something to do with that.

WPC: It's just the small things that give you satisfaction. I remember when I first came here, there were these kids hanging around smoking pot and they were literally screaming abuse at us. We just started talking to them and about ten minutes later they were saying, "You're all right, you two." It's nice. To begin with they're openly hostile and within ten minutes they think you're the best thing since sliced bread.

Sgt: About a year ago we started doing talks in the local schools. One morning we heard the traffic department couldn't send a squad car, so we rang here and got a personnel carrier which, if you listen to the "anti" brigade, is the most hated vehicle ever produced. We ended up keeping it in our repertoire. The kids were fighting to get in to have a ride around the school field. And these are kids who'd been led to believe that once you got inside a police van you'd be beaten to death if you were black.

Their lovely Rasta dads would have strung them up if they'd seen them.

WPC: It's not just here in Toxteth that policemen can be assaulted. A dog handler and his dog were beaten up – the dog as well! They also wrecked his car. They came out with a set of ladders and rammed the lot through his front windscreen till they came out the back. Then they buckled his door. This all happened in seconds. But it can happen anywhere, not just here.

Sgt: Since the riots of 1981, we've got trouble contained in one small street a few yards long. At least while they are there, they're not causing a lot of trouble. We can cope with it. By and large they might be doing some dealing on the streets and doing some catcalling at local bobbies, but as long as you can live with that, the rest of the area is relatively peaceful.

To say you're not frightened under a hail of bricks would be stupid. But you don't come off duty and worry about it for twenty-four hours. It's all so unpredictable. You can walk down the street and there is banter in a light-hearted way. The next day they will throw bricks and be downright rude. It's a shock at first, but it passes.

WPC: This area's wild. A prostitute I was talking to the other night, the man she had been with had played noughts and crosses with a knife across her chest.

Sgt: Any policeman here may get involved in a serious hostile confrontation whilst trying to make an arrest. A police officer in another area might have one in their career and will remember it for evermore. Perhaps tell their grandchildren. But it becomes a usual part of the scene here.

ALL SAINTS ROAD: A NEW STYLE OF COMMUNITY POLICING

In the spring of 1987, violence against the police in All Saints Road in Notting Hill Gate in London had reached distressing levels. Drug dealing was rife and conducted openly. No solution seemed in sight and morale among local police was low. As the police saw it, self-appointed community leaders had senior officers in a corner, through manipulation of the local press and continual complaints of police harassment whenever moves were made to control activity in the road.

When senior officers were changed, a new policy was developed to respond to the problem. A major operation was planned three months ahead: undercover observations were made throughout the preparation to the swoop to ensure that the proof needed for convictions was there. During the surveillance period, anti-police violence continued to escalate and fears grew of revenge during the Notting Hill Carnival two months later. In June 1987, Operation Trident was launched and sixteen major drug dealers were arrested. Hundreds of police were drafted in from all over London and kept on in large numbers for weeks to keep the lid on any reprisals. It was costly in police manpower and risky in relation to the community's reaction. Many black residents objected to the "army of occupation" which relentlessly searched people passing through the area. The Carnival passed off with some violence including a murder – but less organized than expected. One year later, the calm of the area was jeopardized when black community leaders were arrested by drugs squad officers not involved with the local experiment. Like Brixton, the area is being slowly gentrified by the increase in house prices, and All Saints Road is beginning to benefit from increased development funds. The threat of "slow rioting" in this area may have been met for the 1988 Carnival saw a major reduction in crime.

Met superintendent, age 43, twenty-four years service. Formerly in the Notting Hill area of London.

The All Saints Road, it's 100 yards of road. It's a lot of people, it's drug dealing and crime. Where do these people come from? Outside the area. That was the most significant find: you weren't going to have a community problem. So why wasn't anyone doing anything? What is the community? Who represents the community? No one. Residents Association? Tenants Association? Local Council? They won't go up there and clean the place up for fear of being attacked. The community is nothing. The parking meter heads are off. How long have they been off? "For years." Why not replaced? "They'd only get ripped off again." They don't want to park their cars on parking meters, they just want to park their cars full stop. Why don't traffic wardens go up there? Because traffic wardens get attacked.

All the civic services don't want to go up there – it's a no-go area! Speak to residents who've been there for twenty years and they'll tell you that they'd walk half a mile round All Saints Road rather than 100 yards across it. Why? Fear. Why don't they come out at night? Fear. What about the loud music? No one does anything about that. The environmental health services won't come out because they're frightened of going up there. It's like Piccadilly Circus, the punters and the dealers driving round and round, at two o'clock in the morning, it's rush hour up there. The public urinal was absolutely astounding. It was a big corner of the pavement and it was absolutely saturated. It didn't matter what the weather was like, those paving stones were absolutely soaked with urine. People would just go to the toilet, it was accepted. Local residents got fed up with complaining. Who do they complain to? Local residents won't go up to a black man and say "Don't pee up against my door please," because the door will go in and a few other things will happen as well.

You could never actually know how many people were there, because there are little cafés, fish and chip shops, little restaurants, basements, back gardens. You could never say, "There's only two hundred in the road tonight," because there may have been five hundred, just behind doors or down stair-ways. That was very difficult. It set the adrenalin running for several of the coppers, but it was very intimidating for others.

The problems PCs faced on the street included spitting and not being able to do anything about it. Physical assaults – women officers were pushed, not sexually assaulted, but certainly hands on breasts and that sort of thing. There were stones, bottles, bricks, PCs were kicked. One PC was spotted standing in a doorway and was hit over the head with an iron bar. The crowd spat on him when he was on the ground and then closed around the perpetrator to shepherd him away. The verbal abuse was really cutting, not only about police officers – "Pigs", "Fascists", "Shit" and all the rest of it – but about police officers' families: "We'll fuck your mother" or "I'll fuck your wife, but I wouldn't have a go at you." It's one thing to be insulted verbally – you can forget about it. It's another thing to find the graffiti there week after week. Graffiti like "police brutality" or "police harassment". People from the road would either ring the senior officers of the station or actually come direct to the Superintendent's office claiming that PC Bloggs had misbehaved and "Get him transferred, we want him out of the way, he's a disturbance. He's a threat to the stability of the road." They're very shrewd people. Coming in here gave the black person credibility within his own community: he could come and speak to the big white policeman. It demoralized the PCs; they couldn't get access to the big white policeman. It all helped to undermine our role.

Officers started to do things to express their discontent with management, with their lot in life. Graffiti: comments about senior officers. No pride in themselves – rubbish everywhere, filthy faces, totally disorganized, untidiness, absolutely disgraceful. Symptomatic of no care, no pride. It was absolutely astonishing to see.

Police units were not allowed to respond to anything that was happening around the All Saints Road in case it inflamed our relationships with the people in the road. It was a physical, mid-stream restriction on the communications systems. If there was an incident on the All Saints Road, no one was to go in there until the duty officer actually authorized it. No one could go in with blue lights and two tones. Even if a PC was getting punched to death, he himself couldn't call in for aid, it could only come from an Inspector – who might not be in contact. That, more than anything else, was ridiculous. You were denying police support to colleagues when they needed it.

After Trident women now walk down All Saints Road carrying handbags without being molested, because there aren't groups of coloureds loitering about. The shops are being improved. We've actually got Crime Prevention Officers knocking on doors, getting old people's security improved: lights on porches, extra locks, chains on doors. The local Council is back in the area cleaning up regularly. We are ticketing illegally parked vehicles. A year ago, all of my crime problems centred on the All Saints Road area; now, there is probably less crime committed in the All Saints Road area than anywhere else in Division.

The displacement is obvious. You have robberies in the Portobello market, but they tend to be robberies by the next generation of criminals, twelve-, thirteen-, fourteen-year olds, whereas the crime a year ago was directly drug-related and that was seventeen-, eighteen-, nineteen-year-olds. There is less gratuitous violence now with robberies. In a crowd, a quick slash of the hand on the bag and it's gone. Whereas before it might be someone pinning you against the wall, sticking a knife under your throat and saying, "Do you wanna buy a bit of cannabis?"

I don't see it as a race problem. I see it as a consequence of senior police officers not policing in the way they should have; of the agencies not actually coming together with a degree of commitment to help solve the problem; of the media concentrating on one or two vocal people, without giving a balanced story. The main factor must be that it only happens on the street if the police allow it to happen.

PROFESSIONAL STANDING

For all the lip service paid to community policing, many old school senior officers on promotion boards often see it as a "soft option" in place of "feeling collars", so operational experience counts for more in the promotion stakes. They see community policing as in conflict with keeping law and order and that view carries all before it.

Many Community Liaison Officers complain of a lack of support at all ranks. Some have resigned while others are seriously thinking of it. These are men the service can ill afford to lose if the trust of the public is to be regained.

Met Chief Inspector, age 48, twenty-five years service. Now a Met Community Liaison Officer, age 47, twenty-nine years service, in an inner-city area. Just resigned.

I have learnt a lot about the community and about myself, probably for the first time in my life, because I have been privileged to go to all these committees and groups. I would not have seen the frustration and problems that people have got. It has made me more aware of my own abilities, of my own sincerity and in some ways, my own disloyalty.

I am worried that I might become disloyal to the police force if I go on much longer. I might forget this balancing act and go to the side of the community, which I would not want to do as a police officer, if you understand me. I might begin to wonder whether I have done the job for twenty-five years or more in the right manner. I happen to believe that the force, in general, is doing a first-class job. There are so many thoughts I have now which were different even three years ago. That worries me. It is hard to describe. They are inner thoughts.

Take minority groups: every police officer, as far as possible, has got to understand these people. They are to be respected and trusted. Maybe at the end of the day I am considered to be too soft, no cutting edge, not hard enough on the men that work beneath me, too flexible, too understanding, too compassionate, perhaps. Maybe I should be a hard bastard and not worry about the community. I could sit on my arse and do nothing. But what's the point?

IMPLEMENTING THE SCARMAN APPROACH

From 1982 to 1987, a major experiment in neighbourhood policing was held in Surrey and four inner-city areas of London: Kilburn, Brixton, Hackney and Notting Hill. It involved extra training and an elaborate thirty-nine point strategy for improving both crime reporting standards and community involvement. It reflected the Commissioner's hope to put community policing into practice. Its key innovations were:

1. In place of the usual shift coverage, a small team of officers would take twenty-four hour responsibility for a particular patch, with the task of preventing and reducing crime through close cooperation with residents.

2. Greater police teamwork, with cross-rank discussion of local problems and flexible hours to meet local needs.

3. Microcomputers linked to Division to develop local intelligence.

4. More effort on crime prevention, such as Neighbourhood Watch, and victim support schemes.

5. Graded responses to local calls – now known as "case-screening" – to determine the appropriate level of response, if any.

After five years, at a cost of £200,000 per station, the scheme was halted – never having been implemented fully. Although many officers liked the open style of management, and the hi-tech back-up, they felt less in control of the streets. As far as the public was concerned, it did not increase respect for the police nor did it appear to reduce crime.

According to Peter Turner, former head of research at the Treasury, it was not the method, it was the PCs involved that were the problem: "The desired changes in procedure, attitudes and behaviour were too great to be brought about by training, persuasion and edict. Some attitudes acquired over many years of traditional policing needed to be totally reversed." It was "hard" versus "soft" policing again. The Metropolitan Police Policy Committee recognized this too: "The introduction of neighbourhood policing in a largely mechanical way will not force the development of the required attitudes and skills [in the PCs involved]." Their report continued: "These skills did not develop to any marked extent even despite extensive training programmes, and the selection of 'better than average' managers for the experimental sites."

Nevertheless, the Committee report concluded: "We consider that the concept [of neighbourhood policing], refined as a result of deep scrutiny, may offer significant benefits." It has yet to be given a fair chance. But with racial tension still a major issue, it may be that community policing as training for all PCs is the only real alternative to the present stalemate.

CHAPTER FOUR

Race

"No one tells the truth about race," said a white Home Beat Officer raised in Kenya, now policing a multi-racial area in the Met. I am inclined to agree with him. The subject is clouded by rhetoric, ranging from wishful thinking about equal opportunities to fanatical polemics by both black and white extremists. Meanwhile, on the streets, the police and members of the black and Asian communities face each other daily with a collective history of mistrust on both sides.

The riots of 1981 dramatized the feelings of Britain's black youth in an inescapable way. The issue of racial discrimination had been festering on the edges of British politics for many years, but it affected too few people to carry political weight. The riots changed all that. Nearly as many whites as blacks took part in the Toxteth, Moss Side, Brixton and Handsworth disturbances. But Lord Scarman saw the gulf between the black community and the police as a primary cause of the Brixton riots.

Scarman was scrupulous in laying blame: he criticized the black community leaders for withdrawing from the local communication structure with the police in the months before the riots and for being too quick to believe all the rumours of police harassment. While he cleared the police of racism at the top, Scarman blamed senior officers for "inflexible and insensitive policing strategies" by using the Special Patrol Group (SPG) on the streets in plain clothes for three weeks of saturation policing. He confirmed black youth's claims of harassment on the streets and in police cells, although less often than the black community believed. Scarman realized that the climate of suspicion was such that it would only take one incident a year to keep the mistrust alive. And there were and are far more frequent occurrences.

Scarman also confirmed that black youths were stopped far more often than white youths, under the so-called "sus" law. Based on the Vagrancy Act of 1824, the "sus" law gave the police powers to arrest people for "loitering with intent" to commit a criminal offence. They could also stop and search people they reasonably suspected were carrying stolen goods or drugs.

The law has since been changed, and the Code of Practice in the Police and Criminal Evidence Act of 1985 tries to restrict the circumstances in which the police can stop people:

Reasonable suspicion cannot be supported on the basis simply of a higher than average chance that the person has committed or is committing an offence, for example because he belongs to a group within which offenders of a certain kind are relatively common ... a person's colour of itself can never be a reasonable ground for suspicion.

This confronts the police case for stopping black youths because they are generally believed to have committed a higher number of crimes than their proportion of the population as a whole. Some researchers criticize this widely-used police statistic because the figures are drawn from areas of high crime, where the proportion of black residents is also much higher than elsewhere in London, or nationally. In other words, in a black area, more crimes will be committed by blacks. Researchers also suggest that if the police stopped more white youths, their percentage of crimes might go up as well.

Despite the new law, most police officers feel they are right to regard black youths as more likely to be up to something. In the year of the 1981 riots, police in London stopped and searched 1,200,000 people. Only one in twelve stops yielded an arrest, but 100,000 arrests was enough to keep the practice going. Seven years later the law has changed but the presumption of guilt has not.

The police approach to crimes against ethnic minorities has also fed resentment. In the many attacks on Asian families in East London, the police were accused of ignoring possible racial motives despite the active presence of the National Front in the area. There was a growing feeling that the police response *ranged from indifferent to hostile. Marches and vigilante groups were the result. More attention is now being paid to racial attacks as a matter of official Met policy. How much it will reassure anxious families remains to be seen.*

Racial tension in Britain has not been confined to London. The Toxteth riots in Liverpool were triggered by rough handling of a black man suspected of stealing his own motorbike. Relations between the police and black community had been poor for a long time. In Manchester, the report on the Moss Side riot by Sir Beret Hytner, QC, referred to "evidence from highly reliable people both white and black of police spoiling for trouble with young blacks." Police vans were seen touring the area shouting "Oi, oi, nigger!" and pounding their batons on the sides of the van, challenging black youths to come out and fight.

The worst incidents were in 1985. Both the Brixton and Tottenham riots were triggered by aggressive – and fruitless – police searches of black family homes. In each case, the suspect's mother was on the receiving end. In Brixton, Mrs Cherry Groce was shot and paralysed permanently. In Tottenham, Mrs Cynthia Jarrett was knocked to the ground, causing a fatal heart attack. An independent enquiry – with which the police refused to cooperate – held that the police had entered her house without warning, using keys taken improperly from her son, who was being held for questioning. They claimed that he had committed no offence but was stopped after a computer check on his car. It seems that no adequate explanation was offered to the rest of the family at the time of the incident, nor, despite their complaints, was disciplinary action taken against any of the officers involved.

Accidents are inevitable in police work. But it will take the kind of trust that does not yet exist between the police and the black community to calm the anger generated by those events.

To build that trust, Lord Scarman made various suggestions, many of which have been implemented:

1. More recruiting from ethnic minorities. (A significant improvement unlikely until the attitude towards the police within the black community changes.)

2. Police consultative committees. (This has largely been done.

But in areas where suspicion is most intense on both sides, good communication is imperative and yet hardest to achieve.)

3. *The complaints procedure should be improved and made more independent of the police. (The Police Complaints Authority now exists, but there is still little public confidence in the system.)*

4. *More Community Police Officers with a higher standing in the force. (They are in place but still lack status and resources.)*

5. *Closer links with community leaders before major operations are launched in their area. (Made law under the Police and Criminal Evidence Act of 1985, this has helped to reduce local tensions, but is deeply unpopular with rank-and-file PCs for giving privileges to ethnic minorities not accorded to white people.)*

6. *Training to be extended from fourteen weeks to six months, with greater emphasis on ethnic and cultural awareness. (The scope of training has been widened in many forces, and now extends to twenty weeks in the Met. This is still shorter than the rest of Europe.)*

7. *Racial discrimination to be made a discipline offence, "normally punished by dismissal". (It has been made a discipline offence but not a cause for dismissal. Attacked by the Police Federation, it has still to be enforced.)*

8. *More sensitivity to be shown by officers, rather than always moving to arrest. Each situation should be handled with care. (This is taken seriously by senior officers but is often mocked by rank-and-file PCs for being a code which means "turning a blind eye to blacks", "bending over backwards" or "community policing".)*

The collective importance of those moves has involved the police service and the Home Office in a major programme for change, which has been underrated by the black community itself. Dismantling prejudice is a difficult process that takes years of experience, not just changes of official policy.

The nature of the problem can be gauged by the fact that the views expressed in the following interviews are not unusual.

They were repeated over and over again in the course of the past few years, with remarkable consistency. Even officers in forces with no black people in their area shared similar opinions. The details change from officer to officer, but it is clear that when both sides encounter each other on the street, they both often expect the worst. It is hardly surprising they have had so much trouble. The miracle is that there isn't more.

Met Chief Inspector, age 43, twenty-five years service. Now a Community Liaison Officer in an inner-city area of London.

Some of the riots in this country, apart from all the reasons of environment and unemployment, are caused by aggressive policing. Black community workers I know extremely well have said to me that whenever things have gone a bit wrong with the police, and they have asked what is going on, the reply is "Fuck off, you black bastard and mind your own business!" rather than "This guy has mugged that old lady over there and we are arresting him." What is so hard about saying that? They are entitled to ask what their black brothers are being arrested for.

The police don't understand young black people. Black youths do have an aggressive manner, they are very excitable, and they shout and wave their arms about and they sort of sway and stagger around. Now for a young police officer, that can be very frightening.

YOUTH AND THE UNIFORM

Many young PCs, from predominantly white or country areas, may never have had to deal with black youths before. They are easily intimidated, and when their fears are borne out by violence they are unable to act effectively. Their bewilderment may reverberate through the other officers on the relief and in turn affect their dealings with young blacks as well.

Ex-Met PC, age 28, five years service. Just resigned.

Young PCs tend to think that West Indians normally have

drugs, give trouble and are tooled up. A lot of them are, which doesn't help!

I remember being on the Underground one day with an informant. He identified four West Indians who were stealing girls' handbags. They used to work from Holborn to South Kensington for a living. They worked as a group of four, with knives, and they would just surround a girl, take her handbag and stare at her. There was no way she could shout or scream because she felt intimidated. I was down the tube when this actually happened and I didn't do a thing. I felt "Oh dear, I'll get stabbed." So there's a situation where I was supposed to do something. I'd seen someone get robbed but I just couldn't do anything about it, I would have got stabbed, there's no two ways about it. I went down to the police station and at least I know who these people were, and then we got them later – mob-handed. That was the only way you were going to get them in.

Met Inspector, age 45, twenty years service. Now in the TSG.

A lot of the country lads who join the Met have never seen a black face before. In the same way the unemployed coloured youth gets fed up with being stopped all the time by horrible policemen, you've got the young policeman who's fed up with coloured lads who spit at him, verbally abuse him and – if they can – beat him up. It's Catch-22. You go in there and if you're nice to them they'll regard that as a sign of weakness. If you go over the top you're going to provoke some sort of trouble. The answer's in the middle, but you have to learn that.

Even experienced policemen, blokes who've got the same amount of service as me, still don't know how to deal with it properly. One person overreacts, the other overreacts and it builds up. The thing about the coloureds is that they're naturally more excitable. They shout and jump about. That's the way they are.

And the parents expect you to be like a West Indian police-man. They go in there and they're the magistrate They make the decision. Maybe they cuff them round the head, take them away and lock them up for a couple of days, say "Don't be a naughty boy", and send them home again. The parents can't understand why we don't do that.

Met WPC, age 30, nine years service. Now in Central London.

The most sane thing I ever heard a police officer say was when one of the youngsters on a refresher course asked a very old, intelligent, leery Sergeant about racism, and he said: "Look, racism and prejudice you're always going to have. I don't happen to like Scotty dogs. Everybody is going to be prejudiced about something. The only thing I can beg of all of you is not to let it show."

I remember once a very, very stroppy West Indian was brought in. He was absolutely glowering hatred. He'd been caught giving the Old Bill two fingers or something. It went down as insulting behaviour. A few minutes later another West Indian came in – an adorable little bloke, about 5 foot 6 inches, a little tweed cap. He was like a little sort of West Indian Hobbit, he was really cuddly. He said, "Terribly sorry to bother you, but I think my brother might have been brought in here. Somebody said they saw him being carted off in this direction. I don't know what he's done." It was the stroppy bloke and he was bailed. He was let out of the charge room: there he was, bouncing on the soles of his feet, doing the West Indian bounce – which I find very frightening. In my experience they are the dangerous ones.

That sort of prejudice is impossible not to entertain, because it's self-preservation as well. If on a dark night I see a West Indian bouncing towards me, I make damn sure that I'm walking in the middle of the road. You're never going to stamp out prejudice. I don't see how you can. I don't like drunks either.

Met Deputy Assistant Commissioner, age 42, twenty-three years service. In charge of a racially mixed area of London.

A daily report of racial attacks in my area comes to my desk every morning. That's how closely we highlight it. But what we do about it, I'm afraid, is pretty poor. Of course, with a high proportion of Asians you have a closed community, it's very hard to penetrate it. But the amount of under-reporting is changing, I'm glad to say. They are coming forward now more and more – but with what results is quite another question. It all takes time.

One ironic by-product of greater trust will be an apparent increase in the number of racial attacks because more will be reported. Thus, by doing more to help the police will attract more blame.

GROUP CULTURE

Recruits from rural Britain, or graduates from leafy suburbs, join the force with no personal experience of West Indians or Asians, but often sharing national attitudes which are less than friendly. They enter a police culture actively hostile to all minority groups: "Policemen are insulting about everyone. It's not specially against the coons," as one PC put it. "You hear remarks about poofs, Pakis, lesbos, women, students, the rich, the media, politicians, all foreigners, the Scots, the Irish – you name it. We hate everybody."
    Scapegoating is a way of dealing with the outside world seen as hostile to the police. But not all those groups are presumed to commit crime, as black males are. One PC told me the following string of jokes: "What do you call a coon in a three-bedroom semi? A burglar. What's black and brown and red all over? A Doberman with a nigger by the throat." There were more. The Policy Studies Institute Report The Police and People in London shocked the nation in 1983, when it reported in detail how police attitudes to race flow freely in the canteen culture of "nignogs, spooks, sooties, spades, coons, monkeys" and the other common police terms for black people. We also found that Asians are just "Pakis", perhaps because they have far less contact with the police. It is language that again echoes Vietnam, where the enemy were "gooks".
    The interviews suggest that the many officers who do not share the canteen view of black people face several choices – none of them satisfactory. They can shun the group, a lonely option. They can stay and argue – risking exclusion and a permanent label as a "softy" or "pinko lefty". Even supervisors rarely do that. Or they can adopt the protective colouring of

the group – using the language, but not acting on it. This is the most popular option.

PC in a southern Home Counties force, age 28, six years service. Now in a large market town.

There's a difference between somebody who is an out-and-out racist, has a pathological hatred of coloured people and looks upon coloured people of all types as some sort of lower individual to be treated nothing less than scum. That's a racist. But somebody who turns round and says "coon" or "spade" and then turns round to another West Indian bloke and says "Hello, mate, I haven't seen you for ages" – is he a racist?

In all walks of life there are people who despise other groups of people, other ethnic groups. Is a Protestant who despises with every ounce of his being a Catholic, a racist? There are policemen who are racist. There are also many, many more policemen who don't always choose their words wisely. I think there's as much a language problem as there is an ethnic problem. I'll say "spade", but I'm not a racist, because I think a racist is just describing people as he sees them, that's the way he was brought up. A black man calls a white man a "honky"; is the black man a racist?

Met Inspector, age 30, eight years service; Woman Police Sergeant, age 31, eight years service. Both now in a racially mixed residential area of London.

Insp: I often think of Enoch Powell's speeches of the '60s and '70s. The black population of this country do not want to be part of this country. We're the guys at the moment who are picking up the tab. What the hell do we do with people who can't read and write? They don't want a job, they don't want a house, they just want to wreck everything. We think being British is the greatest thing in the world. They think being British is shit. You have to correlate those two philosophies.

WPS: There's no moral leadership. There's a floating younger generation, just grabbing. Our society's in a mess, and one of the few agencies that understands the problem is the police force, because we have to deal with it all the time. What really shocks us in inner cities is that the poor are robbing the poor.

Insp: In an area which is rich and white, as soon as a black guy goes down the street, everyone notices him. That's horribly racist, but it's true. In your white middle-class suburbs, if a group of black youths walk down the street, they're going to be on the phone within thirty seconds. Villages in Staffordshire have had burglaries caused by blacks coming in from elsewhere in carloads. They've asked villagers to clock registration numbers of any car with blacks in it. It's totally correct, but no one wants to say it too loud.

WPS: Why are we being constantly got at because of racism? They can't even get on with themselves. Indian castes can't get on with other Indian castes. We're all racists in our own way. There's a presumption that racism is against blacks, which is rubbish. If you're told that the person you're looking for is a 3 foot midget, then every 3 foot person is going to come under suspicion.

COURTESY UNDER PRESSURE

Both the Policy Studies Institute (PSI) report of 1983 and my own observations on and off over nine years, suggest that many bobbies treat individual Asians and West Indians with far more courtesy than the group attitude suggests. But with black and Asian males, officers often find themselves facing the brick wall of anti-police prejudice. That then feeds the police group view that "You can't win. What's the point of trying to be nice? They're all animals" and so on into the night, as squad cars cruise the streets of the cities. The group culture is reinforced, and younger PCs are that much less willing to try again. This is the vicious circle that must be broken if police relations with the black community are to change.

Met PC, age 24, three years service. Now in an inner-city area of West London.

I was in uniform and stopped a car driven down the road by a

West Indian. He got out of his car and moaned and groaned about: "Why have you stopped me?"

"Because the seat belt on your passenger side is trailing along the floor." You're trying to help him, he still wouldn't thank you.

PC in a large northern force, age 23, three years service. Now in a racially mixed area on the edge of a city.

They're incredible, they're so quick to jump on you before you get them. I had one bloke I stopped for a defective headlamp – waved him down in the middle of the night. He gets out of the car shouting at me, "You've only stopped me because I'm black." I mean even if he was white I couldn't see the bastard at a hundred yards, now could I?

Met PC, age 25, five years service. Now in West London.

When I was first assigned in Brixton, I walked into a pub and saw a sea of black faces – it was a wall of hate. They didn't know me, they just saw the uniform. I was brand new there and all these people already hated me. It felt terrible, absolutely terrible. I thought, "I didn't join the police to be hated." Then I was called to Broadwater Farm. It was my birthday and I was just getting dressed to go out for dinner – and the call came. One hour later I was up there with people I didn't know trying to kill me. Said the same thing to myself – "What the hell is going on? I joined to help people. There are all these strangers trying to kill me."

Met Inspector age 42, twenty-one years experience. Now in the TSG.

This morning, coming in to work, I got off the train at Baker Street and there were two men fighting. Nine o'clock in the morning, rush hour. One's black, one's white. The trains were crowded and running late, there'd been a bit of pushing and shoving, and they'd had a go at each other. Both equally guilty. I didn't want to, but I got involved and arrested them both. The white man calmed down, stood there, knew he was in the wrong, didn't make any moves to run away. The coloured man – I've never heard language like it. Calling me a cocksucker, fat pig, cunt – everything. Said I was only nicking him because he was black. And he'd got a lot of previous. We got into the British Transport Police Station on Baker Street. He was so violent and noisy that he was searched and put in a cell. The other bloke was sitting there quite calm. From what I'd seen of the fight, the white man was by far the most aggressive, he was nutting him and everything else. The coloured boy had blood coming out of his nose but because of their attitudes, the Sergeant of British Transport Police was quite happy to caution the white man and charge the coloured one. I said, "No, they're both guilty." So they were both cautioned and kicked out.

I'm experienced enough to know that with this coloured lad it was all frustration. He was late for work, he'd just got the job after being unemployed for so long, you can see it when you've been about a bit. The lad was twenty-one, he was born the same day I joined the job.

RACIAL HARASSMENT

For the black community, the police are the most obvious symbol of their position in British society. To the extent that harassment takes place, it fulfills their worst expectations. If it didn't happen, they might have to invent it. Sometimes they do invent it to save face with their peers, but real harassment happens often enough to feed their mistrust.

Met PC, age 25, seven years service. Now in South London.

One night a call came over the radio to stop a purple Cortina All the message said was that it was suspected of being involved in drugs. So I stopped it and there were four West Indians in the car and they weren't very happy. All I said was, "Look here, I've stopped you because a police officer has asked me to do so. The police officer is going to come and have a word with you." This police officer got on the radio and said, "Oh, just turn the car over will you? I think they've got drugs on them." I said, "No, I won't. You saw the car, you get down here and do it."

He wouldn't, but another police officer I was working with came over and we did a check driver's licence and things like that. These people were thoroughly annoyed by this. I said, "You were seen coming out of a club in Greek Street." They said they hadn't been anywhere near there. They had just come down from Luton. The driver pulled out a slip showing he'd been stopped by police earlier that night on the A1 – literally half an hour earlier, the time was written on the form – so they couldn't have been anywhere near the club. The other people in the car were getting really stroppy because they felt the police were victimizing them – and essentially we were! They said, "We're not puttin' up with this. We're going."

Because West Indians are a very physical race, they stand too close to police officers. They were standing too near to the face of the police officer I was with. They were pointing their fingers in his face and he just lost his nerve. He flipped and called for "Urgent Assistance". So half the Met turned up, you know, at three in the morning. Then it was, "Right, you're all nicked for a drugs search – everybody into the back of the van."

We got back to the station and dragged these people into the charge room. They were livid. The Station Officer asked me what these people were in for and I said, "Don't ask me. They have got nothing to do with me. As far as I'm concerned, they haven't done anything." He said, "Get elsewhere." It's his job to find out why they'd all been arrested. The original PC made up some kind of story about drugs, I don't know whether it was true or not. I suspect it wasn't. Anyway, they were searched and the car was turned over and there were no drugs. I had a stand-up row with this PC who had put the message on the radio. He said, "You should never let these West Indians take the piss out of you. You are a police officer in uniform." Basically, he had asked me to stop that car because it was four coons driving along at three in the morning.

Later I bumped into one of these chaps. I was off duty at St Thomas' Hospital. he recognized me and I thought, "Oh my God!" He was a doctor! Anyway he came up and said I was the only decent police officer he'd met that night. I'd thought he was going to hit me because they were really mad when they left the police station. I said, "Yeah, the whole thing was really unfortunate." He said, "Do you realize what happened when we left the police station?" They had gone through Trafalgar Square and down Whitehall and were stopped! Four coons in a car. They were stopped three times in less than four hours!

Met Chief Inspector, age 44, twenty-five years service in inner-city areas of London. Formerly a CLO, now just retired.

Being a Community Liaison Officer has been the most rewarding job I have ever had in over twenty-five years in the police force. It has opened my mind a lot, about myself as well. I realize now I was too narrow-minded, probably slightly racist, certainly I was prejudiced.

I don't expect, even now, that many of them fully trust me. I was in one of these black community groups chatting with the leader. He said something like: "I suppose now you've had a look round, you'll go back and tell them the layout of the place and when to raid it." Which I obviously didn't. However, coincidentally, ironically that very night – and unbeknown to me – four police officers raided the place for drugs. You can imagine how I felt. They thought I had set it all up! Trust can be lost so quickly.

HUMAN AWARENESS TRAINING

Human Awareness is the general title of the new courses designed to help officers change their approach to ethnic minorities. They are taught about differences in cultural attitudes, for example that Asian women in purdah are forbidden to speak to strange men, which makes interviewing them as witnesses rather delicate. New recruits are encouraged to admit their prejudices, as a first step to changing them.

This is an important move. In the past, much police time has been spent denying that prejudice existed in the force.

Detective Sergeant in a Home Counties, age 38, sixteen years service. Now in a university city.

You know why there aren't more black coppers? They're too fucking lazy, that's why. I think they're scared of their people. And I don't think they've got the brain power for it either. I'm sorry, but that's how I feel. You can get a whole community, you wouldn't get an O Level between them. They're so bloody arrogant, they really are, certainly the people I come across in the West Indian community. I do know a couple who are quite nice guys, but 90 per cent of them – they really are arrogant. And totally "anti". Most of them are bloody born here. Yet they all live in their own community, which is not right. What's the matter with other people? They think there's a war between them and us.

All too often, such attitudes can lead to more serious problems. Yet they are expressed by conscientious policemen.

Superintendent in a Midlands force. Now in a small industrial city.

There's a lot of misinformation and misunderstanding with Asians and blacks. I had a classic example in my last posting where we had a massive Asian population. Two pigs' heads were thrown into the main mosque, smashed through the window. Immediately the senior Asian elders got together and spoke of racism. They paraded. There were hundreds of them. It created all sorts of problems. They added on to that a load of other allegations and complaints that were a pack of bloody lies to support what they were claiming about the mosque. As far as they were alleging, it was a major racial incident against the Asian community. Turned out to be a couple of drunken yobs who didn't even know it was a mosque. They had gone down to the abattoir, got two bloody pigs' heads out of there, gone on and had a good booze up, intending to drop them in the door of somebody they'd had a disagreement with, decided against it, and just slung them through this window.

That's a problem with Asians: they make so many allegations that are totally a pack of lies.

Met PCs in an inner-city area of West London, average age 37, average service eighteen years.

PC1: Since they made racial discrimination a disciplinary offence on this job, I'm very reluctant to stop a car with blacks in it, and I'd never do it on my own. I could stop that car. "Evening, gents, whose car?" and it's happened so many times, I've heard it from other PCs – you're polite to them, they're polite to you, bona fide owner, "Sorry to have troubled you. Have a nice night." They've turned around, gone in the nick and complained about you. You've got a discipline board with three or four blacks standing there staying: "When that police-man stopped us he said, 'Oi, you black cunts, get out.' He called us wogs." And they're going to believe them.

PC2: They want you to go on a Human Awareness course. I've never been on one;. I think they're leaving the old coppers out, because basically they wouldn't want to do it. By the time you get out you're all brainwashed that the attitude you had when you went in is wrong.

PC1: The prime example: A black bloke walks along a road with a big ghetto blaster on his shoulder. So many decibels it's untrue. He's not there to upset people – he's happy. He wants to share his happiness, his love, with everybody else and he's showing that through his music. Or if he's having a reggae party – it's three o'clock in the morning and it's coming out of his window; he just wants to share that with everybody else.

When you say to him: "I know you're trying to be happy and you want to be in love with everybody, but Mr So-and-So down the road is trying to get a bit of sleep. What about turning it down?" He says, "No." You just leave him alone – that's what we've been told. Now poor Mr Smith down the road who's got to get up at 7 a.m. to go to work, he's got no rights.

PC2: What annoys me is the sheer arrogance of these arseholes who try and teach us Human Awareness. Theirs is only one point of view. In my opinion, that coon with the ghetto blaster is a man who is terribly selfish. He doesn't give a monkey's about anybody else. He could be just as happy more quietly but, having no self-discipline, he doesn't give a shit about anything.

Why is their point of view right and my one wrong? "You're a racist." It's absolute crap. It's become a moron's chant. It implies that somebody just isn't really thinking. English people are generous people. They've got to be the most tolerant of anywhere in the world.

Two Met PCs, average age 23, average service two years in inner London.

PC1: We spent the whole of the first six weeks talking about ethnic minorities. It was a bit boring after a while, you want to get on with real policing. But it was interesting. Like I didn't know about Sikhs carrying little daggers. I can see coming up to a Sikh bloke and searching him and finding this lovely little knife, and taking him down to the station while he insists it's for his religion, and you're going "Oh yeah, pull the other one."

PC2: Yeah, but it all depends on the instructor. If you've got one who thinks it's all a waste of time, he'll just smirk all the way through and you won't get much from that. But if you're lucky and get a straight one, you'll know a lot more about the problems.

PC1: Some people coming down from Shropshire or wherever haven't ever met a coloured person before. For them, these courses are really good. But I don't think they expect you to change your mind. All they want is for you to be more aware of their habits so you know how to deal with them properly. Nobody who's a racist is going to admit it, unless they're stupid. They'd boot you out on your ear.

ETHNIC RECRUITMENT

Lord Scarman recommended recruiting more officers from ethnic minorities, to make the police seem less like an "army of occupation" in the inner cities.

Recruiting drives have been launched, but the response has been slow. The numbers of ethnic officers in the Met increased from just under 50 in 1975 to over 300 in 1986. In 1987, another 114 joined – a rise of one-third. Yet the total of 418 ethnic officers is a tiny proportion – under 2 per cent – of the 27,000 officers in the force as a whole, and considerably smaller than the proportion of ethnic minorities in London. In the whole of England and Wales there were 124,182 police officers as of April 1988. Of those, 1138 are members of ethnic minorities – less than 1 per cent. Yet 5 per cent of the population of Britain are from ethnic minorities.

Among the problems of recruitment are educational standards. In the first years of the recruiting drive, most ethnic applicants were not even interviewed. Now extra help and encouragement is provided at the interview, with reapplication advised in borderline cases. At the time of the first campaign, the rumour spread throughout the Met that standards were to be lowered at entry and at training school, to enlist more black coppers. This set off a fierce debate in police canteens and did not help the already problematic welcome which new ethnic recruits would receive.

Met Superintendent (ex-colonial background), age 40, twenty-five years service. Now in a racially mixed area in South London.

We have got to positively discriminate. One coloured lad we interviewed had everything going for him until we probed a little bit and it turned out that his brother had been kicked out of the police. His other brother is awaiting trial for burglary. He hasn't got a father and everything he has done since school has lacked any guidance from anyone. He was taking O Levels and then decided he couldn't be bothered. He had a job with a security company earning £7500, but gave it up because it was boring. Maybe it was boring, but it was a job and we would have thought, "Well, he's got a bit of commitment."

You could see him wearing a uniform very well – super smart, good-looking bloke. Had a lovely smile all the time, but he was dozy. He would not have lasted more than a few minutes in the interview if it had not been for the fact that he was coloured. We spent about half an hour with him, trying to encourage him to take his O Levels, just to get him to show more than a few months' commitment to something.

There are discipline problems with the West Indians in the force. Probably because we recruit people who are below par and we hope we will train them properly. But we don't give them enough time. They do need more supervision than most to achieve the same, and we just have to accept that. The only way we can recruit other ones is to have a few black faces in there, but generally they don't want to join. The good-quality lad, everyone wants him.

Met WPC, age 24, five years service. Now in a racially mixed area in West London.

I would say that at this station most police officers are racist. That's not because blacks are blacks. It's because of the behaviour of the blacks in this area.

I always go on the basis that you treat each person as you find them, but I think a lot of blacks are very quick to jump up and say you're being racist just because you don't like them as an individual person. I don't come across many black people in my beat. I've got three or four, and they will always stop and talk to me and we'll have a good chat. They're smashing. But you couldn't do that in All Saints Road or Toxteth, or St Paul's.

I think positive discrimination is dreadful. You've either got it or you haven't, and it shouldn't make any difference whether you're black, white or yellow. If I've got to study every night to pass my exams, I don't know why some other bugger shouldn't have to, just because he happens to have a different colour skin. I don't think I am a racist, but it annoys me when I hear of things like that. I'm not saying they should get less chance than we do, but I don't see why they should get any more.

Met Detective Constable, age 28, six years service. Now in South London.

Coloured policemen get a hard time. There are racists – a lot of policemen are very racist.

An Indian PC that I worked with came onto Crime Squad shortly after me. The first day he walked into the police station, an old Inspector called him a "black fucking gupta". I've never ever known him to be called anything since then – just "Gupta"! The guy came onto the Crime Squad and immediately was gunned for, to get him off. On a Crime Squad you work a partner system. A lot of people go through their whole Crime Squads with the same partner. This guy had about six partners, because nobody would work with him. No reflection on his ability, in fact he's just been promoted. It's got to be all credit to that guy, because he is a brilliant copper.

Met PC age 36, fourteen years service. Now in East London.

I would love to see more coloured policemen. There's five or six in the station and not only are they the nicest blokes you'll ever meet, but they are bloody good coppers. I would like to see more. I went to an incident in Central London, turning a black club out – illegal drinking – and all these blacks were coming out, looking daggers at us, ready to have a verbal go or even fisticuffs. And who's standing outside the door? A black skipper. They came out and looked at this bloke, black as what they are, and in our uniform, and didn't do anything. Yes, I'd love to see more black coppers.

If we're racist, Christ, these black coppers are twice as racist. Quality is the thing. I worked with one on a shift. He was an absolute dickhead. I'd stop a car full of blacks and always start: "Hello, good evening." I talk to them like anybody else. This black copper comes up and: "Right, you black bastards, out of the car!" There was only two of us and four of them.

Detective Constable in a large northern force, age 27, eight years service. Now in a city-centre area.

The police problem is that we tend to get the shittier end of the stick from every element of society. When we come into contact with blacks, it's generally with the bad ones. We become racist that way. I'm not sure if "racist" is the right word. Most policemen are anti-villain. Whether that villain is white, yellow, pink, Irish, Catholic – it makes no odds. Though if he's a black villain they are more anti him, because they feel that policemen are being treated like shit by the black community and the bosses are not backing them up.

There's a bobby who's a Muslim. I think he's Iranian. I'm not really sure. He worked in the same station as a white who was born in South Africa. The white bobby continually gave him stick about his colour. It came to a head when this South African poured out tea for all of the section except for the coloured fella. He said, as any bobby would, "Where's my tea?" And the reply was, "You're a fucking nigger. Make your own tea." And he poured the tea on the table. "There's your tea" – not in a cup. The coloured fellow stormed out, didn't know what to do. Rings up a friend of mine who says, "No problem. report him immediately." He says, "I can't do that." My friend says, "Take a few of your mates round. I'll come with you. Say to him, 'Listen, you do that again, I'm going to sort you out.'" "No, I won't do that," so he has been transferred.

He's a great bloke, but now he's having problems with another white bobby who's ex-Met. Apparently the Met call blacks "groids", as in negroids. All "groids" are black bastards to this copper. And this coloured copper has to put up with being told, "Oh well, you're different."

ETHNIC POLICE OFFICERS

The cynicism and bitterness that characterizes the canteen cowboys, and which leaks into the language of many PCs, is strikingly lacking from the interviews with ethnic PCs themselves. Interestingly, they are the ones under the most pressure – sharing all the impossible tasks of their white colleagues, plus the resistance among their home community. By no means all officers from ethnic minorities have been happy in the police. Some have had nervous breakdowns and left. But the ones we interviewed are optimistic – a hopeful sign.

Met WPC, Indian, age 24, three years service. Now in an inner-city area, south London.

I'm a Hindu. Not a practising Hindu, that's my culture. I don't feel anyone's racist towards me. It's banter. When they call the corner shop a "Paki" shop, they get embarrassed and say, "No offence." But I call it that myself. I feel it boils down to our attitude, not to take offence at that. Maybe I'm being naive, but I don't know how much racism there is in the Job. I've never come across it.

I don't care for ethnic recruiting myself. I joined this job of my own accord. I'm quite happy here. I've assisted the Yard with ethnic recruiting. West Indians and Asians would come in and speak to ethnic officers, like myself, and we were meant to discuss how we were treated within the Job. No one wanted to know about that. They just wanted to know what the pay and the social life was like. Obviously you can promote a job by public advertising, but when they campaign just for ethnic officers, lowering standards for them like one O Level instead of two – it's wrong.

An ethnic officer joining this job should anticipate a hard time. I admire the ones that come in wearing turbans. I wouldn't be able to do it. This is a British force. If you're going to join a disciplined force like this – then you should conform.

Because the ethnic population is increasing, we do need people in the Job who will understand them. Some ethnic officers would like to work within their own community. I wouldn't. If you're a police officer you deal with all members of the public. You shouldn't really be restricting yourself to your own little community.

Everybody has their prejudices. I've got mine. That's what it is, not racism. You're trained never to stereotype. But if you're in Brixton or All Saints Road and there are young West Indiams, in their jeans and bomber jackets, you feel they're only there for one reason – and it's true. Nothing else goes on in that road apart from crime. So you do stereotype. But you've got to be able to adjust when you come out of that road.

Met WPC, black, age 23, two years service. Now in an inner-city area of West London.

I haven't met a great deal of prejudice, not as much as all these West Indians with chips on their shoulders. I've only had a little bit, most of it since I've come to London. Everybody calls us "wogs, coons, groids". It doesn't bother me. They're just using it to describe black people generally, as opposed to me individually. A couple of members of the relief though, I feel they meant it – as if to say, "We've hated black people all our life. Now we've got one in our ranks. What's it doing here?" It doesn't upset me as such, but it makes me a bit wary of them.

We were on a football carrier and there were no seats. I went to sit next to the driver and he said, "You're not sitting next to me, go sit at the back." When the next one got in that he didn't like very much, he said, "Go sit next to that grey lady at the back." I thought, "What an out-and-out wanker."

The blacks don't see me as being black and whites don't see me as being white. I'm in a little grey area. A coloured lady screamed at me once: "Take that dirty white man's hat off your head. You're doing the evil white man's work." I thought it was hilarious.

Met PC, black, age 22, three years service. Now in a racially mixed area of West London.

I've just come back from Jamaica, and the corruption over there is incredible compared to here. I'm proud to say that I'm an English policeman.

I had a few friends in the police and they said they were looking for "my kind of people". I didn't think much of the ethnic recruitment side, but it was a career I could make a go of. I didn't fancy sitting in an office, I like getting involved. And it's good money as well.

I've moved from where I lived, but I still have a lot of black friends. They find the job very attractive – just like the normal youth. You grow up and think: "I want to be a police officer." But it's the barriers that make them feel it's unacceptable. They feel that it's dominated by white officers, that they'll get too much stick when they come in. Not only that, their own community will reject them. I can't say to them that it's not true, but when people say, "What about the hassle?" I say: "You went to school. It's nothing more than that. You handled it." Now, because you're being paid, you've got things like a mortgage to support. If they're strong personalities, they could override it easily.

I went through that stage of hating the police for no reason. When I was about fifteen I was in a group who used to go to blues and dances. It was just accepted that you didn't like the police. It was quite a surprise for my school friends when I joined.

I was bracing myself for a real leap over the wall, not knowing what it was like on the other side. In my interview they said, "You're going to get called 'Uncle Tom'," but I thought: "I want to do this. They're not going to stop me."

I had a Street Duties Sergeant who gave me an excessively hard time. I didn't know whether it was because of my colour or because I was a probationer. After a while I thought it was my colour. I wasn't doing any worse than everyone else and yet I got hassled all the time. But I didn't lose sleep over it. You get a few people like that anywhere.

One thing I'll say about policemen: they are the biggest piss-takers in the world. They take the piss out of you whether you're Scottish, Irish, Jewish – whatever. It's just the way they are.

The thing that hits most home to me is protecting South Africa House. I detest the regime, but I have to be there. The demonstrators pick you out and say, "You shouldn't be here, you're a traitor to your race." It just doesn't affect me anymore. I can't go up to my guv'nor and say, "My political allegiances don't allow me to stay outside South Africa House." I'd be out of a job in a month.

I don't think I'm any good to black people if I'm outside the force. It's black policemen that will restore the confidence of young blacks. If I see a crowd of black kids and they shout something at me like "Judas", I'll walk straight into the crowd and say, "Why do you say that? Who am I a traitor to?" They usually haven't got an answer. After a while they start chatting to me. They go away saying, "You're all right. It's the rest of them."

The irritating thing is when white PCs also say,"You're one of us – you're not like the rest." Back to square one. It's meant to be a compliment. You see, policemen don't like "slaggy people", whether they're Gypsies, Irish tinkers – people who are rubbish, whatever colour they are. This is the danger – a lot of them call people slags just by looking at them, which is wrong. If they were living in the community they'd realize that not everyone who wears a Rasta hat or drives a Ford Cortina with furry dice is a slag or up to no good. My brother is a Rasta.

I've been stopped many times after work. One time I was meeting my girlfriend in my white Ford Cortina when a policeman stopped me. Normally I let them know I'm a copper straight away. But this guy was so rude I thought, "All right then, go on."

"This your car, mate?"

"Yeah."

He said. "Makes a change, dunnit." Then he said: "What are you doing here?"

"I'm meeting my girlfriend."

My girlfriend had just come up, so he says: "White slag is it?" I just let him go on. Then he said, "You got a job?"

"Yes."

"You're one in a million then, ain't you? What do you do?"

"I work for the government."

So we went all round the car. He had a WPC in the driver's seat and he was obviously trying to impress her. Eventually he said, "Where are you going?"

"I've got to go to work."

"Where d'you work?"

"In a Police Station. I'm a policeman."

He just looked at me. So I showed him my warrant card and he says, "Sorry, mate." The WPC was cracking up in the car.

If you look at the Holloway Road incident, it's the cover-up people disapprove of. Nobody criticizes their beating the black kids up – that would be too liberal. The police force is ultra right wing, no doubt about it. If you air a left-wing view you're called a lefty pinko faggot! There's a lot of closet lefties, though. There are also some PCs who are out-and-out Nazis. They admit it themselves. They still do their job effectively. I don't think the guv'nors know about it. There's one up Bow Street. He's out and out NF "send them back" kind of thing.

But I honestly haven't seen clear-cut racism in action. They talk about "spades and coons" but when it comes down to it, they do think about their job. They wouldn't get much support from guv'nors if someone made a complaint against them.

Met PC, a Sikh, age 30, three years service. Now in inner London.

The community has got to be a bit more open minded. Before I joined, I would always see it from my point of view, from the outsider's point of view. Once you join the job, you start seeing things both ways. If there was an Asian demonstration or a Moslem march, then the police would be against them. The same policemen could be against the supporters at a football match. Whichever group is facing you, you're against them. The miners probably thought that the police were anti-miners, but the same officers were facing West Indian marchers two months later, who would have the same feelings.

Most of the Asians that I know hold the police in high respect, because most of us remember what the police were like in India! They are a million times better here. In India – you can be picked up and beaten for no reason at all. I have heard of people being killed by the police, for just sending them up. That's why, when I joined as a police officer, most friends supported me.

The British don't realize how good their police force is. The Asian youngsters haven't experienced the police back in India, or Pakistan, they take it for granted. They want a perfect police – which you can never have.

Ten years ago, I would have been treated differently from the way I am now as an ordinary person on the road. It's a lot, lot better. You can't stop a policeman being nasty to you. He's probably nice to you 90 times out of 100. But the other times you don't know whether it's just a bad day or he's nasty. They have off days – who doesn't?

Racial attacks happen, and the police do follow them up. But the police don't publicize the work they do. My wife was attacked by a rifleman. She had an air-rifle pellet in the head. The police were called. I know how much they did to catch him, but the public wouldn't know that.

Nobody saw the attack. There were six people injured. They were all Asians. If you wanted to think of it as a racial attack, you could. You could back it up with the fact that six people were shot at with an air-rifle on the corner of Southall and Hayes. But at that time of day, most of the people there are Asians. It could be just another Asian youngster, shooting at anybody who was available. I think you've got to keep an open mind about these things.

Racial attacks are like burglaries – very difficult to detect. If the police force decided today that they were going to deal with nothing else but racial attack, then they probably could do it.

If they could put enough resources behind it. But there are so many other things, more important things – maybe not to the person who's been attacked, but in a whole perspective. An Asian has been attacked by five skinheads. He's been cut on the head and he wants them caught. At the same time, a two-year-old has wandered off. What's more important at that particular time? To find the lost child or these five skinheads? At that time the force has to concentrate on this child. If you can do both, fine. But, lack of resources make racial attacks low priority.

People come up and say, "It's nice to see an Asian police officer." A lot of others, I can see they snigger. They walk away and laugh behind my back. What can you do? Hopefully they'll get used to it. Hopefully I'll do a good enough job they'll respect me. That's the way I treat it. I can't tell people off for laughing. Some people refuse to believe I'm a police officer when I arrest them. It doesn't happen too often in a uniform because obviously they can see it, but if I'm in plainclothes it's only when I handcuff them that they believe that I am a police officer!

It's not that much of a problem. People get used to seeing me. Also, word of mouth starts spreading, that there is a new police officer. Everybody talks about something they don't see that often. It's getting better.

The public's view of the police as racist is a bit unfair. There are racists in the police force, but because of the disciplinary offences, I think they keep themselves to themselves. If an incident did occur, I would report it without any hesitation, but it would have to be serious. Everybody is wound up once in a while and everybody is on the receiving end of jokes – if you can't deal with it in the parade room, how can you deal with it on the street?

In an ideal world, a policeman should be a policeman. But I am Sikh and if I can do my job more efficiently in Southall I should be there. It's no use having a 10-stone weakling in the TSG. It's a tough job. You have to be in the front line of a riot. People should fit in the jobs they can do best. I speak Punjabi. If members of the public can only speak Punjabi, they're going to have problems trying to speak to policemen who don't speak Punjabi. So there are linguistic and cultural reasons for Asian police officers in Southall. For communication purposes and also to appreciate things which other cultures don't. In Southall you are allowed to carry a sword. I can tell somebody who should be carrying it and somebody who shouldn't. I can tell if somebody is a genuine believer or not. An English person wouldn't be able to. All they cauld see is the turban and somebody who claimed to be a Sikh. You can't train people how to read these signs in a couple of weeks. There must certainly be mistakes made sometimes because of this.

My family are very proud I'm in the British police force. I know they wouldn't have been if I'd been in the Indian police force. Being an officer in the British police force is a highly respected job. My father is always telling his relatives his son is in the police, he can't stop himself. The way our community works, word of mouth gets out to over 2000 friends and relatives, many people who have no connection with me but through friends of friends know I am a police officer. A couple of them have come to ask me advice about joining, in places where I had least expected it. I went to a wedding in Birmingham, 150 miles away and a couple of people pointed at me and I thought maybe I was dressed wrong, but no – they came over and asked about being in the police. They wanted to know how the police would treat them if they joined – I think that's the same fears I had when I joined, of being a minority in a large organization. I told them that they had nothing to worry about.

CHAPTER FIVE

Everyday Policing

Police Constables are the foot soldiers in the War Against Crime, against public disorder, drugs, vandalism, sexual abuse, domestic violence and football hooliganism. But the war they fight daily is less exciting and emotionally more damaging. It is a war of attrition against the police service itself.

Beat policing can be very dull, and bobbies on the beat are notoriously hard to supervise. In the pre-radio days, they had to ring the station from each police box along their route, within a fixed amount of time. The Police and Criminal Evidence Act of 1984, however, obliges most Sergeants to stay in the station, or gives them an excuse to do so, so there is still less pressure on PCs to keep busy. The old worry that the Sergeant might be watching from the corner has been removed.

Beat PCs can spend hours wandering aimlessly, waiting to be called to whatever the 999 operators may turn up next. This mixture of boredom and danger is a perfect recipe for stress. In the middle of the night, it encourages too many squad cars to answer calls for assistance just to keep themselves awake. News of a "shout" draws them like flies to honey – I recall a simple two-handed pub fight to which fifty policemen turned up.

The 1984 Police and Criminal Evidence Act has also made bobbies more wary of contact with the public, as they are now obliged to give anyone they stop their name and number. Many younger ones avoid unnecessary contact altogether, out of shyness, or fear of a complaint of rudeness, or to avoid the heavy load of paperwork that now goes with an arrest.

THE SHIFT SYSTEM

Although work patterns vary from force to force and area to area, uniform Constables, Sergeants and relief Inspectors work a basically similar three shift system, each twenty-four hour day, 365 days a year.

Early turn is usually from 6 a.m. to 2 p.m. and is the least popular, as it involves rising an hour or two earlier to travel to work. On the other hand, it gives family men time with their children in the early evening.

Late turn is from 2 p.m. to 10 p.m., or from 3 p.m. to 11 p.m. in some forces. On the whole it is the most popular with the men and least popular with their wives, as post-shift drinking can go on into the early hours.

Nights are usually from 10 p.m. to 6 a.m. or from 11 p.m. to 7 a.m. The night shift produces the most ambivalent feelings: it comprises both the busiest and quietest hours. The fights and drunks when pubs and then clubs close down are followed by private time known only to night workers like policemen and nurses, when the rest of the city sleeps. The occasional call is usually serious. Burglar alarms are most often assumed to have gone off by themselves and may be passed to private security firms. For the squad cars, or for the beat man walking up and down the same stretch of road testing doors, the sight of a speeding old banger or a stray pedestrian who can be stopped and searched is like finding an oasis in the desert. On a wet night it could lead back to the station, however much bad luck that is for the civilian concerned.

Most uniform officers work seven days on, followed by one or two days off, and shifts are rotated weekly. The end of a night shift at 6 a.m. followed by a new, later turn shift starting at 2 p.m. on the same day allows only a few hours rest. When possible, many married PCs work long hours of overtime or on their rest days to increase their pay. All this, combined with the pressures of the job, and the absence of the civilian weekend break, is a potent formula for short-tempered policing.

POLICING BY OBJECTIVES

Policing by Objectives is one of a number of strategies to give the force and each PC a way of doing something positive instead of aimless patrolling and purely reactive "fire fighting". In theory, area priorities are set in consultation both with station working parties of officers from all ranks as well as with the police liaison committees: problems such as vandalism and graffiti, or car thefts, become the focus for each PC on the beat. Structured patrol schemes can also give a greater sense of purpose to the job, but still do not take away the humdrum nature of many of the tasks. They also tend to be assigned to younger PCs, who often see the beat job as "only" keeping the peace, a relatively meaningless task, while responding to calls in an area car is "enforcing the law", a much more glamorous one.

Senior officers face their own dilemma over the status of the bobby on the beat. Many did their minimum of two years on the street in the early 1970s when Panda cars were all the rage. They may not know the satisfaction that can be gained from gently building bridges rather than just responding to the latest emergency call. They mistrust the very idea of "soft" policing and only go along with putting more men back on the beat because it is politic to do so. The poor quality of middle rank supervision is a serious worry in itself. It leaves bobbies even more isolated.

Current doubts about the real value of beat policing are easily read by all ranks, which undermines force policy as it passes down the line. Even its advocates know that research has yet to prove that it reduces crime, which is the name of the game to "hard" policemen and politicians. Lord Scarman asked for a more complex approach than either hard or soft: he wanted each incident handled with sensitivity.

No one, however, has yet found the optimum between hard and soft policing. Scarman said that it did not matter whether beat policing actually reduced crime. What makes it worthwhile is that local residents think it does. This is a confidence trick that takes confidence to bring off. Without such conviction, it fails just as the sceptics expect it to – a self-fulfilling prophecy that leaves the bobby in limbo.

Met Woman Inspector, age 32, ten years service, and a graduate. Now in an inner-city area of London.

A Royal Commission is needed to clarify the job since Scarman. The government has been sitting on the fence. We have conflicting objectives between upholding the law and maintaining the peace. So we're lost in a melee. Scarman's report was just a convenient get-out. He said all the right things, but we're confused about the force's conclusions. The lads have no idea what would happen in the event of another major disorder. They don't know if they'd be given back-up or just left to run for their lives. It's a scandal, such uncertainty. If senior officers don't know what they want, how can young people just out of school?

GIVING BOBBIES A BOOST

In 1981, Lord Scarman urged that beat policemen be moved from the lowest rank of the pecking order and put into the "forefront of the police team". As with the status of community policemen, this needs more than exhortation to bring about.

Met Inspector, age 36, fourteen years service. Ex-SPG.

Everyone says the job of PC is the most valuable in the force, but it's total bullshit. Why else do they take raw kids just out of training school and throw them into the worst areas of London at the worst hours, while the CID and the rest of the management nine-to-fivers go home early on Fridays? Looking after children is important too, but when the lollipop man goes sick it's a PC who has to cover. You can find a good thief-taker just standing there all day, and it makes him feel rotten.

PC in a southern Home Counties force, age 28, six years service. Now in a large port.

There's been lots of times I wanted to complain about things that are wrong in the police – I've even considered writing to the local paper. But I've reached for my pen, and I've thought about the wife and kiddies and the mortgage. I can't risk anything happening to my career. So I swallow my frustration. It's a shame, but that's the way things are in the police. I wouldn't have signed the letter anyway, but what if they got hold of it from the paper and got my fingerprints off it? Bang goes my promotion. Sorry if I sound paranoid, but everyone watches their backs in the office and their fronts on the street.

RURAL BOBBIES

It is not just urban police who are under pressure. Assaults on police are rising in country areas as well.

Village beats are disappearing, and police cover is extended from the nearest town. The theory is that integrating rural bobbies into thinly manned town reliefs offers better value for money. But like beat and neighbourhood policing, it is impossible to put a value on a rural bobby's contact with the public.

PC in a Midlands rural force, age 36, seventeen years service. Formerly in a village, now in a market town.

They're selling off country beat houses. The police will lose out because country people are much more introverted and won't talk to policemen if they don't know them.

Take cases of burglary. Somebody in the village knows everybody's business. They're usually the quietest. But you go round and they'll say, "Are you going to have a little tot?" and you'll say, "Yes, please" – especially on a cold day with rainwater running down your neck. When they trust you they'll come out with a little bit of information, good as gold. The chap in the village before me was a real stickler. He went down the pub at Christmas time and saw they had a draw and asked to see their gaming licence! Nobody spoke to him after that.

I used to run a youth club in the village. There was a punch-up one time – motorcyclists came in. I was there by myself, and one of the lads went over to the pub, into the public bar and said, "There's trouble over there." They all came over to help, which was just smashing. I could see them coming down the road and I suddenly got all brave and told the bikers to push off. Now if you're the sort of policeman who's a stickler, you won't get cooperation like that.

ALL THINGS TO ALL MEN

In rural areas, the job is much more low key than in the inner cities, though weekends may bring lager louts and violence. More often than not, however, the police are treated as an all-purpose support system, which is impossible to quantify in current police management terms.

Superintendent in a rural area of a Home Counties force, age 45, twenty-three years service.

I picked up the phone the other day and it was one of the locals: "Can I come and talk to you?"
    "Yes, what about?"
    "Well, I've got a summons."
    "What's it for?"
    "That's what I want to talk to you about."
    "Read it out on the phone, then."
    "Well, I'd really like to come down."
    He couldn't read. He's got an official document he doesn't understand and he wants someone to explain. That isn't a policeman's job, to read bloody summonses to people. The public thinks, "I've got a problem. Who's got a twenty-four hour service I can ring?"

BUREAUCRACY

A typical police officer's formal education would only be to O Level standard, and include some police training. Yet there is more writing in their job than in many highly educated professions. All uniform PCs and Detective Constables are pressured by the knowledge that their paperwork will be carefully studied, first by Crown Prosecution Service solicitors and then in court by the defence, for errors that could affect the outcome of a case. The cynicism this engenders discourages arrests and leads PCs to tidy up loose ends by pooling accounts

*of what happened, or even fabricating evidence (see "Law,
Justice and the Courts"). The paperwork also takes them off
their beats, and produces the distinctive and wordy mode of
expression that often sounds comically officious: "As I was
proceeding in a westerly direction ..."*

PC in a southern Home Counties force, age 23, three years service. Now in a large port.

For a shoplifter, if it is going to be a guilty plea, you are looking
at one and a half hours of paperwork. If it's a not guilty plea,
what with taking all the relevant statements, it can take three
or four hours.

If you get a prisoner early in a turn – say 2 pm to 10 pm and
you get him at 3 pm – by the time you've got his solicitor in,
done the interview, taken fingerprints and photos, possibly
searched his home before you release him to check for stolen
property, got back to the station, put all the stolen property
into a bag, got all your statements together – that's the day
gone!

You don't get time to do what the policeman does on the
telly. It doesn't work like that at all. If you're not outside
working, then you're inside doing the paperwork on the work
just done outside.

PC in a West Country force, age 28, seven years service. Now in a city.

Arresting people is quite exciting, but booking people back at
the station is just a drag. It's a lot of bad feeling for no excitement really. I enjoyed arresting people, but the novelty wore
off. You used to wreck their lives so badly, it bothered me after
a while. I did think about it, but the excitement was greater
than the responsibility.

I arrested a nurse who got addicted to drugs and was dipping
her hand in the medicine jar at work. I felt sorry for her because
she was a single mum, not a lot in her life, and she found it
easier when she dipped in the medicine jar and cheered herself
up. The arrest was probably justified in law, but it wasn't a
very nice thing to do to the lady.

Met WPC, age 35, ten years service. Now in an inner-city area of West London.

I began ten years ago in Finchley, in North London, which was a huge area with very few police. But it had decentralized control, so we were really in charge of our own patch. You really felt involved with each case – you arrested them, processed them, followed through the case to court. Now you wade through all this paper and then hand over your case to a central processing office – which several stations feed into. It means losing contact for both the PC and the victim. You even lose contact with the criminal.

There's been such a huge change in the last ten years. Probably the biggest change in the whole history of the police. Nobody cares any more, nobody listens. These days, you're lucky if the Sergeant says, "Good evening." The Inspector probably doesn't even know your name! There's not even any blooming paper to take complaints at the counter or calls when they come in. You just have to write on the back of all these expensive forms. It's crazy.

NORMAL POLICING IN NORTHERN IRELAND

Research shows that even those most harassed by the police – black and white youths, students, gays – still call the police for help. In dangerous parts of Northern Ireland, both Catholics and Protestants still rely on the police to perform their normal duties. It can be dangerous, however, for Catholics to be seen helping the police, so the RUC have a secret hotline for anonymous calls.

Clear-up rates for ordinary crime in the worst area of sectarian violence are among the highest in the UK. Although stress and suicide are serious problems a smaller percentage of officers leave the RUC than any other force, and morale in those areas is high on the constant adrenalin. A form of "ordinary policing" goes on despite the extraordinary circumstances.

RUC Superintendent, age 42, twenty years service. Now in West Belfast.

They don't like police in the sectarian strongholds, a lot of them, but if their house gets broken into they still report it. They still make complaints against the Army. They complain formally about policemen ill-treating them, so even if they don't like the system they still use it. Most of them, if they are honest, realize they are quite fairly looked after. There's a reluctance to meet us, though people do use the hotline, I'll tell you that.

RUC Sergeant and 2 PCs, average age 30, average service nine years. Now in West Belfast.

PC1: We've all been in this long enough to get out if we wanted to. You'll find that serving here a while makes you go hard, but it's also hard to leave because the comradeship is an awful lot stronger than in a less exposed station. They can strike anywhere. You'll find the boys work closely, get on well. You've got to look after each other. You don't just go for a walk, you've got two Land Rovers behind you as well. You can have two police armoured Hotspurs and an Army Land Rover to deal with an ordinary break-in that you'd just jump in a car and go to by yourself in a normal station.

SGT: Everything is checked and rechecked here before you respond. We rely on the uniform lads here to advise us completely. If the boys say don't go, you just don't go.

PC2: On foot, sixteen soldiers accompany you on a walk. They are divided into "bricks", four soldiers each. You have a primary brick, a secondary brick and two satellite bricks. Primary brick is the one the police and the company commander walk with. The second brick follows and the satellites follow 100 or 150 yards behind.

PC1: You don't know how often a rifle has been pointed at you and they can't fire because the soldiers are there. But that won't deter a command-wire initiated explosion, so they can still commit murder when the place is saturated with soldiers.

PC2: I've sat in a Land Rover for two and a half years just getting to know the odd street. As soon as you get out on the beat you want to know everyone, but in a Land Rover you're confined and you can't see what's happening. We can't walk out on our own, they'd just skin us alive.

SGT: If we do a house call, the soldiers wait outside. The police are, let's say, "in charge", no matter who in the military is there for back-up. When the boys take a patrol out, they're the men that say what happens.

RUC Superintendent, age 46, twenty-five years service. Now in Traffic Division.

When there's an accident, the first thing people say is "Get the police." When they've been robbed, house has been burgled, "Get the police." Life goes on here as normal – burglaries, rapes, robberies, accidents, whatever. Life is normal. We've got to support that normality.

Police officers like mine, on Traffic, find it very hard to understand why they have been singled out, targeted, shot, bombed and attacked simply because they're trying to do their best. That's the hardest thing for a policeman to accept. The fellow on the beat at the scene of the accident is just trying to help someone and some bastard takes a shot at him. Traffic officers wear high-visibility jackets and things like that. We do that simply to be seen at night, but it is a very calculated risk.

TRAFFIC COPS

Rudeness from traffic police is a continual source of public irritation. The Traffic Division is set off from other PCs by its duties, and in provincial forces by its separate locations. Much disliked by the rest of the service, traffic cops are known as "black rats" in the Met and are mocked for sitting together in the canteen "flashing their boots like Batman and Robin".

They too feel the pressure of public disapproval and the public's failure to appreciate the positive side of their work. They are the police officers most in contact with the public at large and they resent being seen as "the enemy".

*Recent research by the Police Foundation shows the ambiv-
alence of new officers towards offending motorists. They veer
between teaching them the Highway Code and punishing them.*

**Traffic PC in a Home Counties force, age 30, ten years service.
Now on motorway duties.**

The problem is you can never criticize anyone's driving. It's
like you've attacked his manhood. They all think they're Juan
Fangio no matter what dumbhead thing they've done. The truth
is you could fuck their wives spreadeagled on the bonnet right
in front of them and they wouldn't mind because they're so
intent on proving to you that they couldn't have been doing a
ton or whatever you've clocked them on. They'd stand there all
day arguing if you let them.

*The Police Foundation's research shows that traffic cops are
insufficiently trained to manage delicate encounters with motorists. They are unaware, for example, of the negative impact of
their boots and sunglasses. Nor do they grasp the way the
uneven spread of traffic enforcement across a particular area
makes motorists believe they have been stopped unfairly. Rather
than taking responsibility for breaking the law, it makes them
feel they have been picked on.*

**Traffic Chief Inspector, age 40, nineteen years service; Traffic
Sergeant, age 36, fourteen years service. Both in a large
northern force.**

Sergeant: They complain for being done for 40 mph in a 30 mph
zone: "Why aren't you out arresting burglars?"

CI: One of the favourite things people say is, "I've been driving
for thirteen years and have never been involved in an accident."
You feel like saying, "Well, you probably left a trail of carnage
behind you." It's more by good luck than good judgement: they
want educating. I agree with spot driving tests.

SGT: Why can't we just jump in and say "Give us a quick drive about two miles up the road and back ... I'm sorry, give us your licence – you failed!"

CI: You might find a body in a house with 200 stab wounds in it. You'll get the CID with a couple of hundred men all trying to find out who killed this person. You go to a traffic accident where someone is just as dead as the bloke with the 200 stab wounds. The fellow who caused it all drove off, so nobody knows who it is. One traffic cop or one constable is trying to find out. To me, that person lying in the road is just as serious to his or her family as the one murdered. But no one seems to see it that way. If you get killed by a car, it seems to be acceptable. This goes right through policing. It's the same thing with burglary, rape and domestic attacks. People are just not interested until it hits really close to home.

DOMESTIC DISPUTES

"Domestics" are the single most frustrating task regularly dealt with by ordinary police officers. They are never simple; for police to be called means the incident has already got out of hand. Experienced PCs do their best to avoid them, sending young ones still less prepared emotionally and professionally to sort out highly charged conflicts between two much older people. No one is satisfied, and all too often both parties turn on the PC, sometimes violently.

Former Met PC, age 28, six years service, and a graduate. Resigned in 1988.

Fighting couples just act out their discontent in a very physical manner. I came to the conclusion that that's a perfectly reasonable manner of communication, even though they damage the furniture and each other. It's no worse than saying painful things and picking on each other's emotional soft spots. They are not actually interested in talking about the situation anyway, they are both participating in the fight. And you will never understand what it's about, certainly not if you're a policeman. You're there for thirty minutes maximum.

The answer, if there is one, is a social worker. All I can do is keep the peace. "If you don't stop thumping each other then I'm going to thump you harder than either of you can." When I realized that, my attitude to the job changed quite a lot. We aren't counsellors. The sooner you're out of their house the better, because the radio room want you to do something else anyway.

Chief Inspector, age 43, twenty-one years service in a Scottish force. Now in a suburban council estate.

In the olden days, when there were twenty men on a shift and the pace was slower, you'd go in and chat to a couple. You would find the source of the problem and talk away to them. You would be in effect a marriage counsellor. Even if the wife is willing to press charges, which most times she's not, there's absolutely no point in the police arresting the husband, putting him in jail overnight and appearing in court in the morning. That's the last thing you want. But now there's so much pressure on a PC, he goes in – "What's the problem? Where're the witnesses?" – and locks the husband up. The following morning the wife goes down to the station and says she would like to withdraw the charges. We say: "It's in the Fiscal's hands and that's it." We want to do the job the gentle way it was done before, but we don't have time.

Battered wives present a special problem which the police are just beginning to acknowledge. Because domestics are so fraught and unrewarding, police officers usually register them as "no crime" in the station book, unless one or other party wants an arrest. In 1988, the Met changed its policy and now urges officers to become more involved, arresting the husband if appropriate rather than giving him the benefit of the doubt as was done previously. The new Commissioner of the Met, Sir Peter Imbert, has said that "Domestic disputes are just as serious as assaults on the street." But it will take a long time to change police attitudes.

PC, Acting Sergeant, in a Home Counties force west of London, age 24, four years service, and a graduate. Now in a university town.

We've got a job to do preventing people from killing each other for a start. A lot of murders and woundings are domestic incidents. Even quite reasonable people fall out and strike each other. A lot of it stems from affection. You go to the same address time and time again where he has beaten her up, and she doesn't want to do anything about it. She wants him stopped and perhaps kicked out, but when you ask her if she wants him in court she says no. Some people say you shouldn't bother, but you have to, because you are preserving life. There are different problems in each one. Do you lock a man up every time he beats his wife? No, you don't. We will go in as referee and try and smooth things over and if we can't, then we will remove one of them. If they won't have that, then maybe they get locked up. That is reasonable. But the chances are as soon as he's out he'll hit her again for locking him up. You can't win.

YOUTH TROUBLES

Much the most trouble for beat police officers all over the United Kingdom comes from young people. There are ordinary problems like vandalism, graffiti, litter, under-age drinking and loud music, and at a more serious level joyriding with stolen cars, drugs and petty crime. On a larger scale, football hooliganism, "steaming" (mass shoplifting and street crime by gangs of youths acting together) and full-scale looting and rioting are mainly the work of youths between eighteen and twenty-five. Assaults against the police by young people are now commonplace in both urban and rural areas.

With cinemas closing, and cuts in local authority spending, the problem with policing young people is finding a way of keeping them out of trouble. Many PCs run football teams at the weekend or work in youth clubs, but they often lack support from older members of the community who just want to see rowdy youths disciplined. By far the majority of police officers believe in stopping and searching young people late at night "for their own good", a view not always supported either in law or by the young people themselves.

PC, age 27, six years service. Transferred from a northern city force to a Home Counties force.

Our principal preoccupations are with the local youths. They gather in the shopping centre during the day. They're widely involved in quite a well-organized form of shoplifting and just their presence en masse is a headache. Then in the evening they gather in different parts of the town and you get vandalism, disorder – real trouble.

They are markedly anti-police. They're outwardly abusive and bold, whereas in the northeast I was used to turning up to a situation with perhaps one or two policemen and the group would disperse. Here we've had a number of incidents where a policeman has been lured into a side street and been set upon by a large gang. I was warned about this when I first came here but I took it with a pinch of salt. But a few weeks later we had a policeman put into hospital, unconscious. He'd run after a group of youths and round the corner there were a whole load more who attacked the poor bastard.

PC in a Home Counties force, age 40, twenty years service. Now a village bobby.

Three years ago we'd got two trained youth leaders in the village, but no youth club. So we all got together and started thinking about having our own youth club. We circularized all the businesses, asking for donations, but what has grieved me more than anything is that although some people in the village were right behind us – local tradesmen had offered us help, solicitors gave their services free on the lease – we had no help whatsoever from the Parish Council. Yet, as I pointed out to them, half the trouble in the area would be stopped if they had a youth club open every night of the week. When I talk to the kids and their parents, the first thing I hear is that there's nothing for them to do, nowhere to go.

You've got your "them and us" situation. You've got a lot of the older villagers, the retired or the commuters, who get themselves into positions of authority on Parish Councils, on this and that damn committee. On the other side you've got the council houses, who don't care a toss as long as they can go out and have their drink and betting office.

Now the Parish Council are unfortunately finding out that what I said a long time ago has come true. Now they're on about employing a bloody security firm to walk around the village, because they reckon that their policing isn't enough. If they've got the money to spend on a damn security firm, why couldn't they have given that money to us to help with the bloody youth club?

Inspector in a southern Home Counties force, age 33, twelve years service. Now in a port.

On these huge housing estates, teenagers going through that instinctive territorial phase may have an area of acres and acres and thousands of people. And the gangs may consist of hundreds of youngsters. It is a self-generating thing. Because the groups are so large, they become very confident and violent, and that means the people within that area become more and more insecure. They won't make statements or talk to the police, because they're frightened of what might happen to them. So you have groups of thirteen-year-olds running an area. They try to make it a no-go, certainly an unwelcoming area for any sort of authority. And the poor people who live there are really frightened. They can't shout. They're alone.

Recently there's been a murder and several rapes. We've had a certain amount of public response because it's so extreme. In my street, a woman living on her own with two children had a Persian cat, the joy of her life, one of her few extravagances. A neighbour watched three young lads set their dogs on the cat, tear it apart on this woman's own piece of grass. One of the lads picked up the cat, saw it was dying and slung it over a wall. I've spoken to the woman and to the witnesses, but no one will say who did it, they're too frightened, even though they're appalled. I imagine the lads are only thirteen or fourteen, if that.

PC in a large northern force, age 32, twelve years service. Now in a severely deprived inner-city area with a high proportion of council estates.

The area is quite a quiet one but it's full of old age pensioners, and every now and again something happens. There was some money available from the Council for extra security for pensioners, and I was knocking on doors in full uniform, big hat on, the works. We had a hell of a job convincing these people we were actually the police, because there'd been a couple of fellows knocking on doors pretending they were from the station. They're terrified, their minds are boggled by what they hear on the news and read in the papers about the muggings of old ladies. They don't stop to think that it's come from all over the country. For them it's like living in a war zone.

A lot of teenagers, they've got a chip on their shoulder – no matter what you try to do for them. To them you're a "bizzy", you're out to find something wrong with them, you're not out to help them. You make your way into a house and there's a kid of two. "Here's the 'bizzy'." If they're like that at two, what chance have you got when they're fifteen.

There's a youth club down on the estate, and people are moaning about young people using heroin and chasing the dragon. They know everything, but they won't tell you. They won't let you do the job. It's always been the public's responsibility as much as the police's to maintain any form of law and order. If you neglect that responsibility you end up with places like parts of Toxteth, where there are no rules. To the young especially, if it's not nailed down, they'll steal it. There's no morality at all.

FOOTBALL – FUN AND GAMES

Football duty used to be a perk. They would put the oldest bobby in town by himself on the gate, then he would go in and watch the game. Now it has become dangerous.

Each Saturday, in many parts of Britain, the police and surrounding community pay the price of having a football team. Inside the ground, small numbers of policeman dive into huge crowds to make arrests. They utterly depend on the crowd to let them do it. If the crowd is angered by the decision, the atmosphere may become menacing in a moment. The Bradford City fire showed how easily the situation inside the stands can get out of control. It also showed police heroism at its most extreme.

Policemen resent the time they spend on football duties. They also resent the expense. A big match takes 400 officers off the street for twelve hours in and around the ground, but the club pays only for three hours for the modest number of men actually inside the stadium. One game may therefore cost the public £90,000, to which the club contributes precisely £1000. With police resources overstretched already, the expenditure on football seems like an open tap. One northern town is home to three first division teams, with the result that its annual police overtime allowance goes on a few weekends of football. As a result, on busy Saturday nights, the local force can muster only five men to police 160,000 people.

The FA, League and many club managements have been averse to taking modern preventative measures against hooliganism – and to channel their substantial revenues from television and advertising into doing so. The police are now ready to force their hand by withdrawing their services, which would leave clubs open to major civil actions.

Identity cards and membership schemes are no deterrent to determined youths, nor are they likely to affect mob violence in the streets outside the ground. That is where the trouble starts in earnest, before and after the match. Outnumbered police do their best to control hordes of youths running amok, rampaging down side streets in an echo of primitive warfare. For the officers involved, it is yet another thankless job which exposes them to the taunts and jeers of thousands of their fellow young people.

Sergeant in a Home Counties force, age 31, ten years service. Now in an industrial city.

After a football match once there were about 3000 of them and there were four of us and the Chief Inspector trying to keep this gate shut. We put handcuffs on it, but it began to give way. The Chief Inspector behind me said, "I think it's about time we ran" – so we just turned and fled. We went through the crowd and down some steps and through these big eight-foot gates which we pulled together. By that time they were out of the pen and right behind us. For a few moments we stood on one side and they were on the other side. Then they started lobbing bricks over and the big gates just collapsed under the weight and they all poured through. I thought, "This is it, nowhere else to run to." It was the dog handlers that saved us. If someone with a bit of bottle had had a go at the dogs – Jesus.

PC in a Home Counties force, age 26, six years service. Now in a resort town.

I've worked in plainclothes at football for two years. I did all the home games and quite a few away games. You target people, get in with the away supporters, see what they're like. If there's trouble, you stay with the main perpetrators and get them arrested. Mind you, the guv'nor's quite happy if we have fifty people fighting provided no one is arrested. That is a good result. A bad result is lots of arrests, because someone will say, "You must have policed the game badly and let everyone together." But there is always trouble at football matches and it's getting nasty. They're becoming more devious. They don't wear scarves. They find out addresses in the town where they're going – they clock a road as they arrive, they pick out four or five roads so they've all got one. Then if they get stopped, "Right. That's where I live." That way they get let in on the home supporters' side.

Most policemen don't understand football crowds, the behaviour of people who are out to cause trouble. It isn't because the troublemakers are drunk. Most of them have been drinking, but that isn't the cause of football hooliganism. The cause is human nature. They just want to and they live for it all through the week. To be a football hooligan is a way of life.

They all fight the same people. It's a very small minority, no more than a hundred, perhaps more in the bigger cities. All week in the pub they talk about the fight they had last week, they know everyone's names. They tell you about people from QPR or Millwall and say, "We're going to get the big black bloke, or the skinhead. Do you remember him?" And you say, "Was that last season?" "No, about three seasons ago." Three or four years later, they're waiting to have a go.

The guv'nors just play at it really. I don't think they understand.

Detective Constable in a Home Counties force, age 26, six years service. Now in a large port town.

We had Chelsea down and all the hooligans in the county came over for it. I was spotting troublemakers in the crowd. I was in plainclothes, and because I look young I was just accepted as one of them. But there was no radio for me, so I had to leave the stands to go and tell the uniforms who was doing what and then come back again.

Of course I tried to be discreet, but they're smart. They twigged. The third time I was on my way back some of them grabbed me and pushed me up against a wall underneath the stands and put a knife to my throat. They said I had two choices, either leave them alone or get stabbed. That wasn't much of a choice for a man with a family. I left them alone.

All during the match they were throwing things into the family parts of the stands, where dads and grandads had brought their kids and weren't doing anything to anyone. They were shouting obscenities, throwing sharpened pennies, anything they could find. They never watched the game at all. Then when it was over they chased the families off and ripped the seats from their hinges and just flung them at people like frisbees. If I'd had a gun I'd have happily shot them.

OPERATION OWN GOAL

Early in 1988, the undercover operation codenamed Operation Own Goal was making London policemen proud. In three separate trials, a number of defendants were alleged to have planned an elaborate conspiracy to wreak havoc at matches up and down the country. They were also alleged to have stockpiled a horrifying array of weaponry for the purpose. Undercover operations seemed the answer to the successful prosecution of hitherto invincible thugs. Operation Own Goal was hailed as a triumph of positive policing.

Suddenly the trials were stopped and prosecution evidence was withdrawn. Police evidence was held in court to be "unreliable", implying that it had been fabricated. The release of the accused was yet another scandal for the Met, whose credibility in court was already fragile (see "Fitting Up" in Chapter 9, "Law, Justice and the Courts"). Across the front pages of the press were pictures of defendants sharing a drink with jurors in a pub. It was a dreadful moment for the police.

Sir Peter Imbert, Commissioner of the Met, issued a savage indictment of any officers found to have mishandled evidence. In police canteens, the men were shocked. They had expected him to have defended their colleagues, much as previous senior policemen have done in the face of public criticism. In the end, it seemed Operation Own Goal had lived up to its name.

Met Chief Superintendent, age 46, twenty-six years service. Now in West London.*

It was suggested that we should employ a team of plain clothes officers to infiltrate the gangs. We chose a number of officers – I can't remember how many, about ten or more – who came from not too far away but who hadn't worked here, because there is always a danger they will be recognized. We had got a reasonable amount of intelligence about these people, and using this as a base, off they went. They travelled all round the country, whenever there was an away game they went along, and gradually they started feeding back information.

Ultimately we compiled quite a lengthy report, without statements at this stage, saying what we could give evidence about. This was put up to a barrister, who looked at it and said there was enough evidence to go on. So we got the search warrants and went and raided seven or eight addresses. Obviously when they went out with these people the officers couldn't take anything that would identify them, but when they came back they transposed what they had seen into evidential statements which were then filed away. That was it really, in a nutshell.

* N.B. Interview given before the trials.

Met Commander, age 44, twenty-five years service.

You've got lots of policemen scurrying around with these gangs, getting into all sorts of places where we would normally not want them to go. But they've got to, of course, and they've got to be sharp. You worry about using inexperienced officers from the uniform. Obviously if you're moving with this sort of circle you've got to stand your round of drinks. You can't sit there all night drinking shandy. So you've got policemen drinking perhaps heavily – paid for out of the public purse. And then driving cars afterwards. With that sort of crowd they can't say, "Well, I can't have another one, I'm driving." They'd lose all credibility. They've got to keep up with them.

I don't know whether there'll be any long-term effect on football hooliganism, but if we hadn't done it, would the figures be even worse than they are?

Even when successful, complex undercover operations of that kind always create hazards. The major one is that young officers become over-involved with their targets and "turn", becoming sympathetic to them. To avoid this problem, in the US the FBI has evolved a set of safeguards for their many undercover operations that have yet to be adopted on this side of the Atlantic.

Met Deputy Assistant Commissioner, age 44, twenty years service. Now in West London.

There is a dilemma with regard to the policing of football. We have a small number of officers caught up in an operation (Own Goal) which is more complex than they thought, in which they failed in professional terms. Maybe the organization let them down or the management of those endeavours wasn't thought through enough. Perhaps they were not given the guidance, and supervision they were entitled to. Maybe that's all true, what we've got is no more than officers doing a very dangerous job under cover, subject to exposure at any time and the risk of horrible violence if that did happen. Maybe the actual gathering of evidence to succeed in a criminal conviction is so much of a problem that they felt it necessary to try and make up for some of those shortcomings. It might be fitting up, or just not doing the paperwork very well, or taking the paperwork apart at the wrong time. It may well turn out that names were substituted or changed.

Whether we have officers who were overzealous, or whether we have officers who consciously embarked on a conspiracy to fit people up because they thought they were guilty – what we have now is a morale problem. They are looking towards the leadership of the force to somehow put it right. They feel terribly let down and don't understand why the Commissioner is so condemnatory – that he can "brook no part with officers who do this". He hasn't even tried to qualify his condemnation. But they don't understand that he cannot do otherwise. The level of public concern with this force, and in this case where the force had vaunted it from the rooftops – now it looks like we got it wrong not once, not twice but at least three times. The Commissioner had no choice but to condemn out of hand such behaviour. The feeling is around that we have been less than professional, less than honest, in the way we went to court. If the great organization got it wrong in three cases what else has it got wrong? And then every police officer who goes to court will be called a liar.

SOCIAL SERVICES

Police need the cooperation of the local Council for many tasks: access to Council premises, school visits, joint consideration of cases with the social services – the overlap is continuous, especially now that the police are advocating Lord Scarman's multi-agency approach, developed by John Alderson, formerly Chief Constable of Devon and Cornwall, who called it "proactive" positive policing. But in sensitive areas – such as Tottenham, Lambeth, Islington and Brent in London – Council relations with the police are poor. Scarman blamed both sides for the trouble in the run-up to the Brixton riots. In parts of London and other major cities relations have recently improved, but in the worst areas politics hits policing badly.

Some Councils encourage their police committees to act as watchdogs rather than provide liaison. They are both a reflection of and contributors to the mutual mistrust between the

*police and the public in those areas. It leaves ordinary PCs who
need Council cooperation frustrated and encourages them in the
canteen culture view of left-wingers as agitators and "anti".*

**Met PC, age 23, two years service. Now in an inner-city area
of South London.**

Much as I detest some of the activities of the National Council
for Civil Liberties and lefty pressure groups of that type, I
have to admit that our privacy is being whittled away – very
gradually, but very certainly. But how can we do our jobs if we
can't get information? When you're on a case, someone local,
a key witness maybe – I mean, I can understand ex-directory
numbers not being given out, but when you're making an official
request for a number for a specific reason you can't even ask
the operator to ring the number and ask the person to call you
back. There's noncooperation from the Councils, any statutory
body – nobody wants to help any longer. And we're fucked
without it. Absolutely fucked.

Common Law says that if a police officer calls on a member
of the public to help him, it is their duty as a citizen to do so.
There are a number of reasons why. I once chased a chap, off
duty. I caught him in a doorway and there was a big struggle.
I stood shouting for help and a guy just closed the door on me.
I know of another case where one of the lads was involved in
a fight, arresting somebody, and he called a shopkeeper over to
help. He refused, and the bloke got away. That man was
summonsed for failing to assist a police officer.

**Sergeant in a large northern force, age 36, twelve years service.
Now in a racially mixed inner-city area.**

We've got real problems. Local politics in this city is fraught
with danger. The majority of the community we police are
opposed to the governing party on the council. It makes it very
difficult at times to deal with local politicians. We have to be
very careful so that we appear to be walking down the middle.

Since Scarman, the police, the churches and the probation
service are the main ones to have made the effort. The social
services have been noticeably absent; it is a highly political

organization. During the time the social services were in dispute, nobody would take on the case-load of a sick or absent social worker. I've been to a case conference where we wanted to make several recommendations on the case of a boy who was sniffing glue. But the senior social worker said, "Well, I'm sorry but that case is blacked." So you can't do anything. We'd like to black cases too, but we can't.

Some of them appear to be unaware of reality. A couple of weeks ago, there was a typical case: a couple living together, both drug addicts. The woman was pregnant, one of her children is a druggie, father had a conviction for drugs and was wanted anyway. The case conference was to discuss the future of the unborn child and the possibility that the child would be born with symptoms of heroin addiction. The social services were all for allowing her to keep the child. They seem so removed from reality it's almost unbelievable at times. And it comes to us sooner or later to pick up the pieces.

PC in a large northern force, age 40, twenty-two years service. Now a Home Beat Officer in a poor inner-city area.

I once called out the social services and a surgeon to see someone I would class as mentally ill. The chap in question had set fire to a house. When we asked his occupation, his reply was that he was a secret service officer and his task was to catch any rockets that fell short in the Atlantic from either side when they fired at each other. Totally doo-lally. The surgeon came out with the social worker – because you need two people to certify anyone under the Mental Health Act. They both said all this chap had was a "personality defect", yet both of them asked me what I thought was wrong with him in layman's terms. I said, "Being honest, I would call him a nutter. He's just set fire to a house. We were called out by a local resident who obviously feels the same way as we do. And yet you're telling me that all he has is a personality defect. So what do we do at the end of the day?" He ended up getting charged with arson. He was fined for it and released back onto the streets.

RAPE AND CHILD ABUSE

The police abolished its Women's Department to comply with the Sexual Discrimination Act, but WPCs are still given the vast majority of rape and child abuse cases. It is a deeply troubling area, fraught with all the pain and confusion of domestic incidents, as the Butler-Sloss Report on the Cleveland Child Abuse cases made clear.

Children often do not want to give evidence against beloved or intimidating adults. Statements are crucial and difficult to take, but the law requires both a social worker and a police officer to be present at the interview. Indeed they more or less pursue the case together. This imposed collaboration does not always work and often leads to tension, as each service thinks they have the best interests of the child at heart.

Met WPC, age 24, three years service. Now in a racially mixed area of London.

Since I've been with Beat Crimes, I've dealt with three or four cases of child abuse. Usually with child abuse on this ground the families tend to have a history of it and they're usually from the council estates and places like that.

This particular family were very well-to-do, very intelligent. The little girl was eleven. We were speaking to her and the WPC with me was asking her questions and it got very emotional. You show sympathy and all the rest of it, but you need the information and evidence, so you've got to ask her these questions. Obviously she will get upset and it upsets you as well. You can't be a hard person just because of the job. Everyone's got emotions. I just held back the tears and swallowed. The little girl had tears falling down, but that's just the way it was.

For two weeks solidly, all I dealt with was the child abuse cases. At the end of the second week I'd just about had enough. The old system of WPCs working with kids and females all the time must have been a real strain. It's depressing, especially when you're dealing with all the scum, the criminals. To deal with child abuse you have to change totally.

The recent scandals in Cleveland have highlighted the problems of policing child abuse in a most dramatic way. The report on the Cleveland affair criticized the police for lack of sensitivity in handling the evidence and the families involved. But in child abuse cases evidence is rarely clear-cut. Even broaching the subject leads to highly charged encounters with the family and their supporters. Medical opinions sometimes conflict and police surgeons may be excluded from the initial examination, leaving police officers to weigh the evidence themselves. They are placed in the awkward position of disrupting family life at the request of social services, yet on grounds they cannot satisfactorily test themselves. It is another minefield.

Woman Police Sergeant in a Midlands force, age 32, ten years service. Now with the Vice Squad.

The main thing is that there is no guarantee of where, or in what circumstances, it will happen. I never realized the degree of cruelty people were capable of, physical and mental cruelty towards a defenceless child. How anyone could torment and torture a young child over a prolonged period is beyond my understanding and always will be. There's no way I'm going to understand somebody who puts cigarette burns on a six-month-old baby's legs. I will never ever understand the mentality of a man who systematically commits incest with a young daughter over several years. I don't even try any more. It's just something you have to deal with as professionally as you can.

You always expect it to be somebody from the lower end of the social scale, but it's not. I've been into some of the most luxurious homes, where they have everything they could possibly want, yet the kiddy is badly dressed and neglected. One case involved a doctor. You don't expect it from someone like that. There are policemen who beat their children up, same as anyone, just as there are doctors, teachers, labourers. The problem of child abuse is huge. It's always been there.

Met WPC, age 26, four years service. Now in a suburb.

We got a call from a man to say that his eleven-year-old daughter had been assaulted by his own father. It had been a big family decision as to whether or not they should come to us.

If someone comes straight into the police station, you take

them down to one of the rape suites and the doctor examines them. There's usually some form of evidence. If anything touches anything, there's always a transfer of particles from one thing to another. Hairs, blood, semen, anything like that is all forensic evidence, along with marks, bruising – it's all evidence that what the child said happened, happened.

When "Kate" was examined, it was five weeks later and she'd been bathed, all her clothing had been washed. Grandad had left the premises, removing all his clothing. There just wasn't anything. She wasn't physically hurt, there were no marks. There was no sign of any interference. Even if there'd been evidence of a broken hymen or something like that, defence in court would say that she did it riding a horse. You've got to prove it to the extent of pubic hairs or semen, something like that.

We then started interviewing "Kate". Her mum and dad decided they didn't want social services to be present, though we'd told them, because they felt it would upset her even more – so it was just me, another WPC and the parents. We started at eight o'clock on a Saturday morning and I worked until seven o'clock that night, which is an awful long time with a child. We had lots of breaks. It took me all that time just to get seven pages out of her. That was just the lead up to it, really. So I had to come back on Sunday. I got about sixteen pages in the end, but it took me four hours to get one page out of her on the Sunday, because that was the bit where it actually happened. She wanted to talk about everything else: her new party dress, what she was going to do for Christmas, when she goes to the country. I'd say, "Kate, you've got to get this done."

People say that you should distance yourself and not get too involved. I think you bloody well should get involved, and if you're not interested in getting involved then you shouldn't be doing the job. When somebody is telling you all the intimate details of what's happened to them, you've got to be compassionate. You can't stand back from something like that.

The first time she told me about what had happened, I could see she was getting upset because her bottom lip started going as well. We were all sort of pushing down the tears. When we came out, I said to the other WPC that it was bloody terrible. I'd still got a lump in my throat. She said that she'd had to come out of the room, she couldn't stick with it. Even by the time I'd got the full statement and heard the story about seven or eight times, it still made me want to cry. I'm not going to parade around being a macho policewoman. What I heard would have made blokes cry.

Then Social Services called up and said they should have a copy of the statement. This was absolutely out of order, because it's confidential until such time as the case comes to court. Social Services were saying that they should have been there the whole time to look after the child's welfare. But the parents were looking after the child. Grandfather had gone, there was no chance of it happening to the child again. Social Services as good as told them that the prosecution wasn't in our hands and that they would decide whether the Crown would prosecute – which was a load of rubbish. Dad by this time is tearing his hair out because all he wants is for the police to do their business. It's between him, the police and his dad.

Eventually grandad was nicked and interviewed, with a solicitor. Every time he was asked any kind of question at all, it was just "no reply". So this little girl has gone through the ordeal and there's not an ounce of evidence. It's her word against his. So he's going to get away with it, basically.

There's an awful lot of cases where the parents think: "We'll keep it within the family. We won't put the child through it." I can understand. "Kate" was a damn good witness, the evidence we got in her statement was good. She knew the names of all the bits and pieces. But if she'd gone to court they'd have tied her in knots. It's little things, like when she started to talk about the event she needed somebody to hold her hand the whole time. They don't do that in court. The child just stands there and is on her own.

Met Superintendent, age 52, twenty-six years service. Now in the West End of London.

Child abusers are the worst. I'd hang the lot of them. I had a number of cases in sleepy old Norwood. The terrible thing is the public don't want to believe the truth about how people behave. One case involved a ten-year-old boy being rented out by his parents. We put an observation on him to verify what was going on and managed to get enough to bring him in. We did a long interview with an experienced social worker there, who was great – gave me the nod every time we needed to stop and give the kid a break. But it was clear the lad knew more about homosexuality at ten than I did after twenty-five years in the police. His backside was unbelievable – covered in marks.

But when we got to court the defence brief kept making snide cracks about us. We found out later the jury just couldn't accept that any of it was true. So the case fell apart. The kid's escaped from care, and I imagine he's a rent boy by now.

Scottish Chief Inspector, age 43, twenty-one years service. Now in an industrial suburb.

The offence of incest can be very difficult to prove, but of course you invariably have the identity of the offender easily at hand. It really becomes more of a procedural problem. We rely on the medical evidence associated with that style of offender. The difficulty is the tenderness in many cases of the person that has been assaulted. The children are very young, but of course it's an offence that is fairly prevalent in society. I don't think there's any less today than there was fifty years ago. It's a regular offence. They can be quite distasteful to deal with, but certainly not difficult. I would rather have an allegation of incest; it's easier than an offence of rape with an open-ended case from the investigative point of view. One has to deal with these things in a clinical and compassionate manner. Getting personal is a very dangerous game. But you soon learn to detach yourself. You don't lose your feelings.

The police handling of rape cases has been widely criticized in the past as unsympathetic to the victim, but in the last five years police procedure in many forces has been adjusted to deal with the victim's needs: special rape suites, where possible the use of specially trained WPCs rather than ordinary officers, and recognition that the victim will be in a state of shock. The Catch-22 remains in that there is rarely more than one other witness – the suspected rapist. So unless there is evidence of assault, the case is her word against his, assuming he can be traced. Without clear evidence, rape is the most unsatisfactory of crimes for police to pursue. Even if they are convinced that an allegation is true, proving it in court is another matter.

The reason for the brusque traditional style of handling rape victims' allegations is the presumption taught right from training school that 60 per cent are false. Police have therefore given the man the benefit of the doubt. Court treatment of rape cases has also tended to favour men, and until the law was changed a victim's sexual history could be used as a defence – that is now inadmissible. Another reason why victims found themselves harshly cross-examined at the police station was to see if they could stand up to similar treatment in court.

The handling of rape victims has changed considerably in recent years after the police discovered from their own research that their assumption that the majority of allegations are false was mistaken, despite its wide acceptance in both police and legal circles. Since then they have been developing sophisticated courses for dealing with all forms of sexual abuse. Due to shortages of manpower, however, inexperienced young policewomen are still often assigned to such cases. The new perspective aims to be more humane and to treat the victim as a person first and as a potential witness second, but the lack of maturity and legal expertise of many young WPCs puts heavy pressure on them and on the victim.

RUC Woman Chief Inspector, age 38, nineteen years service. Now in a border town.

About three years ago we realized there was a growing problem with rape and child abuse. The Chief Constable called for a special training unit with resources to train male and female Constables who would be out there touching the community. It's a two-week residential course. Staff have the opportunity to do a lot of work in relation to self-awareness, communication skills, attitude analysis. We have the support of other agencies who come in to talk about their responsibility in sexual offences and child abuse. Attitudes have to change in the force, in that we are looking for evidence. But we have to think primarily of the victim, the trauma that the victim goes through.

We train the PCs to be aware of the victim's position. In one case, a female said: "I can't remember, I can't recall." Forensic officers had visited the scene and taken all the various bits and pieces. From her description, they were looking for a white person, but the examination of the pubic hairs indicated clearly that the person they were looking for was a coloured man. They went back to the victim and said: "Please think about this man again." There was no way way the victim could accept the man was coloured. It is bad enough that any man should have raped her, but that a coloured man had raped her – she had a block, she was in trauma.

When I was a young constable I was inclined to rush in quickly. What about a false allegation? So I'd say, "Come on, tell us the truth." Wrong, totally wrong. Don't ever start condemning someone, because if that person is telling the truth they're condemning themselves sufficiently without you condeming them. It's easy to make a simple remark like, "Taking a lift home at 2 a.m. from the disco – don't you think that's a bit off in this day and age?" Now, the victim is sitting there and she has all these thoughts herself. You're just enforcing her guilt feelings. She may just fall apart. By proper questioning, by sensible questioning, it will all come out eventually.

In my experience few allegations of rape are unfounded, though I have had a few. We had one woman who was "taken away in a van one night". Brought in by the husband. "Raped, two men in a van." When we got down to the nitty-gritty the woman stopped me and said, "Look, I'm behind with the rent and I've a bit of a debt. I go out every Friday and Saturday night. My husband also goes out, but he's usually back later than me. Tonight was the opposite way round." Now I, of course, took a statement about wasting police time, but we are a bit compassionate in these things and she wasn't prosecuted.

Anyone who comes in alleging rape is given the choice of a female officer, or in some cases a male officer who knows the person very well. We would still have a female officer around, to give the victim confidence, to explain to her the medical examination, what going to court may mean; just giving her that little support and help as she goes along, so she doesn't feel alone in the dark or that the police don't care. We keep contact afterwards, not to become a nuisance, just to let them know that "I'm here". A phone call might be enough. But we keep that contact. In our investigations of other crimes, of course, we're criticized for not keeping contact.

PLAIN CLOTHES

Uniform policemen serve in plain clothes on various squads. Depending on the force and station policy, they work on Crime, Drug and Vice Squads, dealing with smaller offences, leaving the CID and specialist detectives to go after the bigger ones. For most policemen, plain clothes duties have a special cachet derived from television series. In Thames Valley no one has shut a car door quietly since Starsky and Hutch appeared on our screens. Plain clothes duties usually involve longer but more flexible hours.

DRUGS

The relationship between the police and drugs has changed over the years, as the problem itself has changed shape. The possession of cannabis was once an automatic crime worth pursuing, but is now so common that it is often ignored. Hard drugs like heroin, cocaine and amphetamines have spread not only in the cities but in country towns as well. That brings many more policemen into contact both with users, who may commit crimes to feed their habits, and the search for pushers who are the real target.

In recent years, big-time criminals have turned to drugs as an easy source of revenue. Drugs are now the international currency between organizations like the Mafia or the IRA and their weapons suppliers. Efforts to combat drug dealing at that level are conducted through the National Drugs Intelligence Unit in Scotland Yard. As was the case with Operation Julie, they involve expensive and lengthy operations any one of which would rate a book in itself.

Despite the scale of the problem – which is sometimes the subject of intense bouts of moral panic in the tabloid press and from politicians, nothing very serious has been done to deal with it. Police involved in fighting drugs feel aggrieved. For all the government rhetoric about its War Against Crime, its

*closure of NHS provision for addicts at NHS hospitals has led
many users to turn to crime to feed their habits. Many addicts
become pushers themselves to ensure their own supply.
Notional increases in manpower for Drugs Squads are more
often men transferred from uniform or CID, but not replaced.
They are seldom extra men.*

*There is little political pressure on senior police officers to
provide more internal resources either, because drugs are so-
called "victimless crimes". No one reports such crimes because
both participants – seller and buyer – are party to it. That
means no embarrassing "unsolved" drugs crimes sit on station
books, as do burglaries or street crimes. The only drugs crimes
to appear in police statistics are those discovered by officers in
the act of solving them by making arrests. So senior officers can
point to a 100 per cent clear-up rate in that category. They see
no reason to invest further resources in drugs when so many
more exposed areas need serious attention. The net effect of
small resources is small results, which makes the problem itself
appear smaller than it is.*

**PC in a large northern force, age 27, eight years service. Now
working in plainclothes in an inner-city area.**

The drugs problem here is incredible. Hard drugs are biggest.
You're talking about mass heroin addiction, almost mass
cocaine use. Crack is openly for sale, though that has been
denied by our Chief Constable. I could take you out to four or
five places and buy it now, no problem. Drugs should have been
nipped in the bud really, years ago. But no Chief Constable
anywhere in the country was going to put his hand up and say,
"Yeah, we've got a drug problem and we are willing to do
something about it." They only recently increased the Drugs
Squad. Plainclothes used to be a licensing section doing the
clubs. Now it's 80 to 90 per cent drugs.

Drugs is very hit and miss, because dealers don't really run
to a system. They do something for maybe two or three weeks,
and then they'll close down. We might get the information in
the third week of their dealing, start watching them and then
all of a sudden they've run out of drugs. Meanwhile there's other
people living around the dealing address and they'll complain to

other police bosses. You're under constant pressure from the community to do something about it, but the public don't understand the strength of evidence we need to bring one of these jobs to court. You've got to have conclusive proof. Nothing less will do.

Nowadays we are the fucking villains. I took a taxi the other day and the driver started talking to me about drugs. He didn't know who I was. He was just saying about the state of the city and how bad it was, blah, blah, blah. He said, "Mind you, it's all down to the police." So I said, "Aye, why's that?" "Because they're all on the take. They are all taking money from drug dealers." I was fuming and thought: "If you knew what we have to go through to get a job to court and through a fucking jury in this city."

Detective Constable in a large urban force, age 32, fourteen years service.

The profit margin on drugs is phenomenal. I mean, if you had £1000 now you could go and buy an ounce of smack, which is going to be street level. You buy it from a dealer, so there's a good chance it's going to be 40 or 50 per cent pure – so the dealer's happy, he's made his 100 per cent. He's added his half of chalk dust, brick dust, talcum powder, Vim. So you buy your ounce for £1000, cut in your ounce of filler and you've got £2000 worth of gear. Brilliant!

It's an epidemic, it really is. We just can't keep the lid on it. They are openly injecting themselves in stairwells, anywhere they can do it. They are selling the drugs to children. I don't put it down to unemployment. I don't put it down to disillusionment with society. I just can't comprehend why people start.

PC in a large northern force, age 30, ten years service. Now in an inner-city area.

It's like the seven-headed Hydra, it always pops its head up somewhere else. Smackheads need the money that's needed to get the gear. That could be £200 a day. They'll do anything, I mean anything, to get it. Rob their mothers, sell their grandmothers, sell their bodies, anything.

I try and think how they must feel, because I've seen reasonably decent lads turn to the complete opposite. I've seen big meaty armed robbers who've gone into drugs, and we've gone round to their house looking for them and we've walked right past them, because there's a 9-stone bloke on the steps, full of spots. He could have done a runner but he'd become too lethargic. We eventually realized he was the same monster that he used to be.

CUSTOMS AND EXCISE: THE HEAVY MOB

Customs and Excise men try to stop the importation of drugs into the United Kingdom. They are supposed to work in tandem with the police, but in practice they are rivals. Each service is back by rival ministries, the Treasury and the Home Office respectively. The police envy the freedom and resources that Customs men have: "They act more like Miami Vice *or the Marines than British law enforcement officers," according to one disgruntled Inspector. "If we threw ourselves around as freely as the V AT and Customs men, people would talk about a police state. But you never get questions in Parliament or leaders in the* Guardian *about them."*

Customs and Excise, on the other hand, simply do not trust the police. Drugs Squad officers figured large in past corruption scandals. Police procedures have tightened up, but the sums of money now involved are huge. Cynics argue that pointing up the risk of police corruption is a ploy by Customs and Excise to justify protecting their sources in order to position themselves as the major anti-drugs agency when 1992 rolls up.

Customs men, local authorities, teachers and social workers all see themselves as civil servants. So do most police officers. But when the others place a cordon sanitaire *around the police it increases their sense of isolation from society.*

Met Commander, age 41, twenty years service. Now in North London.

People assume that an officer fudges issues because he's actually copping money from them. What we have to understand about developing a drugs scenario is that one is trying to use every opportunity when an arrest is made to develop information for the future. It follows that a good drugs officer on making an arrest for possession of a relatively small amount will make a judgement as to whether that individual should face prosecution or whether he should be turned and used to inform on others. Now, that is on the very cutting edge of abuse, of course it is and we realize that. I don't deny that implicitly there is the potential for abuse because we are trusting a maybe fairly young individual to meet unsupervised somebody who is unscrupulous. But we do get results.

ARRESTING DRUG USERS

Policing drugs on the street by arresting users leaves police feeling like Sisyphus, the Greek king eternally condemned to push a boulder up a hill only for it to roll to the bottom again. To go after dealers takes serious manpower. To achieve success in court in front of sceptical juries and artful lawyers, police must prove that dealing has taken place on a number of occasions. This means weeks of observation. Before they commit scarce manpower to a single job, senior officers want proof that dealing is going on. That needs observation: it is yet another Catch-22. The result is that many dealers perform safely under the noses of the local PCs – which does nothing for police morale.

PC in a Home Counties force, age 26, six years service. Now with the Drugs Squad in a port town.

I had some druggies when I was in uniform, people I came across in the street, people in pubs. I was hoping on the Drugs Squad to get at the people that were making the money out of other people's misery, for want of a better cliché, but it doesn't work like that. They are the people that very rarely get touched. They make money out of financing crime from money made out of drugs. It's those people and their immediate lieutenants and their heavy boys who are the real scum. It's not the users on the street that offend me. They would never use drugs if it wasn't put there by someone else saying, "Here it is. Have a go. Go on, go on." If they can get that person to take drugs, then he'll influence his friends – they're making money all the time. And they do say, "You go and sell these drugs for me in two weeks, and if you don't I'm going to break your fucking arm." That's quite a regular occurrence here.

Met PC, age 28, six years service in North London. Resigned in 1988.

For the whole of my last year in the police I stopped arresting addicts. It was a game I just didn't want to play any more. I didn't feel any the worse about these people, they were just unfortunates. I used to spend hours talking to them, I mean sometimes when I was in plain clothes, asking them how they had got into that position. And you realize that most of them are far more intelligent than you, and they are marvellous characters. Yet this drug they are taking has become their god, it has taken their soul. They would steal from their families to get their next fix. They have lost their self-respect.

I was more angry about the dealers. We nicked two doctors once, got in touch with the Home Office and said, "Every Tom, Dick and Harry we come across in Soho and nick for drugs has got one of these doctors' prescriptions. The BMA should take it up." One of the doctors just said, "I couldn't care less. I have a house in Hampstead, I have a yacht in the South of France and a house in Florida. I can justify what I'm doing and in the meantime I'm earning a good living. If I get struck off – big deal!" But he was done in the end.

Two PCs in a large northern force, average age 30, average service ten years. Both now with the Drugs Squad.

PC1: You get a lot of good robbers mugging drug dealers. They can take a stash of, say, an ounce of heroin off them, cut it with all sorts of shit and make two grand on top. So these dealers are carrying weapons to protect themselves from robbers and the likelihood of the police putting their door down with a sledgehammer. I mean, we've gone in where people have had machetes and stuff.

PC2: You don't know – they could be sat there with guns on the table and just blow you away.

PC1: The first two minutes of a raid are terrifying, because we are screaming, "Stand still! Police!" We are dressed like villains so they think we are ripping them off. For two minutes it's literally crazy, till you calm it down and secure the area. It's very difficult to run in with a little piece of plastic with a tiny photograph and say "Police!" when you've got this sledge-hammer in your hand. Your nerves are bloody going. Your hands are shaking like hell.

PC2: We'd done a raid and there was this guy injecting his scrotum. He'd got his trousers round his knees. I'd kicked the kitchen door and he's got his foot on the sink and he's injecting into his sack with the needle. I just backed off and let him carry on, 'cause had he pulled the needle out there was a good chance of hepatitis B blood spurting all over the place, or him plunging the needle into me.

PC1: You could end up going back to your family and saying, "Look, there's a possibiliity of this and that . . ." It's horrendous, especially if you've got kids. I have a shower after every raid and then I go home and have a hot bath and soak in it. Then I feel OK. That's just being in contact with dirty people – druggies, prostitutes. I can't handle the thought of it really.

HOLDING THE BABY

Only in places where drug dealing happens openly on the street – like All Saints Road in West London and Granby Street in Toxteth – have residents put enough pressure on senior officers to act. But in those areas, the fear of public order problems hampers police effectiveness in dealing with crime of all descriptions. Cannabis is part of Rastafarian culture. Recent police policy has been to look the other way to keep the peace. Many feel cannabis should be decriminalized to focus on the drugs that matter like heroin or crack.

Recent signs are that the spread of AIDS among heroin addicts sharing needles is having a deterrent effect. Also wives of hard-drugs users in areas like Toxteth now realize that they too are at risk and have put strong pressure on their men to give up their habits.

The drug most involved in crimes, assaults and accidents is alcohol. Dealing with drunks – often violent – is among the most common and unpleasant of police tasks. Police cells – when not filled with remand prisoners – are mainly used as detoxification centres, to let drunks dry out overnight. Drunks choking on their own vomit has been the primary source of deaths in police custody. Although the police drink heavily themselves, they have pressed the government for tougher measures against alcohol as well. With few results.

Most PCs have a simple moral sense of right and wrong. The lack of action to match the words in the War on Drugs again feeds their cynicism towards politicians and senior officers alike. They feel very much alone with the problem.

PC in a large northern force, age 32, ten years service. Now with the Vice Squad.

About 80 per cent of our prostitutes are heroin addicts. They originally go on the game to make money if they are short. Then they get addicted to heroin. Now they've got to get the money to get the heroin. It's a frightening vicious circle.

You say to the girls, "Why don't you get off the game?" but there's no easier way for them to make £200 or £300 a week, tax free. A lot of them don't even sign on the dole. Why bother?

Society's impression of prostitutes is that they are all horrible, gross things – maybe not agency girls, some of them are quite tasty – but street prostitutes are all meant to be dirty, disgusting people. But some prostitutes are quite intelligent, and they are nice, honest people that will talk to you. We sit them in our car and talk to them.

There's one I know who has used just about every vein in her body: she's injecting into her head, into her neck, in her ankle, at the bottom of her feet – just about every single vein in her body has collapsed. In one of her arms she can just about move her fingers. It's horrible. She's injected into her breasts, behind her ears. Her legs are just withering, and her hands, her fingers, are all just wilting away. In fact her sister's a Page Three girl. When I met her a couple of years ago, she was the spitting image of her sister.

She was sat in our car and all I could think of was to take her away somewhere for a couple of years so she could get off the stuff and build herself up a bit. But she said, "No problem, because I'll be dead next year. I can't get off it." She's twenty-four.

VICE

In 1829, part of the original brief for the police was the improvement of moral standards. It still is. Yet society is divided about prostitution and pornography. In an age of market forces, there is clearly a large demand for both – including from policemen.

This puts the Vice Squad in an awkward bind. They have the task of "cleaning up" their patch, though as with drugs offenders, they know the girls will be back the next day. They can seize the videos and magazines, and know they too will be replaced.

PC in a large northern force, age 32, thirteen years service. Now in a city centre. (Interviewed in a car.)

Look at that wreck! It's horrendous, the thought of giving her one. Horrible! When you think the price is £5 for a wank, £15 for a gobbin' and £15 for sex – it's horrible.

Between five and seven on weekdays is quite a busy period, or lunchtime, when these fellows are coming out of their offices – company executives and whatever, some of our senior officers as well. They know that we know.

I'd rather lift the punters than the girls. We catch a lot of them in compromising positions and the fellow is terrified. We are not concerned he's doing it, but we say: "Do you realize what you could catch? AIDS? VD? Herpes? Explain that to your wife." A lot of the attraction must be this fear of getting caught.

To be honest, these girls are hardly the biggest criminals in the world, and they are easy prey for sex offenders. We had a prostitute murdered last week, a girl working the docks. It's funny how news travels, because they suddenly want to know you again. They're scared. They want us to be around. It's a dangerous game.

I'm bitter and twisted anyway, because of my divorce. But the way I look at women is basically as prostitutes. Only I find the real prostitutes more honest about it. They say, "OK, I'm selling my body," but at least they're not saying, "I want a new three-piece suite and you're not getting it for a month unless I have one."

Met Woman Police Sergeant, age 30, eight years service. Now in an inner-city area of London.

I don't see myself as a social worker. You're dealing with the dregs of society here – not so much the punters as the ponces who run the girls. Obviously you help some people if you can, like a very young girl who's just started on the game. She's here a couple of days and ends up in the charge room. We got one girl's parents to come down. They were decent folk who didn't have a clue. They were horrified.

Greed plays an immense factor in all this. You get a girl from the North who gets £20 on the dole and tell her she can earn £200 in a day – she'll be down here in a flash. They work from cars, flats, hotel rooms, in basements – "Just go down the steps, it's a lot safer." Most of the girls work in twos: one girl holds the bag while the other does the business.

Girls often come in and say they want to turn their ponces in. They'll tell you about him, but at the end of the day they won't go to court. There's a lot of fear. You have to rely on direct observation, but if you're watching someone at four o'clock in the morning you're likely to stand out. Sometimes I dress up as a tart and guys hang around looking like punters. You can blend in quite well that way. It's frustrating, because we're governed by finance and overtime. If you work an eight-hour day there's no way you can do this job because ponces and the like do not keep eight-hour days.

Ponces are a menace all right, but they are not all the archetypal one. We recently nicked a man who works for the BBC. He had a woman who lived in Essex with a husband and two children.

Because vice is a victimless crime, like drugs, few police resources are allocated to it. The only pressure to act comes from residents in areas where the girls ply their trade. But when a Chief Constable like James Anderton in Greater Manchester wants to major on vice, suddenly resources are available. Indeed the Police Authority felt he had gone too far in that direction. Other Chief Constables keep puritanical senior officers in check: campaigns against vice draw attention to how much there is by displaying it in police records, the annual report and the local press. This is not always popular with local politicians.

Met PC, age 39, twenty years service. Now with the Vice Squad in a racially mixed area of London.

If you saw these ponces hanging around on the street and the pressure and violence that's used to get the girls to work for them, and the absolute fear, you'd understand why our job has got to be done. We have five people trying to cope. We can perhaps deal with one ponce a month. We have to keep them under observation for five days to be sure they are not getting income from anywhere else. Then you've got the harder job of proving that they are living on the earnings of prostitution. We have to watch their lifestyle: most of them are drawing the dole but they are running a car and paying hotel bills. Once we've arrested him, there's a mountain of paperwork.

Disorderly houses take about three days' observation. If you nick them and they want to go to trial and plead not guilty, you can write off those officers for at least another two weeks. We really only become involved in disorderly houses when we can find a properly equipped dungeon, a torture chamber. Nobody would believe what they use for the punter's pleasure. It's another side of human nature. It's not illegal so far as the punter is concerned. It's technically an assault, but as it's done at the request of the victim, as it were, we would never proceed. Some girls even get it in writing. There's no chance with a reluctant prosecution witness. We don't usually go in unless the men are coming and going, and there's blood visible. Then it's the offence of "Running a disorderly house." Mostly we ask for a destruction note from the magistrate. That's the worst fine the girls can get. They might get fined a thousand, but their equipment is worth five or six grand – stuff they've built up over the years.

Brothels – two girls or more working from a flat or house – are a much lower priority for us. We do them only when a brothel is in a residential street and we've had a number of complaints from local residents. Basically, we would prefer prostitutes to operate from a house and not from the street. The solution is to legalize it. In the office we all agree about that. But then you've got the problem of housing them. Near where you live?

It's far more interesting than ordinary uniform work. You're dealing with some really bad people, and we get the pleasure of putting some behind bars for long periods of time. Generally the courts differentiate and give the naive and stupid ones a slap on the wrists and a small fine. But the nasty ones, the ones that use violence and intimidate the girls, it's nice to see them go inside for three or four years. And perhaps a girl or two is freed from a bastard like that. Even if they continue being prostitutes, at least they'll be able to keep the money they earn. That's job satisfaction.

PORNOGRAPHY

Pornography has always been a grey area for the police. The Obscene Publications Squad at the Yard was riddled with corruption in the 1970s. Large sums of money are now involved in the international porn trade, but the reputation of the officers involved is now much higher, although one officer challenged me with the notion that taking money from sleazy pornographers did not do anyone any harm. The banned material would circulate in any case as soon as the next shipment arrived from the continent.

Police officers are still less inclined to moral judgements about the material itself. One of their pleasures has been the showing of blue movies or videos seized as evidence. Police parties can be raunchy affairs. Yet the next day the same officers may have to raid a bookshop or warehouse and arrest pornographers for peddling the materials their colleagues have been enjoying at the station.

Met Woman Police Sergeant, age 30, ten years service. Now in a racially mixed inner-city area of London.

We were on a job to do with the importation of pornographic videos – a lot of kiddie porn and homosexual stuff. We had to view all the videos and highlight what is in each one that makes it obscene. We spent the whole week viewing.

I'd never seen a pornographic video before. It was pretty horrible. The kiddie porn was grim and there was a lot of animal pornography. We ran through a typical animal one, a typical homosexual one, a typical kiddie one and a typical very violent one – a video nasty. We made a master plan of all the particular acts and you would go through a particular film and if you saw the actual act of buggery, say, you would tick buggery, and so on.

There were about ninety-five films in total, which is a lot of sordid viewing. There were things I saw which I wouldn't have known the correct term for, not in a million years. I didn't think things like that were possible.

The big operators – we don't even skim the surface. Up at the Yard, storage space would only allow for two major seizures a year, where you take 10,000 items or more. We used to raid three big warehouses in London on a rota basis and each one would take two full days to clear. but you know that ten vanloads are parked up the M1 ready to move back as soon as you're out. They know you don't have the storage, because you could end up holding the stuff for two years until it comes to trial for a destruction order.

I've no great moral view about porn videos for your own entertainment, if it's not doing anyone any harm. So to me, if boys at a stag party want to do that, then boys will be boys.

HOMOSEXUALITY

For years the police have been infamous for their treatment of homosexuals. As a macho group, disapproval of gays is a common feature of the canteen culture, though there are some gay officers. Before sex between consenting males in private became legal, it was common for famous people to be caught importuning in public lavatories by young officers acting as provocateurs. The risk is still there. But the views of the officers involved are no longer just reflex anti-gay sentiments. They take seriously the notion of a public space being open to all the public, children included.

PC in a large northern force, age 27, eight years service.

This place that we are going down to now, the subterranean toilets, the problem has been going on for years. You'll see blokes going down four or five times in the space of ten minutes to meet up with a partner they can masturbate with. Or they masturbate themselves because they see a new punter down there and they'll look over the top of the cubicle. There's only space for eight people, but sometimes there's like twenty-five men down there!

I don't mind gays. They don't bother me at all. If they want to do what they want to do at home in their own place, no problem. But to go to a public toilet is totally disgusting. If you ask them why they are doing it, they say – like with prostitutes – that it's the excitement of going down there, the fear of getting caught.

What frightens me is that there are doctors involved and priests and lay preachers, people that you would look at and think, "I would trust him with my child." But you might be out with your child, and you say to your son, "There's the toilets, go down." Say he's six or seven. He goes down and he's confronted by an old bloke in the middle of a urinal masturbating, or two blokes masturbating each other.

People do complain about it. But all the plain clothes have been told, "Leave it alone." It makes you very angry. Who can say, "I don't want your men going down the toilets and locking up queers"? Why has he got that influence on our boss? Everybody in the police says the best thing is to get the black on somebody else, to protect yourself if you ever drop yourself in the shit. Somebody must have the black on someone somewhere to be able to stop a whole department going to a location.

CHILD PROSTITUTES

The involvement of children in professional sex has gone on since time immemorial with consistent indifference from the authorities. Considering the current attention paid to child abuse inside families, the sexual corruption of children outside the family seems to be ignored. On paper, it is another victimless crime, inasmuch as the boys being paid are unlikely to report themselves. That lets the area commander off the hook. He has no such "crimes" on his books that need attention.

PC in rural force, age 25, five years experience. Now in a coastal town.

Boys as young as ten are selling their posteriors around amusement arcades. It's going on something wicked. I came across a nest of boys aged from ten to seventeen who were actually running a call-boy system out of an amusement arcade. In their statements they referred to orgies where four or five of them would be in bed with two or three blokes at a time. I got statements off all of them, sometimes with their parents' permission, sometimes not. In the end I arrested one gentleman who was buying the boys' time.

I know from the kids that there was a call-boy racket going on in the city as well as here. If kids have learned how to make £10 easy money, it has to be going on elsewhere. I've tried to get senior officers concerned, but it comes down to statistics. We've had thirty cases of buggery in the last ten years and twenty-five of them have been cleared up. So statistics say you've got about a 90 per cent detection rate. But what you've got is nothing. There are hundreds of little boys being buggered regularly for money, and very few of them are ever brought into the station. That's the only way you are going to get a prisoner out of it, so the figures don't mean anything.

The guv'nors don't care. All they are worried about is their bloody figures, because the whole backbone of the police force is based on promotion. All they've got to do is keep themselves clean. You don't have to do anything right. All you've got to do is make sure you don't do anything wrong.

The effect of policing vice can be brutalizing. Most PCs in the Met have come from small villages and towns in the provinces. The sense of futility, the spectacle of the underside of human nature permanently on display, and the hypocrisy of senior officers and politicians who rail against the decline in moral standards but do little about child prostitution – all take their toll on spirit and morale.

Former Met PC, age 28, six years service in East and Central London. Just resigned.

The first time I came across two blokes buggering each other I was in full uniform. I was so disgusted and shocked I couldn't do anything. I couldn't arrest them or anything, I just had to turn and walk out. It made me feel sick. After that I always used to take a very humorous attitude to it, as though it wasn't really happening. I suppose that's how you protect yourself from feeling thoroughly disgusted and nauseated. You tend to feel sorry for them rather than angry. The whole thing is so unnatural.

I used to hang around a toilet in plainclothes, where male prostitution was going on. Inevitably the people concerned come and approach you. You find yourself dragged into being an *agent provocateur*. It didn't do me any good at all. I enjoyed the work inasmuch that it was something new and it broadened my horizons. But in that kind of atmosphere you develop a very cynical attitude towards the public at large, very jaundiced. You tend to see everyone as criminal. I mean, 99 per cent of the population are normal but it just happens that you are always surrounded by the 1 per cent.

In the end I just got pissed off with it. I began to lose my judgement, which is quite frightening. I'd walk around Soho not really knowing what was right and what was wrong. I began to have a really dim view of the law. And nine times out of ten if you got a politician for gross indecency or importuning they wouldn't be charged on the spot. Instead the papers would go up to the DPP who in their infinite wisdom would decide that it was "not in the public interest" to prosecute. That's an example of how the law is designed to protect the people in power.

CHAPTER SIX

Women in the Police

Women make up just under 11 per cent of the police service. For many years there was a Women's Department which specialized in dealing with children and rape victims, but beyond that women were more or less excluded from the normal policing duties of their male colleagues. Since the passage of the Equal Opportunities Act in 1985 and the Sexual Discrimination Act in 1986 which did away with sexual discrimination at work, both the police service and the women in it have been struggling to build a new relationship.

For 150 years, policing has been essentially a man's world, both on and off duty. Women have been granted space in it only grudgingly. Recent legislation notwithstanding, many women police officers complain that they are often treated as sexual objects, secretaries and children's nannies too much of the time.

Women officers are therefore placed in a bind of their own: at one extreme, if they fight for equal treatment by aping male attitudes, they risk losing their femininity. At the other, if they passively accept the sexist attitudes of their male colleagues, they risk losing their identity altogether by conforming to the stereotype men have of them. Some women officers have found a middle path to self-respect while preserving their femininity, but rarely without a struggle.

Not all policemen are sexist. Some treat women as equals and are aware of their own vulnerability. But the brutalizing effect of police experience in general – not only in the canteen – is so pervasive that many men and women lose their sensitivity in a remarkably short time. I have seen gentle young men and women coarsened in a matter of months.

Met WPC in a Home Counties force, age 23, three years service. Now in a large town.

I'm not soft. Some of the women can be very wimpy. Men say, "God, that woman's pathetic. Don't get her on a job with you." They won't say that about me. The number of times I've laddered or ripped my tights climbing through broken windows and over walls . . .

I don't think women have sunk in on the job yet, not really. We still have to wear skirts from April till October, which is awful. It's ridiculous. You try going up a wall without having to hitch your skirt up, and all the blokes behind you are going "Coo, we'll help you over, luv." Then there's the handbag. A great use that is in the kind of fights we get here on Saturday nights. Of course you want to look smart, but it's so stupid.

RITES OF PASSAGE

When they first arrive at a station, all new recruits have to prove themselves before they are accepted by colleagues in the relief. It is a rite of passage into tightly knit groups of men with childish games intended to humiliate the newcomers. It is also a way of welcoming new young versions of themselves. Women – and men from ethnic minorities – have a harder time being accepted. They are alien to the standard group picture of what "real" bobbies are like.

WPC in a large northern urban force, age 23, two years service. Now in an industrial suburb.

When I first came here the Sergeant tended to launch me on difficult things to see how I would cope. I went to one sudden death when an old gentleman suffocated himself with a plastic bag. He'd tied it around his neck. But before he'd done that he'd taken loads of pills and tablets and whisky. The Sergeant looked at me with this cynical grin on his face saying, "Let's see how you cope with this, young lady." He told me to cut the string and take the bag off his head, which I did. The smell that came out was absolutely oh, it was horrible! I said to the

Sergeant: "That's a bit rich, isn't it?" and the Sergeant was out the door gagging. So he didn't bother me again after that.

SPECIAL TREATMENT

Policemen's attitudes to women officers are by no means always hostile. Special treatment can make young WPCs feel looked after, but also patronized.

WPC in a Home Counties force, age 22, two years service.

Most of them are quite protective. If I was out walking on my own at nights when I first started, every five or ten minutes a police car would drive past. It didn't take long to click that they were keeping an eye on me. And the couple of times I've had to call for assistance, it's absolutely amazed me how quickly they've got there. They're quite fatherly towards me, a lot of them. Then in other ways it's the same male/female relationship. A lot of joking and innuendos. If ever I was to take any of them up on it, they'd run six miles in the opposite direction. I know that, so you can quite happily joke about it. They don't mean it – I hope!

WPC in a Midlands force, age 30, eight years service. Now in a racially mixed suburb.

For years and years they said: "We won't issue women with truncheons because there's a danger that they could be taken off them and used against them." Now somebody's decided: "We'll give them a little one – so it will only hurt them a little bit if it's used against them." Bollocks – no one's told me how to use it, though they've shown us how to wear it. I'm not taking it out – I'd rather use a good kick in the groin to protect myself.

THE WEAKER SEX

Manpower shortages have done most to move policewomen into the front line. In one northern force it took five years for an experienced WPC to become their first woman village bobby. Specialist teams like Support Groups, trained to deal with dangerous situations, are now accepting token women. Despite the notion that women are the weaker sex, they often prove braver than men.

WPC in a large northern urban force, age 30, eight years service.

The attitudes towards policewomen are changing. There tends to be a lot more violence than there was even seven years ago. There was a fellow called Andy several years back. Everybody has heard of him and he is the sort of guy that used to bend pumps. "Give us a pint," – if he didn't get a pint, he used to bend the pumps. You didn't argue with him and he didn't pay for many pints. He didn't pay for many taxi fares either.

He was in one of the big clubs on a Saturday night, stoned out of his brains. He comes out and he is still shouting the odds. A little policewoman comes up, taps him on the shoulder – she had to sort of stretch up – and says, "You're locked up for drunk and disorderly." He put his arm down behind her bottom, picked her up and walked from the pub to the station, knocked and said: "She's locked me up for D 'n' D, boss." Had you tried to do him normally it would have taken six or seven men.

The Andy of today would not be that nice mannered to a policewoman. He'd have a go. For the hard nuts, there's no difference between the sexes. That's the difference today.

SOFT TARGETS

Traditionally, women police officers have played a useful role as peacemakers when facing violence on the street. Even violent drunks usually draw the line at hitting women in uniform. In recent years, however, WPCs have often been knocked around with the same ferocity as any male officer. It is a depressing form of emancipation in policewomen's efforts to be treated equally.

Woman Police Sergeant, in large Midlands force, age 32, eleven years service. Now in an industrial suburb.

As most ladies do, I like going to dances, getting dressed up. I like clothes, I like all the usual feminine things. I remember going to a great deal of care to choose this super-duper dress for a dance and then being on night duty the day before and getting a good hiding from two young boys, about nineteen.

They were fighting and I was out on patrol on my own and went over to separate them, and they both started on me, and beat me up instead. They ran away. It was outside a crowded restaurant and no one came to help. Obviously police help arrived, as it usually does. I've always found that encouraging really. If another officer asks for urgent assistance you know everyone will break their necks to get there as quick as they can. But five minutes is a long time when someone is beating you up, they can do a lot of damage. I remember distinctly lying on the ground thinking, "All those people in there, someone must ring 999." I'd already called on the radio and said "Urgent assistance required", but knowing there was only one other car on duty anyway, if they were on the other side of the ground they'd be twenty minutes getting there. Not a soul came out to help.

Met WPC, age 22, three years service in Central London.

I don't think it makes any difference what their occupation is, it's the individual. Class makes no difference. You tend to get very upper-class people who do honestly think that they are above the law. Like where they're parking – simple things – he parks right in front of you and you say, "I'm sorry, you can't park there." "Why not?" They give you quite a hard time: "Do you know who I am?" Quite often there's no difference between the yuppy in his BMW convertible and some glue-sniffing skinhead. They might talk in a different way, but basically they're both rude.

The only time I've ever been badly assaulted was by a merchant banker. He was pissed out of his head and he got nicked for drunk and disorderly. I wasn't even one of the arresting officers. But I got called to the scene. We got him into the back of the van and I sat in the front – He was trying to take swings at me while shouting that I was a "diddicoy", something which I think means gypsy.

We got back to the station. He wouldn't get out of the van and the two PCs had hold of him. I grabbed him by the trousers round his ankles and just pulled him out of the van. He was still struggling and kicking. He calmed down slightly and they'd obviously loosened their grip, because as I opened the door and stepped back to let them in he just lunged at me. He grabbed hold of me and buttons started popping off all over the place. The whole four of us just went careering into the charge room. My chest was hanging out all over the place, and there was a lot of funny comments about that later: "We'll rub them better for you, love." There was nothing I could do. This bloke was right on top of me. Although he was short, he was bloody heavy and I had his full body weight on top of me. He was throttling me and my head was going bang, bang, bang against the desk.

I've never seen so many blokes move so quick. The skipper dived from behind the charge sheet and he's absolutely huge. He just picked the bloke up and he was pounced on by four PCs. But he wasn't slapped about or anything like that. He was put down pretty roughly. He was virtually chucked. He was thrown on the bench and told to bloody sit there. I got up and I would have liked to have gone round and given him a slap, but I was so shocked. It just happened so quickly.

I'm very fair, so I was very badly marked. I was covered in scratches and pressure finger marks all over my neck. My shirt was completely ripped. All the buttons came off my jacket and my cravat was ripped off. All my chest was scratched where he'd grabbed hold of me.

The next day we went to court. When he'd sobered up you couldn't meet a nicer man. I was quite happy because I got awarded £100 compensation on my birthday! He was charged with being drunk and disorderly, assault and criminal damage to my uniform. The magistrate said that in these sort of circumstances he gives a custodial sentence; however, because the man was of previously good character and everything, he gave him eighty days in prison, suspended for two years, for the assault on me and he fined him as well.

Met WPC, age 24, three years service. Now with a special unit policing a violent racially mixed area of London.

When I joined the unit, the blokes on it obviously had this big chat when they found out I was coming in – "Oh God, no – a woman!" It was a matter of proving yourself. I think I did prove myself. They realized I was an asset.

You've also got to go along with them. If the lads want you to do something, you do it. If they ask you to pick up some nutter who's six foot four and coming straight towards you, you don't suddenly say, "I can't see him." You just have to stop him and if something happens, it happens. But you know they're behind you. Once you realize you get back-up when you need it, then you know it can work.

We worked superbly, I think. I was good on the female side of it, when there were females to be searched. It was done there and then on the street, without the lads having to come back in and look for a WPC to search them in the station. So we spent more time on the sharp end and brought in more arrests.

I can understand male colleagues not liking policewomen involved in confrontations, because they feel they have to look out for them. But I would feel the same about them – that I'd be watching their backs as much as they'd be watching mine. I'm the only female in a team of twelve blokes, I can see them not wanting to accept it, but they've got to. Things have changed now.

Met WPC, age 26, four years service in a racially mixed area of London.

I have absolutely no desire to do public order. I don't do the same job as the male officers. I wouldn't wish to try and be like a male officer. I have my uses in other fields. I calm down pub disputes a darn sight quicker than the blokes can, because they go in there with fists flying and, as macho as they are, they're not going to solve it in that way. I go in with a big smile, and they're so astonished that there's a little girl telling them what to do, that they'll do it. Of course, there are times when it doesn't work. If somebody's a bit punchy, they're probably going to have a go anyway.

INTIMATE CONTACT

Everyone who joins the police service suffers from culture shock. Depending on their location, they may face violence, death and squalor on a regular basis. Even the most mundane tasks also present a challenge to each new PC, male or female: talking to strangers, dealing with domestic disputes, coping with drunks and the mentally ill. Body searches present WPCs fresh from nice homes with the task of laying their hands on women who may be either violent, diseased or drunk – often all three.

WPC in a large Midlands force, age 24, three years service. Now in a city centre.

Women are the ones who carry the most diseases. Some of the people who come in here! I have to search prostitutes. I had one who was a heroin addict as well as a prostitute and she had seventy needles on her, in her pockets. Without covers on them. She was quite affable about being brought in, but if she was a fighter she could have done a hell of a lot of damage to me. We have one regular who has every disease known to man! She loves the boys in blue. She frightens the hell out of me, that lady. She is riddled with everything.

You've got to get over a certain amount of shyness to strip-search people. Youngsters just starting on the job think they have done a thorough search, next thing the Sergeant looks through the cell door and the prisoner is smoking a cigarette and they don't know where he got it from. The fact he's been able to light it is the problem. If the cell blanket catches fire, they might damage themselves badly. We do have people who are suicidal and you have to be extremely careful with them.

One female was given a meal with a plastic knife and fork and left for five minutes. When I came back she had snapped them and was slashing herself. The same girl smeared excrement all over the cell. I have even told a prisoner, "Take your bra off. Put your jumper on, but take your bra off," because she looked as if she might choke herself with it. You have got to use your initiative with these people, sus them out quickly. One woman got really upset, I mean *really* upset, when I put a pair of plastic gloves on, so I tried to laugh and say, "You don't know what I've got, never mind what you've got!" She just thought it was disgusting.

BREAKING OUT

Women's Lib is a term of abuse in the police. Feminist notions have made little headway in British society at large; and like attitudes to race, the police reflect popular views reinforced by their own masculine tradition. Research by Sandra Jones at Brunel University suggests recent recruits tend to be even more anti-women than older policemen. Policewomen are up against that resistance when seeking acceptance both on the streets and in the canteen without becoming "one of the boys".

Met Woman Police Sergeant, age 29, ten years service. Now in West London.

I was brought up in Wales in a very small mining village. If you're a boy you go down a mine and if you're a girl you get married at sixteen or seventeen and have however many children. My father wanted us to expand a bit. I was going to be a nurse but decided that wasn't really for me. Two of my brothers left Wales and came to London to be policemen. They were typically male and said it wasn't a job for a girl. They didn't give me any help at all, so I did it under my own steam and came to London at seventeen. I was at a slight disadvantage because I was very short, you have to be five foot four. I said I was five foot four, but I was five foot one and a half so I turned up at the interview with my hair tied up to make me look taller. They said I had some nerve, because I was nowhere near the right height, but they took me on and I've never looked back.

Met WPC, age 28, three years service in central London.

My favourite working companions and indeed my canteen friends are all the older PCs, chaps who've got about eight years in and up, mostly chaps with wives and children. Never the canteen cowboy types. The older senior officers have an awful time dealing with WPCs. They certainly don't know how to handle me at all. When I started I had a Chief Inspector who was a most frightful man, he'd joined the cadets at about sixteen and never looked back, or indeed sideways, but he was exactly my age. I don't mind who I call "sir" or what anybody is called, but he couldn't get used to the fact that here was a red-haired graduate who spoke proper. It used to rattle his cage something rotten, because he wasn't a peaceful, cool chap within himself – of which there are a lot. So this really cruising, promotion-hungry, neurotic, middle-ranking Chief Inspector used to practically gibber at the thought of a confrontation with me. It's a bit naughty to say, but I used to trade on it a bit. I couldn't resist it, the humour element of it was terrific.

WPC, age 28, five years service in a Midlands force. Now in an inner-city area.

The men in this job love to say you're only a "plonk". Then they say, "You get the same money, you should be doing the same job." I know I'm not as good as the blokes physically but I do not accept that I'm some plonk because I'm a woman. Their attitude is, "She wouldn't know, she's only a woman." I could strangle some of them, the things they come out with. I'm a woman, but I've got a good brain – a better brain than they have. If you say anything, it's "Oh, how about more Women's Lib?" There is no consistency. One minute you're holding the baby and the next you're a "Women's Libber" or "If you can't take it you shouldn't have joined." They're very discriminative against women, but they don't know they are, which is the worst thing.

WPC in Home Counties force, age 26, four years service. Now in an industrial town.

If a baby is brought to the station along with a drunk woman, they all start wailing for a WPC to come and look after it. I can't think of anything that annoys me more, because I know nothing about kids. But they say, "Women's instinct. You know all about this." Some bloke walks past as you're struggling with this thing and all he'll say is, "Can't you stop it crying? It wants its nappy changed." They know, because they have got kids of

their own. I've tried pass the parcel – "You take the baby."
"No, you're the WPC, you have the baby" – but the Sergeant
revels in it. If you start objecting, they consider you're not doing
as you are told. They wouldn't think that of a bloke. We used
to have an Inspector who'd call for me whenever there was a
baby. He thought it was a big joke. I really dislike children.

PROMOTION

*Intelligent women often find themselves up against men who
cannot deal with them. In a disciplined force like the police,
there is little they can do to surmount such a barrier. A number
of women officers – graduates in particular – despair at the lack
of opportunity ahead of them. Several have resigned. Many
others are close to it.*

*This is not merely a loss of personnel and the expensive
training invested in them. The resignations of disillusioned
WPCs, Community Liaison Officers and of ambitious graduates
narrows the choice of future leaders who could take the police
service in new and fruitful directions.*

**Met WPC, age 34, four years service in Central London, and
a graduate. Now resigned.**

Probation, as was explained to me by reasonable and understanding senior officers, was a waste of time. Teaching me how
to speak to people about their defective tyres and everything,
forget it. It was really a teeth-cutting period that would have
been the time for a more sympathetic senior officer to say, "OK,
let's get you an interesting job." I then actually had a very
sympathetic senior officer and he was delightful. I got on very
well with him. Then he left and was replaced by the most
frightful little creep, who made life extremely difficult, basically
for the age-old and desperately dull reason that he made a pass
at me and I laughed at him, I thought, "So what? There's
nothing he can do to touch me. OK, he can make life difficult."
He made life extremely dificult. He blocked any applications I
made to do anything more interesting, and I was getting very
fed up with him.

By this time, I'd seen what beat duty could offer and wanted to do something a bit more interesting, a bit more specialized, like clubs or drugs, or even dogs or horses – that kind of thing, but not, please not, the street at three o'clock in the morning with rain dripping down my neck, I think anybody will tell you, once you get over thirty shift work plays absolute havoc with your system. It's pretty bad before thirty, but night duty – when you go on at 10.30 at night and come home at 6.30 in the morning is an absolute stinker. When you come off a week of night duty, you finish at 6.30 in the morning and you go right back on late turn at 2.00 in the afternoon, and finish at 10.30 that night. Then you have two days off, and by God you need it! I used to spend those two days in bed with a bottle of vodka! So I was also keen to get off shift work and, as I say, he made life extremely difficult. It was all so terribly, terribly petty. He took away my right to be a force interpreter because he said it took me away from force duties, but he was quite happy to let other officers go off to play football in police time, or water polo or something. It was a personal vendetta which eventually got so bad I thought: "I don't need this. Stuff it! I'll go." And I put in my papers.

Then I bumped into a high-ranking chap who I'd met before on Scotland Yard squads. He said, "What, you've put in your papers? You must be off your trolley. We've got a vacancy for you. Why on earth didn't you speak to me first?" It honestly hadn't occurred to me to, it would have been arrogant of me. And he said, "Put in a letter rescinding your resignation. Don't say why, just say you thought better of it, and when they've accepted that – as obviously they have to – put in an application to transfer up to me and I'll make sure your transfer goes through. Your cosmetic title will be WPC on the Drugs Squad, but you'll really be working as a trusted interpreter on all the Yard Squads." I was thrilled to bits and shoved in the application to rescind my resignation. I was given a hell of a time by "Hitler" and I just said, "No, I've thought better of it." They told me that my name was due to come off the computer at midnight on Sunday. At two o'clock on the Friday afternoon I was phoned up by a Sergeant in Admin who said, "I'm very sorry, I don't know how to tell you this, but your application to rescind your resignation has been turned down." This was right at the eleventh hour. So I got straight on the phone, and of course Friday afternoon there's nobody there at all. The chap who asked me to stay went into orbit. They'd timed it for when the Commander was going to be away. It's all so pathetic. A petty little vendetta. He went to see the acting Commander, who was a stiff little Scot, and he said, "No, the woman is trouble. We're not having her in." I heard from somebody, outside the room there was the most wonderful confrontation with these two men, who had equal rank you see, thumping the table at each other. The acting Commander had to admit that he had never met me, never spoken to me, never had anything to do with me. But it went through and that was that. There was nothing anyone could do about it on a Friday afternoon, and once you're off, that's it. You're out.

I seethed about it for several months. I was very, very upset about it and felt extremely badly used. I also felt it was bloody poor that a man of senior rank could abuse the privileges conferred by his rank on a personal grievance. At the time everybody was banging on about the cost of training police officers and they were desperate for linguists, and here was a fully trained, fully qualified police officer who the Drugs Squad were crying out to have, not allowed to because of this man.

I was later asked to go back, but I said no. Not out of sour grapes, but simply because I decided that the structure and mentality being what it is, it would only be a matter of time before I came up against yet another unlit tunnel-minded, under-sized, socially complexed, chauvinist arsehole – if you see what I mean! So I didn't go back.

So that was the silly, pathetic, stroppy tale of why I left, I could have stayed on, stuck my head down and kept on with it, but life's too short.

WOMEN FIRST, POLICE OFFICERS SECOND

All police officers sacrifice their private lives to the job, but the men get the extra satisfaction of the camaraderie, the rugby, the drinking and the Masons. Some women officers join the party and enjoy it, but many others wish for a normal social life outside the force. The shift hours and the stigma of the job, however, make this almost impossible to achieve. As women they feel isolated inside the force, and as police officers they are isolated outside it. Black and Asian officers are in the same predicament.

WPC in a Home Counties force, age 25, three years service.

I share a house with four other police officers which is isolating, I suppose. Just socializing with other police officers, you are isolated. Sometimes you make friends with your neighbours, but where I'm living practically the whole household on both sides of us has had confrontations with the police at some point. One time I've actually been there. That's when you try to hide – arresting your neighbours doesn't make you very popular. It's quite awkward, really, because being neighbours they may just have borrowed your mower.

When I was first in the job I used to tell people in nightclubs and pubs exactly what I did for a living. They'd say, "Oh, I'm just going to buy myself a drink." That's it, gone for good. It works a lot easier if I say I'm a civil servant or a secretary or something, because at least they continue to talk to me. It doesn't bother me. It's really quite amusing to see them darting off into the crowd.

ROMANCE

Policemen's protectiveness towards women officers has its more unpleasant side. A WPC who dates a civilian may let both herself and her boyfriend in for harassment. A young man in North London who was going out with a WPC was greeted nightly by a vanload of abusive coppers shouting up at his window. His girlfriend told him that her colleagues had run a computer check on him and warned her (inaccurately) that he was on drugs and had a criminal record.

PC in a West Country force, age 27, six years service. Now in an urban area.

There was a policewoman who joined my group who was very

good. The protocol is they don't get the same work and they don't walk the street alone at night, but this WPC would not have it, she insisted she'd be a real policewoman. She was superb. She used to bring in as many prisoners as the rest of us put together. She wasn't very popular because she was extremely arrogant, but at the end of the day her prisoner tally was very good.

She came from an estate herself and knew what these kids were about. She'd been hanging around with a lad who'd been a petty burglar. He was one of the few who had gone on to get involved in more serious crime. She'd been happy to get to know him because she thought it would help her. That had always been her attitude. She had always mixed with all the other kids who were in trouble and they always stitched each other up horribly. She got involved with this lad – I'd give her the benefit of the doubt and say she got out of her depth. Basically he was using her, she wasn't using him in the way she thought she was.

The Regional Crime Squad were looking at this bloke and would like to have sent him down. They noticed he was mixing with her in social time out of police hours. They started following her, and in the end she resigned. She got called up the second time in front of the Superintendent. She should have taken the warning the first time and not seen him again. She got called up again and the offer she got was: "You can resign or we'll put papers up – conspiracy to burgle" which she said was "totally unfounded". Because she was young and she was a girl, she had an awful lot to prove to be taken seriously. Actually she had done more than enough. She was on this overkill all the time to keep bringing in prisoners. Perhaps they did have evidence, I don't know. But I honestly think it's because she was a girl. She was one of nature's very rare breed of true policemen. A true thief-catcher. She was the only girl I ever saw that could do it.

DANGEROUS GOSSIP

Sexual politics dog the progress of every woman in the police force. As a constable, "being one of the boys" is just code for sleeping around. But the "relief bicycle" who always says yes is no more regarded than the suspected "lesbo" who says no. They are both just "plonks".

At higher rank, jealousy operates the same game. Women officers are still expected to appear in the bedroom, and if they refuse, the rumour mill damns them anyway. In a culture that discourages frank exchanges of opinion, outspoken women officers on the way up collect enemies. Sexual innuendo is the easiest form of damage to inflict, and the hardest to refute. It catches up with some men as well, such as a senior officer interviewing a WPC behind closed doors. But what is seen as a compliment to a man is meant as an insult to a woman.

Like much else in this book, the problem is not unique to the police. But it adds further pressure to the women officers trying to get on with an already difficult job.

Met Woman Inspector, age 35, thirteen years service, and a graduate. Now working in a racially mixed area of London.

The more rank you get, the more difference it makes to your personal life. People will start rumours about you if you're female, whatever you do. If I had done half the things I'm supposed to have done, I'd certainly have enjoyed myself. The present rumour is about me and an Assistant Chief Constable, because we went into a pub and had a drink one evening before a meeting. I'm quite concerned about it, and for God's sake there's nothing in it.

If you've got rank and you want some sort of respect, you need to be whiter than white. You must step away socially from the people you work with. I don't tend to socialize with police officers much anyway, because it makes you too narrow-minded and I don't like talking about the job outside work. But the better reason is that you need to be with people you can really trust. Not many policemen can resist the temptation of telling their mates who they went out with the night before, particularly if it's someone like myself. If a man had rumours like these going around about him, the guys would think it was great. But if you're a woman, watch out – it could affect your promotion board. A senior officer might say, "She's a bit free and easy. We don't want her."

You'll never change the state of women in the police. However many of us get through the ranks, we'll always be a small percentage of senior officers. What are we at now? One or two per cent above Inspector level. In the Met it's no more than one per cent at Chief Inspector and above. It will take many years to become more than that. Anyway, at the moment there is no promotion at all in the middle management ranks for men or women.

A lot of all this is just jealousy, men scared about women getting ahead. Some of them are quite open minded, usually because they've worked with a woman who has been good, but too many others will never change. What can you do? You just carry on and ignore it. I'm now promoted beyond a guy who really upset me at the very beginning and in my own little way I have got my own back. It was nothing malicious, just silly little things, but they meant a lot to me. If he bumps into me again he has got to call me Ma'am. Just a little word, but it means so much to men like that. Yes, I remember them all and I wait! I'm not a vicious person, but they are. They can be so hurtful, they really can.

THE NEED FOR RESPECT

With such a small number of women in senior ranks, promotion can lead quickly to isolation. Senior women officers, who may have authority over large numbers of men, must fight for respect even more intensely than they did on first joining the force as young WPCs. It takes a drastic personal toll on each individual that only those in the same position could ever understand.

Met Woman Chief Inspector, age 36, fourteen years service. Now in an inner-city area.

Most women officers will tell you that you have to put up a façade of hardness at work, every day. But you don't want to go home at night and look hard. People automatically think you are hard by virtue of the job you do, so you are in a vicious circle. In your private life, unless you've got people who know what you are like as a person, they automatically presume that you are hard and cynical and bitter, and all these stereotyped things. I used to pretend that I wasn't in the force, but that gets embarrassing because you are making fools of other people as well as yourself, so I tell the truth now. People don't appreciate that when you are home at night you change into another person and just wish you could be that person naturally without having to put on a façade. It is very difficult.

The sort of circle I want to be in is not available within the force. Because of the age range, the people available to go out with are either divorced or widowed. They've been in a family situation and they want another family. More than likely, they are not used to a woman like me – a woman used to positions of authority who's had to deal with men. They tend to want more of – I don't mean a less intelligent woman – but a woman who is perhaps a bit more narrow-minded. This happened in my last relationship. I'd known the person six months before we had a conversation about current affairs. He turned round in stunned silence and said, "I didn't know you talked about things like that." I said, "How do you think I've got where I have?"

Much precious talent and individuality is lost through the bru-talizing process that turns women into policemen. Many women leave before it is too late. If they marry policemen, the process often continues at home (see Chapter 13, "Sex, Husbands and Wives").

Met Woman Inspector, age 35, twelve years service. Now in an inner-city area of London.

If you are looking for a boyfriend, let's face it, women have got a thing about men in uniform. They think that policemen are attractive and wonderful and hunky and God knows what else, and join the force with this idea. I'm sure a lot of them join looking for husbands and the social life. They get caught up in it and become part of it. They join the canteen culture.

It's really terrible when you listen to the men talking. You accept it and it becomes part of you, part of your life. You either accept it or you become ostracized. It's very difficult to stay as you are. You are suddenly introduced to a new world, something you have never known before. It takes quite a strong character to resist it. You have got to decide whether respect is more important to you than going out with someone different every night of the week. Or having more of a social life and being more accepted. I actually reached the stage where I said, "Right, I'm no longer part of the canteen culture. I'm going to become a lady again and expect to be treated like a lady." Rank helps, obviously, but I would have done that anyway.

Woman Police Sergeant in large northern force, age 30, ten years service. Now in a city centre.

I've experienced severe problems because, on more than a couple of occasions, I wouldn't sleep with senior officers. If you say no, they take it as a personal insult; and no matter what they say, they really do take it out on you. When I was a WPC I was totally ostracized by my superior. Everything I did was wrong. He put me through it so badly I was about to pack it in. Another one gave me a bad report on my Sergeant's course because I failed to give him the goods. Others are more timid and test the ground first, but they are all out there thinking they've got something special in their pants and they try it on you.

Women Police Sergeant in large Midlands force, age 31, eleven years service.

There's a girl at the station on another relief who's got in with a clique of PCs on the relief. She's let everybody down. I'd like to get rid of her, but she's not mine. She'd been told in no uncertain terms what was expected of her and what was wrong. She's a slag, always diving in and out of bed with everybody. Thinks she knows it all. She's a uniform carrier – a lazy, dozy bird. When she first came she looked quite reasonable. You can see the change in her: fag always in one hand, chewing gum. She's a woman and she winds herself down with men. She needs a Woman Sergeant or Inspector, because she needs a woman to sort her out. She'll get no change from a woman because we are not fooled by her little feminine wiles. Men don't have as much control over women, they're stupid enough to fall for all these little tricks.

Another WPC was sent to Coventry by her relief because she *wouldn't* sleep with them. She wouldn't be what they wanted her to be. She was asked out by loads of them, but she didn't want to join the canteen culture. She found all the language upsetting. She found the whole thing upsetting. She was a nice girl and wanted to get on with her job. The pressure on her was so strong that in the end she gave in and soon got pregnant and then married. She ended up with a reputation, leaving the kids at home with her mum and sleeping around. She became all the things she didn't want to and is now divorced and has left the Job. She had great prospects, but the Job had changed her so much she became a different person.

I just decided that's not for me, so I pulled myself together and got on with it. I even changed my hair style. I thought, "If I'm going to be a Sergeant, I better bloody well behave like one."

Met Superintendent, age 44, twenty-three years service. Now in an inner-city area of London.

We restrict the women to about 1 per cent of the force but, in fact, they account for about 30 per cent of the operational office. A woman's probation, although it is only supposed to be two years, is about three or four. It takes them three or four years to gain the competence of a man after two years' service. They are used to having things done for them. It takes them ages to become assertive in the way a man is. They are just not ready for the role yet. Society just hasn't developed women to be equal to a man, certainly not within the police service. A lot of the work is physically demanding. On average the women's sickness rate is about twenty-eight days to the men's fourteen days, which is pretty high. That sickness is often ridiculous things which actually makes it look as though it is stress. Once they get about five years in, they are married and off. Very few last the pace. ...

WOMEN ARE NEEDED

The police are searching for a new relationship with the public – one based more on awareness of community needs and less on conflict and macho shows of strength. The secret may lie with the police – men and women – learning to keep their sensitivity alive through their careers. This means broadening the spectrum of acceptable reactions on the street and in the station. To achieve this cultural revolution, more women must reach senior ranks – with their femininity intact – than the handful who have so far succeeded in rising above the rank of Chief Inspector. Though we have had a strong woman Prime Minister for nine years, it is still an uphill struggle. Meanwhile the vicious spiral of aggression and brutalizing continues.

CHAPTER SEVEN

Violence

Violence separates police officers from the rest of us. We may face it from time to time in our lives, depending on our class and situation. But for most of us, the fear of violence is far more vivid and prevalent than the real thing.

After all, how often do we have to grapple with violent drunks, separate violent couples, face a crowd of rampaging football hooligans or angry black youths? How many of us live like the RUC in Northern Ireland, with the constant threat of fatal attack on ourselves and our families – day and night, off duty and on? Much police duty is spent in more peaceful conditions unless they are actually assigned to the few areas of high crime. But the aura of violence, the imminence of it, informs much of police feeling about the job. Now that assaults against police seem to be increasing in the country as well as in cities, it is taken for granted that "the enemy" is out there and may strike any time, any place. Recent episodes in county towns suggest that "He" is no longer poor and black or a militant picket but white and well off – a worrying new development that leaves the police feeling still more embattled, more isolated.

Yet violence has always been a fundamental part of police experience. Indeed, many researchers feel it is no worse than it ever was, just paid more attention. Even today, more police effort goes into dealing with violent drunks and football hooligans than middle-class crime, though fraud is growing fast and costs the nation far more in what economists call real terms. Many observers still describe the police as the working class keeping the rest of the working class in line. That shared background meant past violence was familiar to everyone involved. Toxteth veterans speak nostalgically of expecting a "friendly fridge" to be thrown at them on Saturday nights, twenty years ago – without the element of pure hatred so corrosive of mutual trust in the 1980s. One senior officer noted that throughout the year-long dispute in Wapping violence was never directed at the News International plant itself, though it was just across the road and not heavily policed during the day. As in the miners' strike, apart from brief outbursts against strike-breakers the pickets' main violence was aimed at the police.

How did it happen? And to what extent have the police brought it on themselves? Is violence the shocking new phenomenon it is imagined to be?

In 1987, Police Review conducted its own study of assaults against the police. They found more than 17,000, the worst year since the riots of 1981. It was an average of fifty assaults per day across Britain, with Strathclyde the most violent area of all. Surprisingly, no official figures of assaults on British police over many years have ever been kept. But in Sweden, where such records date back to the 1890s, cycles of violence against the police are linked directly with war, recession and social change. Similar cycles may apply in Britain. That would make the recent rise in assaults against the police nothing dramatically new and explained by current British economics. Too many people are unhappy at their situation, get angry, perhaps get drunk, and take it out on the first symbol of authority they can find – the police.

That is the familiar bind: the police are again attacked for something well beyond their control. If they retaliate, they risk the complication of a complaint. But they may also bring violence upon themselves. Indeed, assaults on and by the police are their worst current problem.

PC in Midlands force, age 28, six years experience. Recently resigned.

I knew this chap who was a right yob. I got to know his car. He would hang around near a chemist, waiting for any addicts who wanted to sell pills or other drugs, or swap some. He did this in exchange for drugs because he was a junkie himself. The first time I ever stopped him, he had a crowbar by the driver's seat – so he wasn't opposed to violence.

A few months later there were three warrants out for his arrest. I was driving along in an unmarked police car with another officer when we pulled in behind his car and started to follow him. He had three other men in the car with him. After a few minutes he realized and took us into a maze of small roads. They stopped in a blind alley and we got out and I went to arrest the chap. At the same moment one of the other chaps ran off and the officer who was with me ran after him. I was left with the other three ... and got my head kicked in.

It was really odd, I've never been beaten up before and we were rolling around in the road and he was saying, "You can't nick me now – it's too near Christmas. I don't want to be inside for Christmas," and all this, and then a boot would hit you in the head. While I was being beaten up I kind of disassociated myself, I couldn't even summon up enough energy to hit him back. Anyway he got away. I was just lying there in the road. It was strange because I didn't feel any pain and I had always imagined that being beaten up was really painful. The next morning of course, I was covered in bruises and it hurt a lot!

Met WPC, age 30, ten years service. Now in a racially mixed residential area in West London.

I've never – and this is my hand on my heart – seen a prisoner hit in ten years. Obviously prisoners are hit, but I'm just saying I have never, ever seen it. I've seen people use a lot of restraint. I got quite badly beaten up by a guy with another female colleague. We were quite badly hurt.

I'd got my hair up in a bun and he'd pulled it loose and with his hands wrapped up in it he was just hitting my head against the lift door. He punched me in the face, cut my lip. I had two black eyes – scratched and bruised all over.

Quite a few bobbies wanted to knock seven bells out of him because of what he'd done to us, which is a normal reaction when a friend of yours is hurt.

At one stage, I thought: "Yeah, it would be rather nice for him to get a bit battered for what he gave us," because he didn't care we were women. But we know that at the end of the day in court if he looked as bad as we did, we would stand to lose our case. There was no way I was going to do that just so a PC could thump him. But there were quite a few in there straining at the leash, wanting to go in there and do him.

Inner-city areas are acknowledged to be violent: a London bobby has a one in four chance of being assaulted in the course of a year. But the Police Review *league table of assaults against the police puts rural areas like Gwent and Wiltshire ahead of the West Midlands. The cause is most often linked to alcohol, with drunken youths playing havoc at weekends.*

Christmas is the worst time for violence. Families find themselves trapped together for a week in emotionally claustrophobic conditions that keep them inside and encourage drinking. Police officers work their normal roster throughout the holiday and by the end of the Christmas break expect the worst: domestic disputes, suicides, drunken driving, fatal accidents and, as part of the festive rituals, assaults against themselves.

PC in a rural division of a Home Counties force, age 27, seven years service. Now in a market town.

It seems that a lot of sport for youngsters and thugs is police-bashing. Increasingly we find we are not going in to break up fights between groups, we are going into groups whose aggression is aimed solely at us.

New Year's Eve is a prime example. All round the country, at places that are normally very quiet, placid towns, you get a huge mob of so-called revellers who are attacking the police. You can be outside one pub on a New Year's Eve one year and they'll think you're wonderful and put drinks in your hand. Another time they'll be throwing glasses at you and trying to turn your car over. Why? I don't know. It seems that certain elements have just got a hate for the police.

MINIMUM FORCE

Except for the Army in Northern Ireland, the police are the only public service empowered by law (the Criminal Law Act 1967) to use force on fellow citizens. Such use is carefully defined as the minimum necessary to accomplish the task of keeping order and enforcing the law.

Force is used in the course of most policemen's day on drunks or drugged or seriously disturbed people who may need to be arrested or ejected from some public place, or taken to hospital or to jail. But when something goes wrong, if a formal complaint is made, then the assessment of minimum or reasonable force used in the heat of the moment will be made days, weeks, months, or even years later by senior officers in a quiet office, or by magistrates or judges in the calm of a court room – none of whom are likely to have faced a violent situation for many years, if ever.

PC in a southern Home Counties force, age 24, four years service. Now in a large sea port.

There are occasions when you are in the middle of an extremely violent situation, when the pubs and clubs have turned out at 1 a.m. in the morning and there are hundreds of people about. It is a hot night. They have drunk too much because of it. They're unhappy because of the atmospherics about, and you're in for a punch-up. There are only three police officers there and about 400 people milling. A fight starts. You're taking a bit of a hammering and you pull back a fist.

Now there's nothing worse than seeing a police officer strike someone in the street. The public don't like to see that sort of behaviour from the police. You end up with a charge of police brutality. It doesn't matter that there was one officer and twenty yobs there. He's fighting for his life, but it's still police brutality. I've done that, when I was well outnumbered. I have smacked a guy out of sheer self-preservation and there were about forty or fifty people clapping and saying, "Do it again, put the boot in!" – the public have had enough.

If you have one police officer against one violent man and you try to arrest him, you have a fight on your hands. To take him in without hurting him is almost physically impossible. So you'd have to have three or four officers to arrest one man, which looks untidy, but at least you're not hurting him. But to arrest one man these days you have to deck him. You've got to make quite sure he's aware that you're stronger than he is.

Met WPC, age 23, three years service in Inner London.

I will say it and I'm not ashamed to say it: there are times when prisoners have to be slapped. If I'm arresting somebody and they smack me in the face, they get a bloody slap back.

PC in a southern Home Counties force, age 28, eight years service. Now in a large coastal town.

If you go to an incident, it sometimes takes quite a long time to sum up the situation. You get different stories from different people. People start to belt away and they are lost for ever then. So we try to hang on to somebody, whether legally or not. At that stage we don't know what he has done, but I'd rather grab him and say "Just hang on there!" You do put yourself on the line, because technically you are not allowed to restrain anyone unless an arrest is made. On the other hand, if you don't do something, he is going to walk away.

Most policemen work on the basic principle of right and wrong. The law is really in the background. There is, in fact, so much law now you just don't come into contact with it. A policeman will go to a situation and say, "Right. Someone must have committed an offence. We'll work it all out later on."

KNIVES: THE UNKINDEST CUT

In the USA and in television fiction, police seem to be facing guns most of the time. In Britain, however, knives are the principal weapon which threaten officers on the streets. A recent amnesty collected many thousands, and new legislation makes it an offence to carry a knife without good reason. Levels of damage in domestic violence have increased dramatically as parts of the community use knives in place of blunt instruments to settle their grievances.

Scottish PC, age 23, three years service. Now in a Support Group.

When you do stop someone and you think they might have a knife on them, you don't take any messing around. You throw them up against a wall and you frisk them. And you may go physically over the top. Of course, nine times out of ten the people you arrest are non-violent and they are going to think: "God, the police handled me really roughly. I was only arrested for shoplifting and they had me spreadeagled on the floor with their foot in my back."

A POLICEMAN'S POWERS

Until the law changed in 1967, a constable had no more powers than other citizens: anyone could arrest a person in the act of committing a crime. The Criminal Law Act of 1967 abolished the distinction between felony and misdemeanour, and introduced the "arrestable offence" for police officers. This gave them the power to arrest anyone whom they have reason to believe is about to commit an arrestable offence, or may already have done so. An arrestable offence is defined as a crime for which a person of no previous conviction can be sent to prison for five years or more.

Section 3 of the same act gives a police officer the power to use "reasonable force" to make an arrest, or to protect himself. He can also use force to affect an entry on the same grounds of reasonable suspicion. The Act made the subjective notion of reasonableness into an objective measure. But, as public attitudes to the police change, so do juries' notions of what is reasonable for them to do.

Sergeant in a large northern urban force, age 36, sixteen years service. Now in an inner-city area.

If you've got a fighting drunk, trying to get him in the back of a Panda car – maybe a Ford Escort – can be a hell of a job. He can be in one side and out the other. You've got to use a hell of a lot of force to get him in, but it's still reasonable force in my view. What you really need is a carrier van there and then. Open the doors, grab him, in the doors, close the doors and you're away. You'd probably have him in a secure police station in a matter of minutes. Jimmy Kelly – who died in police custody – he was a prime example. An Escort was sent for him. He weighed 17 stone and he was fairly fit. He'd been locked up on numerous occasions, but when these two bobbies tried to get him into the Panda he was in one side and out the other. A van eventually arrived and they got him to the station where he snuffed it.

UNEXPECTED VIOLENCE

Violence comes from unexpected places, at any time of the day or night. Drunks and mental patients can be extremely violent without warning. And their strength is far greater than under normal circumstances.

Sergeant in a large Midlands force, age 40, twenty years service. Now in a racially mixed residential area.

You get some funny things. There was one Sunday afternoon, very quiet, nothing happened. Then a huge "crash" of breaking glass. I went to the door and this fellow said, "It was him, officer." This weedy-looking little fellow. Five big partition windows kicked in. I said, "Hey, did you do that?" "Yes." I thought, here we go. I asked him why. "I was so frustrated." So I said, "I get frustrated but I don't go around kicking in windows."

Then the fellow barked like a dog and told me he was a "protector". I thought "poor bugger" and said, "Come on, you're locked up." As soon as I touched him, he went bloody beserk. I mean crazy violent. He broke my thumb and so I thumped him. It was the only way I could hold him; I just couldn't calm him down. I'm trying to hold him down and get the phone and the mad bugger is trying to bite my hand off.

Eventually a van comes down and we take him to hospital. He was howling and barking like nobody's business, but the psychiatrist just said, "This man has suicidal tendencies, but he is fit for police custody." I said, "If he has suicidal tendencies and thinks he's a guard dog, how the hell can he be fit for police custody?" "Sign here and take him away." So we took him away and charged him.

I had to go and give evidence in court and he had a very elegant barrister, like a very nice chap but totally out of touch. He asked me if I'd hit his client. I said I had. "Why?" "Because he broke my thumb." "Officer, you admit to hitting my client." I said, "Yes, because he broke my thumb." "You can't say that, officer." I said, "It wasn't broken before, but it was broken after and he was the only one I was fighting with."

Of course, this was Monday morning and all the drunks were in the back of the court. The barrister then said, "Officer, did my client say anything to you?" I said, "Yes, he barked at me and told me he was a protector." He said, "How did my client bark?" I said, "He barked like a dog." "Officer, how did my client bark?" I thought, "No, I can't do this." You could see the blokes sitting forward on the edge of their seats and the magistrate was a very austere gentleman. I said, "Your Worship, this is not really going to help this client." He said, "You must answer the question." "OK, Your Worship." The barrister then said: "Again, Officer, how did my client bark?" "Well, he sort of went 'woof, woof, I'm the Protector'," and the bloody place fell apart. I could feel my face like a Belisha beacon.

Experienced men find non-violent ways of coping with threatening situations.

Sergeant in a northern urban force, age 34, twelve years service. Now in a racially mixed residential area.

Give me a drunk man any time as opposed to a drunk woman. How do you handle a drunk woman? Especially when they're violent – they can be bloody strong. There was one brought in a few years ago. She was walking down the middle of the High Street at, perhaps, 3 a.m. Nobody had a mum and nobody had a dad, they were all "bastards". She was chucking bottles and effing and blinding all over the place. A little bobby, not long in: "You're locked up missus, drunk and disorderly." She had a real go at the bobby, so he called for assistance. She was a terror. It took four bobbies to bring her in.

She's brought in forcibly and the Sergeant is one of the old deadpan city bobbies; seen it all, knows it all and done it all. He said, "Now madam, what have you got to say?" "You're all bastards, I'm not effing drunk." She was trying to hit us but was hitting the wall, she was so stoned. So the Sergeant said, "OK, madam, put your property on the counter. You'll get it back when you are released."

Now, I'm not sexist, but women are the best actors in the world. She took her choker off with a flourish. Big production. She should have got an Oscar. Throws it on the counter. Takes her watch off. Now the production was great, except she was stoned and staggering. She gets it off and throws it down and the Sergeant says "Take your ring off, luv." "He's my world." It is half three in the morning, she doesn't know where the hell "he" is, but "he's her world" and she loves him. The Sergeant says, "Take if off, luv, you'll get it back when you go." "You're all bastards." He said, "Take it off, luv, or we will." So she lifted her jumper over her head: "What do you think of those?" She was a bloody big girl, she had no bra on and the Sergeant just sort of looked at her and said, "Madam, you have nothing there." She collapsed in a heap, sobbing her heart out.

Met Sergeant, age 38, sixteen years service. Now in a training department.

I have been in a position where I have hit a prisoner in the face as hard as I possibly could with the intent of really hurting him, because my finger was clamped between his teeth! When it went to court, this chap had a nice face and I was asked, "Did you hit the defendant?" I said, "Yes, as hard as I could." You could have heard a pin drop in the court. I thought: I'm in the soup because it's contrary to normal procedure – you don't put your hand up and admit to whacking the prisoner. I said, "Because he had my finger in his teeth and he was biting it." The magistrate said "Come and show me." So round I went, undid the bandage. You could still see the indentation and the festering from the bite. The comment was, "Animals should be caged." And he was.

THE COMPENSATION TRAP

Recently, a new twist has contributed to the assault figures: injured police may now apply for compensation to the Criminal Injuries Board. But only injuries caused by criminal assaults are taken seriously. Minor injuries do not count. That could lead to officers exaggerating an injury to qualify for compensation and then staying away from duty to bolster their case. (One may stay away from work for seven days without a doctor's certificate.)

This is no small matter. Merseyside and Greater Manchester forces – both areas of inner-city violence - lost an average of nineteen days per officer in 1987 through uncertificated illness, which totals hundreds of thousands of scarce man days lost.

In the old days, PCs came to work no matter how they felt; when they were injured they took it in their stride. Many older senior officers find the current concern with stress and injuries a sign of weakness. Their attitude no doubt hid the true number of assaults on police in the past. Current practice may exaggerate it. Both feed an important but unproven assumption that policing was far safer in the past.

An injured PC finds himself in a new bind; if he stays away and reports his injury, he may get decent compensation – and feel better. But his promotion chances may be harmed if he comes up against a senior officer of the old school. If he buckles down and ignores his injury, his standing with senior officers will improve (assuming they take any notice of him) in inverse proportion to his chances of compensation. If he carries on working while injured, he will be all the more sensitive to the threat of violence, and still less able to take it in his stride. These circumstances lead to premature arrests – and possible violent reactions.

VIOLENCE TO THE POLICE

Met PC, age 28, seven years service. Now in a racially mixed inner-city area of London.

They don't think about the impact of injuries. We've had blokes here – one on the other shift was a long time sick; a back injury just wouldn't let go. He'd been hit with a scaffold pole on the back of the head. He's fit and strong now, but the moment he goes back on the street and gets involved in something, will it go back out? They noticed after Toxteth that people were going sick with backache. Then they realized how many had been injured. After I was beaten up, every time I put my head back my nose hurt. Now, I won't get as close as I used to. When a bloke starts thrashing out with an umbrella, I just grab hold of him and put him on the deck, because I'm scared of getting my nose broken again. You can't help that sort of reaction.

KEEPING FIT

With violence such a regular problem for ordinary bobbies, the need to keep fit should be clear, but unlike the Army, police not involved in public order training have little or no regular physical programme once they leave training school. At the time of writing, only a handful of forces teach their officers the martial arts of self-defence. Most officers do not like such special training, however, as it needs practice to be of use. They are also worried by the ease with which one can accidentally kill someone.

Probationer WPC in a northern force, age 20, thirteen months service.

How do you deal with force when you want to arrest someone who is aggressive? Ours is one of the few forces that do martial arts, so I have no problems. My very first arrest was a violent male shoplifter. I bluffed my way out of it. I said to this chap: "Look, I'm going to warn you now, I'm a black belt in Origami." He was so stupid he believed me! He gasped and said, "I won't cause any trouble." He had smashed this store up. I took him by the hand just in the normal prisoner hold and he was good as gold.

WPC in the same northern force, age 24, three years service. Now in a mixed race area.

Usually you can talk your way out of things. With women you can't, they are the worst people to arrest. They don't fight fair.

They use stilettos and anything they've got at hand – nails. I had one woman, she lunged at me. I'd been brought in to search her and I thought: "No way, I don't like her." She'd been brought in for possession of an offensive weapon anyway. So I walked backwards and she sort of jumped at me. I couldn't believe it. I caught her as she was in mid-air. She started fighting and I said: "There's no need for it. You're being treated all right. What's the problem?" She was so upset, she'd just flipped.

The self-defence training we do is non-aggressive. All you are doing is holding them. If they move they hurt themselves. So really it's in their own interest to be still. In the classes we do the whole spectrum of the jujitsu. There was a Sergeant, about 18 stone. He was a huge rugby player and I floored him with one hold. He tried to run away from me and inflicted so much pain on himself that he fell on the floor! So anyone can do it, no matter how big or how small they are. It's just knowing how to do the holds.

FEAR OF POLICE VIOLENCE

The fear of violence on the streets affects far more people than are actually attacked. It is only for police officers themselves that it is a frequent occurence. For those arrested, the fear of violence at the hands of the police is just as vivid, and is usually a second-hand mixture of rumours, bad publicity – and some reality. The police deal regularly with people to whom accounts of beatings in the back of vans or in cells are as real as if they had happened to them.

PC in a large northern force, age 32, eight years service.

The image I got before I joined was that policemen beat everyone up in the backs of cells, but in eight years I've never seen it. I've seen people get a hiding on the street when they've hit a policeman, but there was none of this systematic beating that I'd expected. I thought, "What am I going to do if I'm put in a situation where some PC beats up someone and I'm there. What am I going to do?" I know what I would do now, but when I first joined I didn't.

We had a thing recently, we bailed a prostitute and two weeks later we were talking to other prostitutes and they said, "What did you do to her? You're right bastards." And I thought, "Fucking bitch, I gave her money to get home." But she'd immediately come out and told her mates, "Oh I've been this, that and the other by them." That sort of spreads. That's not just disheartening, I was fuming about it.

RUC Superintendent, age 40, eighteen years service. Now in Belfast.

The safest place to be if you were suspected of bombings would be in police custody in the Castle because you're documented from the time of arrest. It's not in our interest to beat up our prisoners. If we beat the guy up, we'll spoil the case in court. Any policeman of any worth at all knows that if you hammer a prisoner, it blows your evidence. The doctor examines the prisoner when he comes in. If he has injuries on him, where did he get them? In the van . . .

I had a mother come in when I was commander at a station, and I said to her that it was the safest place in this town for her son. Nothing could happen to him there, with a doctor and everything. They don't believe it. I told her I wasn't going to tell lies and in the end she was quite happy.

When a lad joins the Provos, he's told to make a complaint as a matter of course about his treatment in custody. First of all, he's challenging any evidence based on ill-treatment, and secondly he's tying up two or three policemen while they investigate the complaint.

Met Sergeant, age 38, twelve years service. Now in the East End of London.

Tape-recording interviews is great. The results of the trials are fantastic. We get loads and loads of interviews where people go into court and say "No, I never said that," or "He was standing behind me with a sledgehammer at the time so I signed it."

I mean, people imagine they are going to an interview and will get their heads beaten in. The public actually think we do it. I earn nearly twenty grand a year – I'm not going to throw it away. If someone throws a punch at me, all very well, but they seem to have this image of us beating everybody up all the time. We get them in the back of the van and they still think they're in for a hiding. You know that was stamped out in the dark ages.

Sergeant in a West Country force, age 30, eight years service. Now in a large urban centre.

If you were arrested today for an offence along with another person, and during the interview you admitted it and said, "Joe Bloggs did it with me," you have now got to leave the station and see your friend Joe Bloggs. And tell him you've told the police and he's likely to be arrested any minute. What are you going to say to him? "Oh, I've stuck you in it, best mate. I'm ever so sorry!" You're going to say, "They bloody made me do it. They beat me up." Don't lose sight of that.

Met Sergeant, age 36, eighteen years service. Now in an inner city area in south London.

I've seen prisoners inflict injuries on themselves. It happens quite often. You think they're kicking the door and then when you check on them, they're using their head. It's horrible when you see somebody knock themselves out, smashing their head against cell walls, blood everywhere.

There was one man, he went to one end and ran the whole length of the cell into the door. That was it. He was out cold and had to go to hospital. It not only gets him out of the cells, it doesn't look good for us when he gets into court with a bandage round his head. He says, "I was beaten up in the cells." You say, "Well, Your Honour, he ran the length of the cell head first into an iron door." Everyone thinks you're a complete idiot, but it's not bloody funny if they decide you're lying.

VIOLENCE BY POLICE

As assaults against the police are rising, so too are assaults by the police – despite the Code of Practice. Of the 4148 complaints

*serious enough to be referred to the Police Complaints Authority
in 1987, 3457 – 80 per cent – were for assault causing Actual
Bodily Harm. A further 418 – 10 per cent – were for deaths or
Grievous Bodily Harm.*

*Although policing styles in inner cities reflect the level of
violence on the streets, in the seaside town of Stockport, hardly
an inner-city area, two Constables were sentenced to life imprisonment for beating and kicking to death a drunken ex-guards-
man who had violently resisted arrest. They had intended to
"teach him a lesson he would never forget".*

*It is extremely difficult to establish how widespread the
excessive use of force might be. Many officers insist that they
have never seen the police use violence which was not utterly
justified. Others acknowledge that it happens from time to time,
but only at the hands of a small number of "canteen cowboys",
many of whom are regarded as "dangerous companions" and
are often shunned. In some stations, however, violence is
reckoned to be standard practice. Scottish and Northern
England police officers have a reputation for being handy with
their fists. And television viewers watched North Wales traffic
officers catch a speeding car and beat up the driver. A PC from
Northern Ireland who joined the Met found the behaviour in a
North London police station right to inspector level so violent
towards prisoners, he transferred out again.*

*Police in a crowd can and do go wild, as they did against the
hippies in the Battle of the Beanfield or on the steps of Manchester University Students' Union, attacking a peaceful crowd.
But that is a far cry from the almost intimate violence of one
or two PCs beating a single prisoner. The first is a matter of
crowd psychology – a form of mass hysteria that erupts once
enough pressure has built up an explosive atmosphere. The
second is the number one problem for the police as a service:
how to recruit and train officers with sufficient strength of
character to resist the abuse of power.*

**Chief Inspector in a large Midlands force, age 40, twenty years
service. Now in a large suburban town.**

There are some violent coppers in the force. I don't think they
consciously say, "I'm a policeman, therefore I can beat the

daylights out of whoever I wish and get away with it." But it
is a disease in a human being to have that really violent streak.
I'm talking about the really nasty stage. That is abnormal, and
they are abnormal people.

We arrested this guy – little tiny fellow – and taking him up
the back steps to the police station, they did the business on
him. If a bloke is kicking up violent, you have to use a fair bit
to restrain him. Going even further on, where a bloke gets a
slapping, all right, because he's been making a bloody nuisance
of himself, or he's been totally disrespectful to officers or whatever. What I'm talking about is the level above that, where
you've got officers who have the disease. They go into an area
that is very dangerous. It is not just purely a flash of violence
and loss of temper and bang! – they hit somebody in the face.
They don't do that. They attack that individual very violently
but they do it in such a way that they don't leave any marks on
him. They hit them in the stomach or in the testicles. They
know what they're doing. They are so cold and calculating
about it that even afterwards there's no remorse, no apology.
They know that unless somebody has seen it, they're 100 per
cent safe. And then they wait and look for an opportunity when
they can do it again.

**Superintendent in a Home Counties force, age 46, twenty
years service. Formerly in Complaints and Discipline.**

I know one really punchy, violent PC who's just been taken to
court civilly and the case has been proven against him. The
bloke he assaulted was a renowned villain, a proper hard man,
pain in the arse – but he clearly didn't deserve the outright
beating that the PC gave him in the cell. He had angina. He
said, "Don't hit me, I've got angina," and the PC said, "Go on
then, die on me." Totally out of order.

He was the same guy who was done for a complaint that a
skinhead had been beaten up after a football match. The skinhead hadn't made the complaint, the assault took place outside
this couple's house and they were so upset by what they saw
that they made a complaint.

The PC involved told me: "I'm saying nothing." I was talking to him off the record and said to him, "What have these two witnesses got to gain from telling lies, giving a false complaint? They didn't know the individual, he just appeared out of the blue outside their house on a Saturday afternoon after the football and they reported what they saw. Neither of them have criminal convictions, so they have no axe to grind against the police. With the greatest respect, this is a serious offence. You would be wise to give some explanation because if you don't, what with the two witnesses, and the skinhead's testimony, you're in a spot of trouble." I was known as a straight guy and obviously I was giving him good advice. He was so bent, so punchy, he looked upon me as a bit of shit. He said, "I'll give you my answer, I'm saying nothing." That was it. It went up to the DPP – No further action on the basis of what the other three officers had said. They didn't like him either. It was just a reflex action to protect him.

Within twelve months he was suspended for assaulting a prisoner in the cell. He was charged with ABH, appeared at Crown Court, got away with it and was reinstated. Nine months later he did this other guy. They took him on discipline, proved common assault and he got dismissed from the force.

RESTRAINING YOUNGER OFFICERS

Violence is new for most graduate officers and those with more genteel backgrounds and aspirations. Not for them childhood memories of the "clump around the earhole" in place of a parental lecture or an arrest, which is still common practice in Scotland, Wales and the north of England. Not for them the pub fight on Saturday night. They have never used their fists, as many older bobbies and ex-servicemen have done, so they are more likely to be hurt, and perhaps hurt someone else.

Young officers go over the top in one of two ways. Some want to prove themselves one of the boys. They go looking for trouble, turn up at incidents with which other officers are dealing, wade in and escalate the matter until it gets violent. The other danger is from less aggressive young PCs who lack the confidence to defuse situations on their own. They tend to make an arrest too quickly to avoid what they see as a challenge

to their authority. When the civilian objects in strong language –
the arrest is itself a kind of civil violence, albeit lawful – the
nervous PC will call for back-up. A minor incident suddenly
brings a vanload of policemen at top speed, with flashing lights,
squealing brakes and two-tone blaring. An experienced officer
would walk in slowly and let things cool down. Once blood is
up on both sides, injuries are more likely.

**PC in an East Anglian force, age 30, ten years service working
in a large city.**

What I'm worried about is the young bobbies who are straight
from what they're told on parade. They go out on the street
like bears with a broken bottle up their backside, looking for
trouble – unintentionally maybe – but they're going out wound
up. That frightens me.

I've come across incidents where bobbies have overreacted
because their emotions were running high. We were in a stolen
car chase and the vehicle was stopped. There was no accident.
Nobody was hurt. The driver of the car was only a young lad.
They didn't try to run away. They certainly didn't try and fight.
However, after a high-speed chase emotions are running high.
There were a couple of very narrow misses with other members
of the public, when you think: "Should I break off the chase?
Is it worth it?" So the first thing you do when you get to the
driver is call them everything under the sun, and I've never been
criticized for it yet. But unfortunately one particular bobby
overreacted totally and thumped the lad twice. He was suspended from duty and he's been charged and is going to Crown
Court. What started out as a very good job, a nice little arrest,
has gone totally bitter and twisted because this bobby's feelings
exploded. I'm not being unfair to the bobby to say that it had
been building up like this for a while. It should have been
spotted.

**Met Sergeant, age 34, twelve years service. Now in a training
department.**

Society gets the police force it deserves. In 1977–8, when I was
at the training school watching them come in, we were taking

a particularly aggressive type of person. I don't know why. But when you look outside, there was crowd violence, and gang fights on the street were quite common. It seemed to me that society was venting its spleen.

If you didn't like what someone said or the way he looked, you just took a swipe at him. It could also have been the numbers we were recruiting at the time. It was just after the Edmund Davies Report when our money went up. Sixty a week were going into the system. You cannot monitor those numbers in detail, and some slipped through the net. And we were losing a lot of people from the force who'd got experience. So when the young PCs came into the police force, they couldn't learn from more experienced PCs on their relief.

The problem for the Met now is that these men are the ones with nine or ten years of experience. They are the ones who set the tone in the canteen and in the van. As Sergeants and Inspectors they are part of the canteen culture themselves. It is hard for young PCs to stand up to them and refuse to take part if aggression is in the air.

Met WPC, age 31, six years service in the West End of London.

The most serious problem is the "Jack the Lad" thing with the youngsters. I've heard the boys from different nicks talking to each other before lectures at training school or in the lunch hour, trying to outdo each other. I remember a couple saying, "Oh, we gave him a good and proper thumping." I turned round and said, "You are just bloody stupid! Why on earth do you put your career, your job, maybe your marriage on the line for some revolting little toerag who's going to be passing through the courts for the rest of his life, by exercising your macho tendencies and putting your fist in his face?" "Oh, we didn't mark him" – missing the point completely.

ACCEPTABLE LEVELS

A collective view among a group that violence is acceptable is one of the dangers of a culture that closes ranks. In such an atmosphere casual violence can easily become a much more serious and premeditated affair. The behaviour of younger PCs in south London was directly blamed by Lord Scarman for causing the Brixton riots of 1981. Although senior officers are tempted to blame such violence on a few rotten apples, it is group attitudes and lack of supervision that foster it.

Met Inspector, age 40, fifteen years service. Just resigned.

In the years before the riots, the police in Lambeth treated the community with contempt. There were stories of people having their heads stuffed down lavatories and flushed. Whenever you went into the charge room there was blood on the walls. There were incidents that were just horrendous. We went to one where a coloured boy in a club had hold of a PC by his tie – one reason why PCs now have clip-on ties – and was strangling him. I mean, you could see above the sea of heads this PC's head coming back – the veins popping and everything, and you could not get to him. Until eventually you just saw a truncheon come out and whop the boy who was strangling him, just before he lost consciousness. Of course the PC carried on hitting everyone around him. He was in an absolute frenzy. By the time we'd got the lad back to the nick there were about ten coloured kids with blood everywhere. It was like a butcher's shop. But you can see how it all happened.

Brixton nick also had the reputation that if you went through the front door you came out the back with blood on your face. And that's not one bloke doing it, that was the norm. It almost gets to the point that it has to happen to maintain the nick's reputation.

Actually it happens through lack of supervision, lack of courage on the Station or Custody Sergeant's part to actually deal with it. But if you get a situation where the Sergeant himself does the thumping, then everyone thinks, "That's what's expected of us." The Sergeants should be trying to stop the violence – but if it's the Sergeants and Inspectors doing it, you haven't got a chance. It's usually the PCs, with the Sergeants standing by. They won't participate, but they'll see it as their duty to their lads to square it all up. 85 per cent of the time a prisoner deserves it, and the Sergeant feels under an obligation to protect his men. So you invent a fierce struggle and charges of assaulting the police against the prisoner – and that's how you square up in the cell. Don't get me wrong, it's a tiny minority, but it is a constant problem. Normally we sort it out but it takes time to recognize what's happening.

HOLLOWAY ROAD

One incident clearly reflected the key problems facing the police today – violence, racial harassment and closing ranks to conceal serious misbehaviour. It happened on a summer's evening in the Holloway Road in North London in 1983.

A vanload of PCs and a Sergeant known as a District Support Unit (DSU) were cruising around the area. They had apparently been taunted by a large crowd of youths earlier in the evening but had not confronted them. Some time later they spotted a mixed-race group of youths on the street. Believing them to be part of the same group, they disembarked from the van and attacked the boys. Before making any arrests, they were called to another incident and so left the boys on the street. Their parents complained. Then followed a two-year-long cover-up by the PCs and their Sergeant that withstood a national press campaign and two separate investigations by the Criminal Investigation Branch and the Police Complaints Authority. In response to an amnesty, one of the PCs broke the silence. He has been utterly ostracized for doing so. He has since had a nervous breakdown and left the force. Another PC who testified has transferred to a northern force. Four others were sentenced to two years in prison. The Sergeant was sentenced to four years for organizing the cover-up.

Met PC, age 26, seven years service. Formerly with the SPG, now with the TSG.

The DSU were always on the front line. Any incident, the DSU were always there first. So you'd have all these psyched-up blokes, unsupervised, following the strongest character whether he was good or bad – all of a sudden they'd be deployed and they'd follow whatever he or the group says. If the Sergeant was weak, he'd just sit there. That was what happened at Holloway Road. I can see it now. They'd stopped these blokes and given them a hard time. Urgent assistance call came from round the corner and they decided they'd got to leave them and jump in the old carrier.

The police made it worse by letting them go. That was a stupid act. The common view is that if you do something like that, if you go a little bit over the top, then you've got to arrest the buggers. Don't leave them on the street. You've *got* to arrest them. Everybody thought that what they did was absolutely stupid. There were so many obvious mistakes made – things you learn as a PC just for self-protection. But nobody questions them beating the black kids up. That would be too liberal.

PCs in a large Midlands Force: PC1, age 34, fourteen years service; PC2, age 26, five years service.

PC1: I can't understand a load of disciplined policemen driving along the road, seeing a group of lads and jumping out and beating them up for the fun of it. I can understand if they stopped and the bobbies got out and spoke to them and there was a bit of a fracas with the bobbies jumping in the van and driving off. I can believe that. But I can't believe that they just got out of the van and started smacking them around any way.

I respect the man who came forward more than the others who were keeping quiet about it.
PC2: If he has had a nervous breakdown, that's why. He is a grass. He's got to live with that now. We all stick together and whatever happens happens and we don't tell anybody outside. If that was me, I wouldn't even consider a transfer, I would just leave the fucking force.

Met Sergeant, age 33, twelve years service. Now in a racially mixed area of London.

The Holloway Road verdict was quite right. I've got no sympathy for them at all. The public won't take any notice of violence against the police while you've got complete idiots like that running around doing it to the public. They'll say, "What's

good for the goose is good for the gander." It's fair comment.
We've let ourselves down.

But life isn't always black and white. For a policeman to use
minimum force all the time is very difficult, especially under
pressure. Very occasionally someone might snap and people are
going to get hit. It's difficult to say, but some slight excesses
policemen might cover up because they understand what brings
it about. That sounds awfully corrupt. If you've got friends and
you know you'll put them in prison for the next five years, it's
very difficult. Fortunately, I've never been in that circumstance.

Met PC, age 24, six years service. Now in Central London.

None of us want to work for a police force where people can
do things like at Holloway Road and get away with it. I would
never tolerate that. But you never know the whole story. People
find it very difficult to grass. The villains outside – they don't
like a grass. It's the same in here. You can always think: once
he's grassed on his mates, who's going to trust him again? It's
wrong, but it's human nature.

**Met PC, age 32, seven years service. Now a Home Beat Officer
in a sensitive inner-city area of London.**

Their punishment was not for the offence they committed, it
was the disgrace they brought on the credibility of the uniform.
If one individual sees one police officer behaving like that, then
nine times out of ten it's the uniform they're looking at, and
they say, "If that police officer beats up that individual, then all
police officers act like that." This is not true. Police officers are
individuals the same as anybody else.

I have seen, on rare occasions – very rare occasions I hasten
to add – misbehaviour by a police officer. It doesn't happen
often and it's usually out of panic. He's frightened and scared,
and he misbehaves. There's no such thing as a perfect policeman
who acts perfect all the time.

I think they were very lucky: four years is not bad after they'd
behaved like that. But as for an officer who informs – he's
finished in the Job for ever. However much contempt a bloke
may be held in – thou shall not grass on a colleague. If the price

has got to be that, we should get rid of this comradeship we seem to have aquired, this trust we have in each other. If that's the price then it's too high.

Scottish PC in a large city force, age 29, ten years service. Now in a working-class suburb.

Why did it take so long for Holloway Road to come out? Camaraderie! But there doesn't seem to be much of it at the moment. There used to be. The job's changing. The camaraderie isn't there as much. Perhaps it was a pang of conscience. You get bobbies turning to Christ. We had one here, he said: "I've turned to God, I'm a born-again Christian." He resigned, but he said: "Before I go, I want to clear the air." He told the Chief Super: "I'd like to tell you about the various arrests I've made that have been fictional." All the bobbies were shitting themselves.

Two Met PCs: PC1, age 26, three years service; PC2, age 23, three years service.

PC1: When you come out of training school there's only one thing on your mind and that's being accepted by your relief. You look out for whatever it is you have to do to be accepted and you do it. It may be looking the other way when a bloke's being hammered. If I lose my rag and get out of order and the other blokes look after me, then I'm going to do the same for them if they do something they shouldn't do.

But I'm not doing bird for anybody else, I can tell you. If it comes to that in choosing between being loyal to your mates and maybe doing bird, I'd look out for number one. You've got to in this game.

It's all right for a couple of gobby yobs to get a punch around the earhole, like they did in the Holloway Road. They probably deserved it anyway. I'm not going to cause any trouble about that. And if they'd just held firm, they'd have been all right, wouldn't they?

PC2: These days the new recruits are being taught to report anything they see that might be out of order. It's all changed now. I know one tutor Constable who took out a new probationer and said, "I'm just nipping off my beat for a coffee – and don't tell anyone, all right?" He did this three or four times in the day. The next day the Sergeant asks the probationer how was his day and the lad gives him a list of times and places the tutor Constable had his coffee. Then he did it with two more probationers – he told the second one that he was mad about ducks and was slipping off to Primrose Hill to see some ducks. The next day the Sergeant again asks the probationer how was his day, and the lad says it was all right except for all this bird-watching. The third one just confronted the tutor Constable and said he didn't like wasting his time and wanted to do some proper police work, which was a better way of handling it.

That's the way it works – the relief will sort out any troublemaker. Either they won't work with him so he's got to be moved, or they'll have words with him. We did that with a bloke who was out of order and he's good as gold now.

SUPPORT GROUPS

Every force of any size has its own Support Group of several dozen men chosen for their ability to handle themselves well in dangerous situations. They are called in to deal with sieges, riots, demonstrations and any other situation beyond the means of normal police resources. They train regularly and form a kind of macho elite corps which has its obvious dangers in encouraging aggressive behaviour. The most famous of these groups was the Special Patrol Group in the Met, known as the SPG. Five groups within the SPG were spread across London, and depending on the leadership and general age of the group their skills and discipline varied considerably from very good policemen to uncontrolled cowboys.

After a decade of bad publicity, during which they also did some good ordinary policing in plainclothes, in 1986 the SPG were turned into the TSG, the Territorial Support Group, with many more men and far more supervising officers. Ex-SPG men see this as a retrograde move that simply dilutes the quality of men in the group and makes them top heavy with supervisors, which is how many see the police as an institution.

Met Inspector, formerly with the SPG, age 38, fourteen years service. Now in South London.

I've got rid of people from the unit for being a little bit handy with their fists or feet. After seeing them in action at a demo, I'd say, "Sorry, you're exposed to it too much, and we can't handle you if you behave in that manner." You might be able to hand them on to Division, because then they're sent to violent incidents only occasionally. In a Support Group, where dealing with violence is regular, you can't afford to wait for the next time.

A lot of policemen are not too bright academically, but some of them, they've got quick minds, they're shrewd. But you get the minority – or maybe it's not the minority – who are, quite honestly, a bit dim. They join because they get a police house and a good pension and don't put themselves out very much.

If you've got a situation where some youngster who's quite bright starts making fun of them, some people can't handle it. So they turn round and slap them, because a broken nose is a great leveller. That's unacceptable in any form, where somebody can't ride out the intellectual superiority that another person has over him. You get a lot of police bitterness because people outside are cleverer or richer.

Met Sergeant, formerly with the SPG, age 34, twelve years service. Now in West London.

We used to have guys who would nick people and you'd get a call: "Urgent assistance required. Prisoner attempting to escape." So you'd race around and you'd find the guy holding on to the prisoner and you'd jump out and get him into the carrier and sit him down. Then the PC would come in and kick him. And you'd say, "Oi! What do you think you're doing?" And he'd look at you as if like, "Wait a minute, you're the SPG, don't you always kick everybody? What are you saying? I thought you were my friends." Everybody in the job has got the idea that we kick people, but we never ever do. Put it statistically: we arrested 1800 people in two years and we received only twelve complaints and only about three or four of them were for violence.

At demonstrations SPG officers were kept caged up like animals in a zoo, until things got totally out of hand. Then they'd say, "Shit, the bubble's burst, better call out the SPG." And we'd come running out into mayhem and we'd have to kick people and bang heads together to restore order. Once order was restored it was: "The SPG are animals!"

CLOSING RANKS

The process of closing ranks presents PCs with their greatest moral dilemma. The British ethos is all about people being loyal to their friends. The police culture reinforces that. The remoteness of senior officers throws young PCs into the arms of their relief, their day-to-day working colleagues. Only the training instructors and such Olympian figures as the Commissioner or Chief Constable speak of their need to stand up for what they believe is right. That is the stressful predicament: they know right from wrong very clearly. But ordinary PCs enter a moral limbo in policework that has nothing to do with enforcing the law. Their sense of security is not with the force, or the area, or even the station – it is only with their relief. They know that reporting on the actions of another PC may even help their promotion in the future, but it might put them beyond the pale of their colleagues' trust and company for as long as they remain a PC. Wherever they might go in a move to another station, their reputation will follow them. It is a classic bind in which neither decision has a clear positive outcome. It becomes a double bind because the simple moral language of senior officers takes no account of the complex pull of loyalty to the relief, and the deeply unpleasant consequences of being shunned as a "grass". It is a truly awful choice.

Met WPC, age 30, five years service in Central London.

Remember an Inspector, a Sergeant and some PCs from West End Central up at the Old Bailey on drugs, conspiring to pervert the course of justice? They'd taken some drugs from somebody. They were shopped. Not shopped as simply as that: basically a WPC who's now a Sergeant out in the East End blew the whistle on them because they'd implicated her in their hiding the drugs. They hadn't hidden the drugs for their own use, nothing as imaginative or as fun as that. It was to plant on somebody else when the time came when they hadn't got enough evidence, so they could get the bloke for possession with intent to supply, you see. She was implicated and said, "I'm not having any of this," and blew the whistle. It's all to do with signing things into a book. She knew stuff had been found that didn't appear in the book. She said "What has happened?" and was told "Shush."

She was the victim, while the inquiry was going on, of a horrendous personal vendetta. She literally had human shit smeared over her car after night duty. I think that was the nastiest thing that happened to her. Nobody would work with her. She was locked into rooms. It was an absolute nightmare. That's the sort of vendetta that goes on. There were the most hideous allegations made in the trial, and hideous allegations made personally about her afterwards. She reported the whole thing to a woman Inspector, so what do the yobs do? Allegations of lesbianism between her and the woman. It's bloody tacky, isn't it? She had a very, very nasty time indeed.

Two PCs in a large northern force: PC1, age 27, five years service; age 32, nine years service. Both now in a city centre area.

PC1: You're in a difficult situation where you see things going on out on the street with a colleague. Bobbies might not want to work with him afterwards, but to actually blow him up to a boss, no. I mean fifty uniform bobbies might know about it, because you talk about it in the canteen, and eventually a boss might overhear. But nobody will actually say: "I saw him do it." It's something about our mentality. It's "Us against Them out there" and it's also "Us against Them down the corridor". PC2 If you get a reputation early on for not conforming to what they want you to do, then you can be written off by your peers very quickly. You gain very few friends in the police – friends that will stand by you when something goes wrong. Everyone will turn their back on you, because they don't want to drop themselves in the crap. I could name maybe two or three people

I could trust, that was after three years in the police. That's the reason a lot of naive bobbies will do what their peers tell them to do, because you don't want to walk into the canteen and everybody sits at a different table. And once you're out there, especially a uniform bobby, you could well be on your own if they want you to be.

PC1: Jesus! You know, their radios "didn't work", they "never heard you ask for back-up". That's frightening.

PC2: It gives you a funny sense to back your mates up. You didn't see it, but, "Yeah, I did see it." We all want friends. Nobody wants to come to work and find that everybody hates you.

Sergeant in a large northern force, age 34, fourteen years service. Now in an inner-city area.

Not long ago, a couple of lads from a unit brought in a guy for possession of drugs. The drug is produced to the bobby on duty at the station and he recognizes it. It looks like the same stuff that was produced in another case some time earlier. It was the same forensic analysis. He gets the prisoner to one side, chats to him, finds out he is quite a well-to-do young lad, well spoken, no problems or hang-ups, never been in trouble before. He tells the story that he was walking down the road, two of our lads jump out of a verhicle, grab him, throw him in, tell him he is locked up for drugs, put their hands in his pockets and come out with that. He had never taken drugs in his life, hates them and just had nothing to do with it.

This bobby blew the whistle. There was an investigation and this civilian guy was cleared. He didn't make a complaint. He was told he could have done, but he didn't. He was pro-police, the sort of guy we should be cultivating. Now this bobby has broken the buddy system, but he got 100 per cent support. He was no young bobby, and he had got a lot of service in. He thought very carefully about it beforehand because obviously he knew all the implications. I mean he had balls. He openly said what he had done to anyone who wanted to ask him. Of course the story got around, as it does on the bush telegraph. But I never heard one person say he was wrong.

Met Commander, age 43, twenty years service. Now in Central London.

Some of the injuries inflicted on people who are caught up in this exercise of coercive force are getting worse. We have people who have died in London in the process of being arrested. It isn't just Blair Peach, the teacher who died in Southall, or John Mikkelson, the Hell's Angel. There are others who die each year.

Complaints of assault are by far the highest category of the 5000 or so complaints in London in a given year. Over 1000 will be of assault. Arrest is a conflict situation; there is bound to be some resistance, token or otherwise. The police officer is at one time most likely going to have to get a little heavy. We can handle that. What I cannot live with and increasingly come across is violence inflicted on the public or prisoners after the arrest when they actually presented no threat at all. I'm talking of assaults on people in vans, and it's not just one van in a famous place [Holloway Road]. There are many more than that. I'm talking of violence on prisoners in police stations, within custody suites. They comprise almost half of the complaints of assault made against police. That is worrying.

Why are police officers more violent? You come into this thing about perception. Police officers start their actual duties on the streets of London full of idealism and some excellent training. Some of it gets lost along the way. The intensity of other people's experience and jaundice and cynicism is given full vent in a very short time. The tutor Constable ought to be moderate in the kind of advice and counselling that he gives the young man but not all of them will be like that. And then there is another tutor, who we don't recognize within the system, the guy with five or six years service, the guy in the canteen who is going very quickly to knock all this idealism out of a young man. Very quickly police officers with less than twelve months' experience will become themselves a part of a perception, which I think is flawed, that they are doing a very dangerous job in an almost exclusively hostile world where it's hit first or be hit.

Where we have most difficulty investigating allegations, where we find officers closing ranks and truly believing that it's legitimate to do it, is around this exercise of violence where an officer is alleged to have thumped somebody either in a van on the way to the station, or in the station itself. They will see as quite legitimate the withholding of information about that. That is deeply worrying because some of the injuries inflicted are extremely serious and in a few cases they lead to death. It's not typical but it is part of the extreme. Tapering off the end of this violence is the verbal violence, the antagonism, the attitude problem. It is all part of the same continuum. The problem is one of polarization and of perception. We increasingly have a police service that has this perception of itself as under attack from the whole of society. Therefore to defend itself the use of violence is appropriate.

CHAPTER EIGHT

Complaints

The latest arrangements for complaints against the police reflect the police predicament all too well: both the public and the police mistrust them for opposite reasons. The public see them as weak, unreliable, legalistic, endless and biased against them. Many people do not complain about police behaviour because of this cynicism, or for fear of police harassment. The police, on the other hand, regard the complaints system as ruthless, petty, pandering to the wrong elements of society, legalistic, endless, stressful and biased against them.

When a member of the public complains, he or she must make a statement to set the process in motion. The officer taking that first statement will be from the same station as the officer complained against. He may well be torn between protecting his colleague and his obligation to the public. Frequent attempts are made to dissuade the complainant from proceeding, either warning of the consequences for the officer concerned or the implied consequences for the complainant as well. Forty to fifty per cent of complaints are dropped at this stage. The police believe this proves they were trivial or vexatious, but they do not acknowledge the degree of intimidation often involved. It is now policy to seek informal resolution of complaints where there is no likelihood of disciplinary or criminal proceedings against the officer.

Once a complaint is formally lodged, the PC is notified and a senior officer from another station, or even from another force, begins the investigation. A blanket of silence that can last for years descends on the case, leaving both the complainant and the police officer angry and frustrated.

Met Commander, age 44, twenty-three years service.

At the moment, the single biggest category is a complaint of assault on the way from the site of an arrest to the police station, in a van or whatever. PACE has made violent behaviour inside the police station much riskier, and officers are now less tolerant of it in public, anyway. The majority of allegations are unsubstantiated. We've got to accept, though, in a mature way that the client group of the police [Society], if you like, have nothing to lose by making complaints, so there is an element of maliciousness in it, but a number are undoubtedly true.

Superintendent in a Home Counties force, age 46, twenty years service. Now in an industrial suburb.

Having worked in Complaints and Discipline I know how working policemen operate, the whole strategy, the philosophy that dictates the work. When I was in Discipline there were two definitions with regard to allegations of assault. On one side was the PC who, for no reason other than the fact that he's a bully and a thug, would assault a prisoner where there was no need. When you question him he'd be stone deaf. I'd investigate that like I'd investigate an armed robbery, to get him before a court and convicted of a criminal offence of assault. But then, on the other side of the coin, was the complaint against the good, solid, practical copper, whether he be a PC or an Inspector, don't matter who he was, who was always putting himself in the front line and trying to do the job to the best of his ability. Not easy, because just now he's a minority in the police service. In that situation, he is much more likely to find himself in bother. OK – that fellow is out on the street and he is confronted by a hostile situation. He goes overboard and gives out a fucking good hiding. The chances are he would never, never be thrown out. I would have made sure I interviewed witnesses I knew were going to come down on his side, though I never intentionally suppressed evidence.

For instance – this is a classic. Four Marines: home on Christmas leave got really pissed, were making an absolute fucking nuisance of themselves to women doing their Christmas shopping. Two young bobbies warn them to behave themselves. The Marines get really stroppy and start to take the piss out of the two young bobbies. They call up an experienced PC, a real hard man, to assist. He wades in and really goes to town on these four to tell them that's the finish of it. They have a crack at him. He knocks six bells of shit out of them. But they're Marines and they are bastards. They're drunk but they give him a fair time. The two PCs help as well but they're passengers really. One of the Marines ends up in hospital and his parents go to the police and make a complaint.

Now, members of the public seeing that going on, perhaps in the later stages of the incident, would have said, "Police bastards!" But it's totally out of context; here are Marines, bloody pissed, who'd have been able to look after themselves anyway. Very difficult, you see. It's absolute ignorance on people's part, the general public in a square box – the lowest guy, the road sweeper, to Margaret Thatcher. They are totally ignorant of what a policeman's difficulties are.

Met PC, age 31, three years service. Now in the TSG.

People I know outside come to me and say, "I don't want you to get involved at all because you'll have a really hard time, but this is what happened to me. I'm not making a complaint about it ..." I must admit half the time I've told them to make a complaint because it's been outrageous. Way out of order.

When a policeman gets a complaint made about him, he'll say to his mates: "When I see that bastard, I'll nick him again. I'll give him a real tough time." But it does deter them. They'll think twice about it. It doesn't help, though, that when you're first brought into the force you're told by guv'nors that if you don't get certain numbers of complaints you're not a working policeman. Some people take that to mean you can do things that are out of order and "so what" if you get a complaint. You've got the canteen cowboy who's the only man you can hear in the canteen telling you, "I've had so many complaints it's never affected me. All these wimps in the job, they come here and they're scared of complaints. I've had 342 and I'm still in the job."

The normal, sensible PC who wants to do his job is worried about complaints. Let's face it, in the last years we've seen people getting kicked out. So you try and do your job professionally. Not just for that reason, but because you're proud of being a policeman. I know it sounds corny, but you do feel that.

PC, age 46, twenty-four years service. Now a village bobby in a Home Counties force.

I don't know why discipline slipped. Years ago, in the old style, there was discipline. I can see what's happened with Sergeants and Inspectors; they're too young, too inexperienced. They won't be disciplinarians because they are too close to the PCs. I don't know what's happened to the senior officers. We had an example recently with two probationers who had really been out of order. They had failed to turn up for duty and had lied about it. They had a terrible attitude problem and this was only their first year. The Chief Superintendent said, "We'll let it go with a slap on the wrists." A sit-down with the Chief Superintendent and a slap on the wrists does nothing but send them out afterwards to have a big laugh about it. There's this unwillingness to become unpopular.

When I first joined I was petrified. If I was late I thought my Sergeant would kill me. Now they turn up and they don't even apologize. If you pull them and say, "Where have you been?" they'll say, "What's the big deal?" It's our fault, and it comes from the top. Nowadays a lot of people are just uniform carriers.

The Police Federation points to the 5000 complaints in one year against the Metropolitan Police as a tiny fraction of the several million contacts with the public. Many ordinary PCs fail to see the link between the handling of complaints and the restoration of public confidence, the ultimate weapon in their campaign.

Scottish Inspector, age 35, fourteen years service in a city centre.

We get complaints because we've taken twenty minutes to respond to a call. Even the Gas Board usually aren't that quick when you've got danger. I think people have a high expectation of what they will get from us and then they are quite willing to complain. They've almost been encouraged to complain, it seems.

PC in a southern Home Counties force, age 30, ten years service.

I have been complained against over the years by some real idiots and loonies. The people who have complained have been either malicious or weird, and the complaints have always been unfounded. But each complaint is treated exactly the same way. It is pursued according to the Police Discipline Code. One man who had just left a local hospital complained that I put "rays" in the back of his head to make him go forwards. I had trouble with another bloke who, after getting ten years for conspiracy to rob, and his solicitor has told him there is no way he can appeal, took the only way out, which was to complain against the officers who dealt with it. Even though he had not made these serious allegations before that point they were still investigated enthusiastically. The same waste of manpower; the same idea that because there is a complaint, there must be something behind it.

Met Chief Inspector, age 43, twenty-four years service. Now in Complaints and Discipline.

Some of the trivial complaints are absurd. Someone might complain they have seen an officer on the street sucking a sweet. Vicious complaints where a motorist gets stopped, an arrogant character, doesn't like the police, gives the officer a really hard time, and the officer books him. The bloke will complain thinking the summons will be dropped. When the summons isn't withdrawn they make amazing allegations: the officer was effing and blinding, kicked the car, all that sort of thing.

Then there are internal complaints. An officer is late on duty or is off his patrol, or has a slight accident in a police car and doesn't report it. A police officer complained about another PC who threw a firework in the canteen. As a result, the first PC went a bit deaf – absolutely incredible.

You get complaints involving people off duty, like an officer had a barbecue in his garden and the next-door neighbour didn't like the smell of his pork chops and kebabs. Our Discipline Code is quite clear about "not bringing the force into disrepute" blah, blah, blah. That person made an official complaint; it had to be investigated, costing a few thousand pounds. It's rare, but it has happened. A police officer, off duty, his dog might crap in someone's front garden by accident. It's a complaint.

PC in a large Midlands force, age 26, seven years service. Now in an urban area.

Who are these fucking people? They will take the public's word more than they will take a policeman's word.

About four weeks ago I was off duty with a Special Branch bloke. We went to talk about something, and three fellows asked for directions and I gave them directions. Me and this Special Branch man go in for a meal in a restaurant, and we were just having coffee when the guys walk in and one says, "Excuse me, did you just give me directions?" I says "Yeah" and he punches me in the face. There's a big fight and they get locked up. They got injured; they hit me and I hit them back. One got a bust nose. The very next day, I come in black eye, bruised, sore, swollen. No one had rung up to see if I was all right. But the next day I was in the boss's office and he's saying, "What were you doing?" and such and such. He doesn't believe me that's how it happened. It was in my report. That to me is shit. These three poor innocent fellows, by the way, openly admitted later what they had done.

RUC PC, age 29, eight years service. Now in a border town.

I go and investigate each crime bearing in mind that this could be a genuine claim or it could be a fraud, or just a nutter. You investigate according to the merits. The rule book says a report should be made, but you don't investigate every crime equally tenaciously. When you know the crime is nonexistent, it is a waste of manpower. Yet the Discipline Code shows no such side to it.

THE RUBBER HEELS SQUAD

The investigating officers in Complaints and Discipline, are regarded as part of a different force while they are assigned there. It is a posting few police officers enjoy. Perhaps fuelled by their sense of isolation, the interrogations they conduct of fellow officers are often rough and persistent, leaving interviewees much aggrieved.

PC in a Midlands force, age 35, twelve years service. Now in a racially mixed inner-city area.

Our Complaints Department – even though they're policemen too – seem to want to bring policemen down. There was one case where, even though the court turned down an allegation of assault against a policeman, two Complaints Officers were still determined to get him on something. They went through his pocket notebooks from years back, just trying to find something to fault for a disciplinary offence. They turned up all sorts of things. Obviously things that you sometimes regret. Not serious things. I know I've made mistakes in the past, like how I've spoken rudely to people, but they've been genuine mistakes. We're not just robots roaming the streets.

Inspector in a Home Counties force south of London, age 38, nineteen years service. Now in a suburban town.

I don't think most investigating officers want to get people the sack really, unless they are bad ones and you have great pleasure in getting them by the scruff of the neck. It can be particularly difficult if I work on the same patch as the officer being complained about, I'm treated like some leper. It's not a nice job.

RUC Sergeant, age 30, nine years service. Now in a border town.

You often hear: "He's moved over to Complaints – he must be mad! What does he want to work over there for?" I find it difficult to make out officers who would work in Complaints. I guess they must get some satisfaction from it. A lot of officers look at people who work in Complaints and they say, "They're holier than thou. They feel that they're better than all other officers." They're not. They're just ordinary officers doing rather a difficult and unsavoury job. I think the system that we've got for dealing with police officers that misbehave is adequate, no more than that.

Met Chief Inspector, age 45, twenty-five years service. Now in a racially mixed inner-city area of London.

There are two levels of complaint. There is the Central Investigation Bureau, which is based at Scotland Yard. That team of officers – Chief Inspectors and above – deals with very serious complaints: corruption, burglary, the more serious, criminal type of offences. I was at District Disciplinary Complaints where we dealt with things like allegations of assault. The most serious assault would be what we call a Section 47 assault which would be a hit with the fist where there's a cut. Abuse, bad language, excessive force in arresting people, small thefts – some offences are criminal and some are against the Discipline Code. Some embrace both, for instance, when officers have searched a house for drugs or something and they have gone in and smashed doors down, pulled out drawers and generally thrown their weight around. I investigated about 150 in my time. It is a pretty horrible job. Part of me felt it was an important job. If someone is doing something wrong and upsetting the public then they don't deserve to be in the police force. However, it was quite clear that in a number of cases the officer was carrying out his or her duty in the way they thought best, resulting in a peeved member of the public who just made a complaint. In those cases the officers are under a lot of stress, especially when they feel they haven't done anything wrong. That happens quite often.

THE BURDEN OF DISCRETION

The legal position of the Constable exercising his powers of arrest gives him a certain discretion. This leaves him open to complaint for wrongful arrest, which could lead to disciplinary action against him. In the case of assault, he is vulnerable to criminal prosecution as well. After the officers who shot Stephen Waldorf by mistake went on trial and were acquitted, the Police

Federation actually proposed an immunity from prosecution for officers who wound or kill civilians in the course of their duty. This reflects a general desire by PCs to be given clear directions by their superiors or by the law so that their individual responsibility is lessened. If things go wrong, they feel the system should take more of the blame.

Inspector in a Midlands force, age 30, ten years service. Now in an industrial town.

I've just had the papers through withdrawing a complaint against me. It was a public order situation where a lot of policemen and senior officers ducked and weaved and got out of it, didn't want to know. Because certain of us took on their responsibilities, we ended up being complained about. For two and half years it was up in the air. It goes to headquarters, and then it's got to go through the Deputy Chief Constable, who may send it to the Director of Public Prosecutions. When it comes back from him it has then got to go to the Police Complaints Authority. I can assure you that as police officers we get treated worse than the public from that aspect of complaints. I was lucky I was promoted after all that.

That's how the job works and you have got to accept it, but for eighteen months we were all suspected of perhaps a criminal offence. How are you supposed to go out and work every day? How are you supposed to go out and produce your stick again in a dangerous situation?

Met Superintendent, age 47, twenty years service. Now in an inner-city area of London.

"Little Johnny's never done a wrong thing in his life, it's only you nasty coppers that keep arresting him." When there is an allegation of crime, it gets very tricky. If a chap claims to have been assaulted by a policeman while being arrested, you have to call a doctor to check his injuries. But nearly always those injuries are the result of the man's resisting arrest. If he dies subsequently because he cracked his head on the pavement in the fight, then we just have to put that down to bad luck. There aren't that many people who die as a result of that. In London we have about ten to fifteen a year who die in the cells – of heart attacks, drunkenness, hardly ever from violence from us. But we always have to check it out.

The police officers concerned are notified that a complaint has been made, unless it will impede the investigation, such as in criminal cases where it has been alleged that PC Bloggs is stealing regularly from a shop. The officer may need counselling. If it's a young officer, he might think his world is at an end. More senior PCs have probably had several complaints. The more active a copper is, the more complaints he gets. But the quiet little chap who hasn't done a lot may find he has to arrest some nasty fellow who will make a malicious complaint. Often a malicious complaint won't seem so at first sight.

The judgement as to what should be done is made at the end of the investigation. The poor fellow just has to wait until it is finished.

LAY VISITORS

The Police and Criminal Evidence Act of 1984 attempted to deal with allegations of misconduct within police stations by setting up a system of lay visitors. They must be given access to the charge room and the cells at any hour of the day or night, unannounced. Some officers report this as working well, as it opens the eyes of the public to the reality of policing. In some areas, the major problem is finding people willing to visit once they have discovered how boring life in most police stations can be. But when things do go wrong – most often with drunks in the early morning hours – lay visitors are unlikely to be present.

Met PC, age 28, seven years service. Now in a racially mixed area of West London.

A gang had gone in to have a fight with the occupants of a drinker and the police were called. There was a regular battle going on. Lots of prisoners were brought back and there was this poor Sergeant, the Custody Officer, sitting there having a nice quiet evening and the next thing, chaos descends from on high. There was mayhem in the charge room with people shouting and screaming and blood everywhere – absolute chaos. You've got to keep the prisoners under control, you hold them to try and keep them still for their own safety as well as the safety of the officers present.

One officer did something outrageous. I'm not prepared to say what he did. Suffice to say that it was outrageous, and he is now the subject of a serious complaint. What he did happened in seconds. Unfortunately the skipper didn't see this, he was concentrating on the mayhem, but it happened right next to a solicitor who made a complaint. That was the source of all the prisoners there making complaints against virtually every officer they could see. Certainly one of them had a justifiable complaint. He was the victim of the misbehaviour.

In the end the Sergeant gets a complaint as well about his lack of supervision over the one officer who misbehaved badly towards one of the prisoners. I felt sorry for the Sergeant getting this complaint. How could he see everything that was going on? He was a lovely bloke, one of the old types. I've never seen him do anything wrong. I saw the Sergeant when he came out of the interview – he looked like death warmed up. He was all white, his eyes were glazed. You'd think he'd just had ten pints of beer! He almost looked drunk – a state of shock perhaps. I said, "Christ, Sarge, you look ill!" He said, "So would you if you'd just sat there for the last seven hours!"

Met Superintendent, age 47, twenty-seven years service. Now in a special squad.

In legal language, all these things are tied up with the *mens rea,* which means a man's state of mind at the time he commits an act. Did he ever show any intent, criminal intent, to do harm? It is very difficult to presume that, with a police operation set up in advance. So Complaints Officers will be asking themselves, "Why was he there? – Stopping someone, or going into a cell. Did he want to be there and was he just doing what he's paid for?" The whole ambience of a Complaints inquiry is inflected that way, unless you seriously believe that the officers involved actively stepped outside their role and deliberately did something they knew to be criminal and intended to do it criminally. That's a culture jump. That doesn't say that police officers won't do anything wrong a) in the heat of the moment or b) purely by misjudgement or c) because they get angry and flip. All of those things happen and give rise to the complaints that you see too much daily. Those are roughly the three areas where things can go wrong.

I've been associated with a high-profile squad, constantly examined for so long now that I have come to live with the fact that everything you do will be the subject of an inquiry. I accept that it's necessary. I don't resent that side of my life any more.

STRESSFUL LIMBO

Complaints have always been a sore spot for the police. As a disciplined force they are expected to act in a disciplined way. Yet they have created a bureaucratic system to deal with complaints whose delays insulate officers from the direct consequences of their actions. But it often leaves them in stressful limbo for years.

PC in a northern force, age 30, seven years service. Now in an inner-city area.

It comes down to people's total unreasonableness towards others. You see it all the time on the roads, in the horrendous state of driving. When you stop somebody for going through a red traffic light, he will argue the toss with you until the sun goes down. They say, "Be civil to a member of the public." You get so much aggravation you can't talk to some of these people.

I've been commended at Crown Court by the judge for my tact and diplomacy when this bloke assaulted me. He still made a malicious complaint that I had assaulted him in the back of the van, when he had been taken to the station by *other officers!* The complaint hung over my head. I didn't receive the commendation until the complaint had been quashed. I'd actually received compensation from the court as well, but the commendation came through six months later, after he'd finally agreed the complaint was malicious. But there's nothing done about him. That's besmirched my character. In the front of my file is "Complaint: Assault". That looks bloody marvellous on your record, that. It's never proven, but it stays there on your file. So somebody just reading through records thinks, "This guy's a bit naughty."

DEMOTION AND DISMISSAL

The threat of disciplinary action is more worrying to most officers than its practical reality. The terms for applying it are so strict that it is relatively rare. Demotion, which is a familiar punishment for failure, incompetence or misbehaviour in the world outside is applied much less often in the police. According to the current terms of employment, dismissal is only possible through a full-fledged disciplinary court finding the accused guilty of one of a small number of dismissable offences. In those cases, they first enter the limbo of suspension.

Met Deputy Assistant Commissioner, age 43, twenty-five years service.

One of the fundamental problems is that the job is too protective. We make these great demands about professionalism; we demand a professional salary and so on. But one of the things about professionalism is that we must go on adhering to the tenets of the job, which means to actually carry out your oath. As in all large organizations there are a few officers who gave up working a long time ago. Yet, because of the way the police is structured, they've got a job for thirty years.

Met Chief Superintendent, age 50, twenty-five years service. Now in an inner-city area of London.

There's a Superintendent in this area who has just been demoted to Chief Inspector. He was demoted on discipline because he had certain investigations to carry out in the area and he just didn't do them. We had all sorts of repercussions over it. It was neglect of duty.

There's no way you can demote anybody in this service unless you go through the formal disciplinary procedure. It's a bit unwieldy. I know people who have been suspended from duty two years before the Discipline Court. That is quite wrong. You wouldn't treat criminals like that. I actually put in a long detailed report on this state of affairs on a couple of occasions, right to the top. I got feedback: "Yes, something is going to be done about it." It's improving. We've got it down now from three years to two. But why should that chap be under that sort of pressure for that length of time irrespective of what he's done? It's his family as well. When he's suspended, welfare-wise, people should go and see him. But human nature being what it is, out of sight, out of mind. He's pretty isolated. Having said that, for somebody to be suspended from duty he's got to have done something wrong. Not because Mrs Bloggs complained that he swore at her. It'd be an allegation of corruption, assault or bribery – something pretty serious. We have 200 officers suspended at any one time.

The reason it can take years is that if it's a criminal inquiry, the criminal aspects have got to be investigated. The papers go to the Director of Public Prosecutions. Many months later he makes a decision. Then comes the disciplinary investigation which might take at least three or four months. It'll go to the Director and that can take two or three months because the Director has a pile to start with. He doesn't sort out the policemen and put them on top of the pile. They just take their turn the same as everybody else.

I feel very strongly about it – it could be streamlined dramatically. I think it is pure bureaucracy, people dragging their heels, not moving quick enough from department to department for decisions to be made.

CIVILIAN REVIEW

The apparent failure of the police to investigate themselves has fuelled the pressure for independent bodies to investigate complaints. This has been resisted for the past twenty years. Sir Robert Mark retired early as Commissioner of the Met because Roy Jenkins, then Home Secretary, insisted on pressing ahead with the establishment of the Police Complaints Board, to provide civilian review of police handling of complaints after

*the fact. But the PCB rarely used its modest authority. In some
40,000 cases between 1977 and 1980, the PCB disagreed with
the police in only 65. They never called in a single case to be
reviewed in tribunal. Yet this was the period about which Lord
Scarman was so critical of police behaviour in the inner cities,
when the "sus" law was widely used to stop and search black
youths. Inevitably public disquiet with the police handling of
complaints continued.*

*In 1984, the Police and Criminal Evidence Act established the
Police Complaints Authority with more teeth than the PCB.
They can oversee important cases during investigation, ask for
cases to be referred to them and recommend disciplinary action,
but they still rely on the police to do the actual investigating.
Also their powers are still severely limited. When two old ladies
were killed by a speeding police car, the PCA asked for the case
to be referred to them because the only two civilians to be a
party to the matter were now dead. The force involved simply
refused. Cynics speculated that the limited powers of the Police
Complaints Authority were a Home Office trade off to win
police support for ceding their power to prosecute. An independent Crown Prosecution Service was also established by the
1984 Act (see "Law, Justice and the Courts").*

**Superintendent in a northern force, age 42, seventeen years
service. Now in city centre.**

The Police Complaints Authority is an administrative and investigative nightmare. It doesn't allay public fears and it has no
respect from the police. Less than one per cent of complaints
get acted on, so police now realize there is little chance of
anything serious being done about a complaint. So they don't
worry about it. At public order situations like football matches,
you get this cavalier attitude. They think, "What the hell, it
doesn't matter if I get a complaint for our behaviour, they won't
be able to identify us anyway."

In my day when anyone got a complaint it was the talk of
the division, it was discussed in the canteen for weeks. 80 per
cent of complaints are never substantiated anyway, not because
we don't believe it happened, but just for lack of adequate
evidence. We have to meet the same standard as the criminal

law, "beyond all reasonable doubt." Almost impossible without witnesses willing to verify it. The ironic thing is that since we've had case screening to make better use of our time, if you're burgled, you get a PC at your door to see if there's any hope of tracing the gear or the villains. If the evidence is slight, there'll be no more done about it. But if you complain about that PC's behaviour or tone of voice, an investigation is set in motion that may last months or even years, and involve many hours of police time up to Superintendent level.

Superintendent in a Midlands force, age 43, nineteen years service. Now in a city centre area.

It's reached the point where I was sent to a neighbouring force to do a complaint, and as it's customary, you tell the local Super out of courtesy you're on his patch. But the local Super wasn't there. He'd gone to someone else's patch to do a complaint. When I got back, I found a Super in my office, investigating some of my blokes. It's all going haywire, it's a mismanagement of police resources, which is why for our different reasons, we all want an independent body to conduct those investigations.

I don't go along with the notion that only the police can police the police. I mean look at Customs and Excise, or the Income Tax people. It only takes time to learn the police way of doing things. We don't have a monopoly of investigation.

Superintendent in a Home Counties force, age 48, twenty-three years service. In charge of a large suburban town.

The Police Complaints Authority are doing their absolute level best to try and show the public that they're independent. Consequently, they go in too quickly. When someone has been injured, or there's been some sort of confrontation, the last thing we want is someone on TV saying the Police Complaints Authority is investigating this.

Everyone seems to think there is a manpower allocation in which to do complaints. There isn't. A complaint is something you do in addition to your normal daily work, when you can. It takes bloody months and no one thinks twice about putting resources into matters that are often very trivial.

Take this complaint I've got now. It's at bloody Ramsgate and a hundred people are involved, and I'm up here, hours away. I keep going to Ramsgate on the way home and spending a couple of hours there. I don't think people appreciate exactly what all this costs in time and money. You fetch up forests full of paper. And when you keep coming to see the same people again and again, witnesses start to think they may well have been mistaken in the first place. In the old days, before there was a complaints system, when malicious complaints were made the loyal Sergeant said, "Yes, and pigs have wings."

Met Commander, age 47, twenty-six years service. Now in North London.

I think the police service themselves – myself included – would be quite happy for somebody outside to investigate the complaints against us. Having said that, I'm not sure if an outsider could because everybody would clamp up and not say anything. The only reason they get the inquiries and investigations done now is because there's a common bond between the inquirer and the person who's inquired against. There's a certain amount to be said for ex-policemen doing it. But then again, if it were ex-policemen the public would see it as the same. In this area we've got eight Chief Inspectors and eight Sergeants doing nothing else but investigating complaints against police – that's in this area alone. We're split into eight areas – there's something like sixty Chief Inspectors. A Chief Inspector is a very senior officer. But the law that's laid down states that nobody below the rank of Chief Inspector and, indeed, in the provinces, nobody under the rank of Superintendent can do the investigation. He's a very expensive resource.

THE WALL OF SILENCE

The Police Complaints Authority finds itself neutered by police officers closing ranks – what they call "the wall of silence". In 1987, out of a total of 11,560 cases, there was conflicting evidence or a lack of evidence in 10,018 of them. No one can tell how many of those officers involved are sticking together. One young PC told me how he had been taken aside by a Detective Inspector after telling the truth at a disciplinary inquiry. "First lesson. Never tell the truth. Deny as much as possible." It was exactly this attitude that led to the Holloway Road cover-up.

Met Chief Inspector, age 45, twenty-five years service. Just retired.

There are many complaints where an investigating officer knows the member of the public is not telling "porky pies", they have a real grievance. But it is often very hard to substantiate. You might have an officer who has a record of fifteen assaults, none of which have been substantiated through lack of evidence. Nothing the police can do. You can't sack him. We can't actually do anything but say "watch it".

I don't suppose more than 15 per cent of the complaints I dealt with were actually substantiated. The rest may have been true but could not be proved.

POOR RESULTS

Only 1 per cent of surviving complaints are proven and dealt with in disciplinary hearings. Only 8 per cent produce lighter penalties – warnings or reprimands. By far the greater number are dismissed for lack of adequate evidence. A complaint must be proved beyond all reasonable doubt, the same standard that applies in the criminal courts. Therefore, the Director of Public Prosecutions takes a very strict line with complaints against the police. Of the 1367 cases referred to him in 1987 by the civilian watchdog, the Police Complaints Authority, 440 were for assault. He recommended proceeding with only one case of assault. Under current guidelines a case should only go to trial when there is a better than 51 per cent chance of a conviction.

This is deeply unsatisfactory for both the public and the police. It feeds public suspicion that the police are incapable of investigating themselves. Civil actions against the police in the London area have gone up four-fold in fifteen years. Evidential standards are lower in civil courts: the plaintiff has only to establish a balance of probabilities in his favour rather than prove a case beyond reasonable doubt. This has proved expens-

ive – in 1986 the Met paid out more than £375,000 in com-
pensation compared to £200 in 1973. It also delays any internal
disciplinary hearing until after the trial, leaving the accused
officer's career prospects in jeopardy for as long as six years.

Met PC, age 24, three years service. Now in West London.

What do you do if somebody you work with – a family man
with a wife and a couple of kids, nice bloke not aggressive,
usually good as gold – suddenly flips one day? He goes berserk
and kicks shit out of a prisoner. Fair enough, he's out of order,
but if you grass him up that bloke's going to go to prison – he's
got a wife and kids – just because one day he flips. How am I
going to feel afterwards?

**Met Commander, age 40, eighteen years service in an inner-
city area of London.**

Most police officers would agree that officers who are guilty of
malpractice, of serious misconduct, deserve all they get. If you
look at the level of complaints in London, at the moment it
runs at just over 5000; it was only six years ago running at just
over 8000. It has fallen off. Most of the ones that have gone
have moved into the new category of "informal resolution".
The public don't want this great ritual of formalized investigation. They don't want the prospect of giving evidence in a
hearing. They want the police to do two things: to acknowledge
error and to say "I'm sorry". But policemen by their very
instinct – or is it their training? – find it very hard to say "I'm
sorry".

We have made the whole thing of complaints investigation
terribly difficult. The courts are an enormous legalistic machine,
grinding on remorselessly.

But we produce very little that's useful through the complaints
procedure either by way of punishing guilty officers, or ridding
our ranks of them, in the extreme cases. At worst we catch too
many officers in the machinery itself that ill deserve to be there.
It has less and less to do with justice, either to the complainant
or the officer.

Enormous amounts of money are wasted this way, and the

public is paying. So we've raised the threshold of cases worth running. Now that counsel are in on disciplinary hearings, the investigating officer knows he will be challenged by counsel who has all the luxury of time to dissect your case – just as PCs fear defence counsel dissecting the prosecution case in court. So he's now a lot more circumspect, a lot more cautious about what he brings to court. There are fewer cases going forward, and those that do take far far too long. As the trend for complainants to take civil actions against us grows, it can take five or six years before the police internally address the issues themselves. What I ask is that they cooperate with us at the same time because only in that way can we clean out the stable.

CONVICTION AND GAOL

The number of police officers actually convicted of crimes is very small. Whatever suspicions juries have of police evidence against civilians, they are notoriously reluctant to convict policemen. When they do, it is trouble for the officer concerned from the media, from his family and from other prisoners. The flak hits other police officers as well.

PC in Home Counties force, age 31, nine years service. Now in a coastal town.

I suppose it is a weird form of compliment that whenever a PC or even an ex-PC gets into trouble, the headlines shout "Copper In the Shit Again!" whatever he's done. You don't see "Ex-Plumber in Love Nest" now, do you?

Met PC, age 28, four years service. Resigned from the force in advance of prosecution for theft and criminal damage.

I was driving down the road with three friends and jumped a red light. I was off duty and was pulled by Traffic Division and I can honestly say I was actually frightened. I thought, "For Christ's sake, I'm a police officer," and yet these two people were frightening the life out of me. They were incredibly aggressive. I was driving three people back from a pub. They'd been drinking and I hadn't. It was raining quite heavily and the windows were wound up. It was steamy and you couldn't see a thing and the Traffic guys said, "Right you've been drinking. Get out of the car. We want a breath test." They took the test and much to their amazement I passed it. They genuinely thought that I was paralytic. They stuck me on for the red light. I didn't say I was in the police or anything like that. They said "Have you got any ID?" I said that I'd got a warrant card but I didn't say where from. They probably thought that I was from outside the Met anyway because the car was registered at my parents' address. So they thought, "We'll have him – it's a bit of sport!" The paperwork went to my own police station and was put in the minor process section.

I was too proud to appear at the local court. It's pathetic really. If it happened at any other court I wouldn't have worried because I wouldn't have been known. Unfortunately I was looked upon by other police officers as a kind of model police-man and it felt as if there was this weak link in my armour. So I went into the station one morning very early and removed the books. Stupid, it was stupid. If I had appeared at the court I would have got a £25 fine and three points on my licence, whereas what did happen was I lost my job. I destroyed the papers.

When I was interviewed by Scotland Yard they took con-temporaneous notes and that went to the DPP. I was inter-viewed by them at nine o'clock for about forty minutes, then went down to the Commander who said the best thing I could do was resign. Whatever was going to happen I was going to resign. Some people get suspended and drag it out for a year and a half and stay on full pay until it comes to court. Anyway I resigned, handed in my uniform, my warrant card and left. It was really weird to work for over four years and then come in one day and go through all that and leave. About three months later I heard from the DPP that they were going to charge me. The police treated me really well. My colleagues at the station were really supportive and that made me feel even more ashamed of taking the papers. I felt I'd really let them down. That was more upsetting than actually leaving. If I'd gone to court in the first place they would have taken the piss out of me for a couple of weeks, maybe not even that, it was no big deal. It wasn't as if I'd gone out and mugged somebody.

When I left my flat to go to the Old Bailey the first problem that I had was at the station. I didn't know whether to buy a single ticket or a return! I got a return ticket.

I went into the court and it was really strange to be standing in the dock. You really feel alone and that everyone is deciding your life for you in your absence. You just sit there listening to everyone talking about you, without being able to interrupt. If someone says something nice about you, you feel like standing up and saying "That's not quite true. I'm not as nice as that!"

During the proceedings the court was adjourned for twenty minutes and I was taken out by the prison staff and down into the cells. That was the first time I'd been confronted with the reality of being put inside. You leave all your friends in the court and you're taken away. It's really odd and very frightening. I asked the prison officers what they thought was going to happen to me, would I get a prison sentence? They said, "In our opinion we think you will." I asked, "What's going to happen?" They said, "It's bad news really. You are an ex-policeman and you'll get a really hard time in prison. As far as we're concerned you are a pain in the neck. We'd far rather have normal criminals. You're going to be real bad news to us. We're going to have to try and make sure you don't get your head kicked in. We'd rather you didn't get a prison sentence. Basically what will happen is that you'll be totally dehumanized. You'll be taken downstairs, showered, all your clothes will be taken and you'll be given prison garb, your hair will be cut, you'll be anonymous. The best thing you can do if you do get sent down is make out that you're a fraudster. You look like you could have done that so just try playing it along so they don't know you're a policeman."

The proceedings then continued and the judge said, "I can't decide what to do. Come back at ten to two for my sentence." That was the first time I'd had a glimmer of hope that I wouldn't get locked up. I had written a letter to my parents and left it with my brother-in-law so they would know what had happened to me – a very strange situation, writing a letter that started, "Dear Mum and Dad, As you are aware I'm now locked up in prison. I didn't want to tell you beforehand because I didn't want to drag you through it all. I'll see you in a few months' time. Don't worry about it because I'm strong enough to handle it ..."

When I returned to the court I was told I was going to get a suspended prison sentence and that was the only time I showed any emotion at all. I got six months suspended for a year. When I left the court I met a barrage of photographers – I wasn't expecting that. I thought I'd done something fairly minor and been taken to the cleaners for it. If I'd been a member of the public I would never have ended up at the Old Bailey. But policemen are expected to be perfect, and they threw the book at me. I was in the papers and the television news. It seemed ridiculous, it was no big deal. It seemed an irony that I was some tuppenny ha'penny police officer who had nicked two pieces of paper, and yet in Court Number One there was a terrorist case going on and the previous case to mine in my court was a murder where the judge had given a life sentence. Yet here I was appearing for this!

THE WAY TO A BETTER SYSTEM

The faults of the Complaints system are glaringly obvious to everyone involved in it, including the members of the Police Complaints Authority (PCA), the civilians who rely on police cooperation when they supervise police Complaints investigations. In the Authority's four years of existence, the number of successful cases that have satisfied either the public or the police is tiny out of the many thousands the Authority has dealt with. Its Chairman, Sir Cecil Clothier, recently said in Police Review, *and in his annual report, that he would like to see a number of urgent and basic changes:*

1. There should be a clear definition of a complaint, so that lines can be drawn to limit vexatious ones. Only victims, bystanders or close relatives should have the right to complain.

2. The PCA should have the final word on whether to record a complaint. Too often the local force fails to record a complaint made against one of their officers.

3. A complaint should be enlarged to cover anything wrong

that was done at the time, not just what the complainant refers to.

4. Crucially, the PCA should be able to check on whether those complaints that were withdrawn were done so willingly.

5. There should be a six-month time limit for the start of disciplinary proceedings. Too often police use the sub judice *rule as an excluse for delaying them, yet that requirement only applies to the court case and not to the disciplinary process. The delay hurts both sides.*

6. The PCA should have the power to seize evidence. In too many cases, evidence is destroyed or withheld, or the PCA must ask the Police Authority or the police for crucial evidence that doesn't come.

7. The PCA should be able to publish its findings. It currently cannot do so in order to ensure confidentiality. That leaves the public frustrated in their ignorance of the Authority's findings.

8. Chief Constables should be prevented from using statements made to the PCA for any other purpose than in investigating the complaint. During the inquest into the death of Mrs Cynthia Jarrett at Broadwater Farm, complaints already made to the PCA were used to defend the police and undermine the credibility of complainants. As a result, the Authority's own credibility was also seriously compromised.

9. Most importantly of all, the PCA has urged that provision should be made for the dismissal of unsuitable officers without having to employ the full evidential tests currently in force. Too many people turn out to be unsuitable for police work, yet cannot be disposed of unless a serious complaint against them is proven. This is plainly bad for the public and for police discipline alike. As Sir Cecil puts it:

Being a police officer requires certain abilities, one of which is to be able to tell people to do things without getting their backs up. So many complaints start out on a simple clash of personalities. Disciplinary action is too severe for someone who, perhaps, just does not find police work to his liking. There could be some form of administrative discharge for someone who is just not putting up an adequate performance.

The interviews show that such thoughts run through the police ranks themselves. The Home Office and the Association of Chief Police Officers are currently at work on revised terms of employment that would include such a change as part of shorter-term contracts. Although Police Federation spokesmen already fear it would be abused in an arbitrary way, the power to dismiss an officer for incompetence or ideological unsuitability would allow real discipline to be enforced in a less legalistic way.

Too many complaints against the police arise from the way they initially make contact with the public. The Policy Studies Institute report, The Police and People in London, found that 85 per cent of the Metropolitan police officers they interviewed themselves knew of other officers who were often rude to the public. Two-thirds said that they thought some officers often used more force than was necessary. The British Crime Survey found that 52 per cent of young people felt that the police were rude to them.

In practice, this means that when police officers arrive at the scene of an incident, they all too often behave so provocatively that the civilians involved react unpleasantly. The incident then blows up into an affray which to the officers justifies the use of force. In the Dutch Police force, such a spiral is a disciplinary offence in itself.

CHAPTER NINE

Law, Justice and the Courts

Over the past few years, the legal system has added to the sense of uncertainty in the police about their standing in society. Although they are accused by some of being "an arm of the state", and indeed are servants of the Crown charged with enforcing the law, many officers regard the legal system with roughly the same contempt as many black youths. Both see the system as heavily weighted against them. Both think it is impossible to get a fair trial.

In the police, that feeling began in the 1970s. It stemmed from a number of acquittals in inner-city courts, notably the Old Bailey. Always under pressure for results, police officers saw armed robbers walk away free men after lengthy investigations because of jury "nobbling" through bribery or intimidation, and through what they saw as defence chicanery. There were frequent allegations against the police of mistreatment of prisoners, fabrication of evidence and perjury. Even unproven, such claims cast enough doubt on the police case for many inner-city juries to acquit. Judges and magistrates who had previously been assumed to be on the side of the police became more sceptical of police witnesses. As laws grew more complicated, a growing number of cases were lost through legal technicalities. All told, many officers came to see the legal system as a clumsy, expensive and time-consuming parody of justice.

The late '70s and early '80s were an extremely awkward period for the police. It was the beginning of the major riots: Notting Hill, Lewisham and Southall had already gone up and Blair Peach had been killed. The coverage of the strike at Grunwick had focused on the rough handling of pickets by the Special Patrol Group. The corruption scandals in the Met and the City of London Police were a major embarrassment. A number of widely publicized deaths in custody raised serious questions about the handling of suspects. Even senior police officers warned that the crime rate was "soaring", especially crimes against the person and armed robberies, both of which served as useful material for the tabloid press and politicians to feed public paranoia. Despite a decade of increased professionalism in terms of technology and organization, the police entered the 1980s very much on the defensive. And it affected the minds of judges and juries.

The result was first, in 1979, a Royal Commission on Criminal Procedure and then in 1984, the Police and Criminal Evidence Act (PACE), a far-reaching provision intended to begin the long-term restoration of public confidence in the police. For the first time, police procedures were codified in law and the rights of suspects defined. In 1985, the government introduced an independent Crown Prosecution Service (CPS), which removed the decision to prosecute from police hands. This measure, it was hoped, would both improve the standard of cases reaching the courts and free police time to put more men back on the beat. In practice, since its implementation in early 1986, PACE has made dramatic changes to the way the police conduct themselves. A recent study of custody and interrogations by the Police Foundation, for example, concluded that those parts of the Act were working as intended. But not all police officers see PACE nor the CPS, in such a positive light. In the War Against Crime, there is much cynicism on the front line.

THE CRIME FIGURES

The pressure on police procedures, and therefore the temptation to bend the rules in the interests of rough justice, begins with the laager mentality. With politicians and the public clamouring for results, a beleaguered police service has resorted to cosmetic moves much as any government or business would do: it has massaged the crime figures. It is easy to juggle statistics by varying the definitions of a Crime or No Crime in police records. Among other manoeuvres, this creates whatever impression is required: "Crime Up" or down, "Muggings Up" or down. "Rapes Up" for example, could be said to mean that the number

of actual offences may have dropped, but more were reported
as confidence in police procedures grew. As well over 50 per cent
of crimes go unreported, the figures are guesswork anyway.

Two Met PCs, average age 39, average service eighteen years.
Now in East London.

PC1: Statistics are biased. We have to give figures in terms of
work. I make no secret about it. I tell everybody, including the
skippers and Inspectors, that my records are absolute crap. I'll
make them up to fit in with what's what.

The reason I do it is that about two months ago I put an
attempted burglary in the book. They said, "Oh no, that's not
an attempted burglary." A small pane of glass near the lock, in
French windows, was broken. I said, "That's attempted
burglary, obviously." "No," they said, "that's criminal damage.
You can't prove it was an attempted burglary." That's absolute
crap, because you can't prove it was an accident either. Somebody happened to be mincing through your garden and put his
elbow through it!

I said, "I'm putting it in as an attempted burglary. You do
what you like." And they did, they crossed it out and put
Criminal Damage. At the end of the year, the Commissioner
for the first time in many years reported a drop in burglaries and
attempted burglaries. A quite substantial drop. Unfortunately
Criminal Damage had gone up.

They're liars, some of them. So I said, "If that's what they
want, I'll tell lies."

PC2: It's bollocks. Some months you've got practically nothing,
particularly if you've missed the night shift. But I just have a
quick whizz through what everybody else has put in and Tom's
got 10, Andy's got 2, so I thought: "Right. I'll have 6." I do it
like that. If anybody wants to know, it's crap.

THE SHORT CUT

The police improve their clear-up rates when someone confesses
to a number of unsolved crimes and asks the court that they be

Taken Into Consideration (TIC). This is usually done by a prisoner who wishes to curry favour with the court and the police. At a trial such admissions risk increasing a person's sentence, so the practice now is to deal with serving prisoners whose sentence will be unaffected. The legal guidelines require that each confession be investigated before it is accepted.

TICs are a controversial practice which some forces disapprove of and others regard as normal. Kent police were accused recently by one of their detectives of not only seeking fictitious confessions from their prisoners but also of inventing crimes to match them, in order to improve their crime figures. The Met were called in to investigate and cleared the Kent men involved, but further allegations of destruction of evidence left a nasty cloud hanging over the whole affair.

Sergeant in a Home Counties, age 28, eight years service. Now in a large suburban town.

I've been on prison visits with experienced detectives who say to the con, "Are there any other jobs you want to clear up?" And chummy will say, "Yeah, I've done this, that and the other." And then it's, "We've also got a pile of file cards of unsolved crimes. Do you want to clear them up?" You think to yourself: "Hang on. This isn't right!" That's the way, apparently, it's been done since time immemorial. To me, the whole TIC system is ridiculous.

You'd have to be so naive to think these TIC prison visits don't happen. My parents are both prison officers and they tell me that when these prisoners go back to their cell it's a big joke to them. "I've just coughed up twenty burglaries in the suburbs when I was on holiday in Spain!" "What are you going to cough up tomorrow?" You are meant to check all this out. Was it possible for him to have done all this? Was he in prison at the time? But they are not going to be investigated, and it looks good to clear up all these jobs.

Statistics can be manipulated. All crime statistics rely upon a crime being labelled in relation to a clear-up. You can call something like an alleged rape or domestic a No Crime if there is no evidence or the complaint is withdrawn. Or you can show it being solved. You can put a report in and have it "cleared up" on various criteria. I have worked in a CID office where some experienced old lag of a Detective Sergeant would assess every single crime that went in the book. Half his job was to see whether they were worth investigating, but the other half was to check what everybody had done about them, how they'd labelled them, and then change things to look good.

Met P C, age 28, six years service, and a graduate. Now in police computer services.

The whole recording of crime is going to be computerized within the Met and some other police forces. When this comes in, it will be a thousand times more difficult to manipulate numbers. You can't rip up a computer screen and slip it in the bin. There will suddenly be an enormous "crime wave" appearing to happen. You can virtually guarantee it. At the moment gathering statistics is a colossal mess. In two or three years' time it's going to be at the push of a button. Phoney statistics will be more difficult to do, so the detection rate will fall.

It's a dreadful quandary: proving that the police force are under pressure by increasing the crime rate, and also proving our efficiency by decreasing it. This is where manipulation comes in: if you've got a Chief Superintendent who is looking for more resources, one man stealing ten things goes down as ten crimes. If you've got a Chief Superintendent who is looking to become a Commander, then it's only one crime. But in the future they will lose that choice.

Met Superintendent, age 42, twenty-two years service. Now in an inner-city area of North London.

On Friday night there was a boy who was buggered twice by two queers. He was a queer too, but he didn't ask to be buggered by two people when he came out of a pub. He didn't wish to prosecute, so it was recorded as No Crime. There are loads of things like that.

You get people robbed in markets. Somebody loses their handbag and if they can't prove it's been stolen, it gets shown in the book as lost property. That's ridiculous. People don't lose their handbags by the score in markets. Now if the public knew of those figures, they'd see their MP and ask for a rebate. If the pressure was greater, a law and order party, as the Tories claim to be, would actually do something about it.

THE ANSWER: THE POLICE AND CRIMINAL EVIDENCE ACT

More effective policing and increased public confidence go hand in hand. In the words of the Home Secretary, the Police and Criminal Evidence Act was designed to give the police "adequate and clear powers to conduct the fight against crime on our behalf" while providing the public with "adequate safeguards against abuse". PACE sets out strict rules in a number of areas of public concern: among them are the handling of evidence and "fitting up", police powers of stopping and searching on the street, the treatment of suspects in the police station and in the cells, the length of detention without being formally charged in court, the conduct of interviews and access to solicitors.

In protecting the rights of the accused, PACE is a major advance on the old system of Judges' Rules. Dating back to Edwardian times, the Judges' Rules had no force in law and were sometimes overlooked by officers determined to convict those whom they believed to be guilty. A key instance, in the early 1970s, was the handling of the Maxwell Confait murder case, in which three teenage boys, one mentally retarded, were convicted of murder after "confessing" to a crime which it was later proved they could not possibly have committed. Such cavalier police attitudes led not only to miscarriages of justice but also to sceptical juries refusing to convict on police evidence alone.

But the public debate around PACE resembled a dialogue of the deaf. The government hoped that both the public and the police would be pleased to have clear obligations and rights. A suspect's rights are now protected, for example, and spurious accusations by defence counsel in court are more easily rebutted. But it has not happened that way. Many civilians see PACE as primarily a worrying boost to police powers, while the police feel it to be a severe restriction at a time when they are under pressure to produce better results. Provincial forces feel, with some justice, that they are being made to suffer PACE because of the bad habits of some members of the Metropolitan Police.

FITTING UP

"Fitting up" – framing people on false charges or evidence – has long been a part of police folklore. There is no doubt that the practice has gone on, sometimes on a widespread scale. Although some detectives have fitted up suspects for corrupt reasons, in order to drop false charges in exchange for money, many police officers have done it with good intentions, as it were. The pressure to produce better results, often coupled with a genuine desire to see justice done, encourages officers to fit up people whom they fear might otherwise escape punishment or who are "due" for a conviction, having evaded it for previous crimes. Where evidence is lacking, it is sometimes planted. Interviews produce "confessions" supported by perjury on the witness stand, often with a number of officers involved.

The Police and Criminal Evidence Act was intended to reduce fitting up by changing police procedures, but it is the attitudes behind it that matter more. A Policy Studies Institute report, The Police and the People of London, *concluded that "outright fabrication is probably rare ... departures from rules and procedures affecting evidence are far more common. There will be no fundamental change as long as many police officers believe the job cannot be done effectively within the rules."*

Some sort of "tidying" of evidence, if only PCs writing up their notes together, has long been common practice. It is impossible to measure how common. Recently, two "born again" detectives, one in London and one in Scotland, confessed to fabricating evidence. In Scotland, some thirty-two cases are involved and the officer believed that all the accused were guilty.

Scottish PC, age 26, four years service. Now in a council estate suburb.

If we did everything by the book, nothing would happen. We're the ones who stick our necks out to make the system work. It's all designed to let the guilty go free. They know how to play the system so it works for them, instead of how it was meant to be, a safeguard for the public. If we get caught making sure that guilty men are sent to prison, it's our heads on the block. If we didn't do it, no one would go inside. Maybe that is what needs to happen for people to change the system. I don't mean a wee fiddling at the edges, I mean radical change.

PC in a large northern urban force, age 27, three years service.

There are lots of side steps in the police. They rarely stick to testimony. The classic case is verbals. One of the magistrates actually said, "Well, it's very hard for this court to believe that the PCs, the Sergeants, the Inspectors all collaborated to produce this evidence." Of course this is precisely what they'd bloody done.

The basis of an officer's case is what is written in his police notebook. Now, if you don't get results with the court you're in trouble; particularly in the CID, you get transferred back to the beat. No one wants the job of walking the streets in the cold when you could be driving around in a fast car, with a leather jacket, sitting in pubs all day long.

Even with the best will in the world, when you're arresting somebody you can't be taking notes at the same time. So you've got to do your notebooks retrospectively, and sometimes that means the next day. I've seen officers in the parade room, sitting there and writing out their notes, saying, "Right, yes: 'Excuse me, sir, can I look in the contents of your bag?' And the defendant then says, 'Fuck off, officer!' 'I must insist, sir, that I look in it.' Then, 'OK, guv', fair cop!'" That's how they do it, and it's often totally fabricated. But not only is it fabricated consciously, very often it's fabricated unconsciously. When you're looking back, you don't want to portray yourself in an unfavourable light, because you're going to court and not everyone does everything perfectly in the heat of the moment.

Former Met Inspector, aged 43, sixteen years service. Recently resigned.

I've fitted people up. You go out with the intention of arresting criminals. That was always my intention and has been whatever I did.

The guy gets nicked for burglary and gets off on a technicality. So you say, "OK, you bastard," and you sit outside his house or you find his car outside a pub and wait until eventually you nick him for drinking and driving or whatever. Or you fit him up on a false charge.

You would go out in a car, the two of you, both in uniform and you'd drive around. You would see a guy that you knew was a villain either from repute or from the feeling you get that you can spot thieves. It would invariably be someone who you knew deserved it, somebody that had got away with something in the past. This is where you become judge and jury.

The first time it happened, my partner stopped a car and asked the guy to get out. He gave him a bit of a hard time and then said to me, "You stay with him, I'm going to have a look in the car." I started looking at his driving licence and my mate goes round the car, slips in a piece through the driver's door and says to me, "Now you go and search the car." I then go and "find" something. It was a lump of metal, like a wheel brace, by the driver's seat. I say, "What's this for?" The driver says, "What do you mean?" "Right. Offensive weapon!" He was a minicab driver, so when we got back to the nick, he didn't accuse us of planting it. Instead he said, good as gold, "We've had lots of trouble in the company and I keep it for my own protection." Charged with possession of an offensive weapon, goes to court, £100 fine. The effect it has is of slapping him into line. My partner had put the wheel brace there because the guy stepped out of line before, he had got off with something. This time he pleaded guilty in court; I don't think he even got a lawyer. That's the way the world works. We went out for a drink afterwards and he became an informant.

Met Detective Sergeant, age 34, fifteen years service. Now in central London.

Before PACE, fitting people up was common. Fitting an extra

page in that statement. I have been a party to it, I won't pretend I haven't. And the motive for doing it, certainly in the past, was personal advancement. It was certainly the case on my first tour with the Crime Squad. If you hadn't had your two or three arrests that week, Friday morning you were getting desperate and the guys would go out and just pick somebody up. That was the "sus" business – stopping and searching anyone who fits the bill. Another thing about it was commonplace: nobody can tell me the magistrates did not know that these guys who were coming to them – two, three, four, five a day for "sus" – were being fitted up. Nobody can tell me they didn't know. "Minimum amount of evidence." Bull shit. Absolutely no evidence whatsoever!

Met PC, age 28, seven years service, four with the CID in a racially mixed area of London.

I see corrupton as taking bribes, taking gratuities to influence a prosecution. I've seen very little of that, honestly. I've also seen people fitted up, but the motives for that are perhaps misplaced. It's a misplaced morality, misplaced values. The "verbal", writing up statements, certainly was commonplace; PACE has reduced it drastically. If you want to fit somebody up now, you've first of all got to trust everybody who is in the chain of the custody procedure, because you can't possibly hide an incident through the whole custody procedure without falsification of the records at some point or another. There are occasions when the whole chain can be trusted and then it does occur. It's basically hard work. It takes longer and requires a lot more thought, so PACE has reduced it.

The interview actually means getting a guy out of a cell for five minutes, talking about cricket, putting him back in the cell and then turning it into a forty-five-minute written confession. Forty-five minutes to write it all out and then he "refuses to sign" the statement, which gets taken down to the Duty Officer, who could quite innocently certify on the bottom of the record of interview that it's been presented to the guy at the correct time by the officers who conducted the interview. Then, when you go to court, if you have officers who are competent in presenting that, they very often get away with it. Forging a signature is a fallacy – you don't need to. He just "refused" to sign it. There are still convictions going on where that is occurring, but fewer.

PC in a Midlands force, age 31, nine years service. Now in an inner-city area.

Some policemen have an exaggerated sense of wrong and right, black and white, and a total mistrust and disillusionment with the legal system.

PACE has very clearly laid down to a lot of people the fact that society disapproves. A phrase which appeared three or four years ago was: "If that's what they want, that's the way they're going to get it" – if society doesn't want people fitted up, doesn't want people convicted, then they're not going to have it. Since PACE, I've seen an awful lot of detectives who'd get the guy out and if in ten minutes he wouldn't admit it, they'd kill it there and then. The guy would walk out on the basis of "society doesn't want him to get convicted, so he's not going to get convicted".

STOP AND SEARCH

PACE did away with the legal basis of the notorious "sus" laws, whose overzealous application was one of the primary causes of the inner-city riots. Now, a person cannot be stopped and searched without "reasonable suspicion" that they have committed an offence. That suspicion must be given in writing to the suspect, together with the PC's identification. Officers feel this does away with intuitive policing. They find having to hand out such slips of paper humiliating, so stops have fallen dramatically.

Met PC, age 33, fifteen years service. Now a Home Beat Officer in South London.

Three o'clock in the morning you'd be driving around your beat and, all of a sudden, there's a bloke walking down the road with a bottle. What's he doing out at three o'clock in the morning? So you'd stop and ask: "Where are you going?"

"Home." "Where's home?" It might be miles away. "What are you doing around here?" "Seeing my girlfriend." "Where's she?" "Can't remember." So you think: "I've got a sticky one here," and you get him to turn out his pockets. Out comes a screwdriver, knife, whatever. Now he knows the law better than we do. He doesn't have to worry about being searched, even if you know the man is a villain. PACE specifically says that previous convictions don't count in allowing you to stop and search. I can understand that up to a point, but it's not practical. That's how I used to get a lot of arrests.

This anti-stop/search thing was brought in by the lefties. But now it's got so bad, there's so many people being seriously injured or killed with knives, that the lefties are asking for the rules to be changed to cover the immediate search of any person believed to be carrying a knife.

Nowadays the frustrating part is that you're driving along and you see a car or person, and the old gut will go and you think: "Shit, I can't do anything about it." Because if you do, and it goes bent on you, you're going to get a bullet straight up your arse and you're out on your ear looking for another job.

Met PC, age 45, twenty years service. Now working in a local intelligence office.

Stopping somebody in the street: OK, you might be wrong once in a while, but an experienced officer usually knows when there's something wrong. You get the gut feeling. Just walking along the street you can do that. We notice people you wouldn't even think of looking at. I'll never forget, driving the area car once when we came down to a junction and a car came round the corner. I thought, "We'll have him." The probationer said, "Why did you clock him?" I said, "The way he looked at us." We came back to the same junction. Another car came round the corner and the bloke didn't look at us. I said, "We'll have him as well." The probationer couldn't understand at all.

Scottish PC, age 27, four years service. Now in a Council estate suburb.

Everybody reacts in a different way when they see a policeman.

Some of them get "friendly" and you think why are they being "friendly"? Policemen are suspicious. You don't think bad of everybody, but no one has walked through life without breaking the law. No one. I don't care who they are. Old dears who say, "I've never done anything wrong." What about the pencils at school? "That's not stealing." Course it's stealing. There's always something you do wrong.

Met Superintendent, age 47, twenty-six years service. Now working in a racially mixed area of London.

Every single item that is stolen has got to be carried from A to B, either on foot or by car. There is nothing stolen in this country that isn't moved, probably twice. Once from where it's stolen to its resting place and secondly from its resting place to whoever is going to purchase it. Everything. So what's wrong with stopping people, provided we do it properly? I never had any complaints about stopping people before. We're getting complaints from people now, especially if they are black – that's not a racist comment. If it was I wouldn't have said it.

You see, police see the whole legal framework differently now. It is no longer a tool, it has become a straitjacket. The vast majority of conscientious officers cannot understand why such a weapon has been handed to the other side.

CUSTODY SERGEANT

To deal with complaints of mistreatment of people in the station and in the cells, PACE created a new post of Custody Sergeant whose job is to oversee each prisoner's well-being and property from the moment of arrival in the station to departure. His duties are tightly drawn and can involve some fifty different notations in the handling of a single prisoner.

Not surprisingly, Custody Sergeants complain of too much paperwork, lack of control over the flow of work and lack of understanding and support from above. Such feedback as they get from senior officers is all negative and concerns mistakes. Their worst fear is of a death in custody, which would inevitably be down to them.

Met Sergeant, age 40, twenty-six years service. Now a Custody Officer in East London.

You ask any young probationer what is the worst job in the police force, he'll say Custody Officer. They absolutely hate it. Because if anything goes wrong the buck will definitely land in your lap.

A prisoner is brought in to the table and delivered to the Custody Officer. The arresting officer says what he arrested him for. You've got to do all the paperwork, and then of course you've got to read him his rights and give him a copy of them, ask him if he wants a solicitor, if he wants somebody informed – all this sort of thing takes time. And then if he's waited in custody since midday and you want to interview him, you may have run out of time as he's got to have eight hours of uninterrupted sleep. Unless he is to be released.

I remember when I was working at Holloway. I'd come on duty at six o'clock half asleep. Then those charge room doors would crash open and the Crime Squad's been off and done a load of raids; they're bringing in masses of property that you've got to count, type out the forms – that's your fucking "starter for ten". Then during the middle of the day there's fights, a few assaults, domestic disputes, burglaries, robberies. Some at night, further domestic disputes when dad comes home drunk, beats the living daylights out of mum and the kids. So it carries on twenty-four hours a day, seven days a week. There's no day off, not even for Christmas.

I'll never forget one Christmas, at two minutes past midnight the whole area blew up and it never stopped until six o'clock in the morning. The whole world was out to kill each other. It's rough saying to the fellows, "Keep your sense of humour." The cells were absolutely full. We were banging them in hour after hour, till in the end one Sergeant throws his pen up in the air, says, "Sorry, I can't stand this any longer," and goes out. We thought he was having a breakdown. After an hour he comes back in again, by which time we're all laughing. The queue of prisoners and arresting officers had turned into a three-ring circus.

You have to keep your sense of humour or you'd crack up for sure. There was one time when we distracted this Sergeant, whipped a prisoner out of one cell and into the next one. Then we put the prisoner's jacket on a mannequin and we left it hanging, strung up by a tie. The Sergeant came back, looked into the cell, and his expression! Just then we all popped out and took a photograph of it. He was thinking about all the writing he was going to have to do. He could see his whole career going down the plughole in front of him!

Sergeant in a Home Counties force, age 38, seventeen years service. Now in a seaside town.

On the original charge sheet you were encouraged to make a one-line entry, but now we keep much more detailed notes. In six months' time it goes to Crown Court, the man pleads not guilty and says, "I made that statement under duress" or "I was tired and hungry" or cold, or whatever. We record now whether he was offered a meal, given an extra blanket, exercise in the yard, everything. It pays off in the end. If they can complain about mistreatment, you lose the case.

Former Met Sergeant, age 32, nine years service, and a graduate. Recently resigned.

Since I left the force I have had to attend Crown Court to clear up unfinished cases and it reminded me why I left the police. I stood in the dock for two hours and all I had been was the Custody Sergeant. I wasn't even the arresting officer. I had missed something off the custody record and for two hours I was castigated by a tuppenny ha'penny law-centre brief for not putting something in the record, although it was recorded somewhere else. He was clutching at straws.

I joined the police with certain idea about people working together and very strong socialist views, and there I was giving my evidence and there was this lawyer who probably had similar views to me but his only goal was to knock the police. It is one of the things that shatters your illusions about why you are doing the job.

PERIODS OF DETENTION

PACE did away with another common police practice, that of holding people for extended periods of time without charging them with a specific offence in order to pressure them into confessing. Now, after six hours the duty Inspector must review and authorize further detention. After the prisoner has been held for a total of fifteen hours, the Inspector must review the case again and then authorize further detention. After the prisoner has been in custody for twenty-four hours without charge, a Superintendent must review the case. He can authorize a further twelve hours only for a Serious Arrestable Offence such as murder or rape. He must also be satisfied that the investigation is proceeding apace. After a total of thirty-six hours, the police must have the approval of a magistrate to hold a prisoner for longer. After seventy-two hours in custody, they must charge the suspect or let him go. The object of all these extensions is to allow time to check alibis and for extended interviews within the controlled conditions allowed by the Act.

The purpose of this new system is to eliminate police "fishing expeditions", in which the suspect is left to cool his heels and with any luck, loosen his tongue while the officers on the case go looking for evidence to corroborate their hunches. The independent inquiry into the Broadwater Farm riot concluded that the arrest and detention of Floyd Jarrett, after which officers went to search his house without a proper warrant, was just such a fishing trip. Extended periods of detention without charge may have softened up professional criminals, but innocent people could be panicked into confessing to crimes they could not possibly have committed. Errol John, who was thirteen years old, confessed to stealing two toy cars for which he had the receipt. He was awarded damages for wrongful arrest.

Detective Sergeant in a large northern force, age 38, twenty-eight years service. Now in a racially mixed inner-city area.

The main drawback with PACE is that you have lost control of your prisoner. Before PACE, if you brought a prisoner in he was your prisoner. You would put him in the cell, you'd take him out when you wanted, you would interview him for however long you wanted, within reason, and then you'd put him back. He was yours. He was your responsibility. It was easier to move quickly with the bloke, taking him to places, like taking him out to search his house.

PACE now means that the minute you come back to the station with this guy, he goes straight into the care and control of the Custody Sergeant, whose head is on the block if anything goes awry. It results in long-winded procedures. It can be a couple of hours from the time you want your bloke to the time you actually get him. You are just kicking your heels. The bloke's in the cell, he doesn't want to be there, I don't necessarily want him to be there, all I want is for him to answer some questions.

When you've finally spoken to him and put him back, you make a few inquiries as a result of what he said. You want to ask him a few more questions. You go back and the Custody Sergeant says, "You've had it. You can't have him back for the next half an hour because he's having his meal." So now a number of people are staying in for hours longer than they need to. I don't like spending all day stuck in a cell block. If I can find out what I want and get the bloke out, that suits me fine.

People say that PACE is bad for the police, but on balance I'd say it isn't bad. In some ways, it's done bloody wonders. If someone driving up a one-way street declines to give you his name and address, before PACE there was nowt you could do. Now you arrest him. I think PACE simply codifies a lot of standard police practice. PACE gives us the authority to search a person's house after he's been arrested. We always did it anyway. In certain areas it's restricted us a bit, but it's also made the job a lot clearer. Basically it's made things that we do wrong into disciplinary offences.

It's our fault, I suppose – people who've come before us, like older detectives who bent things. The time was bound to come when we'd be told officially what we can and can't do. The villains don't like the fact – it's frustrating to them that we all lost that freedom of manoeuvre.

CARRYING THE CAN

Under PACE, Superintendents and Inspectors are now personally liable for any errors in authorizing the extended deten-

tion of a prisoner without charge. To hold someone more than 24 hours, it must be for "an offence of a very serious nature, and in order to ensure the investigation will proceed promptly, and in the interests of justice". Under PACE, this can be challenged in court.

No challenge has yet been successfully mounted that made an officer liable, but the Superintendent's Association have arranged an insurance scheme for its members that has been widely taken up. As one Superintendent put it, "It's a pretty heavy burden. Makes you think twice!"

PC in a Home Counties force, age 37, nineteen years service. Now in a market town.

We are so overwhelmed with the rights of the accused that we forget about the rights of people who are trying to live their own lives.

A young lad had been hurt with a bottle. His friends were running around and trying to vent some sort of vengeance on the pub, its occupants, or anyone they could, including police officers. So it's, "Come on, calm down. What happened?" "My mate's dying. I want to hit somebody." "Calm down." He wouldn't listen. He was just trying to vent his feelings on somebody.

He was going to hit me and I caught him and said, "Listen son, behave. I am big enough and old enough and you are going to get hurt" – which is a natural reaction if someone is going to hit you. His immediate response was, "You can't do that. I've read the Code of Practice." A fifteen-year-old lad, pissed out of his skull, quoting the PACE Code of Practice at me! That is the sort of reaction you are getting on the street.

LEGAL UNCERTAINTY

The police needed PACE to clarify their own legal powers. Few civilians realize just how little power police officers have to act as we assume they should. The office of Constable goes back nearly a thousand years. Many police actions are not covered by any specific Act, though the powers of arrest are spread across hundreds. In the end common law and common sense are the twin bases for most police actions.

PACE has codifed much of that, providing under Section 25 a new power of arrest and detention for someone who commits an offence, no matter of what nature, if the person refuses to give his name and address, or gives a name and address which the officer has reason to believe is false.

A police officer can enter any premises if they have reason to believe a breach of the peace is taking place. Otherwise, they can only enter those premises where the public are admitted either free, or on payment of money. Licensed premises can be visited to confirm the terms of the licence are being observed. Otherwise, to enter private property a warrant is needed.

Under PACE, that warrant must now specify under what Act the warrant has been issued, and what precisely the officer is looking for. They must only look for that specified object, and nothing more: if it is a stolen television set no search of a small bedside table is allowed. To get around that officers use "the ways and means Act" – "tv set and spare parts" is added to the warrant to permit the usual wide-ranging hunt for drugs, and other goodies. Although the warrant should be issued by a magistrate, under certain urgent circumstances it can be done by a Superintendent, Inspector, or even in extreme cases the officer himself – when a suspected thief runs back inside his house and may be hiding or destroying evidence.

PC from a large Midlands urban force, age 33, twelve years service in a racially mixed inner-city area.

A few weeks back, the social services contacted us and said they were going to apply for a warrant to search a house under the Mental Health Act, because a chap had not been seen for at least three years. It was believed he was living in the bedroom. His old mother who was eighty-five lived in the house, and his brother. There had been a warrant out to search the house previously because he had not been seen and had been ill-treated by the brother.

The brother was running the household, the mother was senile. Nobody could get into the house at all. They had two chains on the door. The brother would not even let his sisters in and would only talk to people through a crack in the door.

He said this lad was upstairs in the bedroom: "I put food outside the door every night and he eats it. He does go to the toilet and he does have a bath a week, but I don't see him."

So we only had this fellow's word that he was alive.

We got to court and there is an argument over a technicality, so the warrant is denied. The social services then decided to try and talk their way in. We spoke to the brother who said, "No, he is alive."

But as we have no evidence at all, we say, "Well, if you don't let us in we are going to have to break in." There is a power in the PACE Act which says that you can enter a property to save life and limb. I thought that it would cover me, but it was very arguable. I decided that I would rather go to a civil court and be sued for breaking his door than let this fellow suffer. He could have been on the verge of death and twenty-four hours might have made a difference.

So we broke the front door down. We went upstairs, the bedroom door was locked, we got no reply from within the room. So we began to break the bedroom door down. Suddenly he starts shouting from inside: "Don't break the door down, I will pay the money!" So we put a note under the door. A bank statement came out and he kept saying "I have got the money!" There was obviously something going on between the two of them. Eventually he opened the door a crack. He realized it was the police, but he would not come out and he would not allow us in. We got his own doctor down. The social worker eventually took him to the mental hospital. I mean, to lock yourself in the bedroom for three years, you have got to be amiss somewhere.

He went in for seventy-two hours for observation and I went away happy.

However, the hospital decided that he was quite normal, which left me mid-stream. When we first talked to him he was going on about infra-red rays coming through the windows. People who jump off the top of flats and things usually start talking like that, "communists are listening through wires in the walls." The social services said they would make sure they got into the house to check that he was looked after. He had been living on bread and marge for two years.

His solicitor eventually turned up and he said, "I don't agree that you had the power to force an entry." As it happened, he did think we had done the right thing, but who else was going to help the fellow? I'm happy to go to bed knowing he is alive. The purpose of a Constable is to protect life and property, but the law did not give the clear protection that I require. I could have been prosecuted just for doing my job!

SOLICITORS AND INTERVIEWS

Before PACE, the Judges' Rules laid down that prisoners should be given access to solicitors unless this would interfere with the course of justice. That left room for much discretion. Legal advice was often denied to people accused of complex offences but with no knowledge of the law or of the legal process.

PACE guarantees access to a solicitor if the person arrested so chooses, either for advice or to be present during the interview. In police circles, this was widely assumed to be a serious block to confessions. Police Foundation research, however, shows that only 29 per cent of those detained accept the offer of legal advice and only 22 per cent have the solicitor attend the interview.

The major change imposed by PACE on the conduct of interviews is the obligation to take contemporaneous notes, each page of which must be signed by the prisoner. Although many officers complain this cramps their style by giving the suspect time to think, it has also reduced allegations against the police in court.

Met Inspector, age 34, fourteen years service. Now in the East End of London.

The criminal barrister, because of PACE, is not getting the work and his income is decreasing. Before PACE, he could challenge our interviews, which were notes made up afterwards. Now our interviews are written contemporaneously, signed usually in the presence of a solicitor. In court it's a question of just reading these notes and maybe getting one or two little questions from the defence; they cannot attack. Your brief is getting a half-day trial instead of a week's trial, so he's getting a half-day's remuneration instead of five days.

TAPED INTERVIEWS

The use of tape-recordings in interviews has been going on in experimental form all over Britain and has been similarly effective. There are logistical problems to do with typing transcripts and distinguishing between voices when several officers are present, but the experiments are largely regarded as a success.

Detective Inspector in a Midlands force, age 32, twelve years service. Now in a city centre.

They've been trying tape recorders out and we're getting so many guilty pleas from them, it's unbelievable. Solicitors who begged and begged for tape recorders because we were "verballing" everybody now realize that that's the worst thing they could have asked for, because blokes do cough jobs. It's like boasting. You get murderers and sex people, they can't stop talking about it once they start. I think that once we get tape-recorded interviews nationally, it will be much better. If you put the right questions to somebody, they will talk.

Detective Inspector in a large northern force, age 46, twenty-four years service.

I'd like to see videos. I'd like to see the detective interview the suspect. I'd like to see him say whatever he wants to say and see the response from the suspect, and I'd like the whole video to be shown to the jury and let them decide if that person has told the truth. Most prisoners at some stage or other want to talk to police officers about "Will I get bail?" I'd like to see all that go before the jury and let the jury decide, not the legal profession.

THE CROWN PROSECUTION SERVICE

The Crown Prosecution Service was introduced in 1985, to distance the police from the decision to prosecute, to cut down

the unreliable cases being brought to trial, to raise the standards
of criminal evidence and to make better use of the courts. By
drastically reducing police court duties, it was also intended to
put more men back on the beat. As ever, lack of resources has
been a crucial factor. The CPS is staffed largely by overworked,
inexperienced and underpaid solicitors and barristers, some
with scant knowledge of the criminal law. (Wages for a pros-
ecutor start at less than the salary of a good legal secretary.)

The CPS review each case the police bring to court, using a
code which encourages caution: cases may proceed to trial only
when there is a better than 51 per cent chance of a conviction.
Similar criteria are used by the Director of Public Prosecutions.
Cases are also scanned for possible breaches of PACE, for signs
of unreliability in the evidence of witnesses and for any other
flaws that might lead to an acquittal. The existence of a bare
prima facie *case is not sufficient reason to prosecute.*

The way the CPS has used its discretion has greatly dis-
appointed the police. Older officers are used to "having a go"
in cases where their gut feeling tells them that the accused is
guilty. Lacking court experience, of which they will now get
much less, many younger PCs have little grasp of the rules of
evidence. The police suspect the CPS of proceeding with cases
only where the evidence is, as one detective put it, "Gift-
wrapped and handed to them on a plate." The police accuse
the CPS of dropping borderline cases to avoid more work.
(There are only 1500 lawyers to handle over a million cases a
year.) CPS solicitors, on the other hand, complain bitterly of
police tardiness and incompetence in drawing up papers.

Detective Constable in a large northern urban force, age 32,
fourteen years service. Now in a racially mixed inner-city area.

When suspects appear at court and there are no papers, and
they are discharged through lack of evidence, some police feel
a bit strong about that. The court will only accept so many
remands, adjournments. We don't stand there and say, "We've
lost all the papers." They're never lost, they're always "in the
system". But no one knows where to look for them!

The amount of work for the drunks, the simple shop thefts
and so on, where you have to go through the same procedure

even though it might be a guilty plea, is ridiculous. A survey in 1983 reckoned that about 58 per cent of our time was spent inside the police station just doing admin. Now it is well over 60 per cent. It's ludicrous, a waste of time and money.

Although the creation of the CPS was intended to put more men back on the beat, the paperwork required by the new system has had the opposite effect. Even before its introduction, officers reckoned that an arrest in the first half of a shift could take the rest of the shift to process. The threat of more paperwork has been a distinct disincentive to making arrests. If younger PCs, who comprise an increasing proportion of the police service, are not going to court to see how the legal system works in practice, the situation is likely to get worse.

Met Sergeant, age 43, twenty years service. Now in central London.

You're going to see a radical change in the next couple of years. One of the solicitors who was employed by the Crown Prosecution Service went to court, but when the court presentation officer showed her the day's schedule, she said, "That's a week's work," and walked out. The Crown Prosecution Service throws so many cases out. They just don't bother. In the end, we won't bother to nick anybody. Magistrate's courts have now become a complete and utter joke.

The new arrangements also distance ordinary PCs from seeing their work through to fulfilment. They bring in a prisoner, hand him or her over to the Custody Sergeant, hand the prisoner to the CID to be interviewed and hand the evidence to the CPS. If the case is tried, the arresting officer is not even notified of the outcome.

The result is that police officers now feel themselves hemmed in at every corner, by PACE, by the CPS, by magistrates, judges and lawyers who simply do not understand the nature of crime and yet who clamour, together with politicians and the public, for better evidence and more results.

**Detective Constable in a West Country force, age 29, seven
years service. Now in a small city.**

There are very few jobs that go through the court that you're
100 per cent happy with. If it's a loose end and you think you
can get by without tying it up, you will. Every time you get a
not guilty verdict, you wonder which of those loose ends caused
the trouble and you wish you'd done it. It's not really laziness,
a lot of the time, it is simply "Will that do? Will it go through?
That's good enough."

When you first start off, you may have visions of setting the
world on fire and bringing people to justice. They go fairly
swiftly, because the practical aspects of the job take over your
thinking; just the problems of getting shot of paperwork, never
to see it again. In the beginning you may feel strongly about
every crime that comes your way; you think, "God, what a
terrible thing!" But after a few years you become numbed to a
lot of stuff and it doesn't really bother you, it's just something
else to deal with.

THE COURTS

*Since the Crown Prosecution Service was created, police officers
have spent less and less time in court, as was intended.*

*They appear as witnesses only when people plead Not Guilty.
The stronger the prosecution case, the greater the likelihood of
the defence attacking police evidence and harassing the officers
in the witness box. The police feel on trial themselves, an
experience which younger PCs find hard to deal with. They
give a flustered performance which seems to support the defence
allegations, whatever the truth of the matter. One northern
magistrate told me, "I'm very suspicious of them for no evidential reason. Just an intuitive feeling. It's very feminine, I
know. They always used to be nice to us on the bench. Nowadays they just seem to be lying." Such attitudes must give the
benefit of the doubt to the defence.*

*Police officers are vulnerable to such legalistic examination
of their behaviour because they spend so much time in a moral*

limbo, cutting corners, ignoring rules, even breaking the law by speeding or drunk driving or tampering with evidence. This does not necessarily make them bad police officers, however, nor does it cloud their sense of right and wrong as it applies to those outside the force. They are usually crystal clear when it comes to the guilt of people they have brought to court. That juries, magistrates and judges seem to be ranged on the side of the accused confirms the image the police have of themselves as the Thin Blue Line, holding on to moral values at a time when all around are losing theirs.

Training Sergeant in a northern urban force, age 38, eighteen years service.

I don't like the idea of us losing discretion for prosecution to the CPS, that was a bad move. They're not an efficient service because they're not policemen. People say we should be detached, but when you've arrested somebody right at the scene of the crime and you've seen the results of their behaviour, you cannot be otherwise than personally involved and think, "They should be put away." Somebody who only comes in at nine o'clock in the morning, into an office, has got nothing at all to do with the police force and meeting the people who are hit by crime.

THE ENEMY OF JUSTICE

The need for more detached judgement about the quality evidence was one important reason why the CPS was formed. Even to officers more modest about their knowledge of law, the legal profession is seen as the enemy of justice by many police officers. It makes it all the harder for them to work together.

P C in a large Midlands force, age 36, seventeen years service. Now in a city centre.

Try getting a job home in court via jurors that have been nobbled and with the shysters that appear defending guilty people. I would never go into the Chief Constable's office and say, "This man is innocent," when I know he has done it. Yet there are solicitors and barristers that do it all the time. Not only are they doing deals but they are doing trials knowing full well the man has done it, and they are saying the man hasn't. In my opinion, that's conspiracy.

If you do manage to get a job home, then what happens? Do they get sentenced to jail? No, they get a pat on the back and money out of the poor box, and are told not to do it again. That's where it's all going down the drain.

WPC in a Midlands force, age 30, ten years service. Now in a city centre.

Court can be absolute agony. By the very dint of somebody being a police officer and somebody else being a barrister, the barrister is nearly always going to be brighter. It's totally unfair to shove a probationary PC in front of a top barrister who can make practically anybody say black is white, but that's the way it goes. That PC has got to be absolutely spot on with all the details to get a conviction in court, which is why everyone savvies up their notebooks before the case gets going. I don't think this is a particularly brilliant way of training people, because it encourages police officers to lie in the witness box.

Met WPS, age 33, twelve years service. Now in West London.

It's not terribly important whether some horrible rent boy gets another fine for highway obstruction or not, because he's an absolute pest to society. Far more important is that if you start off lying about that, when it comes to the really big time fifteen years later in the CID and nicking armed robbers, you'll be caught out by a top barrister who will make absolute mincemeat out of you. You'll lose the case and somebody extremely dangerous will be unleashed on the public again because of your lies.

If you've got a police force with a reputation, which the Met very sadly has, for being persistent and not very good liars in the witness box, the whole legal structure is going to break down.

PC in a large northern force, age 32, fourteen years service.

The reason for PCs making things up is basically down to the law, what is required to prove an offence – what is admissible as evidence. The evidence of a co-accused is not admissible unless corroborated. You've done your raid, and you've got two people and a pile of drugs. You know one of them is the main dealer because the other one tells you. He pours his heart out to you. He tells you the whole story, all the intelligence you didn't know. You put it to the second one. He says, "Don't know what you're talking about." There's nothing you can do. The first person will not be allowed to stand up in court and say, "He did this, that and the other." If the rules of co-accused could be relaxed, there'd be no need for us to say, "We saw this, that and the other," if people look like they are going to get away with it. It's the way the law is structured. We have to do that to get a result.

JURIES

The continued failure rate of police cases in court is a source of serious distress to many officers. It confirms their suspicions that society is against them. Although inner-city juries are most likely to acquit, the number of rural juries and magistrates that no longer accept a policeman's word is growing as well. The effect of these acquittals on police attitudes is corrosive. It makes them more suspicious of the public and leads to more unpleasantness on the street.

Juries' scepticism means that a higher standard of evidence is required to reach the 51 per cent chance of conviction without which the CPS will not prosecute. The more juries acquit, the higher the standard of evidence demanded. The fewer the cases that get through court, the less police officers are inclined to try, or at least to try by the book. Yet if they resort to fabricating evidence or making up testimony, the defence will challenge and the jury acquit. So the vicious spiral feeds police cynicism and public mistrust. The Police and Criminal Evidence Act was designed to break this spiral and has achieved some success, but this is not yet reflected in the courts.

Superintendent in a Midlands force, age 43, twenty-two years service. Now in an inner-city area.

The jury system wants updating. Hunreds of years ago it was ratepayers, responsible citizens. Now the average jury seems to me to be made up of unemployed eighteen-year-olds. Have they the right to sit and judge a fellow man? Have they the experience in life to do so?

WPC in a West Country force, age 32, ten years service.

How can you sit and judge someone when you don't know anything about that person? Surely you're entitled to know they've been convicted twenty times for indecent assault? If the jury return not guilty you can see the drained look on their faces when all the previous convictions are read out. Equally, when they bring in a verdict of guilty you can see the look of relief. It must be very difficult for them.

Two PCs in a large northern force, average age 34, average service fourteen years. Now in an inner-city area.

PC1: The judges, the magistrates, the solicitors, they come from a very nice environment. They've no idea of how people live down here. You can pull the wool over their eyes so easily it's unbelievable. They genuinely want to believe that the fellow you caught at four o'clock in the morning was looking for somewhere to build a pigeon loft.

PC2: There's also a firm belief among magistrates that if you're nice to villains, it'll do them better than being strict with them. But there comes a time when that goes too far. If the lad's been in trouble several times, after a not guilty verdict, you can see the judge thinking "Oh shit!" when they read out the record at the end of the trial.

PC1: The juries just don't want to convict. In one case of rioting, seventeen of us identified this fellow in court. We all knew his name, where he lived. Even the judge stressed to the jury, "The officers are not giving evidence of identification, they are giving evidence of recognition." And he got away with it! He was "in the pub having a drink". There's no answer to that. The trial should never have been held locally anyway.

Sergeant in a northern force, age 40, twenty-one years service. Now in a training department.

If I go to court and give perjured evidence, tell lies in the witness box, I get done. I lose my job. But every villain goes there and he tells lies. Nothing ever happens to him. Every villain that pleads not guilty and is found guilty has told lies in the witness box and nothing's ever done. Is it fair? Everybody in our country is supposed to be innocent until proven guilty, but as police officers we don't have to hold that view. As far as I'm concerned, if I lock someone up, they're fucking guilty. If you charge somebody, then you've got to have evidence against them. You don't say, "I'm going to charge them for the hell of it."

Scottish Sergeant, age 32, twelve years service. Now in a large town.

Do you really, honestly think that innocent people go to court? They're probably innocent of some of the things they're actually charged with, but they're not innocent a lot of the time. Nine times out of ten you pull somebody in and they're guilty. I accept that there could be people who commit offences and they don't know they're offences. But if I didn't believe they were guilty, I wouldn't lock them up.

CRIME AND PUNISHMENT

In the interviews police officers' views on sentencing were consistent around the country. Officers of all ranks wanted more and longer sentences. Yet the notion that loss of liberty is the only appropriate punishment for criminals is a simple form of retribution. It throws no light on why people commit crime and what might dissuade them from doing so again.

Met Superintendent, age 43, twenty-four years service. Now in a racially mixed area of London.

Custodial sentences are a must. No doubt about it. In the eyes of the villain, if he doesn't get one, he's got away with it. He is not worried about a fine. He is certainly not worried about probation or community service – that's nothing. Think what some people do in motor vehicles, which if they'd done with a weapon they'd go inside for ten years. Instead they get disqualified for ten months and a £100 fine. Rape cases should not be anything less than ten years. Unfortunately, those who do the sentencing have never been at the receiving end. Time and time again we see people released on bail who go out and do the same thing, something like 40 per cent. If we haven't got enough space in the prisons then we have to build more prisons. We are criticized for our poor clear-up rate, particularly in the Met, and yet our clear-up is good enough to fill all the prisons in the country. Let's face it, we can't be that inefficient.

Chief Inspector in a large northern force, age 36, thirteen years experience, and a graduate. Now in charge of a large industrial suburb.

The majority of police officers feel the courts are letting them down. I don't mean "bring back the birch" or "bring back hanging". But the process of getting a custodial sentence these days is unbelievable. You have to be suicidal, you have to positively *want* to go to prison. You have to be already into a wholesale career of crime to get put away. Even when you manage to get a custodial sentence, you're out in no time.

I get the feeling that social services and the courts have given up caring what these kids get up to, so it's left to us to pick up the pieces. When our lads see someone they've sent down for nine months walking around free to commit burglary again after four months, they just say, "What's the point?"

With prisons already overflowing and police cells now used for remand prisoners, the need to find alternatives to prison is all too clear. The possible futility of custodial sentences as a means of reform is also rarely considered by the police.

Met Inspector, age 32, thirteen years service. Now in East London.

Rape is the worst crime there is, it is worse than murder; rape and buggery, and we get quite a bit of that too on males and females. A four-year-old girl was buggered here last week. The only reason that man is being prosecuted is because the mother, who was also buggered, wants him convicted because he did it to her daughter. She was not bothered about herself and that is quite common. These sort of scum are allowed to live. They need locking up forever, or they need the death penalty. That would be much cheaper to society, and it would stop it.

Scottish PC, age 35, thirteen years service. Now in a city centre.

I don't think we will always say no to the death penalty. One day it might come back, because crime is continuing to rise. We have more murders and more people who go to prison who are released and commit further crime. There has to be some way that stops people committing crimes like rape. What do you do, castrate the bloke? They wouldn't commit a rape again. You have to have some answer to it and there isn't one at the moment.

Former Scottish PC, age 30, five years service in an inner-city area of Glasgow. Now in the Met in West London.

All this death sentence business which MPs are getting so uptight about now, it's a total waste of time. It is hard enough to get a jury to convict for handling stolen goods, so they'll never, ever convict for murder. There is a whole generation of people who've been brought up without the death sentence and to whom it is utterly alien. You'll get far more murderers walking free if the jury thinks they're going to be topped.

Met PC, age 22, four years service in an inner-city area of London

A loony judge not long ago gave this guy a suspended sentence for twice raping a six-year-old girl. He just let him go. He said it was an accident that "could happen to anyone"! That is the kind of judicial system we've got. It's absolutely ridiculous. That shows how mad some judges are. They've got so much power, they can let people off for twice raping a girl. I wonder if it would have been different were it his daughter? I get a sense of pleasure when I read that solicitors, defence barristers, magistrates and judges are victims themselves of crime. MPs as well. All of a sudden, it's happened to them and they're on the other side. Long may it continue! Then they might see what the problem is. That's the only way MPs are going to do something about sentences.

THE RIGHT TO SILENCE

The Police and Criminal Evidence Act of 1984 also enshrined the suspect's right to silence, which has been a mainstay of the British legal tradition. In our adversarial system of justice, the accused is presumed innocent until proven guilty. It is for the Crown to establish guilt, and the accused is under no obligation to help them do so.

The right to silence, however, has long been a bone of contention with the police, especially in Northern Ireland where evidence and witnesses are notoriously hard to come by. RUC detectives see it as both a straitjacket and a legal luxury in the face of terrorism. The old supergrass system, in which a coconspirator did the talking, was one way round the problem, but a series of complaints, and a general mistrust of the supergrass's motives, rendered such evidence unreliable. All supergrass testimony must now be corroborated, with the familiar difficulties involved in doing that.

In October 1988, after much pressure to do something about both crime in general and IRA terrorism in particular, the government announced plans to amend the right to silence. It may still be invoked, but the jury can be informed and may draw their own conclusions. The change is at first confined to Northern Ireland but will eventually be extended to the mainland. Civil libertarians – including some Northern Irish judges – are in uproar at the proposal, which they believe will permit police officers to force suspects to answer their questions. The police are sanguine about the change. Prisoners still have the right to stay silent. The police point out that of the small minority of suspects who invoke the right to silence, by far the majority are experienced professional criminals. The trade-off is between additional leverage on them and increasing the likelihood that some members of the public may implicate themselves unwittingly, or wrongly, in a crime they did not commit.

RUC Sergeant, age 33, twelve years service. Now in West Belfast.

The balance has gone too far towards the accused. Like finger-prints: you've got to have sixteen points on a fingerprint to make it admissible in court. If you've only got fourteen, you know it's him. But it's not allowed in court. A lot of people will say nothing. We can put a thousand and one questions to them and they make no reply apart from a shrug. Solicitors will tell their client to make no reply, although they know damn well what's going on, especially with the bigger jobs. Certain infer-ences should be brought out from the no-reply syndrome.

Met Superintendent, age 42, twenty-four years service. Now in an inner-city area of London.

There are many investigations into crimes which can't go any further because PACE blocks interviewing. When a man comes in he has the right of silence. He has the right to have a solicitor and he has the right to have friends informed. That's fine for ordinary Joe Soap, but a professional criminal abuses those rights. The right to silence means that he doesn't say a thing, so we have to rely on what witnesses have seen. You probably haven't got any witnesses, so you have to rely on something in his possession that's stolen. But he's not going to tell you how it came into his possession. You don't really want to tell his friends, because one of them will make sure that his house is cleared of dishonestly handled goods, phone numbers or any-thing connecting him with the stolen bank proceeds or whatever. You don't really want to tell his solicitor because he's probably on 10 per cent of the proceeds of the crime. That's something that's laughable in normal circumstances, but there are professional criminals who have criminal solicitors. That's the deal. It's well known. So PACE actually makes crime pay.

RUC Sergeant, age 44, twenty years service; RUC Detective Constable, age 32, eight years service. Both now in West Belfast.

Sgt: The courts have an awful lot to answer for. There's boys killing people and they're getting ten years. The supergrass trials, like them or hate them, saved us a lot of trouble. Those were hard men, the ones we wanted; there was literally mass genocide in west Belfast.

When the appeals were over, those boys were all released and within no more than a month they were shooting each other in a power struggle. It was a particularly vicious feud, but unfortunately, they didn't go on with it. These are the boys the Lord Chief Justice saw fit to push out. Supergrass trials go on in England day in day out and nobody worries about them.

DC: An awful lot of Loyalists and Republicans who are in prison now will regret the day they ever opened their mouths. The only people who are still in prison now, after the supergrass trials, are those that coughed to their crimes after being interviewed. They are locked up, no problem, but those that said nothing, they are out.

We're playing cricket and they're slaughtering us. It's as simple as that. We have lost murder cases by virtue of a statement which wasn't signed on the right line, that type of thing. Irrelevancies, in other words. Surely there is room for a legal system such as they have in France, where the whole essence is to get to the truth? I feel that sometimes the sacrifice of some rights, given the extraordinary conditions under which we are living, would be justified.

Sgt: "The right to remain silent." You can't operate. The boys will lie in the corner up at Castle Street. "Have a seat." "No." First thing they do is lie in the corner. You can't force a man to sit in a seat. He won't ask you to go to the toilet, he will actually defecate in the corner. Apart from getting down on the floor and lying beside him, with the smell of shit coming off him, how do you question somebody like that? He's under no obligation and he knows he's under no obligation to say "boo" to you. You come out of that interview and you need a drink. You need three or four days to get over it because you've put so much into it and there's nothing coming out. That boy knows the law better than we do.

DC: They're professionally schooled. They know exactly what their rights are.

Sgt: They will tell you that they're entitled to give you their name, their address, and that's it. The law does say that it extends to any reasonable information which you require to establish the history of the individual, but he'll just give you his date of birth. No more.

DC: He doesn't care. If he has done maybe five or seven years just wrapped in a blanket and spread shit and stuff up the walls, if a man can do that ... you are fighting an extraordinary war with extraordinary methods.

Inspector in a southern Home Counties force, age 29, seven years service, and a graduate. Now in a suburban town.

Of course it's tempting to scrap the right to silence. It's easy to see why people want it gone. But British justice relies on being seen to be just. We have to live with the times. We know someone has got off that shouldn't, in the knowledge that we've protected the rights of those who should be free. We're not perfect. We make mistakes. It's the old question: is it better for guilty men to go free so that innocent men should not be hanged, or even just imprisoned? Hard cases make bad law. We shouldn't give up our principles so easily.

OPEN VERDICT

The verdict on PACE is not yet in. It has certainly helped to reduce police misbehaviour in stations and to a lesser extent on the street, although its uneven application nationwide has caused problems for many officers in the provinces. But it has laid the foundations for the long-term restoration of public confidence in the police, and that should eventually bear fruit in jury rooms all over the country. Fitting up is reputed to be on the way out because of PACE, although the interviews suggest that the practice still goes on. Yet, for police evidence to be taken seriously in the courts, the public must believe that things have changed for the better. Sadly, a recent opinion poll (November 1988) indicated that half the country believes the police are prepared to lie under oath. Even if that is no longer true, it is what people think is true that matters. There is still a very steep hill to climb.

CHAPTER TEN

Corruption

Like unreported crime, corruption can only be measured when it is exposed, and proven. All one can do to assess the level of corruption in the British police is to look at the tip of what may or may not be an iceberg, and guess at what lies underneath. This is not a book of investigative journalism, and it is very hard to corroborate police claims about corruption. The interviews convey how police officers themselves perceive the problem.

There are two kinds of corruption worth looking at: hard-core corruption, which involves serious money, senior officers and big-time villains, and soft-core corruption, which largely consists of small-scale local favouritism, usually by junior officers.

Hard-core corruption clearly flourished on a substantial scale in certain sections of the Metropolitan Police and the City of London Police during the 1960s and '70s. The whiter-than-white image fostered by Dixon of Dock Green, and completely accepted by the public in the 1950s, was gradually tarnished by the emergence of serious scandals. The Poulson saga from the northeast, the Rhino Whip in Sheffield and the Challoner case in London were followed by The Times *exposé of what appeared to be an instance of systematic corruption in the Met CID. The tape-recording of two detectives asking for money to drop phoney charges effectively forced Scotland Yard to do more than issue the usual denials. By 1972, the Met's Commissioner, Sir Robert Mark, had tacitly acknowledged the existence of corruption in the CID, if not further afield. He formed A10, a new Criminal Investigation Bureau within the Yard, after learning that the existing Anti-Corruption Squad was headed by a policeman who was corrupt himself. Detective Chief Superintendent Moody, who doubled as head of the*

Obscene Publications Squad, had been extracting protection money from Soho pornographers. He was sent to prison for four years. It was a moment of deep shame for the Met, but Mark's efforts were an encouragement to the honest majority in the force who had known about the corruption but had felt powerless to do more than look the other way.

Mark accepted the resignations of several hundred detectives, an indication not only that corruption was widespread but that it was also almost impossible to obtain court-worthy evidence against suspect officers. But he was unable to stop the rot, and his own premature departure meant that the "years of anarchy", as they were known, continued. Scandals emerged in the Drugs Squad, the Vice Squad, the Obscene Publications Squad and, above all, in the Robbery and Flying Squads, the cream of the CID, where a "firm within a firm" that was a law unto itself was identified. The proceeds of bank robberies, some set up by the police, were shared by senior officers at least to the level of Commander.

With half the detectives in London seemingly on the take, Operation Countryman was launched in 1980 to root out corruption in the Met and City Criminal Investigation Departments. Run by officers from rural Dorset, many of whom were rumoured to have been lured off the beat with promises of overtime, Countryman was a fiasco. The "Swedey", as they were contemptuously called, were no match for shrewd London detectives. Their phones were tapped, evidence was destroyed, avenues of access blocked and morale decimated. Hundreds of officers came under investigation, but only three were ever convicted. Operation Countryman was wound up in 1981, having worsened relations between the Met and provincial forces and reinforced the public impression of corruption and incompetence which Mark and others had been fighting for so long. Operation Carter, run by No. 5 Regional Crime Squad, had better evidence against major London detectives than the Countryman team, but that too was quietly dropped. The official view put to them was that it was better to leave the Met intact, with all its faults, because public confidence was at stake.

Nevertheless, the canteen culture which endorsed corruption, or at least allowed it to flourish, began to change. Geoffrey Sims, the supergrass whose evidence began Operation Countryman, had said, "All the Robbery Squad was bent: one-third took money, one-third did favours, and the other third knew about it and looked the other way." Because the CID and specialist squads answered only to themselves, and because promotion within them led all the way to the top, no one rocked the boat. In the 1970s, however, Sir Robert Mark began a process of shifting power over the CID to the uniform branch which his successors, David MacNee and Kenneth Newman, carried into the 1980s. Uniform officers are now in charge of CID and specialist operations on an area-by-area basis; all promotions within CID require a transfer out to the uniform branch for a period; and tours of duty on specialist squads are limited to three years. This has, it is hoped, abolished the "firm within a firm", the corrupt empire within which corrupt men could promote one another.

The sharp reduction in hard-core corruption is a major social change for which the Met, in particular, has been given far too little credit – but then the Met never publicly acknowledged the extent of corruption in the first place. Detectives who openly admitted to taking money in the past told me they had given up because the chances of getting caught were too great, not a very noble sentiment and one which suggests that in some men the old attitudes are, deep down, still there.

One of the problems with rooting out corruption is that it takes so many forms. The hardened criminal's bribe is a world apart from the moral dilemma of the young PC out on his own. It is a severe test of character for him to choose when and where to draw the line. The bind is not just the obvious fear of getting caught. The materialism of British society today encourages cutting corners to make money and please yourself. Young PCs from rural villages, brought up with traditional values, are posted to cities and find themselves plunged into what seems like Sodom and Gomorrah. Exposed to villainy and cynicism, and joining a canteen culture that bucks the rules, inexperienced officers must steer a course between the high tone of official police protocol, their own family values and a peer group with a crude code of its own. Many young GIs had the same problem in Saigon during the Vietnam war.

Chief Inspector in a large northern force, age 38, fourteen years service, and a graduate.

About corruption, I'd say it has changed, the atmosphere has changed completely, certainly in my force. There's a strong man at the top, he's made it clear he won't stand for anything which maybe in other foces is treated in a more relaxed way. Take drinking and driving: we don't even have leaving do's any more, or if we do, you make sure someone there at least is not drinking. Because our chief made sure everyone knew that if anyone is caught drinking and driving, they're likely to be thrown out, especially if they've given the arresting officer a hard time. He's already slung out two officers and that's put the the fear of God in everybody else.

Superintendent in a large northern force, age 48, twenty-seven years service. Now in a racially mixed inner-city area.

I'm not saying corruption and naughtiness don't go on, but certainly it isn't the norm. I mean, what we call corruption out here is not what they'd call it in London. Free meals, bottles at Christmas and so on, that's just taken for granted there. In the present climate down here you are just leaving yourself wide open to trouble if you do that. I get given bottles at Christmas by the local paper and I send them back, "No thanks, I can do my job without them. I don't drink spirits anyway. I earn good money and it's more than my job's worth to risk it for a drink." You have to be suicidal to do a thing like that. Maybe other people take presents, but they're taking a risk, a foolish risk, in my view.

Inspector in a large northern force, age 30, ten years service. Now in an industrial town.

There was a famous incident when a consulate here – a South American one, I think – sent the Chief Constable a case of whisky, a dozen bottles. He sent them back with a note saying he couldn't accept them. But when the Consul wrote back it emerged that only eight had reached the Chief's desk and only four got back to the consulate. There was a hell of a row and a big investigation, but it was very funny too.

I'm not saying it doesn't go on. I'm not so naive as to say that. But if anyone has been up to no good, he won't be foolish enough to make it known to anyone else in this force, because he wouldn't last five minutes. In fact, I can't think of anyone who has been disciplined for corruption in the last twelve months. Not that it doesn't go on. It's just gone underground. They're getting better at it, I suppose.

At grassroots level, the attitude to corrupt policemen varies according to local style.

Sergeant in a Midlands force, age 45, twenty years service. Now in a residential area.

I hate bent coppers. I've met a few through association. You've just got a feeling, you know by their attitude. They give everyone a bad name. We've just had a couple sent down from this Division, and quite rightly. You watch and they know you are watching. You put pressure on them. You can be ostracized in little ways, or get totally isolated from the group. It's nothing offensive, but that's the way bobbies work. If something upsets them, or they think you are breaking the rules, or just not going along, they have their own system of putting you under pressure and most will crack.

If a dodgy number takes a transfer, someone somewhere will know someone at that station, and it will be, "Hello, John, so-and-so's coming to your area." "Why is he transferring?" "Well, we sorted him out. I wouldn't trust him as far as I could throw him." He might dress up as a woman and walk around the park at night or something. It doesn't matter what it is, the whisper will go round and that guy will walk slap bang into the same sort of reception he has just left.

Met Woman Inspector, age 35, ten years service. Now in a racially mixed inner-city area of London.

Things have changed so much. Ten years ago there was a hierarchy in a relief that wouldn't even speak to you until you had done a few years and proved yourself. Now everyone sits around the same table and talks to each other. They are all young in service and the relief doesn't sort itself out. The bad eggs just carry on being bad and there's no one to give summary justice amongst the relief by ostracizing them. A lot of discipline has gone because of that.

Met PC, age 28, six years service, and a graduate. Now in an inner-city area.

You get an attitude about life that's so cynical your values begin to slip. That's where you get the start of corruption. The bottle of Scotch from the happy victim who got a result – I would take that. The next stage on is where the policing is actually influenced by the gifts given – being in on an observation on a shop which is going to be broken into because you know you're going to get a jumper out of it if you nick the guy. That's the next stage. After that it's tampering with evidence. The sky's the limit really.

At Christmas time, hoteliers, restaurateurs and publicans feel they have no option but to "donate" to CID. I think that's obnoxious. I've been a party to it. It's corruption, maybe it was a weak personality trait being part of it. At the time you don't think – it's just a bottle of Scotch, great! It is obnoxious. There is very little encouragement and reward for resisting temptation. It's a long tradition and you just become part of it. Christmas is a big event in the police force. It's not so much Christmas as all December! You just have a bloody good time. The fact is, you don't have to pay for it.

Scottish PC, age 26, five years service. Now in a city centre.

I'm twenty-six, I've got a wee child, a wife, a permanent over-draft, and if someone offered me a million pounds or an amount that felt like a million pounds, I can't say I wouldn't take it. I would say to you now, sitting here, "I wouldn't take it." But in a situation where no one else is affected, say an embezzlement or an insurance fraud, that's different. Obviously not for some-body who has murdered someone, but where it doesn't affect anybody else you may well be swayed. I can never understand policemen who go out and thieve as such, but if someone who has spent his whole life doing crime offers you £200,000 or something, I can understand some people saying "yes". It's not very nice to think they do, but it's understandable.

SOFT-CORE CORRUPTION

Ordinary coppers are far more prone to soft-core corruption, which ranges from little pay-offs for regular favours to free drinks, free meals and free sex with prostitutes. Traffic cops in Hertfordshire were caught giving a local garage more than its fair share of accident business. That is now harder to arrange because the call-out is done strictly geographically from a list at the station. The bereaved may be directed to certain under-takers. Businesses with a shady reputation – scrap metal, second-hand cars, after-hours clubs – find it helpful to stay friendly with their local bobbies.

Pay is a crucial factor in all this. Since 1979, the police have received a substantial pay rise and greedy officers are now perhaps less tempted to risk their pensions to supplement their wages on a freelance basis. But the small presents, favours and discounts normal to civilian life are still strictly against the police Code of Conduct, if not the law.

Detective Sergeant in a Home Counties force, age 38, eighteen years service. Now in a university town.

Me and a mate went into this tart's place in London with a spy-hole in the door. It was like a fortress. We bullshitted our way in as being local Old Bill and the woman let us in, no questions asked. It wasn't till we actually got into her boudoir that we nicked her. She nearly fainted. It was just an accepted thing that two lads like us would drop in for a quickie.

Two PCs from a large northern force, average age 30, average service ten years. Now with the Vice Squad in a city centre.

PC1: The majority of kerb crawlers we stop are businessmen. Between five and seven o'clock on weekdays is a busy period, or lunchtime, when these fellows are coming out of their offices.

There are just hundreds of cars, brand new cars, Porsches, Jaguars, you know, bank managers, magistrates, police officers driving around.

PC2: Senior police officers.

PC1: Very much so.

PC2: Senior officers from Complaints and Discipline Department. Driving around attempting to pick up and picking up girls, having regular meetings and sexual acts in buildings, in backs of cars. We're up there and we see all this going on. They know we know. That's one reason why they tend to leave us alone.

PC in a large force in the Midlands, age 32, twelve years service. Now in a city centre.

They say everybody has a price and they apparently give us a good wage to stop us being corrupt. But the more money you get, obviously you are going to spend more, and if you spend more you are going to have more debts. It's a vicious circle. There's been a couple of times when people have offered me money. Like if you've pulled someone up for a breathalyzer, they say: "How must is it going to cost, £50?" Fortunately at the time I had a Sergeant with me, but it does happen. If they are a manager of a club or something, they say, "The next time you come round, come in for a few drinks or a bottle of whisky." I don't like corruption at all.

I'd have loved to have been on the investigation of Operation Countryman. If some of our bosses were corrupt, I wouldn't have any hesitation shopping them. If somebody came to me in the street and said, "Look, I've got some information concerning your bosses, can I have a word?" I'd arrange some back-up just in case it was a set-up and I'd go along. Then I have a problem: who do I tell? If this fellow is a Chief Inspector or a Chief Superintendent and he's corrupt, then obviously he knows other people who are too. I could go to another force, but what force did he come from beforehand? Do I tell the press or the radio or something? You talk to your boss – but he used to work with him, didn't he? Maybe he is corrupt.

PC in a Midlands force, age 30, six years service, and a graduate.

Crime Squads, Drugs Squads – a spirit grows up amongst small units, almost incestuous really. They either just think they're the last of the centurions and everybody out there is corrupt and rotten, or they become totally disinterested and "It's just a job and I'm out to get the most I can for me out of it." At which point you start to get financial corruption.

Actually, you get a degree of that sometimes amongst the uniform. I don't mean the financial corruption, I don't think most uniformed bobbies have the temptation. They never see it. But some of them take the line: "I don't care whether it's right or wrong; as long as you pay me I'll do it." There was certainly a lot of that about during the miners' strike, where the political issues were too complex for people to grasp. Besides, they knew that if they decided the miners were right, they weren't going to feel good about going on making all that extra overtime money.

The smaller things like a free meal, or a drink, or presents, become confused where friendship is intended to sway your opinion, I think most policemen faced with a situation where the gift and the favour were visibly and inextricably linked wouldn't take it. It wouldn't be worth it for the small return.

But what about drinking clubs, who often let policemen in on the strength of warrant cards? It's probably an abuse of your authority, but most policemen will do it. It's good for the club, because if there's a rumble there and it's known to be a friendly club, then the policemen are going to be less officious. Shades of grey.

Sergeant in a West Country force, age 28, nine years service. Now in a racially mixed area.

On my patch, if you go into one of the Chinese takeaways and ask to buy some food, they don't want to take your money. Most of them come from Hong Kong and spend all their lives sending money home to buy policemen over there. When you say, "No, I want to pay," they are quite panicked. They're thinking, "My God, what's going to happen?" It seems like a dire warning because the policeman insists on paying for his food! That could be quite awkward, but to be honest, I daresay most policemen say, "Thank you very much," and walk out with it, without thinking about the deeper significance. If later on somebody's in a position of temptation for much larger sums, then in a way they've stepped half-way over the line already with these little things.

The service does try and keep a grip on it – locker raids, when they come and look in the lockers to see what's in them. In our force a couple of fellows were actually charged with theft. A lorry shed its load on the motorway. The lorry driver said, "Take some yourselves lads, if you want." "Oh, thank you very much!" Of course, the things weren't the lorry driver's to give away, so they all ended up inside.

The overwhelming impression gained from the interviews is that corruption in provincial forces is by and large soft-core. Sometimes it goes public as in the case of Stanley Parr, Chief Constable of Lancashire, who was sacked for reducing criminal charges for his friends in Blackpool.

RUC Chief Inspector, age 37, fifteen years service.

Corruption never existed in this force, that's one thing I can say. The most you'd get – and I'm sure it's true today – would be buying a thing wholesale and cutting out the retailer. I remember a policeman so uneasy about buying through a wholesaler that he used to get proper receipts in case there'd be queries. There's nothing wrong with that at all – cutting out the middleman. But the police are so conscious. We're a very honest force. We may have had many faults, but certainly dishonesty was not one.

I've never known any disloyal police in all these years, selling police information. You may have got a touch of smuggling round the border – some policemen were suspected of passing information on police patrols to smugglers – but the police aren't involved, that's Customs and Excise.

THE SHADOW OF SUSPICION AND NOT GUILTY

From time to time the shadow falls on men at the top for conduct which would be considered normal in the business

*world. The Chief Constable of Derbyshire was recently inves-
tigated for spending huge sums on redecorating his office,
though he was cleared of any impropriety. Questions were
asked about Ronald Gregory, the former Chief Constable of
West Yorkshire, in connection with mileage and petrol claims
on personal journeys. Gregory was cleared. However, his successor was Colin Sampson, the man who gave John Stalker such
a hard time over the possible misuse of a Greater Manchester
official car. Stalker was suddenly removed both from his inquiry
into the RUC alleged shoot-to-kill policy – a matter of great
sensitivity – and from his job as Deputy Chief Constable of the
second largest force in England. In Sampson's fifteen-hundred
page report, Stalker was accused of nothing worse than associ-
ating with a man with no criminal record, but dodgy contacts,
and giving lifts to friends. Perhaps because of the Gregory affair,
Sampson chose to see it as the thin end of the wedge.*

TACKLING CORRUPTION

*Research into deviance in the police shows that corruption can
occur in all ranks. Beat men have limited mobility and therefore
little opportunity for graft beyond soft-core activities; it is the
Superintendents, Inspectors and Sergeants who can slip out of
the station for a business meeting without having to account
for their movements.*

*The most common kind of offence is petty: infringements of
the police Code of Discipline, which may have nothing to do
with breaking the law. Not a day goes by without officers
breaking the Code: vehicles should be given a sixteen-point
check before being taken out, but in practice this is ignored,
caps are not worn, smoking takes place in public, lunch breaks
are extended, and so on. Where it creeps into corruption is
through fiddled expenses and presents accepted in return for
real or expected favours. Senior officers are more likely to be
the offenders, and most policemen would say that it is the
beginning of the slippery slope.*

**Detective Constable in a northern force, age 38, eighteen years
service. Now in a costal town.**

I can give you all the things that happen in our office which was straight down the line breaches of disciplines: One, late for duty. Secondly, using your car allowance to do whatever you want to do. Thirdly, using police vehicles other than on police work. Fourthly, claiming expenses, like refreshment allowances when things aren't quite normal. Fifthly, bailing out before time is up. Sixthly, making up your notebook for overtime claims. The majority do it.

GOING WITH THE FLOW

It is the attitudes behind corruption that can be so hard to dislodge, especially in the materialistic 1980s. 'Loadsamoney' has entered the language and police officers are not immune.

PC in a Home Counties force, age 29, eight years service. Now in a large suburban town.

I don't see what all the fuss is about for taking the odd present. I mean, they've got a rule now that we can't use our warrant card to get discounts in shops. Why not? We put up with all the shit the public throws at us, while they have all the short cuts and tax fiddles and all the rest that yuppies and anyone else can use to get on, while we're supposed to sit back and take the minimum we're given. It's one rule for them, and another for us. My wife's a nurse, and she's bloody pissed off with the way this government treats her. All the crap about extra money, and they claw it back on the regrading. I feel the same way. Lots of us do. The government makes a big noise about backing the police, but when it comes down to it, to the bottom bloody line, there's no money for local authorities to pay us overtime, is there? It stands to reason we want discounts, and presents, a free meal, or whatever. It's all right for Maggie and Nigel to preach about values when they're very well looked after by their friends. Why shouldn't we be?

MOONLIGHTING

Avarice is hardly unique to the police, nor is moonlighting. Although it is against the Code of Discipline. So many officers do some sort of extra work that it is barely regarded as an offence. Running a small building company on the side is a popular option.

Sergeant in a northern force, age 34, thirteen years service. Now in a residential suburb.

We had a set-up with a garage open twenty-four hours for which we gave the night cover. The guy who organized it made sure the Inspector's nephew, who was also in the force, did most of the time up there. It all went well until there was an altercation between one of the off-duty PCs and a taxi driver. The PC insisted he was a policeman to settle it, and the taxi driver said, "No, you're not, you're a petrol pump attendant." He reported it, but fortunately it wasn't recorded formally. Our Inspector got it on the grapevine from the Inspector who took the call and he came down to see us and warned us all off. Apart from anything else, strictly speaking we should have paid income tax on it, so there was arguably an offence there too. But to me we weren't doing anything bad, it was just a bit of moonlighting and not affecting our work. We always made sure we did it when we were off the following day, so we weren't paid twice for working the same day. It is accepted that a certain amount of moonlighting goes on, and I think the majority of us feel good luck to the bloke that can get away with it.

GUARDING THE GUARDIANS

The job of investigating other officers is among the least popular in the police service (see "Complaints and Discipline"). Officers know that there's a need for them, but resent their presence none the less. The protection given to officers involved in major public controversies like allegations of brutality in the miners' strike or the Manchester Students' Union are not extended to minor offences which are often treated harshly. This often does not have the desired effect of raising officers' morale – it leaves them feeling as hard done by on the small matters as the public complainants feel about the lack of action on the larger ones.

Former PC in a Home Counties force, east of London, age 28, six years service, and a graduate.

Every policeman gets investigated sooner or later. If you don't get any complaints, you can't be leaving the station. I only had one that got as far as Complaints and Discipline. Some property was in the property store that I had taken as evidence. Between my taking it and the day it went to court, the damn stuff went missing – two Scotch salmon! There was an innocent explanation. Someone had given them away with a load of other frozen food in error. But it took Discipline and Complaints eighteen months to decide that ten quid's worth of fish wasn't that big a deal. I was interviewed three or four times. It did seem like a whole burden of fuss about nothing, but they were just concerned that one of us might have stolen them.

One bloke I can think of, there were rumours about him for donkey's years. In the end, he got caught throwing away prosecution files for a lot of money from an influential, respectable family in the City. And he went down for it. People had known for a long time that he wasn't quite what he appeared to be. They didn't usually let him get into a position where he had any control over sensitive things. So they put him in the court office, which nobody ever had the foresight to realize had the scope for corruption just as much as walking around unguarded houses. Bit slow of them really.

The general standard of behaviour within stations was really not bad at all, considering. Personal property didn't go, though you'd occasionally get the station property going missing. I think most people who become policemen do have a personal code of conduct that they respect.

DETERRING CORRUPTION

As George Bernard Shaw remarked, criminals are punished not for committing crimes but for getting caught. The threat of serious disciplinary action is now a deterrent even in large urban forces. It is vital that it remains so.

Met PC, age 30, eight years service in a racially mixed area of West London.

There was a raid one day on a judge's daughter for drugs. As it happens, she didn't have any personally, but she was having a drugs party. There was one fellow who said, "Yes, I've got some." The fool! Senior officers were there as well. He went to his bedroom and couldn't find the blinking drugs. He was hunting around. The senior officers disappeared out the door and I was the only one with him. Eventually he gets his hand in his jeans and says, "Found it!" It was a bit of cannabis. It was a hot summer's night, so he says, "There's only two people here, can't you just stick it out of the window?" I said, "Well, I get paid about ten grand a year, I've got another twenty years to go in this job. It goes up every year, so by the time I retire I'll have earned about a quarter of a million ..."

"All right," he says, "forget it."

"You're nicked!"

What's it worth to my career if I throw it out the window and somebody sees me? My home, my family, my wife, my integrity. Sitting in prison, getting beaten up by prisoners, eating with plastic forks and knives? No thanks.

THE MET

Corruption in the Met has always been a problem. With more than 27,000 officers, it is the largest single force and lacks the intimate cohesion which serves as a brake in other forces. London presents officers with the greatest temptations: it is Britain's richest and largest city, now thriving in a ruthless climate committed to money as an end in itself. Living on fixed wages since overtime was cut back, and watching soaring house prices push them further out of London, Met officers are asked to observe higher standards than the people they police.

Chief Inspector in a Home Counties force, age 34, ten years service, and a graduate.

I would say that corruption is at a much higher level in the London than in provincial forces. The culture is more inclined to tolerate corruption in the Met. My first sniff of it was when I had a traffic duty, escorting lorries with abnormal loads up to the border of London where they'd be taken over by the Met. The traffic lads at the changeover would have a word with the driver of the lorry, and according to how much they were paid, he either got down by the fast or the slow route through London. That was not the exception, that was the usual practice. It was eight years ago, but after the miners' strike I've no reason to think it's changed. I've worked in Complaints and Discipline, so I've investigated a few cases. There's very little serious corruption out here, though there have been some awful cases. Police officers were dismissed and convicted on two occasions. They'd been investigating serious crime networks and got on to the top villains about when the police raids were going to take place – for a fee. Here you're talking about small things. You aren't there.

RUC Superintendent, age 38, eighteen years service. Now in Belfast.

I sent across two men one time to collect a prisoner who was in custody in the Met. They drove the prisoner and two RUC men to the railway station, and at the station the Met policeman held out his hand for a tip from my colleagues for driving them there. They were horrified. They said: "We told him, if he came across to our force in Ireland, there'd be a man detailed to take him round with a car from Transport, and they'd buy him dinners." They said, "We wouldn't ask you for a tip." The Met officer couldn't believe it. He said, "I've driven you two down. It's a police car and I'm on duty. I've got better things to do than drive you two around." That's their colleague. That's the Metropolitan Police. That's the start of corruption.

London is also the traditional centre for many criminal trades: the armed robbers of South and East London, vice in central London, financial fraudsters in the City – and drug dealers. The bank robberies of the 1970s netted hundreds of thousands of pounds – a share of which was enough to corrupt many London detectives – the fortunes involved in the drugs trade are so enormous as to corrupt whole countries.

Former Met Inspector, age 37, sixteen years service. Now with a provincial force.

The first time it happened to me was after a sudden death. Three of us went to a house where an old lady had died and searched through the premises to find the next of kin – quite legitimate. Any valuables you give to the next-door neighbour or take back to the nick and put in the book – which we did.

I was three or four weeks out of training school and back in the canteen with the two guys. They gave me £5 or something. "What's that for?" "Just put it in your pocket and don't ask any questions." So I did and then felt, "Shit, what have I done? It can only have come from there." They were sitting chatting away as if nothing had happened.

What do you do? You can't go up to a Sergeant and say you're upset about a £5 note. So I waited. A week later I went out with the guys again, still with the note, and I said, "Look, what's going on? What's the score?" They said it was just a way of making a few bob. I said, "But she was an old lady and she only had about forty quid and it's not ours. It should go to the next of kin who may be in similar straits." So I gave the money back. OK, that solved my problem but it did not solve *the* problem. When a sudden death came up the same people would always answer and then you realized the deal.

Four years later when I was made Acting Sergeant I made it my point to get to sudden deaths first and take care of the property. The guys would be looking over your shoulder, saying, "Is there much here, guv? Is there much?" They say it's no big deal because a lot of the time what you find goes to the Exchequer – that's their logic.

The moral climate in the Met is changing as the intake has begun to include more graduates. Nevertheless, the vast sums now available from modern criminal enterprises must be deeply worrying to senior officers. And because there is no provision for dismissal from the force without proof to the standard of the criminal law, bobbies who took money in the past but who were not caught or successfully prosecuted have remained in the force, their cynicism waiting to influence young green PCs.

PC in a Home Counties force, age 44, twenty-two years service. Now a village bobby.

In 1966 I decided for personal reasons that I was going to be a policeman. It was a very sudden decision. I had a sister who lived in a flat in London; my father lived in the North of Scotland, an area the size of Hampshire with a very small population; and I was living in Reading, which was a small borough force. Three totally different types of police work. Which should I choose?

I fancied the bright lights of London and the activity and the high training in the Metropolitan Police area. I went to London and I spoke to a policeman there, to whom I am eternally grateful, because he was honest. I put my dilemma to him and asked what he advised.

He said, "round the corner there is a telly shop; on Friday night there was a smash-and-grab at 2 a.m. Witnesses saw a man running off and they called the police. The van went there three times before the key-holder turned up; two and a half grand's worth of gear had been nicked. The guy who ran off certainly couldn't carry more than one telly. Draw your own conclusions." He said, "Right, you've got the picture? You join the Met and you join a relief and you are put in that van. What would you do?" He said, "You don't know much about life, you have joined the police force to find out. Do you want to find out the hard way? If you join the Met there are so many officers and so many opportunities – if you can cope with that, then make your decision. The Met is the best place, you won't get better training anywhere else in the world. It is a fast life. You will deal with everything here in the first two years – from armed robbery to murder. If you can't handle that, go for a country force." Which I did, because I still don't know how I would have coped with it.

CHANGING THE CANTEEN CULTURE

In recent years, senior officers in the Met have been trying to change the canteen culture and its attitudes towards race, women, violence and corruption. They know its corrosive effect on impressionable young PCs. Attempts to turn it into a positive influence have failed, on the realistic grounds that almost by definition, the canteen culture has to be against authority.

As long as it is just talk, no harm is done. Police officers complain and re-create their dramas for each other as a way of passing the time until the next one. But it is a forum in which echoes of the excesses of the 1970s and early '80s can still be heard. Officers who joined in those days have some years to go.

Met PC, age 45, twenty-two years service. Now in South London.

There used to be horrendous alleged misdoings by squads who thought they were invincible. Other CID officers would never challenge them because they did the same. In fact, the more daring you were, the further you got up the ladder.

Prior to the Mark era, it was getting to such a state that particular squads just ran London. But it kept a lot of the villainy down. Now they're not keeping it down. They're not allowed out drinking so they don't get their informants in pubs. There is no fear of the police anymore. "You catch me pal – prove it!" It has to be proven scientifically, forensically, legally – it all takes time and crime just soars.

Former Met Inspector, age 37, sixteen years service. Now resigned.

I was just leaving the job when my Superindendent came up and said, "You're going. Not a bad time to leave this job. The only thing you can say is that corruption is on the way out." I said, "You must be joking." And he said, "Oh, I think we can pat ourselves on the back here. I think I can happily say that Mark finally put an end to that." And I said, "You are just not looking round you, guv'nor. You should spend a little more time away from your desk. It's nothing to do with me, but don't think it's all gone."

Only three weeks earlier we had a job where we nicked someone for cocaine. It's a long story but the net result is that this guy comes up to me and says he didn't mind being nicked, "But do I get my money back?" Straight up! "I don't want to cause trouble. I just want my cash back." He realized I was in a difficult position, because when it came down to it I couldn't not nick him. "But what about the gaff?" I told him I would look into it but never did.

The trouble is the guys that were DCs and DSs stopped taking money in '73, '75 when Mark actually started hitting them for corruption. But if they start again they are DIs and DCIs and more by now. It doesn't bode well.

Met Sergeant, age 39, twenty years service. Formerly with the CID, now in uniform in West London.

Let's be honest, the CID felt they didn't have anything to worry about. The "Swedey" – the Countryman wallies – there was no way they were going to get a result. What did they get, two people prosecuted? They were just scratching the surface. They must have realized the size of the issues involved and said, "How in Christ's name do we approach them?"

It's some of the best officers that go bent. The chances are that if he goes bent he's a bloody good thief-taker as well. He'll be a good policeman, a guy who gets results through genuine means. He'll walk down the road and arrest a car thief but then try to do a deal with him. The poor coppers never nick anybody. They're never going to be corrupt because they haven't got it in them, they haven't the mind to see what's going on.

All the detectives I've known who've been pretty well bent are very good policemen, and very, very likeable. There was a DCI from the Regional Crime Squad. He owned a big house in Surrey and £100,000 worth of cars but he had "never taken a penny in his life". It's at the Inspector level, both in uniform and in CID, that's where you see it happening: people making deals, wheeling and dealing, getting around the pubs and the clubs.

Everything that was wrong with the police you could see at the CID Christmas party. It was outrageous – all the local villains, publicans, betting-shop owners, girls from everywhere – the whole thing was seedy. I don't want to make myself out to be a crusader. I enjoy a drink like anybody. But inviting all those people, it was just so blatant. I doubt they're so cocky now, though.

Assistant Chief Constable in a large northern force, age 50, twenty-eight years service. Formerly in the Met.

It really was very bad indeed in London, quite horrific. Some could see what was happening, but never said what was happening. They were very clever, some of those guys. And the sad thing is that there are still some people who would like to go back to that era – people who hate and detest the memory of Robert Mark, for what he did to their way of life. I mean, if you're earning that much money it's human nature.

Countryman was a fiasco. The whole world knew it was a fiasco. But there are more ways than one of killing the cat. You only have to look at the major characters involved, if you know who they are: they've either gone from the force or changed their spots very considerably. Even if they haven't changed their attitude, they are not doing it any more because they know people are going to catch them.

But I do find it disappointing that people are still prepared to take money despite all the restrictions. But the situation is 1000 per cent better now, it really is.

Met Superintendent, age 44, nineteen years service. Now in central London.

We are not worried about corruption on the old scale. Not at all. There are bound to be pockets, isolated pockets, but the firm within a firm, the easy attitude towards fitting up, "taking a drink" off villains to leave them out of the frame – all that has really gone. Of course not all the bent coppers have left the force, but their influence is no longer what it was. The top men have gone now, and the others keep their heads down.

CHAPTER ELEVEN

Freemasonry

Whether justly or not, Freemasonry is now widely regarded both inside and outside the police force as another form of corruption. As it is a secret organization, rumours abound about preferments for jobs and promotion, protection from prosecution, destruction of evidence and many other, more ordinary forms of favouritism. Whatever the truth, the impression has lodged itself firmly in the minds of both many policemen and members of the public that Masons in the force do not always act impartially.

The most recent controversy surfaced in early 1988. Brian Woollard, a Met Chief Inspector, alleged that there was masonic bias in Islington Council, in the DPP's office and in the force over the handling of corruption charges against Islington officials who were Masons. The subsequent brouhaha led to Woollard's suspension from duty and to a campaign in the Independent *against Freemasonry in public life. The result was a flurry of concern at the Home Office and at the top of the Met, where the problem has been under consideration for a number of years.*

The previous Commissioner of the Met, Sir Kenneth Newman, had been under pressure to make Freemasonry a disciplinary offence. Instead, he merely advised officers against joining because of a possible conflict of loyalty and urged those already in the Brotherhood to resign. This was not a great success. Far from accepting resignations, in 1985 the Brotherhood founded a new lodge, the Manor of St James, specially for police officers – and right across the road from New Scotland Yard.

When the Woollard affair became a cause célèbre *in 1988, the Home Secretary, Douglas Hurd, announced that there was no need for a full-scale inquiry into masonic influence in the police because he had "looked into it" and found nothing to be concerned about. His remarks did not reassure the critics, as Masonic penetration of the civil service and the DPP's office is believed to be high.*

Though Freemasonry in the police attracted public attention only recently, it has fed force cynicism for many years.

Met Inspector, age 32, eleven years service, and a graduate. Now in a middle-class residential area of London.

I am not a Mason. If I was invited to join, I wouldn't. As a young PC in Holborn, I can remember going to a traffic congestion call in Queen Street. It's chaos, and the reason is that there are eight black Austin Princesses parked outside this lodge. I leap out to move them off and the Area Car driver says, "Put your hat on. Look at the cars!" Of course it was all the Commanders' Princesses. I walked down the street thinking to myself, "I'm totally out of my depth here." That was my introduction to Masons in the police.

A couple of years later I applied for the Drugs Squad and having not got that I considered transferring to the CID, and spoke to an awful lot of people to get advice. One Detective Superintendent, who is a good friend, said: "I can name you no more than a handful of people of the rank of Inspector upwards in the CID who are not Masons." He said that for someone like myself, coming from uniform into CID, it would be "a bad move not to join". It's a closed shop in many ways. I've been at two stations where there was a PC higher in the Masons than the Chief Superintendent. It caused absolute havoc with the whole station management. It's been very blatant.

You can say it's a club, but certainly the atmosphere at those two stations wasn't like any golf club. My knowledge of Masonry is very limited, but there's an alarm bell in the back of my mind that says, "I don't like what I'm seeing."

MASONIC ATTRACTIONS

For those whose upbringing leaves them ill at ease with people of different classes and backgrounds, Freemasonry offers an ideal environment of prescribed routines and male conviviality in which to socialize safely.

Met PC, age 43, twenty-four years service and a masonic officer.

I like the social life of it, the masonic assemblies. I like the people who are involved with it. I joined the Masons, not because I was a policeman but because I wanted to. I had an uncle who was a Mason, though he didn't tell me very much about it. After my father his lifestyle was very much how I'd like to be. He's a very nice man, he's very good to other people. He's been a forester all his life and he's got a very simple life and as I say, I like to model myself on them. My father was a gardener. He was a God-fearing man, though he wasn't a church-goer. He wouldn't do any wrong. These are the types of person I come across in my Masonry. Every lodge has got its two or three who are very different. In ours I'm glad to say they are not policemen, they're in business. I don't get on at all but I speak to them and spend the time of day with them but I don't want to get too friendly with them. I know who I like to be friends with because of their lifestyle. You can trust them, trust them with your wife if you wanted. You could trust them with your bank book.

RUC Inspector, age 37, fourteen years service and a Mason.

Masonry only gets bad publicity because people treat it as a secret service. But it's not really, it's just a club with secrets, you can find them out if you go to the public library. Membership's not secret. Some unsuitable policemen have tried to get into the Masonry and been black-balled, then they will be very aggressive and bitter towards Masons. It comes down to your businessmen who are maybe using it to their advantage and they don't want it broadcast that they are members. If someone asks me if I'm a Mason I will say yes, but I won't tell them I'm a Mason because there's so much ridicule from the public because you are a Mason, perhaps from incidents from the past. They only hear about the bad things they never hear about the good things.

Met Inspector, age 38, sixteen years service. Now in the north-east.

Certainly there's a Met lodge and Met Masons are invited to meetings which no one else knows about and which they don't talk about. I've been asked many times by people of various ranks.

I once went as a guest to the Metropolitan Police Masonic Association annual gentlemen's smoking evening, where we all wore dinner jackets and watched strippers and a couple of comedians. It was crazy – all of a sudden you'd see this face and think, "Crikey! I didn't know he was a Mason." It was just that we were all in D Js watching blue entertainment and strippers with a lot of high-ranking police officers. I hadn't thought about it before. As I went in I thought, "That's So-and-so, that's Inspector So-and-so and Commander So-and-so." They were notorious, these stag nights. Everybody wanted to know when the next one was, especially the CID.

PC in Home Counties force, age 40, twenty-one years service and a masonic officer.

The Masons is a stag do but we only have five a year on Friday nights. You have a weekly one but that's only what they call a lodge of instruction. You go and rehearse something – like an actor, learning your lines – so you do that once a week but that's only for two hours, plus my Friday every second month.

The wife doesn't get jealous. At the Christmas meeting the wives are allowed to come to the ladies' meeting once a year. They have dances and this type of thing. Some of the blokes are in our Masonry darts team, so we have a prize-giving night and make that a dinner and dance evening and so we get the women involved as well, fancy dress night as well. It brings them in and she knows who you're with, so I think I've done it the right way.

I've met blokes in the Masons, like blokes in the police force – like they call them "job-pissed" – they're always there. You have the same thing in Masonry. They go to every meeting they can, but I keep it to my own lodge.

I have one friend who's a Mason and his wife hates Masonry. Not because of what it is but what it's done to him, the way he's let it get hold of him. He's very, very high up in Masonry, in the hierarchy and his home life is absolutely terrible.

PROVINCIAL NETWORK

In the provinces, there are different dangers. Masonic ties may well dominate a smaller force and bind it to local personalities in ways that could not guarantee independence for the police. Masonic influence was suspected for the abrupt removal of John Stalker from his inquiry into the alleged RUC "shoot-to-kill policy" in Northern Ireland just as he was about to interview the Chief Constable and his senior colleagues, but it was never proved. Nevertheless, masonic influence in both the RUC and northern forces has been strong for many years. Detective Chief Superintendent Peter Topping, until recently head of Greater Manchester CID, is a known Mason and is said to have recruited heavily from among the Brotherhood on the grounds that all other things being equal he could trust them.

PC in a Midlands force, age 40, eighteen years service. Now training probationers.

There's no doubt about it, with the invitations I've had to join the Masons, there are definitely favours going on in that department. I've had close friends, very best friends, personally invite me. I've had people who don't know me, at the scene of an accident, whom I'm going to report, invite me to be a Mason. I've had people who know me through sport, who consider, looking at me, that I would make an excellent Mason, invite me to be a Mason. The Masons is like any club: you give or take as little or as much as you want.

The attractions of being a Mason are peer power, to be in with a cliquey environment – which is an attraction to some people. Certain officers want promotion and, whether rightly or wrongly, see that it may assist them. If I wanted to go up the ranks within the police force and that was my sole ambition, I would become a Mason. I would definitely go for it. You've got everything to gain and nothing to lose.

PROMOTION GOSSIP

Police officers are loyal to their own rank but tend to be ungenerous towards those who get promoted. The Police Orders are circulated weekly and list the names of newly promoted officers. They are a source of widespread masonic gossip and become the agenda for canteen assassins.

Former Met PC, age 28, six years service in an inner-city area of south London. Now resigned.

You can always tell who's a Mason in the police – just look at Police Orders. If you are promoted at the Yard, you are a Mason or a Catholic and a member of the Knights of St Columba. One in five of the Met are Catholics, but the Masons get a lot more publicity because they are secret.

I was told at training school, and it stuck with me, that if you are going to be a police officer you must be seen to have integrity. If you haven't, you can't do the job. If you are a Mason, you have a clash of interests and you are opening yourself up to being compromised. If your loyalty is not to the Queen but to your lodge, you can't be a police officer with 100 per cent integrity. If it was down to me, you shouldn't be a police officer and a Mason unless you declare your interests.

RUC Inspector, age 36, fifteen years service. Now in West Belfast.

What I find difficult to take on is that a man goes into a police promotion board to be assessed and he is maybe master of a lodge and perhaps the chairman of the assessing board is junior to him in the hierarchy. The conflicting roles there, and the nature of the Brotherhood, helping other members at all costs – I find it difficult to believe that it doesn't influence a man's decision. Yet there's nothing you can pinpoint.

In a disciplined force, in which distinctions of rank are often jealously guarded, the alternative rank structure of the Masons is another source of tension and mistrust.

Met Detective Constable, age 29, seven years service. Now in the Crime Squad.

There was a Detective Superintendent and his driver. The relationship between the two was so peculiar I couldn't fathom it out until someone told me the driver was a very, very high Mason and the Detective Superintendent was a very low Mason. It was weird. The Superintendent would seek advice from this PC on major investigations. Even going out in the evening, it would be the Superintendent asking the PC, "Where shall we go?" It's the most extreme example I've ever seen.

It was all explained to me at the driver's leaving do – he's now a cabbie, which is inevitable. He gave the most horrific speech you could possibly imagine and ripped the Superintendent apart. It was very, very personal. He just crucified him, a PC ripping apart a Superintendent. "Incompetent ... Can't handle himself ... Never seen such bad interviews." It was at the end of an investigation which had gone badly wrong, and the Superintendent had done the key interview. We all knew he was incompetent but no bugger was going to say so to his face. He just left, walked out. The PC was a wanker as well.

Two PCs in a large northern force, average age 31, average service eight years. Both now in a city-centre area.

PC1: In this division a constable who is high up in the Masons wields more power than the Chief Super. We had two colleagues in this office who were very good policemen but they were under a lot of pressure on jobs and didn't keep an eye on the paperwork. They were got rid of, dropped like a stone. Now this PC with the masonic influence told me two days before it blew that they were in the shit. That to me is incredible.

PC2: That PC very seldom knocks – he just walks in on the boss. He's on first-name terms but he's no senior to us.

PC1: Nobody is nasty to that bobby. Everyone is nice to him, even though lots of people absolutely hate him. He won't be walking out there with a helmet on again, in fact there's a good chance he won't be walking out again at all. He's a desk man now, got a "nine-to-fiver" for life.

PC2: It's very disheartening for somebody who's got eight years' service in to see somebody with less service going way up the ladder because he socializes well and does a lot for the Masons.

PC1: You think, "How the hell did that bloke get promoted? He's a half-wit. You wouldn't trust him with your granny!"

PC2: We can slag them off but we know damn well they're with us. Like we all know there are corrupt policemen but we don't talk about them every day.

STOPPING FAVOURITISM

There have been moves to deal with favouritism, not just as it applies to Masons. The most drastic involved the CID – heavily masonic – in which promotion through the ranks in plain clothes was how the "firm within the firm" was maintained. (It must also be said that detective expertise was preserved as well.) For some years, promoted detectives have had to return to uniform for a spell. But selection for the elite squads – Murder, Serious Crime, Robbery and the Regional Crime Squads among them – has stayed a form of patronage. John Cass, a known Mason, was National Coordinator of the RCS. This has led to much bad feeling in the lower ranks.

Met DC, age 29, seven years service, and a graduate. Now in West London.

What happens with specialist squads now is that you have to make a written application to join and they have to advertise in Police Orders, whereas before people were fixed up on recommendation. One of the people behind this basically wanted to counter "old boys", if not Masons. He himself is a Detective Superintendent and quite a high Mason, but he doesn't like the fact that people who are not competent to fill positions are getting those positions because they are Masons. He's very unpopular, an incredibly unpopular man.

CRIMINAL ASSOCIATION

The Masonic reputation for charity and the Brotherhood's strict code of honour have not prevented police officers from openly socializing with villains who are members of the same lodge. In 1980, Lennie Gibson, a top London armed robber, became master of the Waterways Lodge in Southgate, North London, to which eight Met officers, including one Robbery Squad detective, belonged. The Masonic code states that "While some must rule, others must obey and cheerfully accept their inferior position" – precisely the circumstances that Newman and other critics warned against. In the same year, Gibson was jailed for ten years for his part in what was then Britain's biggest armed robbery. Three of the four villains who took part were Masons, who became "country members" while in prison.

Met Sergeant, age 40, twenty-two years service. Now in a training department.

When I was a DC in the West End, we used to have the annual CID beano at the Hilton. The old Robbery Squad were solidly Masonic. So we'd have a top London villain at every table, because he was in that team's lodge – but he was also a target for another team at a different table. They'd have a different villain sitting with them! That was in the '70s. But even now there are two kinds of Masonic corruption – the leg-up for promotion, and the money and favours for villains in the lodge. I know a lot of examples, but the evidence is hard to produce. I've seen with my own eyes where evidence disappeared just before it went to court on a £20,000 stolen lorry full of food. All the documentation went before the trial. Just disappeared.

Met PC, age 40, twenty-one years service and a Mason.

I suppose if you are a dodgy lodge you have dodgy characters in it but really if you have anyone who does anything criminal he should be thrown out because he's gone against being a Mason. They should be thrown out, they should be reported to the Grand Lodge. In the last quarterly communication there was reports of five people being thrown out because there was one who was convicted of fraud and another for dishonesty. You should get rid of them because they are not doing their lodge any good and they are not doing you any good or Masonry or the craft as we call it. I like my Masonry, but if it came between the police and me, that's a different matter, I would have to reconsider and I'd hate to have to do that. Perhaps it's the mysterious part that makes it inviting for others or, makes it sinister. But in no way are we sinister. If you did live by their morals you'd live quite a good life.

In March 1989, an attempt to expel Gibson failed.

UNPROVEN ALLEGATIONS

Allegations of masonic involvement in police corruption go back as far as Jack the Ripper, but have never been proven. In the corruption scandals of the 1970s masonic links were always in the background, but no hard facts emerged. Even so, it was enough to give the Brotherhood a bad name.

Masonic claims to be "just another club" with no undue influence are received with scepticism by non-masonic officers. And policemen have suspicious minds.

Sergeant in Midlands force, age 36, seventeen years service and a Mason.

The trouble I found, was when I was on a relief and I knew that they knew I was a Mason. They would never ask me outright whether I was but they would hedge around it and they would talk about me behind my back. But only one ever asked me whether I was a Mason and I told him, yes. I have had members of the public give me the handshake but I haven't returned it. You couldn't do your job. You're not obliged to, I just let the signals go over my head and ignore them, and they never knew. That would be to the detriment of my way of life, to my family and to Masonry so I just let it go over my head and they think, "Oh well, he's not a Mason," and I just carry on with the job.

Met PCs, average age 23, average service three years in Central London.

PC1: The masonic thing never used to bother me. Then I saw it work in practice, and it really got to me. I've seen an Inspector come in and fuck up the charge sheets to get someone off. Suddenly there were vacant numbers. Strokes like that – if we pulled them we'd be out on our ears.

PC2: We've seen it, we know about it, but you can't say anything because you don't know who will make what phone calls when you're going up for interview for a squad or for promotion. They look after their own on promotion. They don't like people who don't like them.

PC3: I heard from three different sources about a woman in North London who wouldn't sell her house to the Masons. They wanted it because it was consecrated, or something like that – it had been a temple or whatever they call it, before. She went to the police after all these threats and warnings but they did nothing. It was firebombed, and she died in the fire.*

PC1: The bone of contention that sticks in my throat is the oath they swear when they join the Masons. It must conflict with the oath we all swear to the police. I know their oath says they shouldn't break the law, but that doesn't cover everything that might be a conflict of interests. What about promotion? It's not against the law to prefer one person over another, is it?

PC2: It's when you see them interfering with arrests that I think it's gone too far. We had a list put up at our nick of the membership of the local lodge, wouldn't you know, all the senior officers were on it! Of course it only lasted two minutes.

PC3: The sooner the whole thing's banned for policemen, the

---

* Ten PCs and a Training Sergeant heard this story and no one challenged it, such is the degree of paranoia about Freemasonry among the rank and file.

better. It should be drummed out of the force.

PC4: We had a Chief Inspector at our nick arrested in a public bog giving a blow job to some bloke. He was wearing a suspender belt and a tutu. But he swore he was just an ordinary bloke, that he'd been drinking after a rugby match and it got out of hand. He was a bloody giant. It took two carriers to get him out of there. He'd injured the first lads that tried to arrest him. Anyway, it barely made the papers. It was all hushed up. What do you make of that for a juicy scandal? It's the kind the press all go to town on. It must have been masonic help that did the cover-up. No other explanation.

RESPECT WANTED

Most observers estimate that one in five police officers are Freemasons. The reason so many policemen join is not just for advancement. The conviviality of the lodge and a sense of belonging provide welcome relief from the pressures and unpleasantness of the job.

Freemasons respect police officers, especially in the provinces. The Brotherhood bestows honours on officers accustomed to public indifference or hostility. Masonry offers a way into the Establishment for those who feel neglected by it or who come from working-class origins, as so many policemen do. Indeed, both the Duke of Edinburgh and the Duke of Kent are Freemasons, as are judges, civil servants and many other influential professional people among the estimated 500,000 current and former Brothers in England and Wales (Scotland is estimated to have a further 100,000 and Ulster 45,000).

Police officers are not treated with the same respect we accord to military men of equivalent rank. The Honours List contains hundreds of soldiers and all ranks of public officials but very few police officers, who also see themselves as public servants. The occasional knighthood and the Queen's Police Medal for a few selected senior officers are no substitute for the neglect of achievement among the lower ranks. With its quasi-ancient rituals and bonds of loyalty, Freemasonry is not so different from the quaint ceremonials of the royal establishment.

As some of the interviews suggest, many police officers have been effectively deprived of normal social lives by our ambivalent view of them, while being welcomed by the Masons. If we wish policemen to forego such secret satisfactions, we must give them other, more public ones when deserved.

Sir Peter Imbert, Commissioner of the Metropolitan Police, has pointed out that none of the past three Commissioners has been a Mason and that membership is a possible drawback for higher promotion these days. Some critics argue that membership should be banned altogether for police officers, and for judges as well, to ensure their impartiality. Others have urged the mandatory disclosure of membership. Both have been resisted on the grounds that they invite a loyal Mason to lie about his status. But the secrecy in Masonry is attached formally to its rituals, no longer to membership itself, an innovation introduced by the Brotherhood in response to public disquiet. Masons are now allowed to answer any reasonable enquiry about their activities. Of the many problems now facing the police service in improving its morale and public image, this must be the easiest to solve.

Assistant Chief Constable of a large Midlands force, age 48, twenty-eight years service.

Any officer in the Army above the level of Lieutenant can walk into any social gathering in the country and expect to be welcomed. Assumptions are made about him because of his role, because immediately they think, "an officer and a gentleman." Those two are linked. You would never say, "A policeman and a gentleman." It just wouldn't go together.

CHAPTER TWELVE

Stress

Few jobs are as stressful as that of a police officer. According to a study by Manchester University, policemen come second only to coal miners in the league table of stressful occupations. Accumulated frustrations cost police officers their peace of mind, their job satisfaction, their sense of direction and, crucially, a sense of their own worth. Many officers, particularly those in urban areas, live with the notion that the world outside the station is hostile. They feel despised by the very people for whom they daily risk their physical and mental well being.

Stress is a new concept in police circles and many senior officers are still ambivalent towards it. "Stress is a cushy number," a Superintendent told me. "I'd love to have a nervous breakdown but they'd only cancel it." Senior officers are equally unsympathetic towards allowing time off for the treatment of stress.

For many police officers, the new awareness of stress sits uneasily with their macho image. They know something is wrong, but fear the consequences of finding the cause. In police culture, the classic definition of manliness is that you just get on with the job and put up with the consequences. But what happens if you can't?

Met PCs, average age 23, average service two years in Central London.

PC1: When a police football team plays a civilian team, the police team is far more aggressive. I play football to get rid of some of my aggression. I'm not dirty at football, but I go in hard because you are actually pitting against someone, it's a good way to get rid of aggression. Many policemen just push weights to get rid of it. If you go down to Marylebone gym you can hear them screaming, and that's not just the training. Some people like to listen to music to dissipate the strain. There are different ways.

Met WPC, age 28, seven years service. Now in West London.

I'm lucky – I'm a girl. I've sobbed when people have upset me, but just because I was bloody angry. It comes out, it just happens. But I'm a woman and it's acceptable. If a bloke burst into tears, it'd be, "Look at that faggot bawling his eyes out."

Thank goodness the job is becoming more aware of all this. I had a young PC when I was at Paddington. We had what we call a "sudden death", so they sent him off. Next thing, he radio's in: "I think it's a suicide. She's hanging from the curtain rail." It was a seventeen-year-old girl, everything to live for and she'd hung herself. When he came back, it took me three hours to get him to talk. Three hours. He cried afterwards, at the end of three hours, but not one of his colleagues even mentioned that at all. It was as though it had never happened. He'd been and dealt with it, they understood how he felt, nobody messed him around. It was amazing to me that a place like Paddington Green nick could be so tolerant. As he was the youngest on the relief, I thought there was going to be a lot of ribbing.

Single PCs who are strangers to London are stressed just from being new to the city. When the burden of police work is added, they find it hard to cope. This is reflected in their drinking and tendency to marry young, and it shows on the streets in their unwillingness to risk contact with ordinary people. They frequently overreact to even the slightest challenge. Some PCs are very lonely people.

Met PC, age 25, five years service in West London.

When you're either sharing flats or married – whatever the relationship is – you've got somebody whom you can relate to quite closely. Whereas in section house you've got no one unless you're particularly matey and that might raise a few eyebrows in certain circles. You can't relate to that person in the same way as you can with a wife or girlfriend.

It's hard work trying to keep a very macho image. There are times when you just want to sit down and have a chat to somebody. Get it off your chest. Tell the same story in different ways. If you're talking to somebody who's a close friend, you tell them what really happened. If there's a group of you down the pub, I don't think you really tell them.

Met Inspector, age 33, twelve years service. Now in central London.

Policemen are expected to live in premises suitable for a police officer and that's the reason they don't live any old where. It's not an elitist idea, it's to protect the police officer. One woman officer had a load of villains in the East End who she managed to knock off with a couple of the lads. One was a right villain and she humiliated him in front of his friends by nicking him. So they got at her.

She lived on her own. Her cat was found dead, the car was scratched and had paint thrown over it, they daubed "PIG" on the front wall, took the door off its hinges and smashed the windows. She had to sit in the dark with the lights out because of people coming round and these yobs in a car outside the front door, intimidating her when she came home. I had to get her moved to another station and find her a flat so she could sell her home and get away from it. The pressure from this band of yobs, windows smashed, cat killed, all sorts of subtle pressures – they almost terrorized her. Her name was daubed on blocks of flats where she was on patrol, saying what they were going to do to her. This group of yobs is a notorious bunch of rip-off artists. They're professional crooks. They destroyed this girl. She's been in a nursing home, under considerable stress and anxiety, for a long period of time. It's almost reduced her to a jelly. She can't go home any more. How many people understand what that means – not being able to go home?

THE JOB

A recent Home Office study concluded that the major source of day-to-day stress was the shortcomings of the organization itself.

Inspector in a Home Counties force, age 35, fourteen years service. Now in a busy industrial suburb.

Five years ago, if you talked about stress, you were an officer who wasn't capable of doing the job. It's accepted now that everybody, no matter what rank, has got stress. The only thing is that perhaps we use it too easily. It's very difficult to put a finger on it. I've spoken to policemen who have left or retired and they've said that a weight has been lifted off their shoulders, but when you ask "what weight?" they can't really say. Is it the general public? Is it the job itself? Is it the bosses? They can't say.

The unfortunate thing about this job is that the better you are, the more work you do on the street, the more paper you have and the more likely you are to drop a bollock. So the bloke who is working hard is generally putting himself under more stress.

Scottish PC, age 31, nine years service. Now in a council estate suburb.

Stress is just the on-going work. You know you've got so many cases on your desk today and you know there'll be another five or six tomorrow. It does weigh on you, but you just get used to it. You become very cyincal; it's a defence mechanism. I'm sure most policemen would not want to go home having dealt with incest and talk about it with the wife. It's not a thing one takes up at the dinner table, the goriness of a post-mortem examination. When you've seen a dead body lying about and you talk about it as a piece of meat, a carcass, it's no longer a person. You can't become mentally involved with a dead person, can you?

Superintendent in a Midlands force, age 44, twenty-five years service, and his wife, age 43. Married for twenty-two years.

Supt: I had two main roads running through my beat. I used to have regular traffic accidents, bad ones. The ambulance in those days would never, ever touch a dead body, never take it into the hospital. We would have to arrange with the local undertaker to come out and pick the bodies up in canvas bags. They'd be cut to ribbons. And then we'd take them back to the morgue and undress them – no legs, bloody heads smashed to pieces.

Wife: I'll never forget when we were first married. He was on nights and he came in to see me in bed. He'd been to tie labels on this woman that was knocked off her bike that afternoon. I said, "Don't touch me, don't touch me!" I mean, he'd touched a dead body. I couldn't handle the thought.

PC in a Midlands force, age 34, twelve years service. Now in a city centre.

It is not so much stress from out on the street. The stress really starts when you come in the door downstairs. Internal politics. There are a thousand and one governing rules which can drop you straight in it if you are not aware of them, or if you are negligent and pass them by. There are some 300 pro forma forms used in the police force! Because the paperwork is so visible, the disciplinary results in that field are so high. I'm dyslexic, which doesn't help when dealing with books. I have to discipline myself in order to do paperwork.

I can understand police officers who get snappy. If I'm under stress, I'll go out and lose my problems by taking on the problems of the people I talk to. It's when I come back to the police station that the stress reaffirms itself. I think: "I can't get that report done – I'll go and get another prisoner." But other police officers might go out and threaten to knock seven bells out of the first person that even looks at them – which is the last thing anybody wants. We vent our own stresses, but we exacerbate other people's.

STAGE FRIGHT

Even the most ordinary performance of duty can be stressful for young PCs just starting out. Many are shy and unused to speaking to the public at all, let alone with the authority of the uniform. It is actually a performance on a public stage and so generates stage fright.

Sergeant in a Home Counties force, age 38, sixteen years service. Now in a university city.

It's quite frightening the first time you go on the street. It really is quite terrifying. And you're wearing this peculiar outfit, you know. I remember when I first walked out there, I'd gone a hundred yards up the street and three people had stopped me and asked me things. To all intents and purposes, as far as they're concerned, you're a policeman. Whether a week in the job or ten years in the job, it makes no difference to them. You're expected to know.

DEALING IN MISERY

Much police work deals in human misery. Nothing so distinguishes it from other professions as the ever-present threat from diseases like AIDS and hepatitis; from violence, whether casual or orchestrated; and, above all, from the fact of death. For most of us outside the medical profession, death is a special occasion, and deeply disturbing. For many police officers it is a frequent occurrence, and yet, as with racial prejudice, we expect them to overcome their normal reactions to human tragedy in the space of a few months at training school and emerge ready to take almost any kind of shock in their stride.

PC in a Home Counties force south of London, age 22, three years service. Now in a busy port.

I have thrown up after seeing dead bodies. I have thrown up after a car chase, mainly because I had eaten heavily, and driving for thirty-five minutes at speeds up to eighty miles an hour within city confines at night is a long time. I was so wound up I came back to the station and parked the car, but I couldn't climb the stairs at first as my knees had gone. I sat on the stairs until I had got my breath back, went and puked straight away. I couldn't help it. It was an adrenalin reaction.

I have thrown up over cot deaths – makes you feel very bad. But it is no problem, I have handled it and got on with it. I had three fatals within three months of my joining the job when I was out on patrol. Dealt with them, came back without any adverse reaction. But children are very different altogether. Just looking at pictures chokes me up. You get a lump in your throat and walk away. You mustn't allow any fears to get too close. You can fall apart after an incident, but you know damn well that before an incident you have got to be calm because otherwise you will exacerbate it.

Two PCs in a large northern force, average age 29, average service eight years. Now in an inner-city area.

PC1: There's no support service at all for a young bobby that comes straight out of training and then goes on his beat, and it comes over the radio that someone's died in an accident. The big joke is that the youngest lad will have to go and tell the family. So he's got to knock on the door and say: "Sorry, your daughter and your son-in-law and their two children have just been killed." The whole family are around the fire, waiting for them to come in. It's a double-edged sword. It's hard luck he's got to do that, but it's the only way he's going to learn. But when he gets back to the station there'll be no one to support him. Everybody else is at the bar, grateful that there's a new recruit around to do the job for them. This poor lad, no one gives a hoot about how it's affected him.

PC2: I suppose we all have our way of doing it. Bobbies often say, "All I said was: 'They're dead.'" You can't say just that, can you? I suppose the easiest way is not to beat around the bush, but to say, "Look, do you want to sit down? There's been a bad accident, and your mum and dad have been killed in the accident." When you knock on the door, you obviously have this expression on your face. They realize there's something wrong. Have you done them a favour? Or have you just torn them apart? It's horrible.

PC1: I'd love to knock on someone's door one day and say, "Mr So-and-so, here's a million pounds, you've just won the pools." Or do something nice like return stolen goods. The only thing I've returned is money to drug dealers who've gotten away with it in court.

Sergeant in a large West Country force, age 38, seventeen years service.

I remember walking in on a house fire – it was like looking inside a horrible lump of coal. I turned round and sitting in the chair was a charred body.

After a while, there are few things one human being can do to another that are surprising. You come across just about everything that one person can inflict on another. You tend to get hardened and cynical. You cannot survive unless you do.

Superintendent in a northern force, age 46, twenty-four years service. Now in an inner-city area.

I'll tell you about the sort of thing we have to deal with: a prostitute who came into the station one night, sobbing, with blood running down her legs.

She'd been taken by a client to a flat, and after he'd done his normal business with her, he stuck a brush up her. Then he made her suck off his dog and drink a bowl of piss. After that he beat her about a little, and before kicking her out he robbed her of ten quid. She got seen by the doctor and all that. She didn't look too bad. We tried going down to the flat, but it was empty and there was no listed tenant.

Met PC, age 32, eight years service. Now a Home Beat officer in a racially mixed inner-city area in West London.

I went to a sudden death a few weeks ago. An old bloke and an old woman had died. They were both alcoholics and the place stank like hell. He was a twenty-four-hour drunk, obviously distressed, but the thing I found sad was the conditions they were living under. Absolutely appalling. How can human beings live like that? She was very fresh so she didn't smell as a body can do, but he – I had to come out of there and throw up because of the stink. It had not been washed for years, you could cut the dirt with a knife, it was that deep. The cooker was the most unbelievable sight: the knobs wouldn't turn on any more. It was covered in mould. The dishes hadn't been washed for a couple of years. Cigarettes covered the floor. They stubbed them out and left them there. It was a horrible place. It's appalling that society allows some people to live in those conditions.

Sergeant in a large northern force, age 36, thirteen years service. Now in an inner-city area.

One of the worst things I've seen was somebody leaping off a roof. Eight o'clock in the morning, we'd been on a quick changeover and everybody's knackered, and this young girl is standing there, fourteen storeys up. A bobby's going up in the lift and I'm standing outside with another lad, a very callous lad. They called him on the radio: "Echo Mike Three, what's she doing now?" Just as the controller said that, the girl jumped and he went: "14, 13, 12, 11 – she's right in front of me!" I thought: "You bastard!" He said, "You've got to put your coat over her, boss." Trying to get a new coat is hard work, so I said, "No, you better put yours." But he said, "Oh come on, Sarge. I'll have more problems getting a new one than you will." We're standing there arguing like a couple of kids over this smashed-up body and he turns to me and says, "Never mind, Sergeant. We have the technology, we can rebuild her!"

PC in Home Counties force south of London, age 26, six years service. Now in a large county town.

You go to things that are so horrific or stupid. You've got to laugh at them, otherwise you'd end up in a lunatic asylum. Then you get the sad side of things with death. The worst one was when I had to tell a father his baby had died. It was a cot death. He'd gone out on a stag night, he hadn't wanted to go but he went anyway. It's always very difficult.

I went to tell a woman that her husband was dead. I was dreading it. I thought there'd be a big scene, tears and everything, but she just carried on drinking her tea and said, "Thank God, the bugger's gone." I said, "Don't you want to know where he is?" "No." She just wasn't interested.

POLICE FATALITIES

The injury or death of a fellow officer is the hardest thing for other policemen to handle. Not only are they shocked in the normal way, they are also reminded of their own vulnerability. The RUC are more used to this experience than police on the mainland, where the deaths of Yvonne Fletcher in the Libyan Embassy siege and of Keith Blakelock at Broadwater Farm were traumatic for many officers.

Met WPC, age 38, twelve years service. Now in central London.

There was one lad who'd been at Broadwater Farm who's been off sick since the riots. He injured his hip and has been in continuous pain ever since. The hospital has tried various treatments for his hip, but no one has thought about his mental state.

Last week he was set on by someone in a pub. His friend brought him to the local police station. He's six foot three and seventeen stone – he was crying his eyes out.

He now has an uncontrollable urge to kill black people.

Two Met PCs, average age 24, average service three years. Now in a racially mixed area in North West London.

PC1: On the night of Broadwater Farm, I was called in from my home beat and was glad to get out of the rain. Then I sat in the canteen for twelve hours listening to the World Service coverage, as they knew a lot more than the police. We heard a PC was killed and couldn't believe it. We'd been told there was trouble at Broadwater Farm. "Where's that?" they all said.

PC2: Another mate went with Keith Blakelock to the ambulance, with the knife still sticking out of his neck. He just couldn't take it. He came back and just wept tears of rage – he went sick for three weeks afterwards.

PC1: We'd been sitting in the van for hours and hours getting more and more frustrated. When we finally were used, with heavy shields to clear the area, it was virtually over – just chaos. The shields were too heavy to run with. We were thirty yards away from a mate who was being threatened with a shotgun. The bloke didn't fire it but it sure freaked my mate. He was off sick for eight months after.

PC2: When people go crazy, they really go. One Inspector locked himself in the personal radio cupboard. Another one just took off from the station and took a train to Glasgow for no reason. Another Station Sergeant just sat there painting toy soldiers and never spoke a word to anyone.

RUC Woman Police Sergeant, age 34, eight years service. Now in a large town outside Belfast.

Certainly many senior officers can't cope with the stress of somebody getting killed. They can't actually physically go to the house and say, "I regret to tell you, but your husband has just been shot." So what do they do? They bump it down the ranks until it comes to Inspector or Sergeant or even to a bobby – "You go and tell the wife her husband's dead." It's a disgrace! They're not fit to hold the rank they have.

I'm only a Woman Police Sergeant but after the last bombing killed many of our lads, I was the one they sent for. I could do it. There's lots of people I know, chief officers, and they were pathetic. They would come along with me and just stand there – "What am I going to say?" One actually said that. I had to do it. It's not something you can train people for, it's impossible. It depends on the type of person you are.

I had to go at least two dozen times and break the news to people in a very short period. It got to the stage where as soon as people saw me coming they knew I was bringing bad news – that's how bad it was. I didn't even have to tell them. My one fear is what long-term side effects it will have on me. Some days I feel I'm heading for a nervous breakdown.

NEARLY ALWAYS BAD NEWS

People rarely call the police just for a chat. It is usually some sort of distressing situation. While most of these are fairly straightforward for confident officers, there is always the possibility of danger, if only from a guard dog or a person out of control. Fear is a natural acknowledgement of that possibility. Fear produces adrenalin as an emergency resource. On any regular basis, it becomes a key contribution to stress.

Met PC, aged 31, eight years service, and a Met Sergeant, age 34, ten years service. Now in East London.

PC: Went on a raid yesterday: there was an aggravated burglary with people tied up and that, and I had to go and turn over the house. My partner knows that I am paranoidly terrified of dogs. Now the guy who we were going to get was a fucking hard nut, a real loony. That didn't bother me, but as soon as I heard there was a dog in the house I went white with terror. People in the van thought it was hilarious.

Sgt: They weren't going to tell him, you see. They'd send him to the back and when he got in this bloody dog would put the shits up him and frighten him to death. And he would run out screaming. That was the joke.

We like to keep it to ourselves, to our partners, what we're frightened of. There was a strange light on at a school. It was surrounded by railings, so I climbed over them, went up and shone my torch in the windows. I get round to the front entrance – that's open, and I thought, "Hang on, there's something wrong here." I looked back and there's about six bobbies hanging on to the railings. I said, "Come on, guys," and they say, "They've got g-g-guard dogs!" I'm all alone. It's a good hundred yards to the fence and these four big Alsatians come hurtling out. I thought, "Shit!" and pulled the old, "Right, heel! Heel!"

The dogs are not sure so they just nip me gently. One of the bobbies got his stick out and he's rattling it along the railings and calling the dogs, "Come on boys, get him!" I had to walk saying "Heel! Heel! Heel!" all the way over to the railings.

I got there and said, "Sit!" and they sat, and I jumped over the wall. I changed my underwear as soon as I got back to the station, I can tell you. Bastard bobbies' humour!

PC from a large northern force, age 29, eight years service. Now in a racially mixed inner-city area.

The bosses and the public don't realize the time and stress involved in just doing a simple search on a house. I'm talking about houses that are not like yours or ours, that are tidy, I'm talking about houses full of shit. Until the housing programme here, some of the houses were absolutely disgraceful. I've been to ones where there's been a woman with a baby naked on the floor, with an Alsatian and dog crap, the smell was horrendous. There was one yesterday that had two Dobermans, a ferret and a python. I mean, who wants to put their hand in a drawer? There was a python in a tank, and the kid said, "It's not in the tank anymore. It's somewhere in the house." We stepped outside.

THE LIMBO OF PUBLIC ORDER

Public order generates its own form of stress. Like ordinary policing, it too is a destructive limbo of intense boredom and potential danger.

WPC in a Midlands force, age 30, eight years service. Now in a city centre.

In a public order situation the adrenalin gets going and there's no way you're going to stop it, because of fear as well as the fact that you've got a job to do. There is no way you can stop that fear when the possibility of being injured is high. There's a young officer that I've worked with who was injured in a crowd during the riots and now he will not go into a crowded pub. Yet he's an excellent police officer.

Met PCs, average age 23, average service three years. Now in central London.

PC1: At Wapping, I was two places away from a mate who was concussed by a paling – it split his helmet. I was sympathetic to the strikers' case. They'd never have done that. You'd stand there for hours and they would be happy to talk to you, until rent-a-mob came along after the pubs shut and started to throw things. They wouldn't let the strikers talk to us.

PC2: But the senior officers left the thin blue line there unprotected, just taking it.

PC3: Same as the Anti-Apartheid rally in Trafalgar Square. My mate got hit with a brick – many of us did. A Superintendent from Bow Street just walked up and down with a clipboard and his back turned to the crowd and told us not to raise our truncheons – meanwhile a hail of fucking bricks and bottles was hitting us. It was unbelievably frustrating just standing there. What in Christ's name were we doing there? But our brilliant leader wasn't looking at what was happening, he had his back to the crowd. The best moment was when he got hit on the head and had to be taken out. Then the City of London Chief Inspector came and told us to get stuck in – but, "Don't get caught." So we climbed over the fucking railings and dived into the crowd. Some of us may have gone in a bit enthusiastically, but there's only so much you can take. A lot of cameras were smashed that day.

The most serious danger now facing police officers in inner cities is not from violence. It is from hepatitis and AIDS. As drug addiction spreads, so does the danger of infection.

THE DANGERS OF DISEASE

PC in a large Scottish force, age 28, nine years service. Now in an inner-city area.

The way things are now, these new diseases, it's got to be a worry. You might arrest somebody and put your hand down their pocket and find a needle. You could get hepatitis, AIDS – that's always your worry.

You've got to search everybody. You put your hand gingerly into their pockets, feel from the outside and just hope there's nothing there. Always ask them first: "Are there any sharp implements in your pockets?" And if they say "No" just put your hands in very gingerly. It must be a worry to everybody. I don't know how the wife feels. I've never really asked her.

Met PC, age 32, eight years service. Now in an inner-city area of South London.

This lad went to training school with me, he was a nice lad. Anyway, we brought a prisoner in who had hepatitis, she was female and she was a Tom, a tart, that's how she caught it. It's not immediately contagious but it's treated with great care. When we searched her we used gloves. This young lad was the jailer and we thought, "Magic, we'll have a wind-up."

After the prisoner had been dealt with and taken to another location we phoned up the young jailer and said, "Have you been in contact with the female prisoner?" He said, "Yes." So we said, "Right, go to the interview room and sit there, don't talk to anybody, don't touch anything, just sit there and wait for further instructions – we believe that she has hepatitis B which is extremely contagious and is passed on by air contact." That got him into a right panic.

Then we sent another officer round, dressed appropriately in a paper suit and bringing with him another paper suit, rubber gloves and paper shoes. He said, "Right, take all your clothing off, bag it, label it with your name, put the suit on and the Divisional surgeon will come down and see you." So we sent down somebody to pose as the Divisional surgeon and he said to him, "I'm afraid we've got to go to another station where there is another surgeon because we can't deal with you properly here." We took him out to a van and drove him to the front entrance of the other police station – out on the street. We sent him off with his bag, wearing his paper suit, his plimsoll things and his rubber gloves and said, "Go to the front counter, somebody will meet you there." They were all in on the act too.

He walked in, people looking at him thinking, "What on earth?" He went in and said, "I think I've got hepatitis, I'm supposed to meet someone here." So he was walked through all the different corridors of the station and into the backyard where the entire relief were arranged with all the cars' headlights on, blue lights flashing. Everybody came forward laughing. He got terribly upset, he was almost in tears! It was great!

If police officers take things too seriously or too hard, they get too emotionally involved. Tempting as it is at times, it stops you being a policeman. You become somebody who is no use to the community when you're most needed.

Met Inspector, age 34, twelve years service. Now in central London.

We have a lot of AIDS prisoners in now, both male and female. The guys handle it, we've had some briefings and there isn't the hysterical reaction I'd expected. We have young PCs, nineteen to twenty, and they will hold on to AIDS prisoners and guide them and look after them. I find their lack of prejudice quite impressive. They wear rubber gloves and afterwards they go and wash themselves.

Met PC, age 23, four years service. Now in the West End of London.

There are an awful lot of coppers that have caught hepatitis, it's so simple – a smash and grab. A druggy nicked his arm when he smashed a shop window and put his hand in to get a guitar, then ran off. The area car driver turned up to find out what happened and he nicked his arm on the same piece of glass. It was only a tiny little nick but four days later he crashed out. He was off for about three or four months and when he came back he had to have his whole uniform changed – he had lost over four stone in weight! There's a Chief Inspector I know, he caught hepatitis B. He can only drink a pint of liquid a day because his liver was so badly affected. A cup of tea when he wakes up, one with lunch and another with dinner and that's his pint for the day!

THE SHIFT SYSTEM

Most ordinary bobbies find the station shift system debilitating and itself a principal cause of stress. Early Turn, Late Turn and Nights follow one from the other with monotonous regularity, disrupting sleep patterns and normal social life. Community

and village policemen, headquarters staff, the CID and specialist
squads normally escape night duty, though many are on call
twenty-four hours a day.

Doctors now estimate that our bodies need up to three weeks
to recover from jet lag, and the often abrupt changes of a shift
system are not dissimilar. Lack of regular sleep, long stretches
of boredom with sudden bursts of activity and danger, in an
atmosphere of repressed frustration – this is a classic recipe for
stress.

Two PCs in a large northern force, average age 28, average
service eight years. Both now in an inner-city area.

PC1: For those lads on three shifts, it's a very tiring job.

PC2: I talk to the family, but you can't hold a conversation
when you've been up since half-five in the morning. They're all
full of the joys of spring, all chatty and everything, and you just
don't feel like lending anything to it. You go to sleep for a
couple of hours. You might feel better – in which case when
you wake up they're sulking because you went to sleep. Or you
can stay awake. You won't be talking anyway, because you're
not in a position to hold a conversation. It takes a hell of a lot
out of you.

It took me a while to get into it. I was knackered for about
a fortnight, and then things started sorting themselves out. I'd
literally forgotten what it felt like, to feel human all the time.
It's no way for people to live. It's no way for your body to feel.
You don't know whether you're coming or going half the time.

PC2: In our force we finish nights on a Monday morning at
seven o'clock – and it's your day off, Monday. Nine times out
of ten you go to bed for at least three or four hours. You're off
Tuesday, then you come back Wednesday from three in the
afternoon till eleven at night for two days, then you do five days
starting at seven and finishing at three in the afternoon.

PC1: You do a short change: eleven o'clock at night through
to seven o'clock in the morning. Five days. You wonder why
they're asleep when they're supposed to be on duty. It's true,
and they wonder why the sick record has increased. When we

first went onto this new shift system, the sick record was quite reasonable. Then all of a sudden we're now hitting the highest in the country. It's fatigue on the shift system. Everybody knows what the bloody answer to it is: the answer to it is that in the days when everybody else is working forty-hour weeks, we're working fifty-six. The fifty-six hour week – as far as I'm concerned, the rest of the world would be outraged.

PC2: Last time I went off sick, it lasted over eight days. It was an ear infection I couldn't get rid of. I'm sure it was because I was just run down. You become more prone, because you are not at your physical best, so if there is some flu bug going round, you are more likely to get it.

Superintendent in a northern force, age 42, twenty-two years service. Now in an industrial suburb.

Days lost through illness have just gone through the roof. After introducing a new shift system, both Greater Manchester and Merseyside have seen the same pattern of people taking more and more days off, until we're seriously undermanned. Some of those blokes may be shirking, but the ones who get injured in the town centre on a Saturday night are not coming back to work anything like as quick as they used to. So that puts more pressure on the ones who are on duty, which means that when something happens to them – which is more likely to because they're under pressure – they'll stay away longer themselves, leaving even fewer blokes to do the job. It's a vicious circle, that can only get worse.

Inspector in large northern force, age 34, twelve years service.

There is still a lot of resistance to going for counselling. It happens more and more but in a clandestine way. When I first joined if you had a headache you were a sissy, and there's still a lot of that around. But the Bradford stadium fire and the Manchester air disaster were both so shocking to the people involved that counselling has been available ever since. Keeping it confidential is actually very hard. I understand that senior officers have been trying to find out the names of the men involved, which is completely wrong in my book.

ALCOHOL: THE POLICEMAN'S FRIEND AND ENEMY

Alcohol is an intimate part of modern policing. Much of police work at night is spent dealing with drunks or with the consequences of drinking too much, such as pub fights, accidents and domestic disputes.

Despite such vivid evidence of alcohol's damaging effects, most policemen drink and many drink far too much. Alcohol is both a relief from stress and a cause of it. In a grim mirror image of their work, most police traffic accidents and domestic disputes are also linked to drink. (See Chapter 13, "Sex, Husbands and Wives").

Sergeant in a West Country force, age 28, seven years service. Recently resigned

In the old days there was an almost services ideal of drinking. You had to be able to have a drink and join in at the training centre, otherwise you were an "off" sort of chap. The test of whether you were a mixer was whether you went to the bar for a few jars and fitted in with the lads. It's being a team man.

The bar was also where you scored a lot of points because you went there and you bought the Sergeant a drink, and you bought the Detective Inspector two drinks and if the Chief Inspector came along, blimey, you had to have a very deep pocket!

I was an aide on CID but in the end I went back into uniform. One of the reasons was that I wasn't a drinker. It goes very quickly to my head. I never drink much anyway so I couldn't see myself standing in the pub night after night – which was a regular feature even in nice Metropolitan Surrey. I couldn't afford it, either. I'd only been married a year and didn't have any spare cash.

There are all sorts of things which used to irritate me about drinking and it still goes on. The CID always drank in the pub next to the station, so no self-respecting villain ever went near the place. They wrote in their diaries time and time again, "Entered such and such a public house, bought liquid refreshment for an informant" – they never bought liquid refreshment for an informant in their lives, those guys. The only person they were informing was the officer standing next to them.

Met PC, age 28, eight years service. Now in a racially mixed area of West London.

The drinking tends to be sporadic. It depends what shift you're on. A lot of blokes come off night shift and go to one of the market pubs. That's usually on a Saturday morning. The place is full of policemen from all over the place. You've got to the stage where, after Friday night on duty, your sleep pattern hasn't settled down and you've had a long hard shift. You want a jar so you go and have three or four pints, then you go home and have a good afternoon's kip. Monday Late Turn it's across the road and into the pub for a few jars. That can cause problems; blokes' wives want to see their men home within half an hour of finishing and all this sort of thing. It's a very difficult situation.

Most blokes that I know, know when to stop. I've never known a secret drinker, where you've got a bloke sitting in a car with a bottle, or when he goes walkabout. I've heard of blokes that have had the shakes. They've gone straight out with a bottle of Scotch and drunk the lot, then come back to the nick. A complete and utter bender. You hear about them because they are the oddities.

INITIATION

In the Met, young PCs and WPCs enter police culture with a drink in one hand and too much money in the other. The cost of subsidized living in section houses is extremely low, and new recruits are dangerously well placed in the centre of London with free time and a macho image to establish. Most have no outside friends or family nearby to exert a calming influence. This is not true in provincial forces such as Greater Manchester, where young officers are being stationed near their homes in a new move to keep them settled as they learn the job.

Two Met PCs and a WPC, average age 24, average service three years. All now in central London.

PC1: You just go straight down the pub and talk at each other for an hour. You're not listening to what the other bloke is saying, you're just telling him what you've done. That's some kind of release. Then you settle down into your usual thing. Without that hour in the pub, especially when you've had a bad day, you could climb the bloody walls. I used to go out and drink so much. I had to move out in the end; I'd have been an alcoholic if I hadn't. You'd go out six o'clock in the evening and come back six o'clock the next morning. Regularly.

WPC: That's been going on for donkey's years. Even I've done it, as a girl. All my mates have done it. You go out every night and you get legless because there's nothing else to do. It's a release. All the badness goes by the by. If you look at the lads that have lived in the section house for years, you think: "He drinks a hell of a lot and if something's not done soon . . ."

PC2: I was eighteen when I first came out of school and into section house. I was in for two and a half years. If you were having a good night on the drink, you might be able to make the meat market in the morning when that pub opened, a couple of hours sleep and then you're ready for work. That's when the release becomes another pressure. I think we should sell off section houses, not married quarters.

WPC: After six months in the section house I'd had enough. I started to get worried about my drinking. Being a girl, there were a lot of single blokes on my relief who lived there, so I'd go out and I'd be the only girl in a group of ten blokes. That raised a few eyebrows, but I wasn't sleeping with them all or anything like that – people liked to think you were.

I asked if I could live at home because my parents only live in Highgate. I saw my Chief Superintendent and he refused my application. I said, "Why?" "Because you're eighteen and a half years of age, you're an ex-cadet and I don't want you running home to your Mummy." I was deeply offended at that, but he's the Chief Superintendent so I couldn't blow my top. I had far more freedom at home. I could bring whoever I wanted into my own home.

DRINKING FOR PLEASURE

In some stations work seems merely a prelude to the serious business of pleasure in one another's company, lubricated by an astonishing amount of alcohol. Many CID officers celebrate the end of the week; every retirement, promotion or transfer is an occasion for a party. The pint or two or three with mates has its equivalent in senior officers retiring to the bar or producing a bottle at almost any excuse. Dining clubs are regular occasions for heavyweight drinking among the senior ranks, as are masonic evenings in the lodge.

Most of the police officers I have met are very good company – and with a fund of risqué stories as the drink flows. When we were filming Police *for television, several marriages among the film unit suffered because we were having such a good time that we often could not tear ourselves away from the station.*

Met Sergeant, age 27, six years service, 4 with the CID in a racially mixed area of London.

I got into that macho social life, it was great. I married young as well. In fact, I joined the police at the same time as I got married. I went through the Starsky and Hutch Crime Squad thing. My marriage deteriorated because – with lots of drinking – I was never at home. What finally killed it was the Rape Squad I was on for months and months. It just died in time for me not to transfer to a country force.

PC in a Home Counties force, age 26, six years service. Now in a port town.

You do get sucked into it. You have this absolutely marvellous social life. The thing that really pulled me out was, first of all, my marriage went up the spout. The other thing is that about two or three years ago, I found that all the interests I'd ever had in life had gone. I love theatre and cinema and writing and photography – they'd all gone. So I went into a "sod it" attitude. It was six months working in the suburbs – one crime a week – which brought me out of that and put me into the resolve that I've got now.

Former Met PC, age 27, five years service and a graduate. Recently resigned.

One thing I found difficulty with was that I was such a different person by the time I quit the scene. I'm basically quite liberal, humanitarian, with socialist views – when I have the time to stop and think about it. But sinking into that life with police officers, if people were being extremely racist I certainly wasn't standing up and arguing with them. I was going out with the boys: "Rip your knickers off!" and "Bastard spade!". Then throwing up in the street. This is where the pressure built up for me, because I'd no second thoughts about getting pissed as a skunk, then driving home, and as soon as I set foot in the door there's the woman I love and immediately I'm filled with the most terrible guilt. But still it didn't stop me going out the next night and getting pissed. Weakness of character. I certainly got into that. It's extremely difficult to get out of the circle. I don't know how you can crack it.

CUTTING DOWN

Efforts are currently in train to reduce the amount of alcohol consumed in police stations. Police clubs are closing as more police drivers decide not to take the risk of being breathalyzed on the way home. But drinking is so fundamental to police culture that it will take years before a major shift in attitude takes hold.

Assistant Chief Constable in a Midlands force, age 52, thirty-six years service; and a Chief Inspector, age 41, twenty-two years service.

ACC: There's less drinking by the CID. I think they're getting more conscious of their health. On the other side of the scale,

I would suggest there is more drinking now by uniformed men than there has ever been – not on duty, but drinking generally. Nowadays it's normal for the whole shift to go off either to a police club or to the pub after they've finished.

When I was a young policeman in the East End of London, where there was more drinking probably than most places, the whole population was drinking hard in order to overcome the conditions under which they lived. There was the old ethos of a couple of pints left outside the pub. Immediately after the war that was very common. You know, you walked past the front window and held two fingers up and you went round the back and there was a pint standing on the window sill, because two fingers, three fingers, whatever was the signal for what you wanted.

CI: Drinking on duty is virtually an automatic sack. A drink-driving offence while you're on duty is the sack; no messing, you've got the sack. Now that's a change, isn't it? It used to be you could count on your fellow officers looking the other way.

ACC: You just can't argue about it, can you? Here we are, a police force, we're enforcing the law. How can you possibly condone a policeman on duty openly bringing down the character and image of the force? In the CID they say they did it as part of contacting an informer. And it's sometimes true, but there are as many detectives these days who go into a pub and have a bitter lemon or tonic. There has been a major change in attitude.

Chief Inspector in a northern force, age 38, sixteen years service. Now in an industrial suburb.

We don't have the same drink problem as the Met with our youngsters because they come from the area and we try to station them locally. So they either live with their Mummies and Daddies or they get their own place. They don't live in police quarters anymore like they do in the Met. We used to put them across the city from where they live but now they serve as close to their home as possible. Their friends and family are near them, so you don't get that footloose and fancy-free feeling as you do in the Met.

When I joined you had to be at least thirty-years old to buy your own house, if they gave you the go-ahead. These days we get probationers asking to buy their own place a few weeks after they arrive. And they do. With the rent allowance almost covering their mortgage, they're stupid not to. But in London house prices are so high that allowances don't go nearly as far, so they piss it up against the wall.

DEALING WITH DRUNKS

One of the most sought after changes police officers hope to see is the creation of a nationwide set of drying-out stations, rather than using police cells for the purpose. Much of the night shift is spent handling drunks, often violent, frequently sick, some dying by choking on their own vomit. Handling these cases is squalid, messy, dangerous and unrewarding. The drunks just come back again the next night. It is no wonder PCs form such a jaundiced view of human nature. They spend so much of their time seeing people at their worst.

WPC in a northern rural force, age 22, three years service. Now in a border town.

We were so fed up and bored one night with one particular drunk that we decided to hold a kangaroo court. We woke Frankie up at three in the morning. He was a "regular" and every time he was picked up he would choose his favourite cell. If it were occupied we'd say, "Sorry, you'll have to choose a different one!"

Anyway, we woke him up and he was still drunk and we said, "Come along Frankie, you're in court now!" One of the PCs had found a wig and we'd made a bench, so we brought Frankie into the room. He really didn't know what was going on but we went through the whole court procedure and then our "judge" said, "You will be hanged at dawn." Frankie's face just dropped. We took him back to the cell and one of the PCs put on a black cap and made out that he was the executioner. He said to Frankie, "Come with me, it's nearly dawn – your time is up!" We then all went off duty and left Frankie to fall asleep.

When we saw the relief that took over from us they asked us what we did to Frankie. We said "Nothing – why?" And they said Frankie told them that he'd had the most awful nightmare – he'd been sentenced to hang at dawn!

It sounds cruel but we've got to laugh and have a joke because you'd be ill with all the stress otherwise, after all the abuse you take from everybody.

MONEY TROUBLES

Most of us have money problems, but police officers are especially vulnerable. Their difficulties often stem from the early bad habits of drinking all you earn in the section house. Young PCs earn substantial amounts for their age, with little or no notion of what to do with it. Indeed, the major banks lie in wait outside Hendon Training School at passing-out ceremonies to lure graduating PCs into opening accounts and taking out loans – because they are such good risks. The government will always bail out a police officer in trouble. The miners' strike overtime money produced an overheated economy within the lower ranks of the force. Credit is encouraged with disastrous consequences. A young policeman may be good at his job but still remarkably naive about handling his own affairs.

Two Met PCs, average age 24, average service two years. Both now in an inner-city area of West London.

PC1: I'm from Canterbury originally. I lived in the section house from the time I was eighteen to when I was twenty-one and it was the best time of my life. I had as much money as I could spend, just to go out in the West End drinking and clubbing. For somebody of that age, you couldn't ask for anything better – as much beer money as you could spend in a week, and you got through that quite easily just clubbing in the West End. Looking back now, it's frightening what we used to do. We were eating in restaurants every night, in between pubs.

I never bothered to save, I was just pissing it up against the wall.

Then I started buying a few things, fridges and things like that, with a view to getting my own place. In the police section house all you paid was just £3 a month rent – it's just gone up to £3.50 – and for that you get your own room with electricity and hot water.

PC2: At our section house £3 paid for the sauna, the gym, the free beer at all the discos we used to have, the colour television, the videos that we had every week and everything else. The rest of the money goes in your back pocket. At eighteen, I'd only left school for about six months before I joined and you're just all over the place. You get everyone turning round and saying, "Open this account, open that account . . ."

PC1: Everyone in the section house is overdrawn. When I first moved out I was £400 overdrawn, basically from going out on the hit and miss. I'm still overdrawn now. You buy a nice flash motor with high premium on the HP and all the rest goes down your neck. Before you know it you've spent your money half way through the month and there's still loads of, do's to go to. So you just start overdrawing and then the letters start coming through; you're overdrawn to £400 and it just stays at that for months.

PC2: If the bank manager gets the hump, you think, "Sod it!" and change banks. Anyone is quite happy to take a policeman at a bank. I did it a few times! I used to get the odd nasty letter from the bank manager and I'd think, "Fuck you" and go on to another bank.

It's because you're young. You get that pay packet and you're going to do everything you've wanted to do. Some blokes go out and buy a video and don't go out. Some blokes buy a stereo and records. Almost everyone goes out and gets pissed. I don't regret it. It was great.

PC1: You do learn a lot while you're in section house. Everyone gets fed up with it after a while, I think. They either get a steady girlfriend or the old age lark comes out so they think they'd better change their lifestyle a bit. Then they'll move out. There's only a few left in the trap.

Met PC, age 23, two years service. Now in West London.

When I was at Hendon, a NatWest man came in and gave out all the leaflets and said: "Any of you want a personal loan? Come straight to me and I'll sort it all out." It's just like Satan.

FIREARMS

Handling guns is another special source of stress for Authorized Firearms Officers and the RUC. For those officers who have been involved in either end of a shooting incident, counselling is now available. (See also Chapter 13, "Firearms".)

Met PC, age 37, ten years service. Six years as AFO (Authorized Firearms Officer) and now in PT17 (the specialist firearms squad). He shot and killed someone in the course of duty.

As I knew what I was getting into, I had totally prepared myself. Possibly I would have liked to have had a chat with someone who really knew what they were talking about as regards stress afterwards, but in the run into it I was adequately prepared.

After the incident all I had was a chat with our welfare department. I know it's one of my guv'nor's pet themes, but I thought it was the biggest fucking waste of time in my whole life. The bloke I spoke to was more in need of help than I would ever be. At one stage I was looking for a blunt object because I thought that he was going to attack me, I really did. The aggression in his voice as he was talking to me – I thought, "Hang on, who's looking after who here?" If someone had gone in there in a little trouble they'd have come out feeling a darned sight worse. As far as I can make out, the people who counsel us have got absolutely no formal training or qualifications at all. After I'd been to see them I was told to man the phones for a couple of weeks to give me a chance to sort myself out. Jesus, what wankers. The actual stress side of it isn't looked into at all, really. They keep looking at it from the police point of view and not the medical point of view.

We're lucky in this department. If we hear of an incident we'll be straight on the phone to the bloke. We'll ring him at home or go round and see him. We can at least put our hands on our hearts and say, "I know how you feel, mate." Don't mind doing that in the slightest. But the blokes from district, the AFOs, when they pull the trigger they don't get that support. Here, you are surrounded by people who know exactly what the score is, but the district guys go back to the station and no one knows what to make of them. People don't want to talk to them, don't want to get too close – "it might affect my promotion". They've maybe killed a man, and they're shut off on their own. I think there is a lot of trouble as a result of that.

Met Chief Inspector, age 39, fourteen years service. Now in an inner-city area of East London.

There was a shooting during a wages snatch at one of our pubs. Three officers, just by chance, were doing a crime observation outside. Two of them went in and found the villains, who then fired at them and commandeered the police car. But they couldn't use that because the keys weren't there, so they commandeered another car and made good their escape. Those officers were very stressed for quite a long time. They definitely needed counselling.

I was trying to get hold of one of them and rang his home but he wasn't in. I spoke to his wife and she was very pleased to have the chance to talk about it. The next day he came in and was terribly annoyed that I'd spoken to his wife because he had played it down. I hadn't actually discussed how serious it was, but he'd assumed I had and he said I'd got no right to speak to his wife. I wasn't sure what I'd have to do to straighten him out.

Met PC, age 35, fourteen years service, and now an AFO. He was recently shot by an armed robber.

It was very traumatic. When I got shot and I came out from convalescing, a welfare officer came along, a very nice lady but she had got her hands tied as well. She was very caring, wondering how I was feeling and things like that, and asked me, "What do you think we could do for you?" Me, to alleviate my stress if you like, I like to go and lie on a beach in the sun and do sod all for a week. So I said, "Well, if you really want to do something, send me away for a week in the sun with my young lady, so I can leave all this behind me and come back and say, 'hello, I've got a suntan, had a nice time, I'm ready, give it to me again.'" And they couldn't even do that. You're talking about February, to send you down to the south of Spain costs about £150 per person, so that's £300. The welfare department in this force is geared to debtors. If you're in the hole for £6000 they will say, "Look here's six grand. Get rid of your debts, you silly boy." If they are going to give a bloke that kind of money to clear up his debts, what's wrong with giving me 300 quid when I've got all the aggravation of being shot? No reasons were given. They put it before a committee and the committee decided no we don't go.

If you want to talk about welfare, I've had the fucking welfare. I've been shot and I think my case deserved a damn sight more attention than I've got so far.

NORTHERN IRELAND

In Northern Ireland, the RUC are exposed to all the usual stresses of policing, together with the extraordinary danger as a constant backdrop to their work; yet morale, even in black spots like West Belfast, is higher than in any other force. The number of officers leaving early is one of the lowest rates in the United Kingdom and there are very few requests for transfers elsewhere. Indeed, there are ten applicants for every place. But the RUC suffers from an exceptionally high incidence of alcoholism and suicide – indications that, deep down, there is much despair.

RUC PC, age 50, twenty-nine years service; Woman Police Sergeant, age 34, twelve years service; Inspector, age 35, twelve years service.

PC: The management's attitude to stress is shocking. Five years ago they just didn't want to know. Federation reps could see problems of suicides, drunkenness, debts. They eventually got the Police Authority involved, but headquarters didn't seem to be concerned. The senior officers' attitude was, "There are no problems," That is typical of some management, they don't want to bring problems to the surface because it might reflect badly on them – but it wouldn't necessarily. The Home Office research on stress certainly says that stress is more from things going on inside the force than outside.

Insp: One Chief Superintendent has advised us junior officers to try and make sure our men don't take annual leave. He was trying to save money! Our department is short-staffed but he keeps changing the shifts around – anything to save money. But the men are going to have to get their annual leave sometime.

PC1: One particular case, a young man, three weeks out of the depot, on his first tour of duty, attended five murders in his first week. He'd never seen a dead body before and yet here were people murdered by the IRA and INLA. The force's answer to it? The boss tried to show he was sympathetic by saying, "Have a drink, fellas" – he gave them a bottle of whiskey! That was done with the best intentions, he was a caring senior officer but it became the norm. If they'd had a success and captured some IRA people they'd celebrate their success. If they failed, they'd drown their sorrows. As a result two men in that particular section have alcohol problems.

WPS: Within the force we have a group of alcoholics who meet once a week with the full support and knowledge of headquarters. It helps. Senior officers who may have a man with a drink problem can refer him to this group. The difficulty in going to an outside group like Alcoholics Anonymous is that you don't know who you are going to run into. One chap told me he went in and there was an IRA man getting treatment. Knowing some of the alcoholics, any excuse is an excuse not to go. They don't have an excuse not to go to ours.

RUC PC, age 30, eight years service. Now in a border town.

It's still the old stiff upper lip: "Shape yourself up son, you're all right. When I was young in the force this didn't happen and I had as tough a time as you. Take an aspirin and away you go." There's a total unwillingness to talk about stress. Yet we all suffer from it here.

RUC Inspector, age 37, seventeen years service. Now in a large town outside Belfast.

It's not just terrorist situations. At my station a policewoman was married to a policeman and their marriage broke up after six months. She moved out of their flat to a place five miles from the station and within two days was transferred to the other side of the province. She can't drive, she hasn't a driving licence! They couldn't have sent her further away, yet at the time she needed to be near her husband in case they could work things out. I rang the Subdivisional Commander and said, "In my opinion this transfer was not thought out fully. The girl is going to be very upset and I want you to tell her." All he said is, "That's the transfer. You tell her." That was a job for senior management, to talk to the girl. We get quite a number of marital problems and the answer seems to be, "Let's transfer them apart." Transfers create as much stress as the job itself.

RUC PC, age 31, eleven years service. Now in a large town.

In one period of twelve months we had five suicides in the RUC. That's the problem with carrying guns, suicides are easier and accidents will happen. We had one where two men, absolutely bored out of their minds, just sitting around protecting the station, started fooling around with firearms and one chap shot the other. Or, they were playing Russian roulette.

RUC Sergeant, age 37, eighteen years service. Now in Belfast.

I remember one young lad shot himself dead – he bent over to switch on the telly, the gun dropped out of his holster and went off. There's pressure all the time when you're carrying a firearm.

We've had men's wives taking their husband's gun. One chap went to work and his wife cleaned the house, put fresh flowers in all the rooms, then shot herself. It happened to be on the anniversary of her father's death. It's the combination of being a policeman's wife with the uncertainty whenever he goes out. In nineteen years we've lost 253 officers. I don't know how many we've had injured – it must be thousands.

RUC PC, age 37, sixteen years service, and a Police Federation Representative. Now in Belfast.

I go to as many police funerals as I can. I will meet the next of kin. But what can you say to them? "I'm sorry: I'm here to represent all the people that can't be here and pass on the condolences of all my colleagues." They greet you with great kindness and courtesy. Very rarely have I ever been assaulted. Certainly I've been cornered by a few relatives who say, "What's the police going to do about it?" They let their anger out on me.

I always admired Sir Kenneth Newman when he was Chief Constable: in one particular incident a young policeman got shot in West Belfast and had to be buried in that cemetery with the IRA plot. All the advice to Sir Kenneth was that he shouldn't go to the funeral. He responded very calmly: "He was good enough to wear the uniform, the least I can do is put on my uniform and follow him to his graveside."

RUC Chief Inspector, age 36, sixteen years service. Now in Belfast.

A chap I used to play a lot of golf with up in Derry: he was shot in the head getting into his car after coming out of the golf club. In the north last year a couple of chaps I was stationed with were blown up. About two or three months ago, a chap from Prison Education was shot dead in his car. The police were summoned to investigate the murder and as they were examining the car, it went up. It was a wee trap. When those things happen and you go to the funerals and what have you, it certainly has an effect.

There are a lot of places you worry about going to now. If you are in a hotel, you check who's going in, who is about, who is watching. There is a conscious effort on the part of the Provisional IRA to isolate the police force from the community, so that even those who are quite friendly and reasonably disposed towards the force are nevertheless loathe to socialize with you, largely because of the danger. The Provos have made it quite clear that anybody who fraternizes with the police is a legitimate target. Five people have been shot for supplying policemen with goods, including an electrician. This is what you are left with, people don't go where police go, they don't want to buy your house or car because they are apprehensive. Who wants to live beside a policeman?

We make our own social life. I have been able to make friends with several people from outside the police. I spent the weekend with friends where I used to live and I think it is important to enjoy the company of such people. We were discussing where to go for dinner Saturday night and I had to rule out two or three places where they would automatically have gone. One of them was, in fact, the White Horse, which was blown up.

Your personality can be affected in some ways – because I'm a reasonably outgoing person and yet many social situations outside the force make me feel very reticent. I was at the golf club this Saturday morning. The friend I was with introduced me to some people and, of course, the first thing they wanted to know was my occupation because your social identity revolves around it. You can't live a lie, but you don't want to tell everyone in a place frequented by all sorts of people and where we have been warned there is more than a possibility of being watched. I told his friends who I was, but I felt ill at ease. You always have this thing on your mind; it never goes away.

RUC Sergeant, age 28, six years service. Now in a mixed Catholic and Protestant town north of Belfast.

The trouble with Ireland is that all the ordinary, mundane policing problems still go on and people still report them, so you have to deal with them. It's busy in the ordinary sense and yet there's always this underlying threat.

It's a difficult decision for people to make: do you go to a call, or do you not go to a call? You always try to err on the side of safety, but then one day you're not going to respond to a fire call and you'll suddenly realize that somebody's burnt to death.

The IRA isn't something where you get out of bed in the morning and it's standing beside you. It's not there at lunch time and tea time. Sometimes it mightn't affect you for weeks on end, but it's always there. If they want your house, they'll take your house. A lot of people live with that in the background, hoping it will never happen to them. The last murder we had in this area, the man was in his house with his wife and granddaughter. For the last seventeen years nothing had ever happened to him. He'd lived all through that. Then they shot him.

CHAPTER THIRTEEN

Sex, Husbands and Wives

Talking to people about their private lives has several problems. First, you are probing into their pain and excitement. Second, it is easy to moralize about other people's behaviour. Third, it is impossible to establish the truth about what is being said. Nevertheless, a picture emerges from these interviews that is all too consistent with my own observations: many police marriages are under permanent strain. The reasons are obvious: long, unpredictable hours, shift patterns that destroy normal social life, drinking after work, sexual distractions, money pressures and more.

Looking at the cumulative impact of these diverse pressures on most police marriages, the wonder is that so many last as long as they do. The divorce rate among police families is high, especially in the CID – one Detective Sergeant said quite casually that he was "on number three". There are, however, many thousands of unsung heroines who are expected to put up with the consequences of being a policeman's wife, and do. There are enough successful police marriages to prove it. But the emphasis in this chapter is on the often unacknowledged pressures on all of them.

The interviewees have been selected at random, and in that sense they are "typical" – though, of course, it is impossible to measure how many police marriages are good, bad or indifferent. Many people seemed to be discussing the problem for the first time, especially in those interviews in which both husband and wife were present. Even though the difficulties that emerged are not unique to the police, the nature of police work and police culture exacerbates them in ways that could be changed if the service took domestic problems more seriously.

SEX

Met PC, age 30, eight years service. Now in South London.

There are blokes that feel they've got to prove themselves. I've never quite worked out why blokes go over the side. It's quite difficult to pinpoint. Everybody's got different outlooks, OK, they could be having a problem at home. Why does any bloke look for feminine company? His wife could be eight months pregnant and he has a desperate urge to copulate. You know, when it comes down to it, that can be it. That can be the bottom line.

Or he's going through a difficult spell. The wife's come down from up north or from Wales or Cornwall or somewhere and she's a country girl. She's used to a country life and suddenly she's in the big city. She loses her bearings and she goes charging off. A lot of it is two-sided. As for the drinking side, well blokes have got to have a wind-down. Unless you can relax with your mates after a shift is over, you go away and you're thinking about things all the time. You've got to have a laugh and joke.

PC in a Home Counties force, age 36, fourteen years service. Now in a large university town.

On only one occasion, I can say with my hand on my heart, have I gone over the side. I was stupid enough to be quite open about it to my wife, and as a result there was quite a fraught period of time. Obviously, you manage to survive it.

The opportunities are presented, we do get propositioned occasionally. It is risky to say the least. You go and sort someone's problems out and you say, "Right, I'll be back tomorrow for a statement." When you go back the next morning, she's dropped coffee on the table and she's stretching over in a negligee, saying, "I'm terribly sorry, I got up late today." You think "Whoops, quick statement and out of here." You don't want to embarrass her by turning her down flat, but you have to leg it. It is not infrequent.

LOCAL TEMPTATIONS

For younger officers especially, sexual temptations can be flattering but awkward, particularly in communities where bored housewives are alone at home for much of the time. What sounds exciting can lead to the break-up of a relationship or to the risk of being compromised or of picking up a disease. The macho police culture adds pressure to be virile that further confuses matters. Police language is peppered with sexual slang and most women are referred to in one way or another as sexual targets. Although there is more talk than action, infidelity among married officers is still high.

PC in a Home Counties force, age 26, five years service. Now in a large market town.

I used to work in an area where a lot of Navy lived. The hubbies were away a lot and we had one woman who used to ring up regularly, reporting little things just so she'd have a bit of company during the night. Sometimes she'd strike lucky and other times she wouldn't. I remember we went up there for a broken window. We didn't think any entry had been gained but we said, "You'd better check your meters." The meter was down beneath the sink, and she had this very short nightie on and instead of squatting down she bent over and you saw absolutely everything.

Sergeant in a Home Counties force, age 35, sixteen years experience. Now in a large industrial suburb.

There's ever such a lot of cases where you get young policemen with one or two years of marriage and they're off with someone. They're leaving a wife and kids – totally irresponsible. Happens a lot. This is with people they've met on the streets, and with policewomen as well.

It's there daily if you want it. There's a certain appeal because you're a cop. You're going into situations where a woman is susceptible to an approach, she's emotionally keyed up. Then there are the situations where wives or girlfriends of blokes you're investigating are potentially useful informants. That's happened to me. And of course they are the best informants too. It's a very bloody selfish way of going about it and unfortunately at the end of the day you get caught up in it. But initially the object was purely and simply to get information, and they are the best. The best. You've got to think about it – some of them hate us buggers. The thought of getting to be a snout – a copper's nark – is the furthest thing from their minds. And yet, because you work at it and work at it, eventually you get it, and that's why they are the best.

You get some relationships between a villain and his girlfriend or wife where he thinks he's Jack-the-lad. She think's he's Jack-the-lad. And all of a sudden he's confronted with this policeman, who might be a good-looking guy. He's suave. He's efficient. He nicks the fucking guy and convicts him. He does it in such a professional manner that it's impressive. And it impresses the woman. Sometimes that happens and there is an attraction there. That is one small part of it, anyway. In the main it's just the opportunity, the availability of that policeman. He can go out to work in the morning and go home when he bloody wants to. He doesn't have to be at home at five o'clock. He's available. And he's not accountable, is he? Looking at it objectively, that is a major reason for playing away. I could say to the wife, "I've got to work tomorrow," and it can't be questioned. There's not many people can do that, is there?

TARTS

Police have a special relationship with prostitutes. Depending on the morality of their senior officers, they are obliged to give their local tarts an easy or a hard time. The girls are a vital source of local intelligence. Familiarity with them, however, can impinge on policemen's wives in various ways.

PC in a Midlands force, age 28, nine years service. Now a plainclothes officer with the Vice Squad.

The irony is that we do use our own cars for drug raids and whatever, for picking up prostitutes. So with me having a young baby who goes in the baby seat in the back of the car, villains hide stuff down the back of the seats on the way back if they get the chance to, you don't know what the baby will find. An inquisitive baby on the back seat of your car will find anything, a needle or a wrap – you just don't know. I have to search the car after every single job. Whenever I put somebody in the back of the car, I have to search it. It's frightening, isn't it?

My wife has a good understanding of the problem. The standing joke in our house is that my wife will say to friends who are round, "He's the only fellow that I know that can say, 'A prostitute's just phoned up and I am going out to meet her.'" She just laughs. But like my partner's wife couldn't handle it. She'd have a blazing row with him and end up saying, "Well go on then, fuck off, see one of your prostitute girlfriends." You know, the inference being a sexual liaison. That just used to put me off, you know what I mean?

Most of our informants are women and prostitutes. They could tell you anything. They'd tell you stories that would make your ears curl, but I think most police wives find them ringing up hard to handle, which is sad.

MACHISMO

Machismo isn't just a word. It suggests a whole set of values that are relevant to police work: strength, toughness, street wisdom. Some police work is dangerous and violent and takes a thick skin and strong hands to deal with. The notion that machismo is all bad and should be drummed out of the force – even if that were possible – ignores the reality of the work. But the converse of those virtues is a contempt for sensitivity and softness which is a definite liability in other areas of policing. Handling rape victims, for example, or sudden deaths, child abuse or domestic disputes all requires skill and sensitivity. Yet we expect youngsters still in their teens to handle such events with only a minimum of training. It is a daily miracle they cope as well as they do.

Four Met PCs, average age 23, average service two and a half years. Now in various stations in central London.

PC1: The section house life encourages homosexuality. If I bring a bird back, it's trouble, you get stopped, she has to be out by eleven or twelve o'clock. They don't treat you with respect. But if I brought another bloke back, there'd be no problem at all.

PC2: They treat us like children. What do they expect of a healthy virile bloke of twenty-three, twenty-five? We're going to go out with girls. How can you have a decent sex life in conditions like that?

PC3: It's annoying to be stopped and asked who you're with but just as annoying to watch someone you don't know and you're sure the warden doesn't know walk straight past. There were burglaries in our section house not long ago. There was a blonde girl around several section houses: she befriended a PC, went back to his room, and got a lot of confidential information out of him plus nicking the contents of his wallet. Then there was a girl found wandering around the section house in a stupor by PCs on night duty. You've got to be a bit security minded, with your ID, spare uniform and training notes around.

PC1: Of course it happens all the time. You see the car park full of cars with girls giggling away waiting to go in.

PC4: You see the Old Bill rolling in absolutely rat-arsed with a bird under each arm. There's no security at all. When Paddington section house caught fire, there were all sorts of people coming down half-dressed, lots of females who didn't live there.

PC3: You've got to draw the line, otherwise you get girls moving in permanently, and that would put people's backs up.

SEX IN THE STATION

The encouragement of sexual game-playing is an important part of machismo culture. Friendships between PCs and WPCs are assumed to be sexual, and all women below a certain age are presumed to be fair game, at least for sexual innuendo. Some women officers take this better than others.

Met WPC, age 32, four years service in central London.

They think they invented sex, the canteen cowboys. It's the

ignorant approach, if that doesn't sound horribly patronizing. The only time anyone around here ever made a pass at me he was terribly, terribly pissed and his chat-up line was, "Oh, come on, it'll only take a minute." I thought it was a chat-up line second to none. It's like Australian foreplay. That's the only time I've been at the butt of the gallantry of a PC. There are women who get the names, the relief bicycles and so on, "Martinis: any time, any place, anywhere, preferably on night duty." They say that every relief has got one. But I wouldn't say so at all. I've certainly seen several but by no means on every relief. The other girls are highly amused and don't ostracize the girl for it. It's just part of the fun.

There's an awful lot of divorce. A lot of PCs marry nurses because they understand about shift work and they meet in casualty. They seem to feel safe with each other. The Jack-the-lad ones, the sexual innuendos, the connotations in conversation are desperately dull. I'm amused when I hear of some outraged West Indian Beryl Somebody-or-other alleging sexual harassment in her job because Mr So-and-so pinched her bottom and brushed against her breasts in the canteen. Jesus, if she tried being at any police station. It's just a way of life and you have to take it in good part. It would be impossible for a PC and a WPC to walk around the streets together without everybody being convinced they were having a most torrid affair. It's all part of the image.

Machismo attitudes come home to roost in the treatment of wives and girlfriends. One successful career woman married to a detective described the awkward behaviour of tough policemen at social functions where their wives are present. If they are seen being nice to them, their macho image might slip. Such attitudes spill over into relationships at work. Sexual pressure can cause great confusion for attractive women officers.

WPC in a Home Counties force, age 30, eight years service. Now in a commuter suburb.

Policemen do get offers they find hard to refuse, from outside the force. But the offers I get are from inside, from policemen themselves. And from PC up to Chief Inspector. It's a shame actually, because it puts a lot of pressure on the youngsters. I mean, they can't believe that someone like a Chief Inspector wants to join them for a drink. When I first joined, that would never – not in a million years – happen. A PC would ask you out who was married. That was just part and parcel of the job, but no way would a Chief Inspector do it.

I had one turn up here with a bottle of whisky, in full uniform, on my doorstep one night. I had met him once – he was married with children. He rang the doorbell and I nearly fell over when I saw the uniform and the bottle of wine. I told him no, he couldn't come in for a drink, and I made an excuse. I couldn't believe my eyes, because he was my Chief Inspector and he could make my life bloody difficult, so I had to box a bit clever and think. He turned up again two nights later – the gall of this man – and I then said to him, "If you stand on my doorstep again, if you dare come here again, you and I are going to have a lot of trouble." He said, "All right, all right, no need to get upset. I just thought you might like a bottle of wine and ..." I said, "Take your wine and go!" Which he did. And he then made my life hell for two months. Just being bloody awkward, being rude to me, not letting me do things I should have been allowed to do.

I then got called up to his office. I'd had a complaint for rudeness, it had been investigated and they'd decided it wasn't my fault. But he said, "I don't want heavy-handed officers in my police station," and he went on and on at me. As I left the office he said, "By the way, there's something else. This came through for you today." And he gave me a commendation for bravery. For bravery and courage. I read it and thought, "Well, you've made your point." I went downstairs and I was just boiling. I thought, "It's no good, I've got to go in there and see him." So I just walked into his office the next day and said, "Right, you're going to sit there and you're going to listen. I don't care about male pride, I don't care about the three pips on your shoulder, I don't care about bloody any of it, but don't you ever treat me like that again." He sat there with his mouth open and said, "I'm very sorry."

SEX AT HOME

Sex may be a favourite subject in station canteens and in the vans, but is not necessarily so at home. Lack of sexual excitement was a recurring theme in the interviews, and tiredness laced with alcohol after work does not help. The saddest loss to be inferred is a loss of intimacy. One marriage guidance counsellor asked an Inspector when he had last taken his wife out for a treat. "Last week," he replied, "for a few drinks down the pub with friends." The wife could not remember. She thought it was two or three years ago on their wedding anniversary.

Wife of a Sergeant in a Scottish force, age 33, married for ten years with two children.

He used to be in the Navy. We thought we'd see more of each other when he joined the force, but with the hours it works out not much better. The last year or two, now the kids are getting older, I've started to think of myself more. You have to, with sex and everything else. Otherwise they just get what they want and you get nothing.

Wife of a Sergeant in a large northern force, age 36, married twelve years. Works in marketing. One child.

How do I cope with him never being there? The lack of sex? The lack of attention. One time I had to go to a sales conference in London with my boss. He's very attractive and quite a boy, if you know what I mean. He'd always made it plain he wouldn't be adverse to sleeping with me, although he's married too. I'm sure he plays around all the time. On this particular occasion, and I'd thought it out beforehand, I decided I would. It would release the tension. I badly needed to be affectionate with someone, to feel wanted. Our sex life was nil, he was working all the time. I decided it would be a one-off thing. So off I went. I had a wonderful time, he's a very nice man. I felt wonderful, and although I knew he was a playboy, he made me feel loved for that night and that was all I wanted. Later he wanted to turn it into an affair, but I refused and he was gracious about it. And really that one night helped me to keep going. I love my husband, I just needed some attention.

When I came back from London, I told him he'd got to take notice of me because I felt as if I'd had enough. He was doing his promotion exams to make sergeant, and couldn't respond. Then I had another go at him a few months later and that time it seemed to go in. I talked to other wives, and I trained him to remember to phone me and let me know what he was doing, instead of waiting till 1 a.m. and then saying, "Oh, she'll be asleep," because chances are I won't. I'll be worrying. So he does that now, most of the time. It's better than nothing.

Former wife of a Sergeant in a Home Counties force, age 30, married for three years and with one child. Now divorced.

It's me. I don't attract him any more. I don't do the right things. I don't say the right things. So I read books. I went and asked people. I read articles. You name it. I tried to do it. At the end of the day you get the same result, which is nothing.

I got quite close to having an affair. This person just happened to come along. He was a policeman, but he actually used to find me interesting. And treat me like a woman. All those things I desperately wanted from my husband. Then I suddenly thought: "God, you've only been married a year, and here you are, nearly having an affair. This is crazy." So I went on holiday with a girlfriend and I thought: "You stick it out, try and find a solution, blah, blah, blah."

I came home – and I got pregnant. I must be the only person in the world who does it once in a year and gets pregnant. So that's it, I'm stuck.

I looked for all the signs that he was messing about. And in a way I wanted to find out he'd been unfaithful. It would have taken it all off me. Perhaps it was me that drove him to another woman, but I never came up with anything. I'm feminine enough, I'm attractive enough. But he just didn't want me.

When I got pregnant I had a threatened miscarriage. The doctor said to us, "Right, that's it. No more intercourse until the baby's born." And his eyes went ping! I could see it in the surgery – the relief, joy written all over his face. And I thought, "Doctor, you have just put the knockers on my marriage."

Wife of a Chief Inspector in a Midlands force, age 38, married for nineteen years and with two children.

Sex? Zilch – well, not exactly, but pretty bloody awkward. Particularly when he was in uniform and on shifts. If you're working as well, or have young kids, you can forget about sex. I've got to a stage where even if I'm tired and he's in the mood, I force myself because really it's not much to ask. And once you get going you forget you're tired. You have to do that in order to maintain a sex life at all. Even then it's once a fortnight – if you're lucky. That's why a holiday is so important. We make up for it then. But the rest of the time you could say I have schooled myself into doing it when I'm shattered just because it's rare and I don't want to hurt his feelings. Sex is important to keep you close together.

HUSBANDS

A police officer's job dominates and defines the individual in a way that most ordinary work does not. Committed policemen are workaholics: one Met local intelligence officer regularly clocked up hundred-hour weeks. Current restrictions on overtime have sent more officers home earlier, but have thereby brought pressure to bear on family budgets built on the extra money. Now that remand prisoners are kept in police cells, PCs can volunteer to work their rest days on prisoner duty and earn more money.

For all the talk about sexual antics, most policemen marry very young, at twenty-two or twenty-three, settle down in a new house (often with a large mortgage) and have babies. In fact they settle down far too young to have much experience of the world outside the police, and the long hours of work see to it that they stay that way. When "normal" domestic crises hit them, they are often ill prepared.

PC in a northern force, age 31, ten years service. Now a plain clothes officer with a Crime Squad in a city centre.

We just have a compulsion inside. We go out and just do it. It's hard to explain, once the job's bitten into you and you are there and you've done your bit, you've just got to carry on. It's difficult to half do a job and then say, "Sod it! I'm not doing that anymore." You could go home, but it would play on your mind, and it would destroy your home life. That's probably why we do get divorced, because I'm sat at home sometimes after we've gone half way through a job and I'm thinking, "Maybe we should have done an extra hour." It could be two o'clock in the morning and I go, "We should have done that extra hour." It's constantly on your mind all the time.

Met Superintendent, age 47, eight years service. Now in a busy inner-city station in North London.

Officers will volunteer to be on duty just to sit about with our remand prisoners. Now that's fine, not everybody wants rest. But they need it. How do you stop people volunteering or doing these jobs unless you've got more men? And there will always be astute officers who will wangle a job on their day off, and they'll tell their wives, "Sorry, love, I've been told to do it." You'll never stop these blokes unless they say, "No way are you being paid for that. You'll have another day off, in lieu." As it is, we are obliged to pay them.

People who engineer their overtime are a real problem. They annoy me, these money-grabbers. Not a big proportion, but very hard to stop. They are nearly always people who themselves can take the stress, but I don't know if their families can.

STAYING AWAY FROM HOME.

Because the job is so unpredictable within its eight-hourly routine, drinking after work is a form of enjoyable therapy. The environment of the police club is itself seductive and hard to break away from. On top of the normal conviviality of a good pub, there is the intimacy of shared experience. This puts the wives at home at a distinct disadvantage.

PC in a large northern force, age 32, ten years service. Now in an inner-city area.

For the majority of people, they work seven days and their wife finds that once every month or so they've got a weekend off. And on that weekend off there's about three million things to do. It's very, very easy to grow apart without wanting to. If you're on nights, well, if you have a couple of pints before you go home – I mean a couple of pints, that's the most you can have before you start – that means when there's a really enjoyable party to be at, you can't stay. It's a really weird feeling on New Year's Eve or something, when everyone's really getting into the swing of enjoying themselves and you leave like Cinderella, because at eleven o'clock you're here.

You know, it's a natural thing if you finish work. You could be dying for a pint in the club at eleven o'clock at night, but if you get home at one o'clock in the morning there's going to be hell to pay: "Why the fucking hell didn't you ring up?" It's a lot to expect someone to understand, I suppose.

You go home half the time and all you ever hear is snores. You go in and you're waking every bugger up for a start. You know, the dog starts barking and you're having a couple of pints out of the fridge on your tod, because sometimes you just can't sleep, there's that much been going on. Normally it's worse when you know you're finishing one shift at 11 p.m. and you're back on duty at 7 a.m. A couple of pints when I come off means I might be able to sleep when I get back in.

It's finding a happy medium, isn't it? Some way of letting down with a couple of pints after work and then go home. I'm not advocating that anyone has twelve pints of bitter, but I know some of them do.

Quite recently it was a lad's wedding anniversary and they'd booked a table and everything else. Just before he got off duty, the silly bugger went and locked someone up. So he had to do the paperwork, didn't he? He said exactly the same frigging thing happened last year. So he had to ring his wife and say, "Put the meal back. Ring the restaurant, tell them what's happening and put it back an hour." Last year he never got away at all. How do you explain that to someone?

NO SAFETY VALVE

The macho husband has no place to turn with his feelings. Turning to the welfare department or even to his wife is held to be "soft". Weeping is taboo, though the aftermath of the Broadwater Farm riot and the Bradford City Stadium disaster has eased that somewhat.

With no obvious safety valve, the pressures of the job are fed straight into the home. Wives are a safe target. Drinking plays a big part in appearing to help the men wind down, but also in releasing stoked-up emotions that have been kept under control earlier in the day. The alternative – talking it through – is rarely an option, because by its very nature police work is difficult to discuss with outsiders. As one Sergeant said to me, "No normal PC is going to come home after a sudden death and say to his wife, 'The head was over here, and the legs were there and there.' Only if the wife was a PC could she understand." Others feel they want to leave the job behind – to protect themselves as well as their families.

PC in a Home Counties force west of London, age 43, twenty-four years service. Now a village bobby.

When I first joined if the phone rang the wife always answered it. She knew the gossip and what was going on. There was a rapport and a team between husband and wife. That has now been discouraged.

I personally very rarely discuss work at home. If there's a report of a punch-up in the paper, I will try and play it down. I rarely go into specifics. I feel protective both for myself and for the family. I am aware that at times it is not very productive. They do ask. A complaint often is: "You never talk to me about your work. You talk to other people. I've seen you in the police club talking to your mates. Why don't you talk to me?" And you feel guilty about it. You feel defensive because you don't want to trouble her with it. Occasionally something good comes up and I think she will be interested in it, but she's never as interested as when I'm defensive.

When you are in trouble, it is a very difficult thing to talk to somebody you are close to. There are times when you are at risk, but you think, "Will she worry the next time I am out there?" You are defensive, but you know at the same time it is not very constructive. As a result, there can be an awful lot of tension.

RUC Sergeant, age 30, ten years service. Now in a border town.

We don't go and discuss details with our wives every night, it's the last thing you want when you finish work. But it's fair to say that you have to say something to your wife. I might say, "There's a new Inspector on and he's a nice fellow." Now that gives your wife a sense of his identity, because that Inspector may ring looking for you. It brings her into the team a little bit. I used to go home and say nothing, but as years went by I would say little things to her. Sometimes you work long hours and you do get a wee bit uptight if something hasn't worked right for you. Certainly, I remember when I was in CID spending days on end at Castlereagh, where the IRA guy was sitting on the ground and getting up and pissing in the corner, and you have to continue interviewing with the smell. Things like that did not worry me as long as I got there in the end. But even if you did get there in the end, it was two or three days where the boy was laughing at you. And then you go home and the wife's broken the cooker or something.

Met PC, age 43, twenty years service. Now in traffic patrol.

It's put a tremendous pressure on my married life, especially when our children were young and they were off to bed and the wife was on her own. She felt trapped, she was in the house the whole evening and she couldn't leave the house. When I was on night shift I suppose there was always this fear of break-ins and just general insecurity. Drinking wasn't too bad. Just a pint with the lads most nights. I'd come home, she'd always be in bed, I'd have a cup of tea and I saw her the next day in the morning. Now we are having a bit of a problem, the children are grown up, nineteen and sixteen, and they're off in the evening, and she's all alone. So it does create a bit of pressure and stress on the marriage. But I make a point of taking her out quite a lot. I do work overtime so I have the money, and once a week I take her out for a meal or a drink. You've got to do this. Some other lads they go out all the time but they're going out with other women. I'm quite happy to go home and take my wife out and it keeps her nice and quiet and it keeps her satisfied. I'm the only PC here still on wife number one.

The "buddy" system – whether involving male or both male and female officers – can generate an intimacy which often surpasses and excludes wives, husbands and other civilian companions. Long hours of working closely together encourages loyalty to your partner which is fed by loyalty to the force. Criticism from outsiders only reinforces the bond, leaving wives, girlfriends and boyfriends in an uncomfortable limbo: they are unable to share the experience, and yet they know that to comment on it may provoke a hostile reaction. They are obliged to support the job, even though they may be suffering from its worst characteristics, lest they suffer more from criticizing it. It is a full-scale double bind.

PC in a northern force, age 27, eight years service. Now with the Vice Squad.

A girl informant I used to have regular meetings with, she occasionally phones me up at home and my wife answers. This girl's only young and she's good looking. A very beautiful girl. My wife understands that. Obviously other wives can't accept that a girl phones up their husband. I could be just about to go through the door to take the wife shopping, love and cuddles and everything, then all of a sudden the phone rings, she answers, passes it to me and then I drop everything. She doesn't mind that I can't go shopping now because for the next three hours I'm going to meet somebody. But other wives can't accept that. "Is it the job or me?" and that's it. "If you want the job then go to work, if you want me then I'll be home when you get home, and if you don't want me then I won't be here." They disappear and they do go. Wives will go.

Met WPC, age 27, five years service in West London.

Propinquity, isn't it? I mean, if a WPC is there with big tits, big bum, partridge pouting lips, day after day, night after night, in sticky situation after sticky situation, the poor bloke is obviously going to feel tempted. Much more so than meeting her in a café after work where he'd have to make an effort.

The thing that bugs me is the sordidity of it, the publicity. Nobody worries about it at all. It just doesn't matter. What every senior officer likes to avoid is the missus getting on the phone and ringing him up and saying, "My Bert's having it off with a WPC on relief." Then it is official and it's carpet time and Bert will be pulled up and told to keep his trousers shut.

WIVES

To be a policeman's wife takes unusual patience and resilience. Early marriage – the norm in police culture – is a sobering experience for both partners, but it is the wife who is left holding the home together, and guiding the children, for long stretches of time.

Living a life of your own, however, is not an option for a policeman's wife. You are judged and constricted in many ways. The wives of men in other professions – diplomats, clergymen, politicians – face similar restrictions, but are usually compensated by the higher social status that comes with the job. Too often, police wives seem to suffer all the disadvantages of belonging to the police service while enjoying none of the satisfactions that might otherwise come with it.

Wife of a Met Sergeant, age 32, married for ten years. Works as a travel agent.

The worst time was 1983–5, because I just couldn't get used to the shifts. There was Brixton and Tottenham and on top of it all the miners' strike. He kept going back and back to that strike. Arthur Scargill paid for a winter sun holiday and a new car, but it was a dreadful time for all the wives.

People have no idea how hard policemen work sometimes.

Even the bosses don't realize. It makes me furious. How can anyone do their job when they're bloody knackered? He has his leave cancelled with no warning. The quick changeover between shifts is terrible – he finishes night shift in the morning and then has to start work again in the afternoon. For some reason the police force can't cope with giving them a day off to recover.

And they never admit they're tired. It's this image they have, they can cope with anything. It's ridiculous. He's destroying his health and his home life and me, because I'm bloody wound up all the time on his behalf.

Wife of a Met Sergeant, age 38, married for nearly thirteen years and with two children. She works in a health centre. Her husband, age 38, fourteen years service, is stationed in the south.

Wife: People gave me a hard time when we were first married. We moved into a police flat and I got a job in a cosmetics factory. I'd only been married a week when I started the job, and it was: "Don't talk in front of her, her husband's a policeman." You'd go into the ladies' room and they'd all stop talking. I stuck it for three days.

Where we lived before, my husband was stationed nearby, so the people we would see when we went shopping were the people that he quite easily could have arrested. We did meet some on a few occasions. People would be very abusive to us. When we moved to the suburbs our neighbours used to think it was wonderful. I got the feeling that I was put in the same sort of position as the vicar's wife. Anything they wanted, they'd come and knock on my door. "My child's not back. What should I do?"

It's all my husband's ever wanted to do since he's been a boy. He's just been selected for Inspector and he's worked hard for it. His last year's annual leave was study leave. When he was studying for the Sergeant exams he went away on his own in our touring caravan. He took nothing with him but his study books and isolated himself in a field and studied for a fortnight. I thought it was fair. I didn't have a holiday, but you can't have everything.

When they're doing shift work, they get one weekend off in

four, which means you build everything up for your long weekend. You plan to have him for two whole days. Maybe you could go away for a weekend. And often it all would be messed up at the last minute.

We've been married nearly thirteen years and I worry about him as much as I did before. Not all the time, but things like the Tottenham riot. He phoned me up at 8 p.m. and said that he was going up there. He was due off at 11 p.m. He got in about eight the following morning. I sat up all night. Every time a car stopped out the front you think, "Oh no, he's copped it." You've got the television on, you see the scenes from the riot. You've got the radio on and every half hour they're updating what's going on. And you wait and you wait and wait.

You get used to the shifts. When I got married and was working full time there would be weeks when we would not see each other. We'd just leave notes in the kitchen. I'd work all day and he'd work all night. You just make the most of the days when you are both at home.

And when he's on a late shift, the children don't see him for a week because they're in bed before he gets home and he's not up when they go to school. I wait up for him. We sit around for a couple of hours, until the early hours of the morning. He can't go straight to bed.

Sgt: Sometimes I go to the pub after work. Now that's a real cause of friction, after a late turn and a busy day you go for a pint.

Wife: I've been up since seven in the morning, and he comes home late and all the cupboard doors get slammed because I've gone to bed. I do get a bit humpy about that. I get up each day early with the children and it's, "Quiet! Quiet! Daddy's in bed," until they go to school. When I get back from work I do all the chores. The kids are there and after they go to bed, I sit up and wait. Two minutes past ten the phone rings and I think "swine" because I know what it is: "I'm just going to go for a quick pint." There have been times when he's got back at 3 a.m., legless and stupid. He's really suffered for it because I make a point of waking him up before I go to work. I don't think he'd be too impressed if it was me out to three in the morning.

Sgt: That was just proving a point, because on the late turn I went out Wednesday night and I got told off. I went out Thursday night and got told off.

Wife: Wednesday and Thursday at three o'clock he returns.

Sgt: I went out Friday night too and it was, "You dare go out there tomorrow night, the door will be locked." So I thought I'd see if it would be.

Wife: It wasn't. I can be soft-hearted. But the only reason I wouldn't lock the door is because I know he would kick it down.

Wife of a PC in a southern Home Counties force, age 28, married for four years. Now living in police married quarters.

The children: they've both got asthma and now my husband is on these long hours so all he wants to do is sleep. Of course, with having asthma attacks they cry all the time. So I sleep in our bedroom with them and he sleeps in their room for some peace and quiet. If he's all right, I'm all right. But I can't cope if he's been working sixteen hours and then can't get any sleep because of the kids. It puts him in a temper. I can't cope with that. So I don't mind the way things are. If he's all right, it's fine.

I'd love to go back to work, have my own space, talk with adults. But it's difficult at the moment. There are the kids. I can't work round that yet.

Scottish Chief Inspector, age 43, twenty-three years service. Now in a rural area.

It's astonishing how unfriendly other people can be. We've got an officer stationed on one of the farthest islands, and he's got to fit in with the local community, which is tiny, of course, and very closed in. He's a young lad with a wee young wife and bairn. But because they're police, the locals will have nothing to do with her. She tried to invite them to her house for coffee after church, just to break the ice. But they wouldn't come. They don't invite her to anything either, which makes it rather lonely in a small place like that, especially after they'd lived in

Glasgow, where her mum would always do the babysitting. He's got to go back to the mainland from time to time, and that makes it pretty hard on the girl.

FAMILY TIES

A police officer's job may seem to be no more than an ordinary one with uncomfortable hours, like being a taxi driver or an airline pilot. But few ordinary jobs place such a moral obligation on the rest of the family as well to behave themselves. Some police officers may get away with breaking the force disciplinary code, but their families are under pressure to be more circumspect in ways that seem to me unfair. They also have to endure the local community's attitude towards the police, which can often seem still more unfair.

Wife of a Met Chief Inspector, age 43, married for twenty-one years and with two children.

I'm very conscious of my husband's job, particularly with the children. My son has passed his driving test now, but what if he said, "I'm going to go down the road in my car and I haven't passed my test, what are you going to do about it?" In fact, I do know of policemen's children getting into trouble, terrible things that are typical teenage pranks. They get in with a gang. You hope it's never going to happen – touch wood. I may have been very lucky with both of mine, no problems at all. You get policemen's sons and daughters who take drugs and things like that, they're no different to anybody else. You just hope you've brought them up properly.

Wife of Met PC, age 35, married fourteen years, with four children.

It can be difficult with the kids. You're sitting watching the riot on the telly and they're asking questions: "Why did Dad, being as how he's in the police, do all these terrible things?" They listen to the telly, and their schoolmates and teachers, and they all bad-mouth the police. My seven-year-old got cornered by some coloured kids at her school after Brixton. She was all right but a bit upset when she came in from school.

Superintendent in a Home Counties force, age 46, twenty-four years service. Now in a country town.

My two are fourteen and eleven, they go to the comprehensive but they don't have any trouble. They are both girls, perhaps it would be different if they were boys. After the first was born the wife had six months off, we knew a vacancy coming up in the country beat and I put in for a transfer. During those six months we lived on a council estate in police houses that were supposed to be part of the community. They used to put you in the shittiest roads. You asked for a move, you wouldn't get it. We had half a telegraph pole shoved into the garden, dog turd on the door handle and she went down to the shops one day and she was spat on and called names. But that was on a busy council estate where they haven't got time to know the policemen and "they're shit anyway".

Wife of a Met Superintendent, age 47, married for twenty years. Now living in a London suburb.

If we want to start a business it has to be approved, whatever sort of business. If I wanted to open a shop I would have to get permission, or my husband would have to, from the Yard. It would have to come from the top. If you want to have a lodger you have to get permission.

   Police marriages have to be approved and require permission. Your family background is looked into. My parents were vetted. I don't know how they do it, but they've got computers now – there wouldn't have been computers then – to make sure you haven't got previous convictions or if you have, what. Oh yes, it was a big deal.

MOVING HOME

Nothing expresses the impact of the police service on wives and families more than the frequency and suddenness with which they have to move home. It is not quite compulsory, but there is little choice if you want to get ahead.

Wife of an Assistant Chief Constable of a southern Home Counties force, age 49, married for twenty-eight years.

We have moved eighteen times since we were married. I think they are a bit more understanding now. I still remember one time when my husband was a Sergeant. They had just moved him about fifteen miles to another station and insisted we moved house as well. When he objected, they said that he didn't have to move, but then he didn't have to be promoted either.

Wife of a Chief Constable of a Midlands force, age 45, married for twenty-three years.

They pay for your moving costs, but there's no allowance for the emotional disruption. Actually, the money they give you covers the move but there's always the curtains and the fitted carpets. Each house you go to never fits your curtains and carpets. So you sort out new ones, and just settle into the house, and get the kids settled into school and they start to make new friends, and you get to know the neighbours and bingo, he comes home and tells you you're moving again, just like that. It really works out quite expensive, you know.

Superintendent in a northern force, age 48, twenty-seven years service. Now in a coastal town.

Our son was born on 18 November and the very next day we were transferred somewhere else! And we have moved around within the area again.

My wife has always liked a challenging job. You tend to marry people who are of a lively intelligence, who want a career of their own. The problem is, they can't have a career because they are dependent. My wife had a job at a department store; she took charge of all the wages. But she couldn't go any further because she knew and they knew that eventually she would have to move. Some policemen marry nurses. Quite regularly, you find they try to work themselves up in the hospital structure, then bang, their home is shifted across the country and they have to start all over again. A policeman's wife is a very special person. They have got to be, haven't they?

PC in a West Country force, age 26, five years service. Now in a city centre.

My wife basically doesn't mind. But she's not too bad. She doesn't get on my nerves, she doesn't get at me. She runs the house totally by herself. Pays all the bills, sorts out all the problems at home totally by herself and I just come in, go to work. I'd love to spend more time at home, but we've got to pay the fucking bills. Got off at eleven last night, quarter to twelve the night before. If it's there you've got to work, if you want the money. I need the money, what with being a new home owner with a young family and a very large mortgage. But even if I didn't want to work, I'd still have to do it. I'm going to have to. We've got a young baby that's a year old now. That's the thing I miss, the way things are going now, I'm missing him grow up.

STRAINED LOYALTY

How can a wife hope to rival the excitement and companionship on offer from the job? Being mother and father to the children, dealing with the finances, as so many do, and reflecting on her own wish to have a normal social life, she is a living reproach. As one constable poignantly put it: "There's no room to grow together."

Social life in many police marriages seems wary of intimacy. Partners take shelter in the group. Perhaps intimacy and time together might bring a painful awareness that there is often not enough of either. In their place there is only trust, and trust can be a very lonely business.

Wife of an Inspector in a northern urban force, age 40, married for twenty years and with three children.

You've got to learn to cope. You can't rely on him to change the fuse or deal with the kids. When the pipes burst he'll probably be on duty. You don't get married and expect this sort of thing. You know, you expect to be able to work things out together. But he's not there half the time. You're a one-parent family, really.

Have your own job if you possibly can. If you're not going to go under and turn into a bitter and miserable person, a shrew, someone who's going to nag the minute he gets through the door – which I suspect a lot of police wives do – then you've got to have your own resources. You've got to have the strength of character to go out and do things on your own and have friends of your own who are nothing to do with the police.

Now that our kids are gone, I build up my expectations. I sit here in the evening waiting for him to get back. I watch the telly and think of a couple of things I want to say. And of course he'll walk through the door at 10.30 p.m. and you'll say everything you wanted to say and he's not listening. He'll go and read the paper. It's not to relax, because he's already done that with a couple of pints at the pub – always. He's got an office job, you see. He's off by 5.30, 6 p.m. We have this myth that he has to let the traffic die down. The traffic dies down before seven. It's only twenty minutes' drive home, but he never gets in before nine or ten. I'd much prefer he was honest with me.

I'm quite lucky, though. When I look at other police marriages I thank God I'm me. If he stays out till 2 a.m. for a few nights running he starts to feel guilty. I think we've got it about as good as it's going to get, this marriage. We phone each other up during the day. When I first started ringing, they were always saying they didn't know where he was, but now they're more used to it. I know they find it odd that we phone each other. We are lucky, we can communicate. There was a time when he wouldn't talk to me, but he had to, I made him, because I just wasn't getting enough attention.

Wife of a Met PC, age 38, married for eight years. Now living in police married quarters.

When we were courting, I used to go drinking with my husband in the evenings and his pals thought it was really, really strange.

I remember going up to West End Central one night to meet him and I felt such a prat! I was there in my frock, dressed up, they were all taking a good look at me, I could have died. I sat there in that nick, waiting for four blooming hours. I'm sure they were all whispering about me and looking at my legs. In the end I left, I couldn't take it any more. I didn't know where he was. They couldn't say, or wouldn't say. Of course, I wouldn't ever do that now, never. But it was early days and I was young and naive. Well, twenty-nine actually. We didn't marry till we were over thirty. My little boy's seven now and the girl's four. We have a 50/50 rule about housework, because I still have my hairdressing job. But of course, I do all the washing, cleaning and cooking because when he comes in he has a bath and then he just sits there. It's no good talking about it because it just never happens. I am permanently shattered, what with them and the house and him and my job.

Assistant Chief Constable in a Midlands force, age 52, twenty-eight years service.

I had a chap who lived round the corner from me when I was an Inspector. His wife didn't know how to get hold of him at any time. His wife and my wife were good friends – we both had kids about the same age and that sort of thing. She never knew how much he earned, *ever*. My wife at first used to say to her, "Oh, that was nice, that pay rise we got, wasn't it?" This woman would just say, "What are you talking about?" Eventually my wife stopped talking about anything to do with the police with her because she was just too embarrassed. This particular girl didn't have a clue, because her husband never said a word to her.

He would come home occasionally at weekends and then disappear off again – that was the sort of life he led with her. He was a driver for one of the senior officers who move about the country, but there's no excuse for it really. I don't think my wife is prepared to put up with that sort of thing, you know. Wives realize, now, they can come and talk to senior officers in the force if that's happening.

Wife of a Met PC, age 33, married for twelve years and with three children. Living in a police house.

I admire the police. I think they're marvellous. I hate it when you see the ones in disgrace, the bent ones. I hate them, they let us down. It's different being married to a policeman because you have to think twice before you tell people what your husband does. If I don't know someone, I usually say he's in the civil service.

To cope you have to be the tolerant kind of woman. You *never* ask about work, unless he brings it up. I know women who try and plan their lives around their husbands' shifts. Well, you just learn not to. My husband left on a call in the middle of Christmas dinner and I didn't see him for three days. But that's the way it is. I'm a very placid person so I got used to it.

I had high expectations of the social life. I was very disappointed. You don't really meet any other police people except for two do's, one in the summer and one at Christmas. Unless you're on a police estate you're quite out on a limb. It's a common complaint that the wives don't mix. But a lot of husbands wouldn't want you to. That's how you find things out. Your husband says he was working late with so-and-so's husband, and if you know her you might mention it and get the wrong answer: "My husband wasn't at work that night." So it suits them if we don't mix.

I used to cry every day from loneliness the first few years we were married. I used to walk back with the kids from school and I'd cry as I walked. I couldn't stop. I was so lonely. I never told him. He has enough on his plate at work without worrying about me.

The only place you meet people to talk to is the antenatal clinic. I've had three children. Night time is always the worst, I hate it when he's away even now. We used to be in a block of flats, known police quarters. You'd find broken bottles under the car tyres and things like that. I never really knew if it was on purpose or just some drunk.

I don't worry about him getting hurt. I know he can handle anything. I do worry that he might hurt someone else. And then I worry how he would feel. I've told him that – he says it's not a problem, he wouldn't feel bad. But they all say that. I think it would disturb him.

He really looks forward to coming home. I'm his stability. Nothing changes. This is his den of safety away from the force. I know when something's bothering him at work. He'll never say so, but doors get slammed, he gets short-tempered. Nowadays I try to make him talk more. I worry he'll have a heart attack – he bottles everything up. If I want to talk about something really important, like moving out of London, I have to take the light-hearted approach, never make it sound desperate. If it doesn't work out it will be my fault, you see, for bringing it up in the first place. You've got to be very careful.

I'm always trying to keep the kids quiet when he's asleep after a shift. You have to. It's very important. If his rest is disturbed, then he might not be alert on the job, and if something were to happen to him because he wasn't getting proper rest at home, then it'd be down to me. I've explained to the kids, but you know what they're like. I know women who tape their doorbells over when their husband's on a late shift and take the phone off. They have to be alert on the job, you see. I want to move because we've never had our own house and I'd like to be able to do it out how we would like it. And the neighbours always think you get everything free because you're in the force. When we had the front garden done the man next door said, "I expect you get that done free." Same with the living room carpet. Everyone knows it's a police house so they kind of look down their noses a bit, because they own theirs.

Early on, when I had my first kiddie to look after and I was lonely all the time and tired, the sex stopped. He thought I didn't care and I thought he didn't, and it just stopped happening. So he had an affair. It had been going on about six months when I found out. I'm glad now that I found out. It brought us closer together. He was very worried in case I'd leave him, but in my book everyone's allowed just one mistake and that was his. We became really close and sorted things out between us.

I can't look to the future. I want to move to the country with the kids. The problem is finding a suitable job for him, unless he went back on the beat and lost his rank. I know he wouldn't be happy. I don't know what will happen, but I can't put it off any longer. If we move back North, perhaps I'll be able to hold my head up and say my husband is a policeman, without getting slagged off like in London. Sometimes he says he might leave the job, but I wouldn't like him to. He'd just get bored. He's never bored in the force. I used to be naive, but now I'm more cynical. I see the world for what it is through him.

VIOLENCE IN THE HOME

Violence in the home is a growing problem, but it is notoriously hard to document. Most wives and children never report it, whether from loyalty or fear, or both. It spans all social classes and professions, but few men are prepared to admit to violence against their own family. Figures are derived with difficulty from the few refuges for battered wives, police contacts and so forth. The current figures suggest that three out of every ten relationships contain violence. As the job of a police officer is one of the most stressful of all occupations, it stands to reason, therefore, that police marriages at all ranks are likely to be more prone to serious disputes and to violence in the home than the average relationship among civilians.

Senior officers who feel they know their men resist the idea that violence in police marriages is a problem. Because the subject is taboo in police circles, there is no knowing how widespread it is – and for the wives, the pressure not to come forward is even greater than in civilian life because of the potential repercussions for a husband's career. One agency for battered wives, however, told me that out of every thousand women who contact them "several hundred" are married to policemen. The Chaplain of the Met sees five couples a week in marital trouble, of which one case at least involves domestic violence. He has been doing that for years.

Domestic violence is hardly unique to the police, of course. However, recent police recognition of the need to take more vigorous action in civilian domestic disputes has yet to extend to the same problems within their own ranks.

Met WPC, age 28, seven years service. Divorced from a PC, after three years of marriage.

It's easy to say, "I'm violent with you because I have to deal with so much violence at work." I have been in far more violent situations than my husband was ever in, like at Wapping or the Brixton riots. They were absolute hell, and you feel angry you were ever put in that position, but it doesn't make me feel that I want to come home and knock seven bells out of my husband.

Policemen are no different from other people, although one would hope they would be. A lot of them become punchy when they've had a drink. My husband would get drunk, come home and hit me. Then he'd go off to work the next day and chances are he'd be dealing with domestic situations, same as the one we'd had the night before. It just seemed ridiculous.

There have been times, here at home, when I've actually thought to myself, "God, I get called to sort this out, and here I am in my own home and I haven't got a clue what to do." But if you put me in uniform in somebody else's house, I could sort it out in ten minutes. It's a very weird situation to find yourself in.

Even if I had phoned the police, as the wife of a policeman, he wouldn't have been treated like Joe Public. I don't think they would be terribly fair about it. You all stick together in your profession. If it was a case of severe violence, then something would be done. But if it was not too bad, I think it would be a case of taking the bloke outside and saying, "Look, come on mate, you're in the Job. As far as I'm concerned, I haven't been called here."

Just sitting here, I can think of seven women I know who have been assaulted by their husbands who are policemen. One of them is a nurse. Her husband has had so many girlfriends, though I'm not sure whether she knows. And he knocks her about. Not regularly, but he has done over the years. For no particular reason that she can see. He'd come home with stories about "being on a raid all night" or he'd "been on an observation all night", and she just accepted that for a while. But in the end, she thought, "I can't take it any more, but I can't get out. I've got three children, I've got nowhere to go. I'll find a job." She's put all her energies into her job. It's a form of escapism.

They are all basically in the same boat. They're trapped in so far as they have all got children. Because their husband is a policeman they don't feel they can go and seek help anywhere, in case their husbands get into trouble. I wish to God I knew what the answer was. I looked at lots of avenues, because divorce wasn't what I wanted. I did try counselling. Twice. The first time I went, we'd been married a year, but he wouldn't come with me. He told me there was nothing wrong with his marriage, so he didn't need to go. He saw the thumping as something that I should accept, that I provoked him. He's put his fist through doors in this house, "Well, that could have been your face – so thank your lucky stars it was the door!" We've had food mixers and toasters go through these windows. And it was only the last few times it happened that he finally decided there was something wrong with him and he went to see the welfare, who put him onto a psychotherapist. By the time I got to see him he'd decided what I was like and whose problems were whose – and I just felt I was battling my way against them both.

He sat there and justified my husband's behaviour towards me. He told me that I should have tried harder to talk to him: "The times you chose to speak to him were always in the middle of the night and he was always very tired. You should have spoken to him during the day." And I said, "But I couldn't. I felt frightened of him. And the subject was too . . . I don't know, I didn't feel I could sit down at two o'clock after lunch and say, 'Well, let's talk about our sex life.' When we were in bed, to me that seemed like the time to talk about it."

But that was wrong, and I should have been able to forgive the violence "because he loved me" – which I didn't find acceptable. In my book, when you love somebody you're not violent with them. OK, you have arguments and you might throw something across the room, but if you really do love somebody, do you enjoy physically hurting them?

Wife of a Sergeant in a Midlands force, age 36, married for fourteen years and with two children. Now working as a volunteer on a "Helpline" telephone service for police wives during public order disturbances.

It's not what we're here for, but we do have police wives ringing up because hubby has beaten them. One girl was on the phone for an hour absolutely ranting and raving. So I just let her carry on and afterwards I said to her, "Have you finished? What time is your husband due in?" She said he was due in five minutes. So I said, "I know you've had a good old go. Why don't you wash your face and put on some make up, then make a cup of tea? You'll feel so much better" – this is midnight, by the way. I don't have a clue who she was, because we only ever use Christian names for security. She phoned me back the next day and said, "Thank you very much for listening. I feel great now. I went and washed my face and I felt much better for it." So that was a case where it helped.

Sometimes you do wonder if they are making it all up – lonely, nothing to do. You're never going to know if it is a fairy tale. Do they let you know everything? Have they asked for it? Do they give him a hard time when he comes home? If only some of them would put themselves in their husband's position – though I know it can be very hard to do. I don't know how much wife-beating goes on because they are too frightened to tell anybody. It's like a drink problem, a smoking problem, only worse, people won't admit to it.

Former wife of a Sergeant in a Midlands force, age 30, married for four years and with one child. Now divorced.

I should have known on our wedding night, when he said he was too tired. Everything was fine up until the ring was on my finger. He just thought, "That's it, I'm married. I've now got a wife, so I don't have to do anything any more. I don't have to try." I don't think I actually saw the real him until after we were married. I think I just saw the person I wanted to see.

A month after we were married he came home very late, about three in the morning. He was very drunk, and I had waited up for him, which was "wrong". I asked him where he'd been. He said it had nothing to do with me. He said he'd been at work first of all, then I said I'd phoned work, and they'd said he wasn't there. He accused me of checking up on him. He just wouldn't tell me where he'd been. Then he hit me. That was the first time. We'd been married four weeks.

I was in shock. All of a sudden I realized who I was married to. I couldn't believe it had happened. I never really forgave him for it, and I never will. Not for any of the times he hit me. I could never trust him again. Every night you think, "Oh, he's not home yet. I wonder where he is? Will he come back drunk? Is he in a good mood? Is he going to hit me again?" You live with that every day.

He used to come home in such a temper. He used to really, really bitch about everybody, what a load of wankers they were and "they haven't got a clue". He just moaned and moaned. I used to say to him, "Well, look for the good bits," but he was hellbent on self-destruction, it seemed to me. The rot had set in and that was that. It seems like I spent the last three years crying.

The next time it happened, I said to him afterwards that if he ever laid a finger on me again, I would go. He clocked that, because he held himself back for a while, but one night he came home at just gone one o'clock. I asked him where he'd been. I could see he was swaying. He went into the bathroom and he told me, in a very polite manner, just to go to bed and go to sleep. Then I thought to myself, "No, I'm not having this any more. If he can keep coming home drunk and me saying nothing because I don't want an argument ..." So I went into the bathroom and repeated my question. He was drinking a glass of water and he just smashed it on the sink. Then it all sort of started from there. He eventually ended up saying he was going to keep me captive. I tried to get out of the house, and he made me go back inside. I went back because I thought he was going to hurt me. He's a hell of a lot stronger than I am. I eventually got out because he was on the phone. Luckily I'd got my keys, so I just grabbed the baby and went out of the house with nothing on my feet. I walked over to my neighbour's and then my brother came and got us in the early hours of the morning.

He calmed down by then and was full of remorse. But the next day he was very aggressive. It was my fault. I'd "driven him to it".

Scottish PC and his wife, both age 25, married for one year. He has four years service, she has a good office job.

Wife: I know there are people in the police who misuse their authority, and some of them go home and bash up their wives. But the truth is you're mad if you marry a policeman and don't expect he'll be bringing the job back home. You've got to be available to him from the moment he walks through that door. It doesn't matter what sort of day you've had, you've just got to be there for him to let down. Otherwise, if you let him have all your frustrations, he's got no place to go with his own, so naturally he's going to get wound up. It's really no wonder some of the wives get a bashing. Some of them ask for it. They really do.

PC: On the other hand, far too much is made of the "pressures of the job" bit. We were posted to a small town near the border where nothing ever happened, yet you had people in the force knocking their wives around and blaming the pressures of work, like they were in some inner-city area. It's rubbish. There's no excuse for hitting a woman, none whatsoever.

WPC in a Home Counties force, age 30, eight years service. Now divorced from a PC after four years of marriage and with one child.

It did get really bad. He smashed dishes and glasses and pictures and toys. He was just insane. He got me on the floor and bruised my arms and legs. He said he was going to kill me rather than let me go, and at the time I honestly believed it. I thought to myself, "I'm not a silly namby-pamby little housewife who hasn't come up against this sort of thing before." But when it's your husband it's totally different. The violence is directed at you as a person, not just at your uniform. I kept saying to him, "But that means the baby won't have a mother. If you kill me you'll be put away." It sounds crazy to say it now. He said, 'I don't care." It was just ridiculous.

I didn't want the baby to grow up in that environment. Perhaps it's not ideal just having one parent, but I would far rather he had one parent who he can trust, than to have two and one of them saying to him: "Quickly, go to your bedroom, Daddy's come home." Some coppers hit their kids, too. There's nothing on earth that would make me put him in line for that.

I've never, ever heard a policeman admit to hitting his wife. It doesn't go with the image. Sitting in a canteen, you wouldn't hear a policeman say. "Like I hit my woman last night." "Oh, she made me so mad I could have hit her" – that's usual conversation. If somebody actually admitted it, I think he'd find he had quite a bit in common with some of the others.

The women I know who have been hit by their husbands don't talk about it. They know it shouldn't have happened, particularly as they are policemen. They would only talk about it if they had total trust in someone. I've spoken about it to one of my friends who is a policeman's wife. Just her. And I don't think to anybody else.

THE THICK BLUE WALL

The real threat to police marriages is not from other women, nor from macho camaraderie, nor from domestic violence, serious though those problems are. It is from the job itself. Some men go home and listen to music or collect stamps. Others enter the long spiral of heavy drinking. Some try not to go home at all. Like any cross-section of society, the police service has strong and weak, balanced and unbalanced individuals, but the long hours and poor working conditions put pressure on a policeman's personality that sooner or later is brought to bear on the wife. The nature of the service can smother a marriage, or cut it in two, putting the wife on the outside of things, and a thick blue wall around her husband and his job.

Wife of a Met PC, married for eleven years and with two children. Now living in police married quarters.

Before we were married I used to go on jobs with him. We would go to the pub and he was working, dippers or something – that's pickpockets. I was a nurse and so I went with him, because otherwise we wouldn't have seen each other. So when we got married I was prepared not to see him much, but not prepared for the violent mood changes.

When we'd been married two years we moved. The first baby was ten weeks old and I had to pack the house up. That was the first time I had seen him in uniform. He's horrible in uniform, really rotten. Walking the beat, checking doorways – that was when the mood changed. He used to sit in the corner not talking, because he hated the job so much.

I used to dread him coming in. I had to tiptoe around and make sure that everything was just right, otherwise he'd get in a temper and start knocking me around. Fortunately we moved again eighteen months later. He was still in uniform, but it wasn't so bad because he got a place in the SPG. I was happy to be back in police quarters because I was in a place with people I knew. I didn't see him much, though, because being in that crew, he took off drinking and being one of the boys.

The crunch came when he joined the Vice Squad. The things he came across were absolutely sordid and revolting. He was doing tremendously long hours on it. I very rarely saw him and when he did come home at three in the morning he'd just sit in the front room because he couldn't get out of his mind what he'd seen and the people he had to deal with. He had to go to clubs and witness things that normal people don't usually see. The terrible things that go on, the sexual abuse. It upset all the people in the squad.

I couldn't cope with it. I was pregnant, and lost the baby. I miscarried at four months. Then he went over the side. Of course, I was the last one to know about it.

I smashed the wedding photos. I took the towels and toilet rolls and the light bulbs. I thought, "This will make him realize." You're not supposed to disturb them, but I got him to the phone. I still didn't admit I knew. I said, "I've had a phone call from my sister and I'm going." I left my wedding ring on the kitchen table and I went home to Wales.

Then I got a call from him, asking me back. He took all the blame, I'll say that. And after two months I came back and it was lovely. We talked and talked and it was the saving of our marriage.

It's the job. The job changes them according to what's going on. He was moved to south London. And then it was "the boys" again, not quite as bad as before, but it was at the back of my mind all the time, "It's happened once, it can happen again." But I couldn't say: "Don't go for a drink." It's the pressure of his work and I know that he's got to unwind. This was leading up to my third pregnancy. It took me years to think it was all right to have another baby. Things were getting better, so I thought, "Well, it's now or never."

Now he's realized that after ten years of marriage we've got nothing to show for it. It was good money, but he drank it away. We're trying to clear our debts so we can get a mortgage. He's in Firearms now. That's long hours, it really is. But at least I know he's really there and working.

PC in a Midlands force, age 29, nine years service in an inner-city area. Now married for four years to a WPC.

Last year, my home life was completely altered. My wife had left me with the baby. We were just about to get divorced. We had the papers all ready to be signed. We got back together again, and a month later I was posted to the plain clothes.

Knowing that this department is renowned for breaking up marriages, I thought: "Jesus, obviously we are going to get divorced now." So I went home and told her. She was a bit apprehensive. So I said, "Look, if you want me to, I won't go." She knew, her being a policewoman, that if I didn't go, that would be it with my career. Because if you turn down a department, you get a "no" mark on your file. So I said, "Well, I'll give it a try." It's done the opposite for us. It's brought us closer together.

That was really lucky, but it galls me. The invasion of my private life by this job takes me apart. I still do it because I need the money.

Former wife of a Met Detective Inspector, age 40, married for fifteen years. Divorced four years ago.

When we got married, I was running a sales operation and he was already a policeman. He thought he would have a bright future. He did quite well. He had already passed his Sergeant's exam. He had been in the police ever since his national service. His brother and uncle were policemen as well; it was in the family.

He was in uniform, so he was doing nights and all sorts of shift work. I always had a career, so it suited me. I could do my own thing. I don't know whether policemen like having someone who is successful in another career, because they want a wife at home as well.

When I look back, I wonder if I knew him very well. I know there was a very soft side. I think he would have been better being a gardener or a farmer because that is something he really wanted to do. He used to say things like, "I don't like people very much; I prefer plants and animals." He found it very difficult being in the company of people who were not connected with the police in some way; that camaraderie was always something he felt most comfortable with. Out of that environment he was a fish out of water.

My career was all-important to me. He didn't make it his business to find out what I was doing, but on the other hand, he came to resent it terribly. He embarrassed me many times in public situations to prove he was in charge. In the same evening he could be bragging to somebody about my independence and how well my sales were going, and the next minute he would embarrass me by making me feel small and putting me in my place. He used to be terribly jealous.

I eventually found out that he had gone to a police social function with another woman – when I went to the station for something they were doubting I was his wife, having met the other girl. I don't think he cared whether I found out or not. He was definitely unfaithful and admitted it. He said everybody was. I got upset when I first discovered it and he said, "Well, surely you are?" But why should I? I'm married. He said he couldn't believe I wasn't – during sales campaigns and all the opportunities I must have. I said, "It doesn't occur to me. I do my job and, of course, I am friendly with people on a sales tour, but not going over the side." He would never admit we had a problem. Even when I finally said there was no point in our staying together, he said he thought we were getting along fine. He couldn't see it at all.

The police changed him over the years. He was attracted to the uniform because he loved being in the army, then he enjoyed being a detective, but that changed him even more, because the drinking started and got worse as the years went on. When you are in uniform, you don't have those opportunities. It got much worse when he was moved to East London. Usually, they give you a three-year stint in any one department, but this one went on and I saw hatred develop in him for black people. He saw some really terrible things, and he came to believe that black people were all the same. Then the miners' strike happened and he felt the same about the pickets. He became so bigoted that he couldn't see where there was good and where there was bad. It was either black or white – not just in his job, but everything in life.

He voted for the National Front once. I suspect quite a few of them in his department did, because they also probably felt that as black people were responsible for so many evil things, it must be in them in some way. He told friends and was quite proud of the fact. It really did something to me when he told me. I asked him if he would have supported Hitler. Had the time been right, he might have joined a movement like that.

He couldn't ever be off duty, even in the moments we were at home. If he saw anything going on, he would be there. We would be coming back from an evening out, and suddenly the car would stop and he would be out chasing someone along the road in his best suit. He would take them to the police station and charge them. For so much of the time I didn't exist.

He was always getting angry. I don't think he ever meant to hurt me, but he couldn't help it. He got into a really terrible state. He would throw things. The dog and the cat used to run away to get out of his way. Often, he didn't remember a thing afterwards because he had had so much to drink. I was strong enough to stand up for myself and walk away from it, but I wonder how many other wives can do that?

He couldn't communicate terribly well as a person, which is why he enjoyed being a policeman. He was dominating the situation all the time and had the power to do it. I don't even know if he liked himself. Maybe he was sick in his mind. He used to say that I didn't live in the real world, when I tried to understand why he felt the way he did. He said the world I was in was like fairyland. I told him he only saw the black side of life, so how could he call his world real? It was black and white to him, the other worlds in between just didn't exist.

Detective Chief Inspector in a Home Counties force, age 47, twenty-six years service, and his wife, age 42, married for twenty years and with two grown-up children. Interviewed together in their semi-detached suburban house with a well-kept garden behind.

Wife: The way you are at work, there's no space for anything else, is there?

DCI: Except for weekends . . .

Wife: And then you're in the garden and I'm in here. And our day out together: a couple of hours to do the shopping – he goes off with one trolley and I go off with the other. Even then we're not together. At least at our last posting I had some friends there. I haven't made any friends here apart from the girls I work with, and they're just acquaintances. I was just sort of wrenched from there on his transfer. I don't like it here.

I don't mind him working extra hours, but it is every single day. And he's not healthy. Although his heart's strong, he's unfit. That worries me.

I'm the one that does everything, but who else is going to do it? I'm rushing about in the morning. The boy is nasty to me, but he won't be nasty to his Dad. He's given our son a lot more time than he ever gave the girl.

DCI: Lost the girl, I lost the girl while I was in CID all those years. I'm just getting her back now.

Wife: But I'm the old dragon, because I'm the one that tells them off. Even if they're cheeky to me he won't say nothing. Just wants a quiet life. He worries about people outside much more than he does me because he feels sorry for them. I cope, I get on and do what I have to. If I'd been a whingy, whiny wife he might have paid more attention to me.

DCI: Anybody listening would think what a disastrous time we've had. But we haven't.

Wife: He doesn't like me to discuss anything, so he shuts up. When I try to discuss something with him, or to present my feelings, he'll say something so stupid, totally irrelevant, and I think: "Sod you! What's the point?"

DCI: Oh, that's totally wrong, is it? I try to make life a little bit more humorous, brighten your day.

Wife: We've had lots of love in between the bad times, but we've gone through bad patches and he would never have entertained the idea of going to see a marriage guidance counsellor. I've been to see one. And it did help me. I couldn't tell him, because he would have blown his top.

DCI: Anyhow, we haven't done too bad. But I know she's fed up with the whole situation. Of me coming home bloody exhausted. Not spending any time with her. Not going out with her. Not being able to have a bloody discussion with her about anything. At weekends, because I've worked my backside off all week, I've had to spend all weekend getting the bloody garden up to scratch, because we do like a nice garden.

Wife: He won't go visiting with me, he never likes visiting. We never go shopping apart from a little groceries.

DCI: But I don't have the bloody time, do I?

Wife: You should make time. Every morning he says to me, "I'll be home at seven tonight." He's got a desk job now. He's a nine-to-fiver. He never is – never. I phoned him up at ten o'clock the other night and said, "Don't you think it's time you came home?" And then I feel bad because I've had to do that.

I don't ask to be taken to the cinema, the theatre. Don't want to be wined and dined. It don't bother me, not particularly. I just like him to be home, to be part of me.

Two weekends ago we had a row and he went to bed on that Sunday afternoon. He was totally exhausted. He was almost on the point of tears. And I said, "Look, if your job's doing this to you, is it really worth it?"

In our twenties, I thought I had something to look forward to in the future, but I've done all that and the future is here. I want those things now.

DCI: I feel that too. I've worked for twenty-six years in the police force, grafting my backside off to get where we've got. Not where I've got, where we've got. Grafted my bloody arse off. And I don't want it no more. I've had it.

Wife: And you've been saying that as well for I don't know how long. I'm not waiting another ten years. But now it's come to a crunch. They say everybody reaches a crossroads. And you have now, haven't you? With your job.

DCI: Christ, I have. And I'm doing something about it. If things don't put themselves right by the end of the year I shall be positively leaving. We'll just have to struggle on financially. I shall do it and we will have to manage. We're totally in agreement. I'm doing it because I'm fearful of you going. It's because I appreciate that it's got to come to a stop.

Wife: And I'm not prepared to play games and go away just to test him out. If I do it, I shall do it for real.

DCI: There's no doubt about it, that a wife of a dedicated serving officer is a very special sort of human being.

Wife: Yeah, not to be taken advantage of. Nobody's ever taken my side except my sister. But all I get from her is: "You ought to leave, I wouldn't stand for that! Get out now." But where do you go?

DCI: You'd be gone by now, if you wanted to go.

Wife: There's still time, there's still time.

DCI: You wouldn't go anyway.

Wife: I want some life time before I'm too old.

DCI: I've told you what'd happen if you go. I've got a plum tree at the bottom of the garden, I've shorn all the little branches off it ... and I shall be swinging off the end of that plum tree.

Wife: That's emotional blackmail. I could say that to you: "If you don't start coming home to me, I'm going to hang myself from the apple tree!"

DCI: We haven't got an apple tree.

Wife: But next door have.

THE PRICE

If the police themselves pay a large personal price for being in the service, their wives and children pay the lion's share of that, largely unnoticed even by their husbands. Inviting wives to the odd police social is no substitute for official recognition of the way families are taking the consequences of the strains of the job and the insensitivity of the system. Just as the service is now promoting greater awareness of its impact on the public, it behoves them to show similar concern for their impact on the women and children who play a crucial role in the mental health of so many officers. Simple fairness suggests they deserve a better deal.

On a personal level, the men themselves may be aware of the problem, feel badly about it, and yet feel unable to improve it. There is an apparent inevitability about the pattern of long hours, the drinking after work that leaves domestic concerns outside. The women and children must fend for themselves much of the time, like one-parent families. Indeed, feeling guilty about it often makes matters worse. After a point, the long hours make it harder to go home in a normal way.

There are signs that more of the new generation of recruits go their own way and avoid the attractive net of post-shift socializing. I know from personal experience how difficult that choice can be. During the year we spent with Thames Valley Police, all the film-unit marriages were under strain, and three ended in divorce, including mine.

CHAPTER FOURTEEN

Firearms

Guns present the British police with yet another bind: serious villains commit armed robberies, against which the police are empowered to use firearms themselves. Yet their public image rests on being an unarmed force. That is a difficult choice.

A number of myths confuse the situation still further. First, for all the gun battles on our television and cinema screens, police use their guns very rarely. Even in the United States in high-crime cities like Los Angeles, Joseph Wambargh, an ex-cop and author of The Choir Boys, *wrote that he and many of his colleagues went through their careers without ever using their weapons. In Britain, although the Home Office has unhelpfully stopped providing figures, the number of police shootings is tiny, though the frequency with which the police are issued with firearms is very much greater.*

Secondly, the British police have never been completely unarmed. As Tank Waddington shows in Arming an Unarmed Police, *the Met have always had firearms available. In the 1890s, they began carrying them regularly in the outlying districts of London at night. But they maintained their public image of unarmed vulnerability by playing down their interest and involvement with firearms. They made a virtue of their amateur approach to firearms training by minimizing it.*

In the 1960s, the move towards police professionalism extended to firearms as well. As criminals carried guns more often, so did the police. Terrorism was growing in London, which led to the Diplomatic and Royalty Protection officers always going armed. In 1972, increasing sectarian violence in Northern Ireland led to the RUC being authorized to carry guns at all times. Some officers regard this as a fatal escalation.

In the 1970s, as armed robberies increased on the mainland, many more CID detectives and other officers were authorized to draw weapons and were issued with them. This coincided with a third myth, drawn from cinema and television fiction, of the macho gun-toting detective who always gets his man. By 1980 an estimated 15 per cent of the Met also were Authorized Firearms Officers. The training was a modest five-day basic course and the odd day on the range as a refresher. This was itself a dangerous state of affairs.

Just how dangerous became clear with the shooting of a young film editor named Stephen Waldorf. He was shot and pistol-whipped by local Met detectives while driving a Mini in central London during the rush hour. He was mistakenly believed to be David Martin, a wanted villain who had previously shot at the police.

Virtually every aspect of standard police firearms practice was violated in the Waldorf incident: there was no liason between the three teams who were after Martin. The public were endangered unnecessarily, Waldorf was unarmed, yet no warning appeared to have been given, and he was shot and then beaten badly about the head after he was already incapacitated. But the judge and the PCA accepted that the officers had acted in self-defence rather than out of revenge for what Martin had done to their fellow officers.

The trial of the officers involved alarmed many Authorized Firearms Officers, who realized they were vulnerable to prosecution for carrying out their duty. Despite the acquittal, the Police Federation called for immunity from prosecution for AFOs, many of whom tore up their authorizations.

The Waldorf furore was followed by two more mistakes which led to a major Home Office reappraisal of police firearms practice: the first was the shooting of five-year-old John Storthouse in his bed during a house search by PC Brian Chester of the West Midlands Police. The second was the shooting of Mrs Cherry Groce in Brixton during a dawn raid on her house by Met Inspector Douglas Lovelock. This incident sparked off the 1985 Brixton riot.

Both officers were acquitted after emotive trials that showed them to be good policemen who had made basic mistakes under stress. But the trio of events prompted a change from the relatively relaxed issuance of firearms and training towards the *current policy of fewer but better trained specialists accounting for the bulk of police involvement with guns.*

The frequency with which guns are used in fiction, and their finality when used whether by mistake or on purpose, has given firearms a symbolic importance out of all proportion to their rarity in real life. It adds to the impression that violent "crime-busting" is central to police activity. That emphasis in turn has hindered the effort to restore the less glamorous image of the bobby on the beat, now at the centre of current police strategy.

2 PCs in a large Midlands Force, average age 30, ten years service.

PC1: We're like cannon fodder to these firearms blokes. We're asked to back up the arms officers, but we're not authorized ourselves. They are the ones with the flak jackets under their overcoats and we're the ones who never get one. They go on a raid and we're expected to cover the back end in case anyone runs out. You're expecting shotguns. It's a horrible feeling.

PC2: One beat lad – unarmed of course – chased a man into a block of flats. This guy stops, comes up behind him and sticks a gun to his throat. He was there for two minutes with a gun against his jaw, trying to talk him out of it. Luckily my friend managed to grab the gun. Then he nearly murdered the bloke. I can quite understand why.

PC1: No one is to know, tomorrow afternoon, three o'clock we go out. Five past three, you could be wiped off the face of the earth.

GOING IN UNARMED

Time and time again, unarmed British police officers are up against villains whom they believe or know to be carrying guns. Although they should call for armed police back-up, some choose or are forced to deal with the situation themselves. This heroism often goes unnoticed unless some dramatic rescue or arrest is involved – or the officer is wounded or killed. It is a common feature of police life that their bravest acts often achieve the least public recognition. They accept this and carry on, but their resentment emerges when the occasional scandal becomes a major focus of attention.

Two PCs in a large northern force, average age 29, average service ten years. Now in an inner-city area.

PC1: When you first join you'll be full of enthusiasm at the thought of an armed robbery. After a couple of years you'll go "Oh shite" because you'll have grown up a little.

You're just patrolling and you get these calls out of the blue. The banks and the building societies in town have personal attack alarms. They just hit the button under the counter and you don't know what the hell it's all about until you get there. You sometimes wish your tyre would blow out or your car won't start.

PC2: The bloke on the radio just circulates the number plate and says, "Go after it." Doesn't tell us why. Then you say, "We're behind it now," and he says, "The fellow's supposed to be armed. Approach with caution." So you say, "Do you want me to stop him or are you sending someone with a gun down for back-up?" "No, it's yours," he says. Not a nice feeling.

PC1: We were on our way to one armed robbery in town when they circulated the car that had been used in the offence. And it was all of three feet in front of us! There's four men in the car who have already fired their guns once. You think, "Oh shit! I hope to Christ we can't catch the frigging thing." As it happened, with the car we were in, we couldn't.

PC2: Another time, we were looking for a loony that had already used his gun, but none of us had a bloody gun, a flak jacket, nobody had anything. You think, "What bloody moron is in charge?" because some effing DI decides it's too difficult to get firearms authorized. "Well, you'll just have to go and sweet-talk this bloke out of it." That's all right till he comes out of the back door waving a sawn-off. It's like having nine lives. You can escape just so long.

PC in a Home Counties force age 27, six years service on the beat in a socially mixed inner-city area. Just retired.

I was on attachment to the CID and was sent to get sandwiches when the alarm went off at a bank close by. I was the first bloke to arrive at the bank, which was a bad thing to be. If I'd known they had guns, I wouldn't have gone anywhere near it.

Me and my partner chased them up the street and tried to tackle them by their car. I tried to open the door, but they drove off with my mate riding on the bonnet. We then stopped a member of the public and said, "Police! Follow that car!" They didn't want to, but they did. The robbers abandoned their car very soon and got into a large Mercedes. It was in a mortuary car park, believe it or not.

As soon as we found a uniformed patrol we gave the licence number out. A traffic car happened to be two cars behind it and gave chase. A Panda joined in, stopped the car, and one of the men in the Panda got shot in the head. He survived. They didn't shoot us, I reckon because we were in plainclothes and they didn't realize.

The next car they see is a standard squad car coming up behind them. What they don't know is that this is a gun crew. They'd been tipped off that a robbery was going to happen, but they'd been sitting outside the wrong bank. Anyway, they'd finally got themselves into this Granada and zoomed off.

It gets much worse, because all police cars have baby latches on so you can't get out from the inside. So three police gunmen are sitting in the back of this car. The Merc stops. The villains get out with guns and start running towards them, firing. The police marksmen can't get out of the car because the latches are on. So they tell the guys who are driving to get their heads down, and they start firing through the windscreen. They shot one of the blokes. The other decides discretion is the better part and runs back to his car. He abandons it fairly soon and hijacks a lorry.

The lorry driver is amazingly cool. He says, "You've got the wrong lorry here, pal. It only does 55 mph." Which wasn't true! So he's driving off down the M4 with a convoy of police cars following behind. Finally we manage to get a road block across the motorway further down with another gun crew. The lorry stops and he decides to surrender.

But he says to the lorry driver that he doesn't much fancy getting out of the lorry because the police will shoot him, so the driver gets out first and tells the villain to stand behind him. Then he walks him to the police so they have to deal with him properly! The lorry driver going in front saved his life. Our blokes wouldn't have wasted much time talking to him before pulling the trigger. If he'd moved they'd have shot him for making "threatening gestures". Anything they could hang the label on. Why shouldn't they?

After that it seemed to me that policemen carrying guns was quite reasonable in these situations.

Station Sergeant in a northern force, age 36, eighteen years service. Now in a residential suburb.

I've been stabbed twice and I have been shot at. I had a shotgun straight at my head. I used a ton of toilet paper! You don't react at the time. It's afterwards. It's weird.

It was a post office robbery. It was getting turned over by a couple of hooligans with shotguns. I just happened to draw up outside because it was where I used to get my fags. Always in the wrong place at the wrong time, me! I drew up, there was a car parked in front and that little "ding dong!" was going at the back of my mind, but not to any great extent. The next minute, there was a double-barrelled shotgun pointed at my head. I went down and the shot took off the roof of the car, fortunately. Then I just sort of banged the handle and pushed the door. He let go of the gun and went backwards. Another one came out and took a shot at me, then they jumped in their car and were away. We got them about an hour later. This was seventeen years ago. I still remember it like it was yesterday.

ARMED POLICE

Each police authority has a number of Authorized Firearms Officer (AFOs). Apart from special squads like the Anti-Terrorist or Royalty and Diplomatic Protection Groups, most authorized "shots" are ordinary PCs who are unarmed most of the time. They are often the first to be called out when a gun is

wanted to deal with a particular situation. In the past, autho-
rization for a weapon to be issued could be given by as low a
rank as Sergeant so a PC as Acting Sergeant could give one out.
Now guns are normally to be issued only when approved by
Assistant Chief Constables, Chief Superintendents and Com-
manders or Deputy Commanders in the Met.

There are 30,000 AFOs out of 120,000 officers in the whole
UK police service. Some 9000 belong to the RUC where every
male officer is armed. After the Waldorf and Groce shootings,,
the Met cut its AFOs from 5000 to just under 3000. They also
changed the emphasis to rely far more on the Met's specialist
firearms squad whenever guns are needed, PT 17, the "blue
berets". They use a two-tier response: Level 2 is the all-purpose
full-time team used for most situations, like searching houses
or managing the surrender of gunmen. Level 1 are the force
instructors, who do the most dangerous tasks such as forced
entry into a house where arms are expected, or an ambush of
armed robbers or a hostage rescue. That is the way it should
work now.

Met PC, age 34, twelve years service, six as an AFO. Now in PT 17.

It is very, very rare that we zoom straight out. In the eighteen months I've been here on only one occasion have we gone straight out with everything going. We got there and we had a five-minute briefing and we had to go in. That was only search-ing for someone. Those are the ones that are less likely to result in a firearms incident for the reason that you are doing everything so slowly. You've got so much chance that you will see him from a position of safety before he sees you. The dodgy one is the ambush situation. Because of the surprise factor, you're often in a position without adequate cover and in effect it's going to be me jumping out and going, "Boo!" They're going to be as shaken as we are. Those are the occasions where shots are fired. If we thought we wouldn't have enough time for adequate planning, we'd just get a very large, marked police vehicle, put it outside the bank they were planning to rob and scare them off that way.

NO FIRST STRIKE

Despite public criticism of trigger-happy policemen, official policy about firearms is clearly "soft" – they should be used only in extremis. A successful mission by the firearms squad is one where the situation is resolved peacefully. This happens time and again without press attention. Because only those incidents where shots have been fired tend to make the news, the impression is created that when guns are issued, they are used.

Met PC, age 32, ten years service, five as an AFO. Now in PT 17.

I reckon I've personally been out on up to 100 jobs. Overall I'd say we've done 250 jobs in 18 months. If you include the special jobs by the instructors it probably goes up to 300 or 350. Shots have been fired on only one of those jobs. I think the bulk of villains take firearms as frighteners. They don't want to use them. At the end of the day, very few are prepared to. You get the occasional nutter, the occasional one high on drugs, but the bulk of them, no.

Chief Inspector in charge of firearms training in a northern force, age 48, thirty years service.

Officers are trained never to fire unless their life or somebody else's life is in danger. Now that means to say that if some villain has a shotgun in his hand and it's pointing at the floor when we come in, we can't shoot. We've got to challenge him, tell him to drop the gun and do as he's told.

There was a case, in Essex I think, when a member of the tactical firearms team was shot. It happened within months of the Stephen Waldorf shooting. They were waiting to ambush this chap who had a sawn-off shotgun in a plastic bag. They challenged him to put the bag down, but he didn't. He put his hand inside, pulled the trigger and killed a police officer. At the time, the PC didn't know there was a shotgun in the bag and I'm sure he was thinking, in a flash of a second, "This is dangerous, yet I can't do anything unless I see a gun." I sometimes think that the Waldorf affair and criticisms of the police on that occasion were perhaps made in haste. If Waldorf had never happened, we might have done something different and that PC would never had died.

I'm really conscious of the trauma officers experience even when they're 100 per cent justified in pulling the trigger. In this country, any officer who shoots somebody, justified or not, is going to go through hell. The general attitude from the public or our own supervisors will be, "He was wrong." In the United States, they'd probably think, "Well, he must have been right otherwise he wouldn't have opened fire."

Sergeant in a Midlands force, age 31, twelve years service, four as an AFO.

Guns are still too easily obtainable. The problem is that they get no stiffer penalty for doing a robbery with a gun than they would if they did one with a knife or without a gun. If they shoot someone, what are they going to get? Life. Life is what – fifteen years? They think they're going to get away with it if they shoot someone, so it's a fair gamble to them. That thing in London at Greenwich where two of them were shot on the payroll snatch, tragic as it may be, it's quite good for us because it lets villains know that if they want to point a gun at a policeman they've got a good chance of being killed. That's the best deterrent of all.

HOLDING THE FORT

Current policy calls for AFOs to "contain" the situation until the specialist team arrives. Other forces deal with their specialist teams in similar ways. Nottinghamshire has theirs cruising the force area with weapons in the back of an "armed response vehicle", and authorization is given by radio by an Assistant Chief Constable. In 1986, guns were issued to AFOs some 1700 times in London alone. They are the ones most vulnerable to making mistakes from a mixture of stress, confusion, and sheer lack of practice.

Met PC, age 34, twelve years service, seven as an Authorized Firearms Officer. Now in South London.

Procedures have changed because of the mistakes that were made, but I think they overreacted. They have now loaded the authority level needed for firearms so high that the system is virtually unworkable. If a man was outside there now using a shotgun, I couldn't draw a firearm and go and tackle him. As it's "life in danger", I'd still have to hassle with a Chief Superintendent. Many officers will tell you they don't want to bother with guns any more.

I try to take the opportunity of playing with my gun, but I don't use any bullets. I don't think I am adequately trained. I can go literally three or four months without touching a firearm.

Met PC, age 34, twelve years service, seven as an AFO. Now in PT 17, Level 2.

I don't think you'll ever do away with the need for AFOs on district, for the simple reason that we can't always guarantee to get the special team there, sort of like "now". At night they've got to bleep the Level 1 Instructor at home, then they've got to get in and get their kit. So you're usually looking at an hour minimum. If you've got a bloke hanging out of the window stoned out of his skull just blasting away with a shotgun down the street, you've got to have someone there who can at least try and contain the situation until you arrive. So of course there will always be a need, though I can't see the point in arming everyone.

But it's the unfortunate situation you're going to get where maybe some unarmed district PCs are driving past an incident, a bank robbery or whatever, and they're obliged to get out of their car and do something. Personally I'd drive the car at the bloke, but they normally get out and try to deal with it. That can be very dodgy.

Ex-Met Firearms Instructor in a Home Counties force, age 36, twelve years service, eight as an AFO.

You're restricted in the number of days' training you can give these guys because of economic constraints. Every firearms officer should come up at least once a month to fire his gun, so that he's familiar with it, so he's not frightened of it. If you go to a normal police station and say to an officer, "We've got a situation – get your gun out," he'll be shaking and nervous by the time he gets there because he's not used to picking up that gun on a regular basis.

In the Met, I was on a Diplomatic Protection Group where we took the gun out every day. Blokes up there are completely different because they're picking it up, loading it, unloading it, in and out of the holster. The normal AFO doesn't do that, so when he picks up a gun he's nervous.

ACCIDENTS

It is more than a truism to say that policemen are human. In their daily work they encounter far more emergencies than the rest of us do in a year. We make mistakes in our work, policemen make mistakes in theirs. Being under pressure in an emergency makes mistakes more likely. Police traffic accidents, often involving innocent pedestrians or other cars caught up in a car chase, are a common calamity. The CID frequently raid the wrong address. With firearms issued by the thousand every year, it is hardly surprising that some mistakes happen. With the meagre training given to most AFOs, who are themselves under pressure, the wonder is not that there are so many shooting accidents but that there are so few. In the USA, 25 per cent of police casualties are caused by their own guns.

Met PC, age 32, ten years service, five as an AFO. Now in PT 17.

With Cherry Groce I understand that it was basically down to tiredness and the fact that the officer involved was told to do something he didn't want to do. It's the one thing that is always stressed in the firearms authorization – the bloke with the gun is the one who calls the shots. He should have turned round and said, "No, I'm tired. Get someone else to do it." He broke that rule. It is there to stop incidents like that happening, but if you break it, well, you've only got yourself to blame, haven't you?

HARD POLICING

There is a hard and soft style to the use of firearms as well. The alleged "shoot to kill' policy is the hard end. Without it being a formal policy, in some situations the police have taken no chances by shooting first and asking questions later. Sometimes they discover that their targets are unarmed, as in the Hayshed killings by the RUC Special Squad which the Stalker team investigated; or that a suspect's gun is a replica, as in the India House killings by the SPG; or that an innocent hostage is involved, as in the killing of Gail Kinchin in Birmingham; or that the wrong person is involved, as in the shooting of Stephen Waldorf.

Sergeant in a northern force, age 38, twelve years service, eight as an AFO. Now in an inner-city area.

Each firearms officer is given a training and when he's given that gun it's his decision whether he uses it. You can't say to me, "Shoot that man!' because it's not your responsibility. If I shoot him it's not you that's going to be standing in the dock, it's me.

You can never accept mistaken shootings as a part of life, you've got to try and change things. Waldorf was a tragedy, but if you look at it from the police point of view, they were told that this man Martin had shot a policeman and he was dangerous. He was the most wanted man in London. The girl in the car with Waldorf was Martin's girlfriend. They were wrong to do it where they did it, but the car stopped and as they approached he made a move. They thought he was going for a gun. If you've got a gun in your hand and a man in front of you who you think has shot a policeman, your bottle's going to go. What I think happened is that one man's bottle went – you're never going to be able to prevent that – he pulled the trigger and the other bloke, believing that shots were coming from the car, opened up. They said it at the trial* and got off, but you could never explain that to the satisfaction of the public never in a million years.

The Cherry Groce shooting was a similar incident. They went to search the house, they were looking for a man known to be armed and who had, again, shot at policemen before. If you do a search like that, you've got to take guns and you've got to have them ready in your hand. So your finger is on the trigger. It's a 10–12 lb strain. It's a definite strain – you can't just twitch and fire it. It was a tragic accident, no doubt about it, but to the public it's another thing that shouldn't have happened.

The John Shorthouse case – how he got shot, God only knows. My view is that the weapon must have been on single action, which means that he must have cocked the trigger, pulled the hammer back, and then you have got a hair trigger. You touch it and it's off. There's no way you should ever do anything on single action – in fact, that's been taken out of our training completely now. Apparently the PC had only just got into the tactical team. In this force new boys get the back door to guard. To do the sharp end you'll probably have been in the group a couple of years, ten to twenty operations. We've got a black-ball system here if you're not up to it.

PC in a West Country force, age 29, eight years service. Now in a city centre.

They cannot get the blokes to become firearms users. If you are a firearms user you're more likely to get shot, and if you shoot somebody, like the Cherry Groce incident, people are calling for your head. The PC in the West Midlands who shot five-year-old John Shorthouse went through terrible psychological problems. You can't win. So the blokes think, "Is it worth it?" It's the whole force. They just don't want the hassle.

UNARMED POLICE

Going in unarmed against the known threat of weapons is the ultimate in "soft" policing. It exposes officers to great risks, but it protects civilians against police mistakes.

---

* N.B. The officer had previously been threatened by Martin and was terrified.

Sergeant in a large northern force, age 38, twelve years service. Now in an industrial suburb.

One time a chap had broken into a shop down on the council estate. We were told he'd smashed a window and that a shot had been fired. We get down there, and as we started to get out of the car, suddenly this chap appears at the door. He's pissed – not totally, but he's got a Kalashnikov rifle and you think, "This should not be happening to me."

My partner was crouching behind the engine block. He was a firearms user but obviously didn't have a gun with him. I'm feeling in my pocket for my keys, which are mixed up with my house keys, to try and start the car. The man says, "Fuck off, copper!" and I say, "I'm trying to . . ."

I get the keys out, start the car up and we seal off the area. Then his wife comes running down, calling. "It's all right! It's all right! He carved it out of wood." He had done. It was a wooden one, painted. But with this thing being pointed at you – I suppose he was 15 feet away – in the half light it looked like a proper gun. Now if we'd been the Armed Response unit and we'd been told beforehand that he'd got a gun, he'd have been fucking shot, wouldn't he? It could have been dreadful and we'd have been labelled "police murderers". No, I don't care for firearms at all.

TRAINING

The three major accidents – the Waldorf and Groce woundings and the baby Storthouse killing – confronted the police establishment with a most unwelcome problem: how to improve firearms training and the selection of Authorized Firearms Officers and at the same time meet the political clamour for more action against armed robbery. All this came at a time when government cutbacks on local government spending were hitting police authorities hard, so the proposed answer has been only partially acted on.

Inspector in a Home Counties force, age 40, twenty years service. Now a Firearms Supervisor.

Every initial course is a psychological test. There's more emphasis on tactical training now. You can call it cowboys and Indians if you like.

We set up a disused building, where a whole load of things happen. It's far worse than we would ever imagine anybody getting into. They come out at the end having lost half a stone. You're facing eighteen targets on the way through. Each one in effect would be a separate incident. We invariably feed into the exercise things we know they'll make a mistake on. When they come out, often the comment is: "I'll never do that again." Hopefully that trains them to think just that second longer if the real thing comes up. We can only try to stop mistakes being made, we're not infallible.

We also use a video for training. You project a film onto a screen and stand the officer in front of it with a loaded firearm and he has to try to react to what is on the screen.

When a shot is fired a microphone picks up the sound and stops the film. There's one part of the film where the camera is going down a drive and you can see a shadow with a gun in its hand. The next minute out pops the gun. Now the lad is well aware that there's somebody there with a gun in his hand and that's the moment he has to make the decision to fire or not. The gunman, when he comes out, is a ten-year-old kid with a green plastic water pistol in his hand. Someone did shoot the kid once, but at the last second he realized and deliberately fired high.

It sounds easy, everybody knows it's a film and nothing's going to happen, but lads come out of that with sweat pouring down their faces. They're really into it within the first few seconds of the film running. It isn't a film to them any more. It has become real life.

Chief Inspector in charge of firearms training in a large northern force, age 38, fourteen years service.

We only train a small number of specialists, only sixteen or twenty, including reserves. I would say that we are probably better trained than the rest of Europe. I've put the question to the chap in charge of the Hamburg police training centre: "What do you do when you have a student who is going to make a first-class police officer, but when you put him on the range he can't handle a gun?" His answer was that they'd still take him. That fellow will be walking around with a firearm all the time. If he ever drew it, he'd be a danger to himself and everyone else. That just wouldn't happen in this country.

Although I know every force does it their own way, in our force every Authorized Firearms Officer requalifies every three months. He probably shoots under supervision once a month. In the United States they qualify once a year. Even if they fail, they don't sack them. Here, if you fail requalification once, that's the end of your role as a firearms officer. Anything else, and if the bloke makes a mistake with a firearm the following day, he isn't going to thank you.

We get a 20 per cent fail rate on ability, but there's a percentage we fail on general attitude. I'm not happy about one in the group we're assessing now – he can't keep his mouth shut.

Met PC, age 36, fifteen years service, seven as an AFO. Now a Level 1 Firearms Instructor with PT 17.

Although we train other people, in this unit we don't train ourselves properly. Our basic job is hostage rescue and things like that. Now for hostage rescue you need to train in all sorts of buildings, you need variation. We've only got one house in which we can train and we use plastic ammunition. By now the blokes know all the floorboards, they know every nail in the place. It's no good, you need constant change. If you don't vary your training you become lethargic, complacent. They get bored with it.

They recently changed the shift system and they've taken away our training week. If you don't train for the job you're going to have problems and accidents. We don't even gear ourselves towards fitness training. Who wants a big fat belly on a firearms officer?

ARMED RAIDS

The official policy of containment calls for the armed suspect to be surrounded and all efforts to persuade him to surrender to be made first. Depending on the situation, and the attitude of the senior officers involved, many hours or even days of waiting and negotiation may be involved before the decision is taken to go in.

Armed raids, on the other hand, have involved AFOs in uniform and/or armed detectives making dawn raids on suspect houses in a manner quite the opposite of the measured calm of the siege. Bursting through the door with sledgehammers and flooding the house with officers who have been up all night high on the adrenalin of danger is a recipe for potential disaster, as happened with Mrs Cherry Groce. Such tactics are based on the standard CID raid without guns and make no real allowance for the need of the firearms officer to have a clear view and to make a slow and careful entry into each room. Some raids send men through front and back entrances, risking dangerous confrontations.

If the senior officer is not firearms-trained, he may not be prepared to defer to the advice of a AFO of much junior rank, even if it is force policy in such situations.

Inspector in a northern force, age 37, nineteen years service, ten as an AFO. Now a Firearms Instructor.

If you go to a house to arrest somebody and he's known to be into firearms, you go in early. If you hit him at 5 a.m. he's going to be in a deep sleep. There's very little passing traffic. No pedestrians. You'll be in and out before anything starts.

You always think, "What if something goes wrong? What if he decides, 'Fuck this. I'm going to shoot my way out?'" Luckily, it's never happened. But you've always got to be prepared for that one occasion when everything goes wrong. You can avoid a lot of the pitfalls if you plan it right. I have grave responsibility for my men and therefore when I do a job I want the best possible intelligence. If I don't get my own way and think that I am putting my team in danger, I will refuse to do the job.

The ideal solution to any firearms situation is that it is resolved without any shots being fired, and that's what we go for every time. Our whole firearms training is based on defence rather than attack. In this force, apart from one incident, I don't think we have actually had a shot fired. We've certainly never had anybody seriously injured by gunfire. We try to catch them unawares. If you go in screaming "Do as you're told or else!" they don't know that the "or else" would never happen unless there is a real threat to us. That's far less frightening than having him get a little overconfident and having a go.

PC in a large northern force, age 27, six years service. Now in a racially mixed inner-city area.

Our Firearms Instructors are all fat old bobbies who just sit around and occasionally go and do a raid somewhere. One time, when I'd only been in about six months, someone said: "The firearms squad are doing a job with the CID raiding the local estate, and they want you to sit with them in the van." So I got in the van and they all came out of the canteen with their pistols hanging off their belt, shotguns over their shoulders and baseball caps on, sunglasses. They've all got big bellies, these blokes.

So we're going up the street with all these blokes in the van, gun cases, bloody gas masks and riot kit, everything, and the Sergeant in front turns round and says, "Right. Who's going in through the back?"

"I am."

"No you're fucking not, you went in the fucking back last week."

"No, I'm going in the back."

"Oh no you're not, I'm going in the back."

So the Sergeant says, "John and Dave, you go in the back."

"Oh fucking hell, Sarge, he went in last week – let me. Have they got a back door?"

"No, I don't think they've got a back door. It backs onto a yard. There's probably a big dog in there."

"A guard dog? Shit, I'm going in with a bit more than a fucking stick."

The van stops, they jump out with the shotguns, and where's

the CID? It's a quarter to seven in the morning, no one about apart from a milk float going round, and there's this gang of blokes with pump-action shotguns standing about in the middle of the road. These blokes didn't have a clue. And they train *us* how to use guns? Jesus Christ! If they arm the whole force 800 will probably kill themselves and they'll have to start a big recruitment drive!

WEEDING OUT THE GUNG-HO MEN

Another part of the shock to the system administered as a result of the Waldorf and other shootings was the need for more careful screening of firearms officers. Officers who may be good shots but show signs of stress or personal instability are weeded out where possible. Recent changes now involve senior officers on Division having to recommend those officers who want to become part of the specialist squads, so the responsibility for screening is fed back to their home station and both the Squad Commander and the instructors must be satisfied as well that each candidate is suitable for firearms training. It has proved hard to devise any systematic means of screening. Psychological tests have been tried and so far rejected in favour of the true source of police wisdom, gut feeling by the instructors.

Met PC, age 36, fourteen years service, eight as an AFO. Now a Firearms Instructor in PT 17.

There are "gung-ho" blokes in the department. Everyone would admit that if they were being honest. But we always work in the same teams and we know within our group who those people are. Obviously there is a time when you need people like that, but no way are they going to be allowed to go steaming off on their own on a banzai charge. We just keep a bit of a tight leash on them, a little word here or there and they'll keep quiet and keep in the background.

You're more likely to get the "gung-ho" types as AFOs than you are in a department like this. A really serious nutter only has to act sane for a fortnight and he's slipped through the net, gets his course, passes. After that no one has a chance to have a really good look at him. But here you're with the team all the time so you can't hide it. I've never known anyone get thrown out. It's a very difficult selection process to get in here.

Met Superintendent, age 44, twenty-six years service. An ex-Firearms Instructor, now in East London.

Television affects society, and that includes police officers and potential police officers. That worries me very much, not quite so much now because the selection process is better, but at one time I was pleading with senior officers to for God's sake look at the people they were sending us. If a person makes a habit of always wearing a bomber jacket and jeans and is always on his toes with a bunch of keys hanging off his side, his profile is straight off the TV. Not only should he not be sent to me for firearms training but he should be looked at seriously in terms of education and attitude.

Yes, we do suffer from that at the sharp end and at one stage a few years ago it became very, very sharp. We actually had instructors spotting it on the range. Every move belied police culture and emulated TV culture. I don't believe it is any less true in the force as a whole today, but the selection process is better.

SELECTION

The current two weeks of basic training in firearms is less than half the time spent training advanced police drivers who practise driving daily. Four days a year of refresher training on a range is hardly enough to prepare for what needs to be automatic behaviour in a crisis.

The only sources of already trained firepower are ex-soldiers who regard police attitudes towards firearms as amateur, or gun enthusiasts, who are regarded with suspicion by most senior officers as trigger-happy. They are discouraged, if not actually banned, from joining the specialist squads.

Inspector in charge of firearms training in a Midlands force, age 39, nineteen years service, 14 as an AFO.

If everything changed tomorrow and we were told that we had

to train every member of the police force in firearms, I would be most unhappy. Some people are frightened of guns. Before we take anyone on a course, we give them a one-day assessment, not to see how good they are, but to see whether we can train them. Recently I took a fellow for a session – he only fired about twelve shots in half an hour. I took him to one side and said, "You're not going to make it." He said, "I know." Because every time a gun went off, you could see three foot of daylight under his feet.

PC in a Home Counties force, age 31, eleven years service, six as an AFO. Now in a large suburban town.

I know I'm considered by some to be slightly odd because I own a gun. I don't mix with a lot of policemen socially, all my friends belong to a gun club. And they are a lovely group of guys. You go shooting and in the line you've got the director of a computer company, a couple of diplomats, a plumber, a truck driver and an out-of-work electronics salesman – all kinds of people, all of them white, all of them good friends. We've got the common bond of the love of shooting and I don't know of any other sport that is such an equalizer.

And they say it's wrong what we want to do. We want to go down and shoot holes in a piece of paper. Because I do that, people think I'm crazy. When I come into work, I'll read a book on guns, I'm interested in the history of them, but the other PCs look at me oddly.

I grew up with guns. They don't hold any illusions for me. They are a tool. You go riding and hunting with them. They do a job.

PC in a large Midlands force, age 28, eight years service. Now in an inner-city area.

I'm very wary of policemen with guns, of the policemen who are into guns in their private life as well. Something's seriously wrong with their psyche. This Inspector has a silver magnum and he took up this silly position where he sat cross-legged, aiming for about three minutes – an endless wait. Then he shoots, and he hasn't even loaded the bloody thing! It's frightening that he's training people.

If they said all policemen should be armed, can you imagine giving guns to bobbies now? Some of them will be walking round having had a few to drink. Jesus, it would frighten me to bloody death. I'd go to Northern Ireland and join the RUC.

PC in a Midlands force, age 28, nine years service, five as an AFO. Now in a city centre.

There are a few coppers who get an erection every time they see a gun – the John Wayne syndrome. There are policemen like that, I don't care what anybody says. They got rid of a lot when they started vetting, but no system is foolproof.

As for all this crap about the Job looking for special weapons which fire a nonlethal drug: someone who's gone absolutely bananas – like the guy in Hungerford – you've got to be able to take him out like *that*! Not wait ten minutes. I think the job at the moment is just pandering to public opinion.

A FAR CRY FROM CLINT EASTWOOD

If armed police officers wound or kill a suspect, they find themselves no longer protected by their job description: they are individually at risk of being charged with a criminal offence.

Even in legally airtight situations, there is usually a public outcry that puts the police on the defensive. The officer who pulled the trigger may face not only a draining investigation but serious and long-term trauma, including sleeplessness, bouts of uncontrollable crying, depression and guilt. This is a far cry from the Clint Eastwood image of the implacable police gunman wreaking vengeance. Both for the police as a whole, and for individual AFOs, the issue of weapons is a legal and emotional minefield.

Met PC, age 34, twelve years service, six as an AFO. Now in East London.

I get shot. I'm out there doing my job. Some bad guys go out and rob a jeweller's, and I get shot. I'm lying in hospital and the local MP comes on saying, "I'm fed up with all these policemen going out and shooting." This is an MP representing the very people that's being robbed. He's talking about "gun warfare on the streets", for Christ's sake. These people are so out of touch. It was the robbers who started it, we didn't. We told them to put down their guns and they went "bang, bang, bang". And then I get a Chief Constable investigating me to see if I've done my job properly. They start talking about stress: "Why did you use your gun?" I've only been shot in the shoulder! It really pisses me off.

I have no feelings about the guy who shot me. He's a bad guy and I'm a good guy. I shall meet him in court. His brief will be asking me questions, he'll be telling me what I did wrong and I've got to stand there like Mr Joe Cool and take it all.

Met PC, age 33, twelve years service, seven as an AFO.

When we go out there and something goes wrong, instead of all hell breaking loose and everyone coming up and saying, "You're in the shit, you've done it wrong," I'd like to think they'd come up and say, "You've done the right thing. I know you have a problem, but we'll try and help you." It pisses me off. Let's face it, tragic mistakes are made every day on the bloody road out there. But because we as a police force must be seen to be right all the time, we put people's necks on the line.

That guy who shot Cherry Groce down at Brixton, I don't think he should have gone to court. His training was inadequate I think, he was put in a situation by a senior officer, he should never have gone there on his own. There should have been at least five or six AFOs there. So he's nervous and he doesn't have any back-up because his senior officers don't give him back-up. But he is dropped like a hot cake when he drops in the shit. He gets charged with attempted murder, yet he's stayed in the Job. I'd stick two fingers at the Job, I would, because the Job did not do the right thing by that guy, they didn't back him up.

POST-SHOOTING TRAUMA

As part of the new awareness of stress in the job the Association of Chief Police Officers (ACPO) asked the Home Office in 1986 to do a study on the emotional impact of shooting people, an area that, as the report itself points out, has been completely neglected in firearms training.

They studied twenty-five officers who had wounded or killed other people. They found that the difference in their temperaments was far outweighed by the difference in the circumstances of each shooting in determining how each officer reacted to the event.

When they had time to wait, especially if they were vulnerable or passive themselves, officers grew tense and anxious, whereas in quick showdowns they felt completely calm and in control. At the moment of maximum danger, most felt clear-headed. Time slowed down. Some had tunnel vision and saw only the target. Others went deaf and heard nothing, not even their partner's warnings. Some were deafened for several hours by the sound of the gunshots. One fell apart completely and started firing into a swinging door.

Most interesting was the reaction of four out of the twenty-five, nearly a fifth, who felt intense fear, quickly turning to fury of a kind none had felt before. They were so angry they needed to do more physical damage than just shooting their targets. According to the report, this reaction has never been exposed before either in Britain or in the USA, where researchers did know about it. Its implications are serious and may explain why, for example, the officers pistol-whipped Stephen Waldorf after he was shot or the SAS men put so many extra bullets into their IRA targets in Gibraltar. Hiding such reactions merely prolongs the false image of the cool, detached act of marksmanship that is prepared for in the training, and echoed in police fiction.

Met PC, age 33, twelve years service, six years as an AFO. Now in PT 17. Shot and killed an armed robber a few years ago.

I didn't personally shout a warning. By the time I arrived, as far as I was concerned they knew what the score was, shots had already been fired, so there was no point. He saw me.

When it all happened I was looking at him and he turned towards me, he saw me and his gun started coming up towards me and it all went very, very slow. I thought to myself, "That bastard is going to make me fire." I pulled the trigger and I thought to myself, "That bastard has made me fire." And then he went down.

Afterwards I was, for a couple of days, shaken.

That first night or two I didn't sleep all that clever, but it didn't take me long to settle down. The way I've chosen to treat it is that someone started to point a gun at me, I shot him and he died, unfortunately he died. If I hadn't shot him, he'd have shot me, I've no doubts about that at all. I understand he has a young son and I feel sorry for him, but I don't get upset about it. It's the job I've been trained to do. As far as I'm concerned, it was a training exercise that went a little bit deeper. Switch off and walk away.

It gave me a strange feeling over the next couple of days coming into work on the Tube and seeing everybody reading it splashed over the front covers of their newspaper and I'm thinking, "If only these buggers knew." That gives a strange feeling, but then as it all dies away you forget about it. The papers will twist anything to get their best story. If anyone was upset it was my Mum. They never got my name or picture, but she knew it was me and she was very upset by the fact that they were picking on her little baby. But myself, no, I gave up with the press a long time ago.

After it all happened we went and spoke to the welfare department. The impression I got was that everyone was expected within two or three days to collapse in a jibbering heap in the corner somewhere and burst into tears. What welfare base their ideas on is from the States. The way I look at it is that people who join PT17 know what they are coming into, they have talked it through with their colleagues and they know that one day it is going to happen. They are going to shoot someone or they are just going to be standing there with bullets flying around.

UNDER THE SKIN

Of the twenty-five men involved in the Home Office study, half had no regrets. One or two were sad for the dead man's family. The rest felt sad or guilty for a long while, though they came to terms with it. One man had attempted to resuscitate his target and remained distressed for a very long time. Two-thirds had a strong emotional reaction of some kind. Among all of them, there was a general sense of being utterly unprepared for the effects of the experience. No psychological preparation was involved in training at all.

Although in American police circles there has been an acceptance and understanding of the effects of post-shooting trauma for some years, in Britain resistance to things psychological has meant that this problem has only just been acknowledged. Sympathetic handling of an officer involved in a shooting by senior officers and by his colleagues can make all the difference to his return to normal duty. His need to be accepted may mask his vulnerability, which can make the jokes and nervous reaction of his colleagues all the more painful.

Met Sergeant, age 35, sixteen years service. Now in East London.

I was the first person in this department to get shot. It had only happened an hour and already the rumours started up, "Oh, he shot himself" and things like that. It is really pathetic. It doesn't help you when you're in hospital, either. You feel very cut off. I felt very shut off by the police force as a whole. I had my own personal problems at the time – I was about to get divorced. I was living with a very nice young lady, she's already lost a husband so she could to without me getting shot. The only people that looked after her were the Flying Squad. We, as a force, talk about welfare, but we just publicize it. It's a load of crap. This job hasn't got a clue what welfare is about. The Flying Squad got hold of my young lady, they put her up in a hotel for the night, they looked after her. No one from this department, no one from the uniform force, just the Flying Squad. I'll be forever grateful.

Some PCs seem able to take shooting and being shot in their stride. At least that was how they described themselves to us.

Met PC, age 33, fourteen years service, eight as an AFO. Now in PT17.

When I got hit I didn't know if it was a ricochet from the wall or whatever. The first couple of seconds I was able to get two shots back at the guy, to react. I got hit in the leg just below the knee but it went right through, it missed the bone. It's number now, I get cramp, it aggravates me at times. They tell me it might heal, it might not, but it doesn't stop me running on it or anything like that. It certainly doesn't stop me doing my job, I don't go out there thinking, "Oh God, I may get shot again." There'd be no point in doing the job if it affected you that way.

NORTHERN IRELAND

The RUC offer a useful comparison to the mainland forces which are for the most part unarmed. The RUC is more like the rest of the world's police in that since 1971 its male officers carry guns at all times. This seems to be a mixed blessing. It produces a more relaxed attitude to guns, which lowers the level of stress from carrying them, but it also raises the degree of stress: terrorists know that arms will be present at every encounter, and so the stakes are potentially lethal every time.

SHOOTING TO KILL

The "shoot to kill" allegation was that in the early 1980s, IRA men were being targeted and killed by a special squad of the RUC as a matter of policy, whether or not they presented a genuine danger to the lives of the policemen who confronted them. The Stalker investigation revealed that mistaken identities or misinformation had led to several such killings in 1982 in circumstances suggesting that revenge by RUC officers was a

*possible motive. His efforts to establish the policy were stopped
by his removal.*

*At the time, the RUC men involved were tried and acquitted
of murder using the same defence as the SAS in Gibraltar: that
they genuinely believed the suspects presented a threat to their
lives. But Stalker's team found that the post-shooting investigation had been so careless as to undermine the verdict of the
trial. Meanwhile the accused PCs had been abandoned by their
senior officers. They had endured six months of solitary confinement. They even had to raise funds from their fellow PCs
to pay for their defence.*

*The trial was held to show the sceptical Catholic community
that justice was being done. Their trust is needed in the fight
against terrorism. Yet the impact of the killings, the trial, the
Stalker inquiry, and then his sacking and suspension all had
the opposite effect. In 1988, six years after the events, Colin
Sampson's report completing Stalker's work has led to disciplinary and legal moves against RUC officers up to Superintendent level. It will take strong action to restore the faith of
the Catholic community in police fairness.*

*The SAS killings in Gibraltar have been handled in a similar
way. Misinformation leads to killings. The post-shooting investigation is careless. Key witnesses and evidence are not collected,
or withheld from the inquest, and the same defence is presented
and accepted by the coroner's court. Far from uniting the
country against the terrorists, it fans the divisions and suspicions
between the supporters of the police and security services and
their critics, most notably among Catholics. The police in their
turn feel unfairly attacked by media liberals yet again, who
seem not to understand there is a war on.*

*Ironically, though no such "shoot to kill" policy was found
as a directive from the top, there was no doubt among many
RUC officers that it would be welcomed.*

**RUC Sergeant, age 36, fourteen years service. Now in a coastal
town.**

It's almost laughable, the way the English over the water get so
excited about Stalker, and the SAS and the "shoot to kill"
business. Who cares if they made a threatening gesture or not?

They're terrorists, pure and simple. Nobody questions that. Their very existence is a threat, while they're running around loose. I say "Thank God they're dead". It saves us the trouble of putting them away. They'd only be plotting more trouble for us while they're inside.

RUC PC, age 25, four years service. Now in a border town.

In the absence of capital punishment, I think the policemen across the water are sitting ducks. How many have been shot? If I were faced with a pump-action shotgun, I'd get in first. They might not want to, but I think a time will come when they will not be able to do their jobs unless they are armed.

RUC Inspector in charge of firearms training, age 33, twelve years service.

We are in a different situation from the rest of the UK forces, although we try to apply all the basic guidelines which are laid down throughout the UK for police firearms. First of all, a man joining the RUC does so with the knowledge that he is going to be required to carry firearms as a matter of course, not just something which you pull out for a special task, unlike an Englishman who, having joined the force, may have a moral objection to carrying guns. Secondly, people who have grown up in Northern Ireland have, to a certain extent, a security awareness within them, which your average person in England won't have.

Before we get him, a very young recruit has already been exposed for fourteen weeks to a certain degree of discipline and has begun to learn self-discipline. We get him for firearms training when he's open to us.

They watch themselves on video. There are lots and lots of mistakes, and people under stress do things they wouldn't do otherwise. I've seen one policeman, deciding what to do, scratching his head with the barrel of his own gun! He wouldn't believe it until he was on the video – and this was an experienced officer. Or we might set up a bedroom with a child coming out from under the bed. What is a policeman going to do? Shoot it? A naked child. Yes, the child might get shot in the situation there. That's good, because the policeman has learnt his lesson.

We try to implant a positive attitude towards firearms. By that I mean getting rid of the fear of weapons, although maintaining a healthy respect for them. We try and teach them to see that weapons are only one of the many tools available to policemen. The only time we jump behind a heavy word is when safety is completely and utterly disregarded. You can be very nice to the lads but it will boil down, at the end of the day, to a boy in court and the Lord Chief Justice saying, "Ten years imprisonment." Every policeman who has so far used his firearm conscientiously in the course of his duty has got off. But the day will come when a policeman is sent down. The more intensely you train people, the more accountable they are.

RUC Superintendent, age 51, thirty-three years service. Now in a large town.

There are officers in the RUC like myself with thirty-odd years service who have never used a firearm, although they have had occasions where they could have used them. It's unbelievable, the infrequency of use.

Once I stopped a car, it was right in the middle of Belfast. I called on the radio for assistance and when they arrived I got out and approached the vehicle. There were two men with loaded revolvers, and 400 lb of explosive sitting on the back seat of the car. I had a gun on me. There's a situation where I could easily have shot both of them.

The fellow who was driving had his gun at his feet and the other had it in his hand. They just froze. By then they were covered from all sides, so there was no question of them using their weapons. They were taken out of the car and disarmed. They said the bomb hadn't been primed because they were on their way to the explosives officer to have it done. So I got into the car with the driver and we went round the block to some waste ground where we parked in safety. It was summertime and the smell brought tears to my eyes.

RUC Chief Inspector, age 40, twenty years service; RUC Sergeant and PC, average age 30, average service twelve years. All now in west Belfast.

Chief Insp: Notwithstanding that we have 10,000 people carrying guns, there's not been one case I can think of in this past ten years where we have accidentally shot a member of the public. You've no sense of excitement here because you are carrying a gun. Across the water, once you've got a gun in your hand the adrenalin increases. There's a nervousness there.

Sgt: We have got so used to carrying guns that they don't mean anything. The average member of the public, if they walk up to a policeman to ask something, they're not conscious of that pistol. It's a policeman doing his job just as if he were in Birmingham or London.

PC: If I didn't need to, I'd never carry a gun. But I know others who won't leave home without one. It depends on the individual. My feeling is that if they are going to get me on the way to work, they aren't going to have any difficulty because I won't get the chance to use my gun.

Chief Insp: I haven't carried a personal firearm for eight or nine years – and I was working in Londonderry until five years ago. Because your best chance in an ambush is to get out of the way of the fire, jump over a wall or, in a car, jam it into low gear and drive off.

SHOOTING TO KILL

The debate about the RUC's "shoot to kill" policy was wrongly believed in the press to be about aiming to wound, as a compromise between going unarmed and killing people. It was not, as no such compromise is possible. The Police "shoot to stop".

RUC PC, age 28, nine years service. Now in West Belfast.

I think the shoot to kill, shoot to stop is an academic distinction because you don't shoot to kill, otherwise you'd make every shot go into his head. The way I look at it, you've got a very high chance of killing someone if you shoot them in the body where all the vital organs are. As regards giving a warning, 95 per cent of blokes would give a warning anyway, automatically, if there's time and you're not being threatened. All right, if he's got his back to you and is about to shoot someone you're not going to think twice, same as if you come round a corner and a bloke's pointing a gun at you.

But all the firearms officers I spoke to feel that shooting to wound still leaves you vulnerable to being shot. Waiting for the gunman to shoot first is suicide.

RUC Superintendent, age 43, twenty-one years service. Now in Belfast.

I used to be an authorized shot. We don't go in for wounding people. We go in to kill them. We are all surprised if there are survivors. If that person has got a gun and is threatening you, and you get your shots off, the person should be dead. You've got to be good enough to take him out. All your training comes down to that.

The control of firearms in London after the Stephen Waldorf case has been tightened up, quite rightly. But a tragic accident can always happen because in the split second when you pull the trigger you are either shooting at the right person or the wrong person.

RUC Sergeant, age 30, ten years service. Now in Belfast.

We know just where they are. They drink in a club not far from here all day, except when they go to draw their dole. It's maddening to know they're just sitting there free as air, and we haven't the evidence to put them away. But we know who each of them are and what they've done. You just say the word, we'd happily go in and do away with your top 150 IRA men, and that's the end of it. Your troubles are over.

FIREARMS AT HOME

Having weapons always with them presents RUC officers with

special problems. Both children and other members of the family
may get hold of the gun and damage themselves with it. In a
highly charged emotional situation, having a ready weapon can
make it just that crucial bit easier to take your own life. The
suicide rate in the RUC is worryingly high.

RUC PC, age 27, seven years service. Now in Londonderry.

I detest the sight of arms personally, though I've no com-
punction about using them. But with a young family, there are
all the problems of loading and unloading it at home. Do you
make sure the blinds are closed? Make sure the neighbours
don't know what you're doing? If you show the youngsters,
they might like to do it sometime. It wouldn't be the first
policeman's little son got shot by one of the other sons. "Bang!
Bang! I got you!" He thinks it's a toy. There's a boy who's a
cripple in Londonderry. He shot himself by accident.

The suicide rate for this force is high. Everybody gets
depressed from time to time. A policeman is no different from
anyone else. Broken marriage or you've made a mistake at
work, nineteen or twenty years old, go out for a drink ... and
the gun's very handy. These are sad things to me. They're
punches against me as a policeman.

RUC Chief Inspector, age 43, twenty years service. Now in Belfast.

Down on the border one time, there was a child which was
almost shot dead by a soldier. He was playing cowboys and
Indians. He came up in the darkness, crawling through under-
growth, and then this gun suddenly appears out of the blue. A
soldier suddenly found a gun pointing at him. Do you shoot or
don't you? He couldn't see the child. Fortunately he did not
shoot and the child's life was saved.

We are living in a rather abnormal situation in Northern
Ireland and at Christmas we appeal to parents not to buy their
children guns of any description. But there's always the person
who won't listen, thinking it will happen to any other child but
not theirs. It's like other aspects of life – you don't face up to
the reality until it hits you.

RUC PC, age 28, nine years service. Now in Londonderry.

It bothers the wife if she sees the gun. She says, "Get the thing out of here," and I try to put it as high as possible. You can see the child getting interested if he sees it. But what do you do? Do you say, "If you ever see that lying there, don't touch it," or do you hide it carefully? The boy is told not to touch it, but I think he will. It's part of the cult of being a boy.

I'm from Londonderry and I assume they're out to get me at all times. I have to keep the gun in the same place in the house, because if I leave it in different places I'll panic. You must know exactly where it is, because in an emergency you don't have time to stand around and stare. In Ireland you have to operate a gun from instinct. You don't think about it. You just react automatically. It's a split-second decision.

Superintendent in a Midlands force, age 43, twenty-six years service. Now in a city centre.

When we first got Panda cars, eighteen or twenty years ago, policemen started rushing off to calls and jumping out of the car to deal with it. Whereas before that you got called to a pub disturbance and as you approached in the full majesty of the law, people called, "Watch out, there's a policeman coming," and they'd have calmed down by the time you got there. Now, you fall out of your Panda and before they can recognize you as a policeman you get hit.

The same goes for arming policemen. If you give policemen arms, they are going to shoot people. If you don't give them guns, they are going to have to think first. That is why policemen have been so good in this country. Because they've had to improvise and think their way out of things. You don't have to be intellectually brilliant to work out you're in danger. Most problems have been solved by good coppering. You don't have to have a degree or anything special about you.

STOPPING THE RATCHET EFFECT

Is there a way out of the ratchet effect, in which as villains carry guns more often, the police must do so as well, until inevitably the British bobby is armed? Some senior policemen and Home Office officials believe there is an alternative. They have been cutting back the number of guns in mainland police hands, as well as slowly improving the training of those that carry them. Better screening, and awareness of post-shooting trauma all help to reduce the John Wayne syndrome.

But what about the public and their right to carry guns? In the wake of the Hungerford massacre, the Home Secretary tried to restrict firearms to those who clearly needed them for work. The formidable gun lobby outshouted supporters of the moves, such as the Police Federation, who had lost two members in the massacre. In the end, Douglas Hurd settled for a ban on semi-automatic self-loading weapons of the kind Michael Ryan had used at Hungerford. Even these measures were criticized by gun enthusiasts as infringing their liberties.

The police and Home Office scientists are pursuing non-lethal alternatives to firearms that would immobilize an armed target. They have also collected thousands of guns and knives in a recent amnesty. But this only skims the surface of the pool of available firearms. When in the cause of security, both freedom of the press and the right to silence have been curtailed, and serious efforts have been made to restrict the supply of knives and other weapons, it seems perverse to preserve access to firearms in the name of respecting civil rights. It certainly makes the policeman's lot more dangerous.

CHAPTER FIFTEEN

Leadership and Promotion

The paradox of the police service is that it is disciplined and hierarchical – senior officers speak for the force and have the power to make or break those who serve under them – and yet the actual work of policing is done by those at the bottom in a series of discrete, individual acts. Of course, officers should work within the law, the Code of Discipline and the training they have been given. Many do. Some do not.

Quite how many do not is open to question: the Police Federation point to five million contacts between police and public every year in London alone that pass off without complaint, as against ten thousand or so that do not. But fairly or unfairly, ever since the inner-city riots, those ten thousand complaints annually have cast a shadow far larger than their percentage of the whole might seem to justify.

The police have taken stock and have decided they must change. In principle, it should be no harder than turning a supertanker in the English Channel: the first move is at the wheel, and then the rest of the ship slowly responds. In a disciplined, hierarchical structure, orders from the top should be obeyed.

To generalize about "the police" does no justice to the many variations within each force, and the old and new guard are now ranged all across the service. Home Office guidelines have backed both the Scarman "soft" policing policies – community policing and all that entails – along with enough "hard" policing to please the old school and worry civil libertarians.

The legal tools are now in place to go either way: The Public Order Act, together with new training and equipment – computers, CS gas, plastic bullets and the like – and the help of the National Reporting Centre (NRC) could produce over-

night as heavy a police presence anywhere in Britain as any "hard" policeman ever dreamt of. On the other hand, the restraints of the Police and Criminal Evidence Act (PACE), the growing numbers of recruits exposed to new and more liberal training courses, the continued emphasis on closer links with the community and more sophisticated leadership in key police posts point in the opposite direction.

Good leadership can resolve this apparent contradiction. The latest generation of senior officers accepts that a judicious mix of both "hard" and "soft" techniques is needed in modern Britain. But riding two horses pulling together is hard enough. It takes confidence and great flexibility to avoid a painful fall when they are pulling in opposite directions.

Embarrassment and failure are serious taboos in police culture. Many senior officers build their careers on the skill with which they avoid both. Faced with the need to take decisions, to lead officers below them through the paradoxical demands of daily police work, too many pass the buck. They opt for being managers instead of leaders. When a crunch comes, as it did during the inner-city riots, some officer-managers suddenly find themselves forced to take decisions in difficult situations for which they have not been trained. That problem has been tackled by selecting certain senior officers for the specialized public-order training that has evolved in recent years (though their workload makes them less than regular participants).

The more pressing need for leadership is less dramatic, and yet more important to the well-being of the service. A recent report on the Met by the management consultants Wolff Olins points to confused management goals as a major source of stress and low morale. Competitive, defensive attitudes allied to vague notions of a sense of purpose simply smother new initiatives. As in so many large institutions, the gap between lower and upper ranks is deeply destructive of both day-to-day organizational activity and of the major efforts now under way to change the way Britain is policed.

LEADERSHIP

Met Inspector, age 34, twelve years service. Now in an inner-city area of London.

You have a Deputy Assistant Commissioner in charge of a Division with two, three or four Commanders; God knows how many Chief Superintendents, Superintendents in abundance, dozens of Chief Inspectors, hundreds of Inspectors packing the place out; but you still have only five guys going out of the door at two o'clock in the afternoon, all thinking: "What the hell's going on?" This enormous upside-down pyramid causes complete disillusion.

STARTING AT THE SHARP END

All British police officers start at the bottom with two years on the beat until they complete their initial training and probation. Efforts at creating an officer class like the Army or administrative grade like the civil service have been fiercely resisted. But memories of beat policing fade as the incentive of promotion and internal politics take over from the daily contact with the public. As in many organizations, senior management are measured by the lower ranks by their awareness – or lack of it – of life "at the sharp end" or "at the coalface". Geoffrey Dear came from the Met to become Chief Constable of West Midlands Police, and won the respect of his new force immediately by changing their uniforms from the standard issue heavy serge to lighter weight, better tailored and more comfortable material.

Although it is now common practise among well-run businesses for senior managers to spend as much time as possible on the shop floor or its equivalent, talking to the workforce informally, it seems to be something of a rarity in the police. Those senior officers who do it are noticed and remarked on. The rest are deemed to have turned their back on their own past as a bobby, and are focused exclusively on the ladder stretching above them. The only nostalgia they express for their previous experience emerges when they resist new ideas and changes because "in my day, we always did it that way".

Superintendent in a northern force, age 40, nineteen years service. Now in an industrial suburb.

My normal day is eight to four, so when I'm on duty cover for the evening, I go home and have my tea at four, then come back at seven and stay out until it's quiet. Mid-week that's usually eleven or so, at the weekends it can be one o'clock or later. You have to play it by ear. After all, you're on again at eight the next morning, and if you don't pace yourself you're shattered and no good to anyone. I find the evening hours the best time of all to go out with the lads and make proper contact, find out what's happening. No telephone, you can go out in cars, do a parade, really see what's going on. It's much the most productive time.

For all the talk about resistance to new ideas at the top, I have to say there's trouble the other way as well. I don't call it Policing by Objectives because that's got a bad name now, I call it Problem Policing – find your problem and solve it. But PBO is a brilliant concept, nowt wrong with it at all. The problem is in the implementation. There's no amount of selling a good proposal to Sergeants and Inspectors and PCs who just want to thwart it. You get the "we've always done it our way for the past twenty years" excuse – to which I say, "All right, maybe you've always done it badly for twenty years."

Relations between the police and the public are vulnerable to all sorts of verbal and non-verbal signals being misunderstood on the basis of class, politics, ethnic and religious background or just mood and timing. Police training is now designed to help recruits, accommodate those differences in the way they deal with people. But relations within the police service suffer from a full set of distinctions including all the above, plus many more linked to the police culture: specialist squads look down on bobbies on the beat, CID look down on uniform. They both look down on Traffic cops. All the police look down on their civilian colleagues with particular contempt for Special Constables. Distinctions abound within the anonymous and often disagreeable conditions of police stations. Senior officers have their own dining room with waitress service, while lower ranks eat in a grim cafeteria. Although it varies according to attitudes of senior officers, in the police service, rank is there to be pulled.

Scottish PC, age 43, eighteen years service. Now in a city centre area.

There is an assumption within the service that if you carry a rank, you must be more intelligent than the rank below you.

A Chief Superintendent phoned the station one Friday: "Is Inspector So-and-so there?" "No, I'm sorry, he's not." "Who's speaking?" "Constable Smith. Can I answer your question?" "No, I'll phone back on Monday when the Inspector is there." He phoned back on Monday, by which time the constable had been promoted. "Who's there?" "Sergeant Smith." "Ah, I've a query for you ..." On Friday he was a cop. On Monday he could be talked to.

Assistant Chief Constable of a West Country force, age 44, twenty years service.

Rank is much more important in the police than in the military. I can tell you that.

Met Commander, age 43, twenty-five years service. Now in East London.

It's terribly hard to make people see this, but we are trying to show other senior and middle rank officers that to improve the way the police talk to the public, we must first improve the way the police talk to each other. If we treat the lower ranks like shit, they'll treat the public that way.

Of course we train them to do it properly at training school, but in their first two years probationers are faced with a set of values in the canteen and in the station generally they must at least pretend to go along with in order to be accepted. We don't communicate well at the top, either. Kenneth Newman used to say, "I've consulted all my Chief Superintendents and they didn't say a word against it." It never seemed to occur to him that they might just be keeping their heads down.

SETTING STANDARDS

In large forces like the Met, most PCs relate only to their Sergeant, Inspector and Chief Inspector. They may only see their Chief Superintendent at their annual interview. If their immediate supervisors are corrupt, amoral, or just indifferent, it can be very demoralizing. Many young PCs said that their Inspectors never even said "hello" to them.

Met Sergeant, age 33, eleven years service. Formerly in the RUC, now in South London.

I am shocked by some of the really appalling people I've had to work with. I imagined the police to be in a higher social group than they are, perhaps because I went to public school and had quite high principles about what policemen actually stood for.

I joined from the RUC. I was very disappointed. I thought local people would come up and shake your hand and say, "How are you?" It wasn't like that. I was just on my own. I was also alarmed at the behaviour of some officers. There are still people who have a positive attitude to the job and go about it in the right sort of way – they are the people you try to model yourself on. But we do tend to pick up on negative rather than positive things, which means that somethimes the bad boy is more of a thrill than, say, the way of a model officer. That is partly because policemen suffer from a moral dilemma a heck of a lot. You are always dealing with grey areas where it is damned hard to separate right and wrong. On paper a thing may appear to be right but in practical terms it may not work.

Someone is always going to be stronger than you, even if you have more service in. They'll carry more influence. It's particularly frustrating if you feel that the chap in charge is a bad guy. I was in an East London station and just couldn't take it because of the Inspector there. It is totally wrong that unfair pressure is put on people because of one man's influence. You feel that you have to conform to something you don't want to conform to, that there's a lack of respect for your point of view. It comes back to, "I have my standards, you have yours, don't try to interfere with mine."

BEARERS OF BAD NEWS

Middle-ranking officers often face the uncomfortable task of transmitting criticisms and demands from higher up or outside the force which lower ranks believe to be irrelevant or ill-informed. The respect of the men lies in the degree to which their officers stand up for them. This is one reason why many officers of Greater Manchester like their Chief Constable, whatever outsiders may think of him.

Detective Constable in a large urban force, age 30, six years service. Now with the Drugs Squad.

The other day our DCI came down. He said to me, "How many drug arrests do you think each uniformed policeman has had this year?" And I said, "I'd be very surprised if it was one each." And he said, "That's quite right, and I think it's disgusting." So I said to him, "Hang on a minute, sir. There's eight policemen to man a police station per shift. That only leaves one man to go out on the streets and do all the calls for eight hours."

If you're the one out on the street, you don't get arrests for drugs every day, either. Because there's old ladies need their pension books returning and there's shoplifters that need arresting, there's double yellow lines that people don't want cars parked on; a thousand and one other jobs." So the DCI said, "Well, that's management's fault, not ours." I said, "Why can't you tell them that? Tell them that's one of the reasons why we have a drug problem and supposedly the police aren't doing anything about it. We haven't got the manpower." And he said to me, "You have to be a little bit tactful." And I thought, "What you're saying is, you're not prepared to put your neck on the line and say we can't cope."

LEADERSHIP QUALITY

Elaborate management structures are no substitute for good leadership. The indecisiveness of senior officers in the British police has too often left a moral vacuum on the streets, no more so than during the inner-city riots when, in time-honoured amateur fashion, senior officers were expected to cope with any task that came their way. It throws the onus back on the individual PC, who often has only his colleagues and their shared frustration and common sense for guidance.

Met Inspector, age 39, sixteen years service. Formerly with the SPG.

Demonstrations are the easiest place to pick out those with no leadership quality. You can always tell a senior officer at a demonstration – they walk around and do pirouettes, listening to the radio and saying, "No, no – it's OK, it's all right." They just can't handle it.

You know if you are going to have a good demonstration, because you know beforehand who's going to be in charge. If it's a wanker, you think: "Oh Christ, we've got a problem here." Invariably at some point the bloke will not make a decision, or will make the wrong one.

Met Chief Superintendent, age 48, twenty-six years service. Now in the East End of London.

The service has rarely trained senior officers for particular tasks: we're expected to be masters of everything – good admin men, good trainers, good CID officers, good at community relations and dealing with the public. We're also expected to be exceptional individuals who can perform to a high standard in an extremely hostile, volatile situation. But after the 1985 riots in Brixton and Broadwater Farm, they chose particular men in certain districts – I am one of them – who had the experience and decisiveness to deal with this kind of problem. There are some twenty of us in the Met now, and we have been trained to deploy shield formations and horses to best effect and to make split-second decisions on the ground.

DISCIPLINE

Discipline goes to the heart of the debate between "hard" and "soft" policing. It is also an indicator of the emerging generation gap between the old school of senior officers, groomed in a more military tradition, and the bright new recruits who ask questions, seek consensus and expect to be trained for management. But discipline – and self-discipline – has implications far beyond rolled up sleeves inside the station and caps on in cars.

RUC Woman Police Sergeant, age 32, twelve years service. Now in a border town; and PC, age 30, nine years service.

PC: You have to remember supervisors are there along with everything else to make sure their men do not carry out criminal acts, that not only are they good officers, they're not screwing shops into the bargain. They're there to spot the bad apples, and catch them before the rest turn bad.

Sgt: I'll tell you about good supervision. After one of the bombings when nine of our lads were killed, I took some of the PCs home from Belfast, and stopped at my father's pub along the way. One fella, it must have been stress, ended up putting his head through the window at the back of the van – which was borrowed from another station. I was in charge, but I never expected that. I stopped the van and calmed him down. It was a mix of drink and stress – the lad couldn't cope. He was very immature, very, very young.

But as I'm driving back I go through all the panic, "What the hell will happen when they see this damage?" They knew we'd been boozing because I rang and told them we'd be late, but the van wasn't ours and had to be returned to its station in the morning.

So we get back and I go to tell the Super, and this is where personalities come in. He was a Superintendent and a gentleman. He said, "You got back all right." I said, "Yes, but I've got to tell you I put the window out of the van on the motorway." "Anyone injured?" "No. One of the lads has a bump and will have a sore head in the morning, but it won't be the bump, it'll be the effect of the drink." So he said, "There's been nine men killed here, and I couldn't care less if a window's been put out. No one's been injured and you're back safe. That's the end of it as far as I'm concerned."

Met WPC, age 24, four years service. Now in a racially mixed area of London.

Our Superintendent Ops is good. He's keen. He's still got his feet on the ground. He hasn't lost it – he's still a PC. He will come out walking with you, not to catch you out but because he is interested, because he wants to walk round and meet people. I am sure if something happened he would leg after them and arrest them. I'd probably have to do the paperwork, but he would get involved.

At the other extreme, we've got this Chief Inspector who makes a mountain out of a molehill with paperwork. The guy hasn't got a clue. For example, here's a chap put his six shirts in to be washed at home and somehow the kid's red football socks got into the washing machine. You can guess: the shirts came out pink. So he gave them to his kids' nursery school – the kids wore them while they were painting. They were no good to the job. So he puts in a "728" explaining what had happened and pays for the shirts. Then he gets a memo down from the Chief Inspector saying: "Why was your wife washing more than three shirts at once? Bring the shirts into the station for inspection!" How ridiculous! So out of touch.

We have a new Chief Inspector. She's marvellous. Everything about the way she approaches things is nice. She called a Permanent Beat Officers' meeting and everyone thought it was going to be: "You do this and that." We all got up there thinking, "Here we go." We had tea and biscuits. "What's your problem? Right, I'll see what I can do about that." Within a week we all had a memo back with our moans on it and what she had done about them. She had sorted everything out within a week, yet her predecessor worried about six shirts.

What is seen as petty discipline in the Met is regarded as good leadership in the provinces.

Met Chief Inspector, age 45, twenty-six years service. Formerly with a northern force, now in an inner-city area of West London.

I suppose I'm a mixture of provincial and Met attitudes to

discipline. When I became a Chief Inspector in the Met I arrived at the station and said, "Don't get up lads" – motioning them with my hands to stay seated. They just said, "Who the fuck does he think he is that we'd stand up for him anyway?"

Superintendent in a Home Counties force, age 43, twenty-one years service. Formerly with the Met, now in a county town.

I remember trying to get people to behave properly in the Met. It was hopeless. One time I went up to some PCs dealing with a four-car pile-up and told them to put on their flat caps because they were policemen, after all. One said, "But sir, if you put your cap on you find it much harder to make eye contact with the public." I'm afraid I didn't have an answer to that one.

Chief Inspector in a Midlands force, age 38, fourteen years service, and a graduate.

At the pettiest level, as Inspector when I took over a shift, I expected my men to stand up when I walked into a room. When they saw me in the street they would always salute, they would always be smartly dressed, they would always refer to me as "Sir". It's the petty bullshit things which give the sense of pride, of doing the job properly. If there's an institutional acceptance of seniority and of the superiority of senior officers, you're making people receptive to commands. The army has done it for years. But chaps in the Met still say, "We'd never stand up for an Inspector. We'd like to see someone telling *us* to do that." You even get this from Training Sergeants who are themselves going to be Inspectors very shortly. The discipline we accept as the norm out here they see as oppressive and unnecessary.

The Met still don't want to upset their PCs – so they don't have proper control of them. Take drinking on duty. On my unit no one drank on duty, strictly no one. That would be impossible in the Met. Maybe it's because people in London move so often they don't have time to establish themselves. I'm young in service, but when I go into a Met station I'm always shocked by how young their Station Sergeants and Inspectors are.

Ex-Met Chief Inspector, age 43, sixteen years service. Resigned.

Ask any PC or Sergeant or Inspector what the biggest problem is in the Met and they'll all reply "the guv'nors". It's always "the guv'nors", the lack of leadership. Watching them swan off, get pissed and being driven home, listening to their lectures about drinking and driving.

As an Inspector I made it clear that I would tolerate no trouble in the charge room, no assaulting prisoners, no drinking on duty, and so on, knowing full well that as soon as my men got into their own circles drinking was inevitable. It was to establish in their minds that I was going to be more than a supervisor. I was going to be there constantly to put them on the right road as policemen. And I didn't just send them out. If some poor bastard is going to have to stand outside an embassy for eight hours, doing nothing, it's my job to motivate him – so I made it a policy to visit them at least twice a day. Actually that's what matters to people when they have got nothing else to do, when they've got boring jobs.

There are too many graduates being recruited. They're tempted by the idea of becoming an Inspector in three or four years. But the important one is the Police Constable – he's the one who makes the arrests. Half the battle lay in trying to persuade people that being a Police Constable was a good career in itself. You can run demonstrations without the bosses. It's the infantry that you need.

Scottish Inspector, age 41, nineteen years service. Now in an administrative job.

Discipline is going out the window. When I left my shift there were two good Sergeants and fourteen good cops. I didn't allow the men to drink on duty and I expected eight hours' hard work. On many occasions I was an out-and-out bastard, but I was working alongside the men. My successor came out from a city division. He didn't mind a wee pint, he'd log off for hours, nobody knew where he was. If a cop shouts for supervisory help then we know he's having difficulty. Two minutes and we've got to be there.

I watched a good shift deteriorate. There's an inherent fear at the end of the day that if the wheel comes off, the cop's going to be standing on his own, no superior officer beside him saying, "I told him to do it," or "I agree with what he did." Cops have to make decisions in the heat of the moment. Their bosses then sit for weeks over the log books and all the rest of it, and they'll come out with, "You made the wrong decision." Which is fine, but put the bosses in a cop's position. They never are.

WASTAGE

Wastage is a serious and continuing problem, especially for the Met. In 1987, 1621 officers left the Met altogether of whom 19 per cent transferred to provincial forces in search of a better quality of life for their families. A total of 483 officers retired from the Met, emphasizing the move towards a younger force. At the current rate of 2000 new recruits per year against 1600 departures, within seven years half the officers in the Met will have less than seven years' experience. All the new ones will be on the street dealing with the public. As the cycle continues, the loss of experienced men close to the PCs on the street leaves a leadership gap of serious proportions.

PC in a Midlands force, age 38, fourteen years service.

The main difference between now and the old days is that you used to have a tremendous range of age and experience. You could be working alongside men with 23, 24 or 29 years service. Out of twenty in a section you might find two or three with less than five years' service, so the example was always there. I've been with older bobbies who have gone into situations that have made the hair on my neck stand up, and they have come out of it unscathed. Their expertise is fantastic. The younger bobbies talk about it for weeks afterwards.

There is not that experience on the streets now. A Tutor Constable has only got a couple more years of service than the pupils he is taking on. In this job, experience is everything. You find now that younger PCs will go into situations and exacerbate them. Instead of the old bobby going in slowly and getting it right, they will go in brusquely and if someone puts a foot wrong it's the cavalry syndrome – everyone piles in. You don't get the young ones stopping and saying, "Hang on, what's all this about?" It's just straight in and start feeling collars.

Superintendent in a large northern force, age 41, twenty years service, and a graduate. Now in an inner-city area.

The difficulty is that you are looking for thirty-year privates as well as for generals, and for all sorts of specialists in between – dog handlers, detectives, traffic men. But we're certainly getting far fewer wankers through now than we did in the late '70s. Then, if you had two of everything, eyes, ears, arms and legs – and could read and write, you were in. We were practically dragging people off the streets. Many of those people are now in middle management, and it shows. Sergeants, Inspectors who have no ambition, no sensitivity to situations – they are not all bad, but they are shown up by the quality of the new entrants who are on the whole much brighter, better educated, more independent, quicker thinking and more receptive. We have to adopt a much more *laissez faire* style of management to adapt to them.

They are also much more career-minded, and the backlash will come when they ask themselves at five or six years in: why am I not a Sergeant? The answer is that there are no places. We've got four hundred PCs who have qualified as Sergeants, and we're only promoting fifty a year. It will take four years just to clear that lot.

The other problem of improving middle management is that the way we promote people only tests their performance in the job they have been doing, not in the one they are applying for. And the present system just tests their skill at interview boards, not at doing the job under pressure. So Greater Manchester and West Yorkshire have a new scheme for assessing candidates for promotion over twelve months, in which they are given specific bursts as Acting Sergeant or Acting Inspector and assessed on their performance every three months. If they get through that stage, they go to Phase Two, a weekend session with paper tests and other kinds of assessment, and if they get through that, then they go for their traditional board. Now that will take eighteen months but should produce a much better candidate.

The problem is what will happen when there still aren't enough places up the ladder?

PROMOTION

In any organization, there is backbiting and cynicism about promotion. It is especially vivid in the police for several reasons: first, the system of promotion has been based on written examinations for Sergeant and Inspector that reflect traditional reliance on learning by rote rather than judgement, common sense and leadership qualities.

Secondly, there are too few vacancies for Sergeant, Inspector and above to absorb the many officers who have studied and passed the examinations. In the Met recently, 280 officers satisfactorily "passed" the Sergeant's exam, but only 32 were deemed to have passed because there were only 12 vacancies. In provincial forces, there is still less movement in the ranks. Frustrated officers can pass both the Sergeant's and Inspector's examination and still wait years for promotion. In other words, there are too many potential Chiefs among the Indians, who take a jaundiced view of those above them.

Thirdly, the higher the rank, the fewer the vacancies, and so the greater the scope for personal recommendation. Both on promotion boards and in the assignment of key jobs, the opinion of a senior officer can be decisive. Hence the view that being a Freemason makes a difference. Ambitious officers avoid taking risks which may incur the disapproval of those likely to sit in judgement on them in the future. As they see it, the more independence they display in lower ranks the less likely they are to reach higher rank. Yet more than ever independent thinking is badly needed at all ranks in the service.

Fourthly, like all policemen senior officers draw on stereotypes. In their appointments and promotions they have a tendency to replicate themselves. So the notion of a "good candidate" is narrowly defined. As in most huge organizations, risk-taking, imagination, questioning, are not always seen as virtues in this process. Promotion to the most senior ranks requires a three-day extended interview with a variety of civil service tests and a display of policing skills. It is a most impress-

ive and exhaustive test, but the choice is made by the most established Chief Constables and civil servants, so there is still a conservative bent to the final selection.

Chief Inspector in a Home Counties force, age 35, twelve years service and a graduate.

Encouragement for innovative and creative thinking, tolerance of error – there isn't any of that at the moment. The Situation Book covers every conceivable thing that's going to happen. Woe betide you if you make a mistake; the organization remembers it for a long time. I'm thinking about little notes scribbled on your personal file, saying "this officer lacks judgement", which will come back to haunt you five years later when you're on a promotion board. A lot of officers really do worry about what's going secretly on their file.

As Chief Inspector at a local police station, I tell all my probationers when they arrive: "There's hardly anything you can do that we can't put right, provided you tell us about it. If you're going to learn the business of policing, you are going to make mistakes." There was a young girl who goes out and gets herself a commendation for disarming a guy with a knife on a Saturday night. A few days later she makes a mistake. She's investigating a road traffic accident and she phones up the local hospital asking for a particular nurse who she thinks is involved in this accident. It turns out that it's not the right nurse, somebody's misidentified her. Anyway, she doesn't speak to this nurse, she speaks to somebody else and says, "I'm WPC So-and-so, I want to speak to Mrs Bloggs about an accident she's been involved in."

Two days later we get a very irate nurse at the police station saying, "Your WPC is telling my work colleagues I've been involved in an accident and I wasn't even there. I was in Liverpool on that day." This was quite a troublesome woman, she took some sorting out. I sent an Inspector off to see her eventually and said, "Look, we've got nothing to hide. Tell this lady that this was a young, inexperienced WPC. She knows she's caused you some aggravation." First of all I had to argue this with the Inspector. He said, "Make that sort of admission and we could be sued." I said, "That's a risk I'm prepared to take. Most people accept an honest mistake. She's demanding a written apology. Try and get her to accept a verbal apology, some explanation as to how it came about."

The following day I was sitting in my office and this WPC came in. She was almost crying. She said, "I'm awfully sorry about this business ..." I said, "What on earth are you talking about?' It's all right. It's dealt with. No problem any more. I'm glad you were honest and told us what you'd done." She wasn't comforted by what I told her. I said, "What's really bothering you?" She said, "They told me this would go on my file." I said, "Unless I choose to write it on your file, there's no way of it getting on your file. Forget about it." All of a sudden she's happier. Terribly grateful. It had been drummed into her – she'd only been in the force nine months – that a mistake like that is a black mark on your record. How can you expect people to put forward new ideas, try things out, in that sort of environment?

The two most common complaints are too much petty discipline and not enough leadership at Sergeant/Inspector level. Both of those are true. I would also add a much more serious one: not enough leadership at the very top of the force. That's much harder to put your finger on. But unless you know what your Chief Constable thinks about you, your career, about the way policemen should behave, there's a big hole in your occupational direction.

Scottish PC, age 25, three years service, and a graduate. Now in a support group.

You get these fat-headed types who want to be big fish in small ponds. Our Chief Inspector in a previous posting was one of those. We were in the van, one Christmas Eve. It was quiet and bloody cold. We were parked up in the town centre, just waiting in case we were needed. He walks by in civvies with his woman on his arm, and he doesn't even say "Hello", let alone, "Happy Christmas". Just pretended we weren't there.

You never know for sure why someone gets promoted. In Scotland they do you the favour as a PC of making you up to Sergeant for the last few years just so you get the bigger pension. That's grand for the laddie, but not the best for commanding respect from the rest of us.

Scottish Inspector, age 44, twenty-two years service. Now in a city centre.

In Scotland what normally happens is that a promotion is made and a telex comes in. In years gone by, you would look down the list and out of twenty you'd say, "I don't know how one or two of them got there." The rest deserved it. Latterly, you're lucky if you find two out of twenty promotions you agree with.

Met PC, age 38, sixteen years service. Now in the TSG.

The system is simple: you take the exam and if you pass it you get promoted. Whether you're any good or not doesn't have anything to do with it. I can't think of another job where you're promoted even though you're totally useless at what you're doing. If you're a completely useless Sergeant, you can, by studying, be promoted to Inspector. After that it goes on selection. But then the people doing the selection have got there through that system. It's amazing how many blokes are promoted to get them out of an area.

DEMOTION

Astonishingly for a disciplined service with so many rules and regulations, there is no provision for the demotion – or dismissal – of an officer unsuited to police work or to his current rank. This is a serious handicap to good leadership.

Both ACPO and the Home Office have acknowledged the problem, and a working party has been drafting terms for a new contract of employment that does not offer tenure. The Police Federation is alarmed at the prospect, however, fearing that the provision for dismissal will be abused by petty middle managers.

Met Sergeant, age 32, twelve years service. Now in Central London.

This is one of the few jobs that's a lifetime employment. You can't get yourself thrown out without committing a crime. It's the kind of job where you can go out, book the radio out, do fuck all, come in eight hours later and carry on for thirty years and stay in the job – and some people do.

You can write horrendous reports about people and nothing happens. They move sideways, or up, in fact. If we give someone a really horrendous report and say they will never be a copper – they'll go through life pushing doors marked "pull" – the guv'nors won't accept it. Fortunately there aren't very many.

Chief Inspector in a Home Counties force, age 39, eighteen years service and a graduate. Now in a small city.

What I would like to see changed is this thing about not being able to be sacked. It's absolutely ludicrous that someone can scrape through their probation because people close ranks. And once they've done two years you can't get rid of them. You would just not tolerate it in private industry, would you? If you were on a profit or loss situation, anyone who is dead wood would go. We carry an awful lot of dead wood and there is nothing we can do about it.

Another thing I would like to see is demotion. If someone can't do their job they should be told, "Look, thanks very much. You were great as an Inspector, but you are not really a Chief Inspector." I know they have a year's probation, but it's just a token thing really. If someone is wrong for the situation, what they do is promote them to an office job. How can that be in a so-called professional body, which is meant to have the trust and respect of everyone in the country? You've got someone who can't run a police station, so what do they do? Instead of kicking him out or demoting him they say: "Thank you very much. Be a Chief Inspector at headquarters and do a desk job." The bloke is laughing, isn't he?

GRADUATES

The police were originally drawn solely from the working class. Since the Second World War, efforts have been made to enlist graduates to cope with increasingly complex management tasks. Everyone does the same probationary training in the first two years, but career graduates on the Special Entry Scheme are given additional training and accelerated promotion. After five years' service they will be promoted to Inspector.

Although numbers vary in different forces, some 5 per cent of the total number of police officers are graduates.

Sergeant in a Midlands force, age 46, twenty-six years service. Now in an inner-city area.

A police officer is not a particularly super-intelligent person. The average police officer is reasonably intelligent. Most of them have common sense, which makes them able to do the job. It's unfair to generalize, but certain people come into the police force believing, rightly or wrongly, that they are more intelligent than the average policeman. They can pass the exams, which they do pretty quickly. They usually end up doing a short time, perhaps two or three years, on operational duties, and they will spend perhaps four or five years doing forward planning or some sort of desk job at headquarters. During that time they will be promoted to Inspector or Chief Inspector. They think that because their rank is higher than a uniform or CID PC or Sergeant, that they are more intelligent and therefore better policemen. They will not consult people with more experience than them. They only talk to their peers or superior officers. These people are geared to promotion. A lot of them come in not to be policemen but to be senior officers, and the system seems to be assisting them extremely well.

The Graduate Entry Scheme and the Special Course was designed for rapid promotion for people with leadership ability. You don't actually have to be brilliant at driving police cars or nuts-and-bolts jobs. You have to be able to get other people to do that. If you can't do that and you also lack credibility because you've never done it, you're lost.

PC in a northern force, age 36, fifteen years service. Now in a market town.

We had a graduate PC. He was going to go to Bramshill eventually. He was bright, but had no common sense. We didn't like him and decided to get rid of him. We knew he didn't like dead bodies because he would never answer the radio when there was a sudden death – so we played the "mortuary trick" on him. A PC put on a nasty mask and rolled up his trousers, and lay under a sheet on the mortuary slab. I told the PC that he had to go down to the mortuary and identify a body. It was 2 o'clock in the morning . He said that he had this and that to do but I said, "No. You've got to do this." I said all he needed to do was put a name on a label and attach it to the big toe of one of the body's feet. Then he had to look at the face so he could identify the body to the mortician the next day. So he went off and I joined him. When we got there he was shaking so much that I said I'd write the label and sent him to look at the face.

The PC on the slab had begun to laugh and you could see his tummy going up and down under the sheet. The graduate saw this and said "Look, he's breathing!" I said, "Oh no, He's just expelling air – all bodies do that!" He believed me and went over to the body. At that moment the PC sat up and screamed. The graduate wet himself on the spot – literally! He was off for the next six weeks from nervous tension. We told the guv'nor what we had done and he laughed and said he wished he had been the "body". Anyway the graduate was moved to a different station. We told him to keep quiet because it wouldn't look good on his record if they knew he couldn't cope with dead bodies. He learnt later though, because there was a sudden death where he was, and he was the only person on duty.

Met WPC, age 30, eight years service in a racially mixed area of London.

I want to be a Home Beat Officer. Not for ever, obviously, but you should be an efficient relief officer before you start training for anything else. There is nothing worse than someone who does their two years' probation and then goes straight off into Traffic Division or does their promotion exams. A couple of years later you get a Sergeant who knows absolutely nothing. Worse still, you might get a graduate who knows even less, is promoted after three years and is then telling someone with fifteen years' service what to do.

After probation, chosen graduates go to Bramshill Police Staff College to do the year-long Special Course. Bramshill was founded in the 1960s as part of the gradual amalgamation of several hundred forces into forty-three larger units, with common training standards set by the Home Office.

In the setting of a Jacobean country house in Hampshire, Bramshill is meant to provide professional training for high flyers. Its commanders are often distinguished officers near the end of their career, but its academic staff are less respected. The qualifying examinations for the Senior Command Course – future Assistant Chief Constables and above – are formidably difficult. But Bramshill only teaches a small percentage of officers. Its range of courses is impressive but the value of its instruction is seen as doubtful. Most police officers are rude about Bramshill, but it is a source of brownie points to go there!

To the lower ranks, as one PC brutally put it, Bramshill is where "mock gentlemen teach other would-be mock gentlemen to hold a knife and fork properly".

Met Deputy Assistant Commissioner, age 43, twenty-four years service, and a graduate.

A lot of things were said after the Tottenham riots about how things might have been, that Bramshill had failed to prepare people for them. In fairness, though, right through the '60s and '70s we never thought that public order would become a major focus for policing.

Bramshill is often slagged off, but personally I believe in command training. Fairly lengthy blocks of broad training for middle–senior ranks did a lot for me. In all about two years of my life have been spent in the staff college and the Special Course did a lot to develop my intellectual skills. It was a cumulative effect of exposure to a whole variety of individuals and an opportunity to think.

The college has never attracted good-quality, credible instructors on the police side, it has tended to be a haven for people approaching the end of their career. People are trying to change that, but I have my doubts whether they will succeed. The best innovation has been the development of short carousel courses of a few weeks' length.

In the military, selection for staff college and for the general staff is an enormous career enhancement. The same has never been true in the police and I think we need to look at why that is. Why is it that the majority of our officers do not see that people who are better educated than them, who have a broader experience of life, will make better police officers?

We will never have an officer entry system into the service because this pavement thing is too strong. But proving yourself on the street before going on to university or whatever in service training is a contradiction when we have more graduates in the service than ever before.

Former Chief Inspector in a Home Counties force, age 34, ten years service, and a graduate. Now resigned.

I got married between university and joining the force. My wife didn't really know what she was in for, but she was very supportive. She was one of the very few people that were. It was quite clear that after a good degree you don't go into the police! I remember the comment of one of my professors: he said scornfully, "The army need good people too. Why don't you join the army and get shot at?"

As I was a graduate entry, I went to Bramshill on the Special Course. Bramshill is a very second-rate institution. In particular, the academic staff. Who would want to go to Bramshill if they could get a decent job at a university? I was incredibly disappointed with them. I spent a year there. We had the opportunity to learn a tremendous amount but learned next to nothing. It was not an educational experience, it was more a measure of your diplomacy – political skills, the learning of – to keep on the right side of the staff.

They've done a lot more to make up decent professional packages at Bramshill now. They do much shorter courses on particular subjects – there's one on dealing with the press, another on public-order management – that they can get specific experts on. They are generally rated pretty high. The Human Awareness thing they're doing is terrific.

An awful lot of people join the force for ideological reasons. I don't think I've ever met a collection of people who are more versatile – not robust, but they bounce back after a knock. For a long while, that's it. Then there comes a point when you've had enough. When you criticize senior managers, it's mostly because they should never have got there, because they're not equipped to do the job. I think it surprised Bramshill that a lot of extremely well-motivated and capable people in the middle ranks were stifled and frustrated, immeasurably, by the culture of the job they'd been given, or not given, by their senior officers. That is certainly why I left, sad as I was to do it. The future was just too far away.

Although the Special Entry graduates have their way through the ranks protected, they have to prove themselves on the ground. Policing takes skills not taught in academic circles, and leadership is an elusive quality. For graduates in their middle twenties, often from sheltered homes, the jobs of Sergeant and Inspector are serious challenges. They must test their authority in a sceptical if not downright hostile climate. Many fall into the trap of going native, trying too hard to be one of the boys, preferring to be liked rather than respected, though how this respect is won is problematic.

Met Sergeant, age 26, four years service, and a graduate. Now in a racially mixed area of West London.

It's the macho image of the police force, that if there is a fight you must be seen to pull your weight. I waded into one: there was a PC who was on the floor and some people were kicking him. I had to get my stick out and hit a lot of people. Then I said, "Everyone out!" Outside, I picked two of the older PCs, the most responsible ones, and we went back in and calmed things down. Then, in true Bramshill terms, I wrote it down in my diary and thought what a success that had been. I had calmed things down.

A few months later someone came up to me and said, "Do you remember the night when everyone started to think that you were all right?" I said, "No." He explained that it was the night of the fight, after which all the PCs in the charge room were saying: "Did you see Sarge wading in there with his truncheon? He's a boy, isn't he!" There I was, thinking that I'd achieved something by minimizing the trouble and that, but no. The whole culture is so strong that you've got to physically prove yourself and that's how you get respect. I can't see how that can be got rid of, and that's dangerous.

Graduates often have a hard time on the street. They are plunged into a world the polar opposite of university, where bravery and common sense are not often required.

PC in a Midlands force, age 28, six years service, and a graduate.

I was Acting Sergeant and I got a call from one of the cars to consult at the scene of an incident. There was this very irate Asian taxi driver – an Irishman had just run into his house without paying. We knew the Irishman. He could be quite unpleasant, particularly when he was drunk, and we'd had great difficulty arresting him after domestic disputes. I tried to talk to him through the door and then looked through the window. That was when he picked up the breadknife and started brandishing it.

I decided we ought to arrest him. My plan was to get a dog handler there and put the dog in through the back. But the next message I got was that the Inspector had heard my request for a dog and didn't want me to do anything till she got there. She was a Bramshill rapid promotion Inspector. At the time I was only about twenty-three and she was about twenty-five. She thought my plan was a bit gratuitously violent and decided to try and talk him out. It made me despair – you couldn't communicate with this Irishman even when he was sober.

The next thing the bloke is hanging out the window saying he won't talk to anyone without his mother there. So we go and get the woman – she was used to this sort of fuss. She goes into the house and we wait outside and then there's the Irishman at the window upstairs with the breadknife at his mother's throat, saying, "Bejasus, if anyone comes in I'll do for her!"

Nine of us were there till about five in the morning. Eventually, the Inspector decided there was nothing to do but put the dog in and storm the house! But by this time the Irishman had sobered up and didn't want the bother. As they dragged him off to the car, his mother said, "How am I going to get home?" His parting shot was, "Call a taxi. I'll pay the fare!"

It was ridiculous. The Inspector was struggling to make a good impression, but had we gone in immediately with the dog I suspect the Irishman would have quietened down. Everyone on duty that night was seething for weeks afterwards because they all felt they had been made a spectacle in public. The whole street though it was the best entertainment they'd had in years. I don't think this Inspector was terribly liked by the Super-intendent. He was an old-fashioned soul. I don't think he was very impressed by a twenty-five-year-old woman being an Inspector of a Sub-Division. In the "proper" world you'd have to be at least forty and fourteen stone to be conceivably an Inspector. He was called at some point in the night and he said, "She can sort it out for her bloody self!"

Met Inspector, age 44, twenty years service. Now in the TSG.

As a PC I could do what I wanted. If I didn't want to walk that way I could walk the other way. As a Sergeant I liked the freedom I was given by my Inspectors to say to my men: "This is what we're going to do . . ." As an Inspector I like the freedom I've got to direct the Sergeants within their bounds, and they can use their initiative. That's one of the joys of the job – you're given a task and you do it your way.

Look at the responsibility that an Inspector has got – it's quite awesome really. Not just for twenty or thirty men working for him, but for a whole area of London. Anything that happens is down to him. That's one of the things I like about the job. But we have some very intelligent blokes in the job, lots of them with degrees, and some of them are absolutely atrocious as policemen – no common sense at all. Yet they're the ones who are going on to senior management. There's one graduate we tried to get rid of when he was a PC. He's now an Inspector and he's been passed on to his second or third station because everyone knows he's a liability. But no one is ever going to say, "Right, you're not doing what you're paid for – on your bike!"

THE GENERATION GAP

Security and pension rights are the major reasons for most recruits joining up. As unemployment falls, however, more bright youngsters will turn away from choosing a career in the police. Although the pay is good, shift work and the sordid nature of much ordinary policing compare badly with other white-collar jobs, often at higher rates of pay. To ambitious young men and women, the queue for promotion and the conservative attitude to new initiatives are both discouraging. It has led many idealistic young people to leave the service already – a pointless loss of talent and of the investment in their training.

Met Woman Police Inspector, age 32, ten years service, and a graduate. Formerly in a racially mixed area of London.

We look at other organizations and see such forward thinking, such innovative ideas, that it's frustrating to come into an organization that behaves like this. You don't get the support. You don't get the help. You don't get the feedback. You feel that you've achieved not terribly much because you don't get that openness. You can try and be an individual. You can try and shine and want to come to notice, because everybody does. They want to be thanked for something they've done. But you find that you just hit a brick wall every time. You end up stepping back into a cocoon. You put a wall around yourself, and you say: "Well, I'm not getting anywhere and I tried so hard. How much more do I have to keep bashing away at this until someone actually says "Thank you" and recognizes what I'm doing and that I'm better than the others?" And you start questioning yourself: "Am I really better than the others? What am I achieving? I need somebody to tell me. I have to ask my supervisor and say: "Can I have some feedback on my performance, sir?"

I've mentioned twice along the way to senior officers that I'm restless and frustrated and that my capabilities are not being extended to the full. I've now been told by someone in the careers section not to say that again to anyone. It is "disruptive" and they look on it badly. It would be misinterpreted and it would not go well for me in the future. I was never, ever to confide it to anyone again.

So I keep my frustrations to myself. I can't talk to anyone about them. I see that as the force's inability to recognize what the people in it are worth. They try to attract all these intelligent, educated people who are supposed to have all this ability, but they fail to give them a job to do which will stimulate them and keep them in the force.

Met Commander, age 43, twenty-four years service. Now in East London.

In recent years we have been able to recruit a better-educated, brighter class of officer. We find that now on Division, where they're more articulate, more assertive and perhaps make more demands of middle management. Some people say this is all out of lack of respect, but I don't agree. They don't want any longer blindly to follow a set of dictates, they expect an explanation of what they're being asked to do.

If participating in the management of the Met is to mean anything it has got to absorb the energy, vitality and enthusiasm of the young officers who are the most important part of the whole machine. One of the elements of the whole neighbourhood policing project is that it is a very broad consultative process. One or two PCs, a Sergeant or even an Inspector from each relief come together every fortnight or month with the Chief Superintendent and the Planning Committee to talk through what they ought to be doing. So that is truly participatory management in determining future strategy.

BUREAUCRACY

What passes for management procedures in the police are often parodies of bureaucracy that would make a Soviet official feel at home. For all the emphasis on discretion on the streets to do the major job, there is little room to operate within the station. Take equipment: radios are often faulty and in short supply. Cameras for observation can only be obtained with difficulty – often borrowed for a day or two from central stores at headquarters, involving lengthy drives and paperwork. One PC told us that to buy £19- mats to lie on for observations, he had to submit two invoices at £9.50 each because his Superintendent could not authorize more than £10 at a time.

Inspector in a Midlands force, age 33, ten years service and a graduate.

There's such a resistance to change, it's unbelievable. I had a serious new idea about seeing the number of complaints we get not as a public relations problem but as a resource, a performance indicator. I did a report, which the Deputy Chief thought was great. It pointed the way to a complete change of mission. No more meaningless statistics to placate the public. Instead a new role using different analysis and statistics about complaints – much less about the admin of how they were dealt with, and much more about their substance, what we're doing wrong.

But the chap in charge of Complaints was an old school type and wasn't interested. I never heard any more about it until I read it in the Chief Constable's annual report: there it was, "a complete change of mission", "huge amount of valuable information" and this, that and the other. So I asked my friends in the department, "What's changed?" They said, "Nothing." So I went to see the old Chief Superintendent at Complaints and Discipline and said I thought I recognized parts of my report in the annual report. He said, "Yes, you did a great job there. We're going to take little bits of your report and that will keep us going for the next five or ten years!"

I was asked to show it to the incoming Chief Superintendent at C & D. I told him I'd give him a copy (a) if he gave it back, and (b) if he told me what he thought of it. I didn't need it back but I wanted his opinion.

Weeks later I went to him and asked if he'd read it. He said he had, a bit sheepishly. I asked him what he thought. "I didn't disagree with it." "Does that mean you agree with it?" I asked. "I didn't disagree with much of it." I said he was avoiding saying that he actually agreed with it, and that if he did, would he act on it? It had already been through the channels, and been approved by those above him, so he had no need to worry on that score. He was free to do what he liked. I was very nice about it, and gave him all sorts of outs because there was nothing to be gained by pinning him to the wall. But I realized it was hard for him. To give him his due, he was honest with me. "Listen," he said. "You've got to believe me that I mean well. But my brain hurts." And I thought, you poor sod. He could not cope. There was nothing in his education, in the way he'd come up through the police institution that equipped him to think about issues like that, let alone take decisions. At least he was honest about it.

HER MAJESTY'S INSPECTORATE OF CONSTABULARY

PCs and Sergeants feel especially vulnerable to criticism and complaint. Senior officers are more protected. They rarely criticize one another. The higher they go, the more insulated they become inside the service – although they are the spokesmen who must field the press and politicians. In the interviews, Chief Constables in Northern Ireland, Scotland and England were all accused by their colleagues of surrounding themselves with "yes-men", officers who tell them what they want to hear.

For the force as a whole, policing standards are supposed to be measured by Her Majesty's Inspectorate of Constabulary. Britain is divided into large areas, each "covered" by an ex-Chief Constable and a minuscule staff. It is a pale shadow of what serious monitoring entails.

In schools, there is one inspector to every four hundred teachers and a visit to inspect a school involves close involvement over several weeks. To monitor the police, there is one inspector to every 20,000 officers. Force visits last for only a few days and have all the surprise and informality of a visit from the Queen.

It is only human to put one's best foot forward, but with so little real accountability for Chief Constables, the ineffectiveness of the HMI is serious. In a police culture that hides mistakes and sees apologies and regrets as signs of weakness, constructive critics play an important role.

Chief Inspector in a northern force, age 36, thirteen years service.

Their visits are a complete whitewash. Everyone knows where the Inspectors are going, they know roughly what questions they're going to be asked and the Inspectors are very careful with police officers they speak to. The Chief Constable normally goes round with them, so any time an Inspector asks a PC a question the Chief is listening to the answer. Woe betide the PC that embarrasses his Chief! It's bad enough embarrassing your Sergeant – that could end your career. One of the firmest rules is that you never tell a guy two ranks above you something the guy one rank above you doesn't know, because he could be caught out. It's crazy – that it should be such a bad thing to be caught out. It's so stifling in terms of proper communication between top and bottom.

An inspection by the Chief Constable is as well prepared as an inspection by Her Majesty's Inspector of Constabulary. The officers who are going to see him are carefully selected; the others are sent out of the police station and told not to come back. The current force objectives are pinned up on the wall – the fact that no one's paid any attention to them for the past two years is not important. The officers going to be interviewed are asked to memorize their answers so they can spit them straight out. It's a parody. The leaders have lost touch. The "nine to fiver" – as far as the guy walking the high street in the middle of the night is concerned, he has lost touch instantly. He's "one of them".

The best simple formula for new police leadership is that a Chief Constable should spend at least half his day talking to his Constables. It would be so refreshing. At the moment they spend only a quarter of the time in the force area. Where he is for the other three-quarters, only his secretary knows.

CHIEF CONSTABLES

The independence of Chief Constables has become a thorny issue over the past two decades, as they fought to "keep politics out of policing" during a time when the police became deeply involved in political controversy themselves. Formally, Chief

Constables are chosen by the local Police Authority, itself a political body, subject to Home Office approval. That tri-partite relationship is supposed to be the basis of their accountability. The local authority pays half the cost of policing, and controls the budget. They are supposed to be involved in broad policy decisions, and in many instances they are. But their role in rendering the Chief Constable accountable is vague and often ineffective. There is little they can do if the Chief Constable refuses to cooperate, and has Home Office backing.

Kenneth Oxford, Chief Constable of Merseyside, had a running battle with his authority over his handling of the Toxteth riots and the use of CS gas which in most ways he won. He has refused to allow his force to participate in the local authority inquiry into Toxteth since the riots, although relations with the police are a central issue. James Anderton, Chief Constable of Greater Manchester, ignored his police authority when ordering sub-machine guns from the Home Office. The Police Authority tried to sack him for refusing to curtail his remarks on AIDS and homosexuals. The Home Office vetoed this in exchange for Anderton's promise not to speak in public on moral issues. Characteristically, such attempts at informal resolution happen behind closed doors rather than at full authority meetings where press and public are present.

The important Home Office role behind the scenes becomes public through its circulars, guidelines and directives, as well as new equipment and legislation which have far more impact on policing than police authority decisions.

The Metropolitan police are accountable directly to the Home Secretary. At Scotland Yard, the Receiver, a Home Office official, monitors the spending of a billion pounds of public money not otherwise publicly accounted for. Recent pressure from the National Accounting Office on "value for money" in policing is having great impact on operational activity.

Judges also affect police policy through their decisions, comments, and judgements in the Court of Appeal. And the Police and Criminal Evidence Act called for local consultative bodies to provide more communication between the police and the community, though they have no legal powers.

Some Chief Constables feel so boxed in by the various limits to their authority, they are unable to try new strategies.

Roger Birch, Chief Constable of Sussex, provoked a legal tempest when he pressed for random breath tests using existing law.

On the other hand, Labour attempts in Parliament to make Chief Constables legally more accountable to local police authorities have failed.

Chief Constable's Staff Officer, Chief Inspector, in a northern force, age 36, nine years service, and a graduate.

The key lesson I've learnt is that a Chief Constable's job is not as easy as I thought it was. I assumed that the Chief Constable was all powerful, that he had the power, if he didn't like it, to change something. He hasn't. The Chief Constable has to negotiate. If I took over a force as Chief Constable and didn't like my Assistant Chief Constables, what could I do about it? Nothing, absolutely nothing. I'd go in and I'd get a management team I've no control over. I couldn't sack them, because they're not incompetent, not corrupt. They just think differently to me. There's nothing I can do. They can stymie every suggestion of mine, they can delay it, they can corrupt all my initiatives and I can't do anything about it.

Given that sort of inadequacy of power what you do is just move people out. So the bad chaps with the CID, you move them somewhere completely different to disorient them and put in good people, at every level you can. But that presupposes you're going to bring in good cronies, not bad ones.

Looking at the new Chief Constables and the new Commissioner of the Met, they're a far better breed. The senior officers coming through are of a very different ilk to the old style. Nearly all of them will be graduates, all have had an exposure to a far more liberal world and they've looked outside an ivory tower. Another myth of the service is that because the police mix with the worst parts of the community they must be aware of what society is really like. They're not. The police are in an ivory tower, they touch everything with rubber gloves, they observe but they're never part of it. And they only observe a small part of society. There's a vast area of society they're not even aware of. A lot of policemen are not aware of respectable middle-class society because they only get called in when there's been a burglary. They hector the lowest levels, they fawn to the highest levels – they're seen as servants. That's not talking to all levels of society, that's not being able to change gear and deal with everyone as an equal.

Chief Constable of a Home Counties force, age 56, forty years service.

More and more of my colleagues are trying to learn the art of communicating with their fingertips. One way is through what we call a "service" in which the Deputy Chief Constable and the three Assistant Chief Constables arrange with the staff association to go around to different stations over a year and sit down over a pie and a pint with anyone who wants to let their hair down.

The feeling I get from them is that there are a hell of a lot of people between me and the front line who are too conscious of the bits of brass on their shoulders. It's not unique to the police service. It applies to any quasi-military organization – and while we pretend not to be, let's face it, we are. That's how people see us. Despite all the talk of management techniques and changes, it's the middle rankers who find it most difficult to adjust to them, to be accountable to their men. They like it when it's done to and for them by those above them, but they don't feel any obligation to do the same down the line.

I make it my job to see the people who are leaving after twenty-five years and I ask them to tell me honestly if there's anything that's gone on in our stations that shouldn't have, about which they're ashamed. Occasionally I get an honest answer: "I've seen people being coarse, indifferent, rude." I ask if they've told the copper involved that it wasn't good enough. They always say "It's not my job." I say, "He'll take far more notice of you sitting in a car beside him if you say 'Why do you have to be so bloody rude? That could have been my aunt or my sister or brother,' than if the Chief Constable writes some bloody memo."

I believe you can change people's attitudes, but I don't just rely on persuasion. When we had a real balls-up of a public order incident, I called everyone in for a *post mortem*, showed them the television films of some of our officers going berserk –

that's what really happened, I'm afraid. I said that if there was a repeat of that incident, *they*'d be the ones who got bloody arrested.

STYLE WARS

To the lower ranks, current senior management styles leave much to be desired: decisions seem arbitrary, almost random, as changes descend from the top. Explanations are often couched in incomprehensible jargon, using initials known as "alphabet soup". In some areas the vogue for consultation and communication is often seen as a bad joke, coming from people presiding over an organization in which real consultation is actively discouraged. The reversal of such attitudes will be a major challenge to the next generation of senior managers.

Met PC, age 25, five years service. Now in Central London.

One of our great guv'nors came down to hear what we had to say, supposedly, as part of this great new consultation exercise. But you could see his eyes glaze over as we said a few things. We could see he wasn't listening. He was just fed up. He didn't answer our points. He just turned to his minder and said, "I think they've had their say." And left. He just left.

Met Chief Superintendent, age 46, twenty-seven years service. Now in charge of a specialist squad.

In this force, and I should think elsewhere, discipline at the normal, day-to-day level was replaced a little over ten years ago by a form of "creeping management" that had been picked up by bright young policemen studying commercial management techniques. It started as a good idea that should have been overlaid by the old discipline structure, but it replaced it.

Sergeants and Inspectors stopped being Sergeants and Inspectors. The structured behaviour patterns handed down from generation to generation slowly melted away. It stopped the interplay between senior PCs and newly joined PCs in the way the job should be done, like the fact that you don't turn up for inspection five minutes late. What we have now is a pseudo-management system that never really suited the police – "ask" instead of "tell", "supervise" instead of "inspect", "be there and talk to the chaps and see how things are going" instead of "stand in a line with your kit". Briefings sitting down round a table with cigarettes. Discipline has deteriorated to the point where people think nothing of being rude to each other and so they think nothing of being rude to the public out there either.

Without a structure and a set of role models, and the knowledge that you will be corrected every time you veer off course, it is very difficult to set performance levels, for a person at the bottom end to know when he is doing well and when he isn't. All these "up" boys, these bright boys, have got a bit too clever. I suspect, in my heart, that the world out there would like to see a more placid, easily understood set of behaviour patterns in the police that they know will always be there. You can trust that. But it's gone, I'm afraid. Again, you're talking to an old copper yearning for the old days.

Met Inspector, age 39, nineteen years service. Now in the TSG.

When I was a relief Inspector a PC got shot at. Two of us were shots, so we got a gun out each – this was before the present guidelines. We got down there and I had the area sealed off. We had assistance coming in, but the two of us who were armed went into the block of flats to search it. Somebody's got to stay at the bottom of the stairs and somebody's got to go to the top, so I thought I'd go to the top because I wouldn't send anyone out on something I wouldn't do myself. Leading from the front and all that bullshit.

So I'm searching the building and the radio is blaring for information and I'm giving that while I'm searching. I'm going down each floor and thinking, "For Christ's sake, you've been involved in things like this before and you've sat there and thought: 'Why the fuck doesn't the guv'nor do something?' For fuck's sake, you're in charge now, do something! What do I do? I don't know. Fucking do it! You're the guv'nor now, for Christ's sake – you do it."

There are good leaders in the police at all levels. Good Constables who set an example to their colleagues need as much courage as a senior officer in a riot. In recent years, firm policing, with close links to the men on the ground, has raised morale. A new generation of technocratically minded senior officers have in some cases been able to bring modern management techniques into play, with a willingness to be critical about force objectives and strategies.

Both Geoffrey Dear in the West Midlands and Sir Peter Imbert in the Met are two such men, and they have a number of shrewd and resourceful officers below them. But they are in the minority. They are pushing the great boulder of police culture and cynicism up the hill. It will be back down on top of them unless the dynamism and energy of ambitious and imaginative officers in the lower ranks is released to keep the momentum of change going. At the moment, they are being thwarted. It is a tragic loss of opportunity.

CHAPTER SIXTEEN

Epilogue

What have we done to these men and women in asking so much of them? As the social services cuts close mental hospitals, as social workers' case loads render them unable to support their clients, who will end up dealing with the lost sheep? The police: as young as 19, with only a few months' training behind them.

Yet as one PC with two years experience put it, "The public doesn't see you as a young person just starting out. The day you go on the street in your uniform you're a policeman, and they expect you to know everything."

The toll of all the pressure is being paid not just by the families of police officers, but by the police officers themselves. Days off through sickness have risen dramatically in large urban forces – making deep inroads into already reduced manning levels. As employment and wages rise, more policemen and women will leave the force for more comfortable jobs. Good graduates can get far more money without enduring the harassment of the early years in the police, and so will choose other professions, leaving a lower quality of graduate available to become instant leaders.

Some of the most poignant of the interviews are with embittered graduates, who left or are considering leaving because of what they feel the job has done to them. Like Dr Jekyll observing Mr Hyde, they have discovered evil feelings in themselves that they never dreamt existed, nor wish to encourage.

Met Sergeant and Woman Police Sergeant average age 31, average service eleven years, and both graduates. Now in a racially mixed area of London.

WPS: I think I probably am a little bit schizo, because I am different at work to what I am at home. The real me is the me at home. Me at work is a part of me at home, but I adapt it to what's expected of me.

SGT: When we were younger and we used to work together, ten years ago, we used to talk about what we liked about the force and what we didn't like. One of the things we used to talk about a lot was people's attitudes and the way they talk to the public. We are often on duty together. One time I suddenly heard her talking to somebody in exactly the way she told me she couldn't bear being spoken to, and I thought "I wonder if she realizes?" But I never told her until tonight.

WPS: Everybody develops a shell. You have to in this job, you can't survive without one.

SGT: One of the reasons I'm thinking of leaving is that I see changes in me that I don't like. In many ways I like me better as a twenty-two-year-old out of university than a twenty-two-year-old in the police. It's not that I'm more aggressive, but I'm harder, coarser, less patient. I realize I have a capacity for evil, it's there.

WPS: It sounds awful, but I know exactly what you mean.

SGT: I could do things which are evil, which I couldn't dream of doing before. I could do them now. I can see how Hitler got there. If you take it to the extreme from beating people up – I couldn't do it but I can see how it happens, how violence is applied, how people are fitted up, where all the nasty, sordid signs of facism start from. I can see them all now.

I feel now that there is always an element of being dragged into a horror story. It's there and you've got to know it's there and try to fight against it. I could never have been evil before, I feel now that I could – if I was pushed in certain circumstances.

WPS: Oh yes, I can *see* them. But I'd hate to feel I could do that.

SGT: If you take it to the extreme and develop what we're talking about to the nth degree, I can see how you could develop that total heartlessness, viciousness, uncaring. The sight of people screaming in pain I have seen so many times now it doesn't actually stop me in my tracks. The sight of people screaming that they're innocent, they've been fitted up, doesn't worry me any more, because I know they haven't been. The sight of blood and people that have been viciously assaulted by somebody else, for no damned good reason except that they were pissed out of their brains – I've seen it all before and it's just a numbness you feel. Dead bodies. Knocking on a door and saying, "Sorry, little Johnny just got run over," I don't feel pain any more for that. The first time you do it, you're ripping yourself to pieces, but now I don't particularly care. I can't stop people getting killed in road accidents, it's going to happen, but for the person whose door you're knocking on – it's going to destroy their life.

WPS: I think you can cope with it, because I know you better than that. You do care, that's half your hang-up. You care too much. I think what you're saying is that you understand how those things can come about.

SGT: I have actually said to myself since I've been in a black area, "I understand what Hitler was doing."

WPS: You mean getting rid of people, racially?

SGT: Yes. You see all this, well, I'd call it slag or whatever – they're not slag, they're human beings, but to me in my professional capacity they are slag. You think: "What the hell are we doing? Why don't we get rid of them?" But I don't know whether I would be capable of doing it. You sit back and think, "Christ! What did I say?" It's not the inclination. It's not that I want to do it. I feel now that I could do it. Before I couldn't.

WPS: I joined as a naïve student, same as you did, twenty-one years old. I thought the world was a wonderful place and we were going to go out and change it and make it even better, but after ten years now ... maybe it's part of the growing up process, I don't know.

You go into a world which suddenly begins to take you over. You're trying to understand all these ridiculous things taking place day after day – the violence, what people can do to other people, the arguments. Ridiculous fights that take place where you knocked a pint of beer over or you didn't like the colour of his shirt or something. All pissed out of their brains. The viciousness and callousness, the lying and the cheating that goes on amongst humanity. Somewhere you've got to wind your way through this and try to find a path which is called the law. The damage that is done to you as you try to find this path – I don't think we've even thought about looking at it in those terms. They talk about the effects Vietnam had on the Americans. In this country we've got police officers who are facing, over a longer period of time, much the same sort of frightening experience. What is that doing to people? After ten years of going through all this shit, how the hell is a PC meant to think?

What I'm trying to say is that we've got to decide what sort of society we want. The police have got to contribute to steering society to that end. But in this country, we're not even discussing with each other what we really want. We're being asked at the moment to do all sorts of different things which are all pulling against each other.

Met Inspector, age 35, fourteen years service, and a graduate.

We're trying to do a job that other people do not understand. Joe Public out there has no idea of what we do. People have got the impression that the police spend their time nicking criminals, all the rest of it. That's only a very small part of our job. There are an awful lot of individuals in the police service who came into it with very good values and ideals, and they're trying to struggle with all the pressures in society.

There's no real debate in society in Britain at this moment as to what sort of police service we want. I think that is extremely sad and frustrating for a lot of people in the force, because every day of the week we see the problems that are going to be accentuated in ten or fifteen years' time. And a lot of us don't like what we see.

Quite frequently, I go home at night feeling totally depressed about what we've got in the inner cities. The slag that we've got and the crappy places. The children being brought up in that slag, who haven't got a hope in hell. Then you've got the senior people who have the say as to how we apply our resources and manpower, who haven't a clue of what's happening around the corner. The young bobby on that beat, nineteen or twenty years of age, who probably comes from some poxy little village in Scotland, is stuck in the middle. He doesn't quite know what he's doing because nobody really understands the situation. The lack of debate in this country is quite terrifying.

What's at stake is normal law and order. I think it goes deep. One of the problems in London that is perhaps accentuated more than anything is the divide between the rich and the poor. It's quite frightening. None of us would want to describe ourselves as yuppies, but we're all people at the thick end of the wedge. We've all got a good job, good money and a good stake in society. If we are even the slightest bit materialistic, we all want society to be conducted roughly as it is, because we're all right.

The unfortunate thing, which is a product of the political climate – particularly Mrs Thatcher – is that there's a thin end. And the thing about policemen is that they may be living at the thick end, but they're working at the thin end. The thin end is full of three million people. There are about two million people who will never have a job. I go to one and say; "Don't steal." He says, "Why?" I say, "Because property is one of the rights we have." But if you're at the thin end, you're *never* going to have a say in the society that demands those rights. Why the hell should you not steal? I've got no answer to that.

Their honesty makes sobering reading for those of us who can choose other ways of living and working, but still rely on these men and women to keep the peace. Unless we pay more regard to their predicament, we will find only younger people willing to put up with it – the older ones will simply give up, and choose a more civilized life. If that happens, all the risks attendant on younger coppers will become more prevalent. They will not have the wisdom to handle domestics, to comfort rape victims, to spot lies when doing interrogations, to show patience in the face of provocation. The collective wisdom of police culture that enables it to cope with a wide variety of stressful situations will simply evaporate through the loss of experienced men on the ground.

This is not a fantastical scenario. There are an estimated 2,000 men in the Met applying to transfer to provincial forces – more than 300 are allowed to do so every year. Half the entire force of 27,000 men is lost every ten years through resignation or transfer. It is a serious concern both for the Commissioner of the Met and for the Chief Constables of southern forces who face a drift to the North. As our lives become more complicated, we need a more experienced, more flexible, more sophisticated force – not a younger one. Only by paying them the attention which they deserve, and incorporating them into our midst to a far greater extent than we do now, will we rebuild the confidence that police officers need, to feel that they are indeed public servants – rather than an army of occupation in their own country.

Former PC from a West Country force, aged 28, six years service, and a graduate. Now resigned.

There was never a shortage of volunteers to go on big operations like the miners' strike. It really was very exciting. You'd come back at the end of the week feeling tired but definitely elated, definitely buzzing – given that most of your life is fairly mundane when you come home, I mean dog bites and traffic offences. There is that excitement factor.

That was why I jacked the job in really, because it was so hard to go back to ordinary policing afterwards. It breaks innocences. You can't rebuild that when it's gone.

I used to walk up the main street here on a Saturday night, when the pubs were kicking out, and you'd get a certain amount of verbal flak from the lads falling out of the pub. It never bothered me before. I laughed it off as an excess of drink. Fair game, really. But when I got back from the strike I found that my attitude had changed fundamentally and, well, I didn't trust them any longer. I had never really thought that groups of lads coming out of a pub were a threat, I thought they were revelling and if people got a bit carried away some nights, that was just an excess of the moment.

But after the strike, I saw them as a threat to public order, a breakdown of civilized standards. I definitely found them threatening. And I did not know how to confront them except forcibly. Whereas once I had made a point of walking through them, I suppose to demonstrate that I didn't see them as a threat, now I found myself stepping back into doorways and avoiding coming into conflict with them. I had a feeling that if one of them said something too loose to me, I would probably try to make an issue of it. It's quite easy to arrest someone really: you've got Section 5 of the Public Order Act, "Abusive behaviour likely to cause a breach of the peace," and you just colour it up.

I had a feeling that I could end up making these arrests I used to despise other policemen for making. I could not be bothered to talk it out with people any longer. I was happy to stand back and say, "Because I say so, you cunt. And I don't have to explain why to you. Get funny about it and you could find yourself arrested." Before that paramilitary operation, that would have been an absolutely last resort. I came back much harder. I'd seen large crowds of people doing really quite hostile and unpleasant things, no matter how good the cause.

Policing in general colours the way you see people as you get old in the job. As the years pass, very few policemen like to live in the area they work, and I don't think that's just the fear of bumping into someone you've just had to deal with. It's more subtle than that. If you live away, you can imagine there are two sorts of people in the world, like good people where I live and the rubbish where I work.

I've never viewed it like that, I've made a point of living in the area where I worked and was quite happy to do so. But I could not maintain that, I wasn't happy with all those people around me. As I say, it's like a lost innocence. Once you've lost it there isn't a path back. You can't recreate that trust any more. I came to the conclusion that for a lot of young working-class men, the hostility they express in a joking manner to the policeman as he walks past on Saturday night is probably very genuine, and quite probably well founded. Because, after all, part of the role of the police force is to maintain order among groups where it may be a bit tenuous.

I think you make a better policeman if you have not got too wild an imagination, actually. It's a job that's much better done by people who don't think too long and hard about what's going on, because your imagination only gives you nightmares. For anyone who's at all sensitive, it is becoming a harder job to do.

I've watched a number of my peers leave the force for the

same reasons. One was a young graduate who took over my beat. He just had his two years in and was very glad to be leaving. He used to pop in for tea and moral support. One day he told me he'd been to a domestic and found himself so pissed off and disillusioned by the job that he couldn't bring himself to talk to either one of them. He just shouted at them to shut up or else he would arrest them. Then he thought about it over night and realized what had happened to him. He was only twenty-two.

Met Inspector, age 36, fourteen years service in an inner-city area of London.

Disillusionment is rife. They are disillusioned with what being a police officer is all about, lack of manpower, PACE, increased legislation. They've totally disrupted the force, put everyone under so much stress and strain that it's really not the police force any more. We're just an ambulance service.

At six o'clock, two o'clock, ten o'clock, a dozen disillusioned guys turn up to do a job in conditions they think are appalling. They think "Fuck this!" and count the hours till they get out. Now the lads are almost sticking two fingers up at overtime. That's what's wrong. They are at the sharp end, dealing all the time with situations of conflict where nobody likes them. Nobody says, "Come on in, have a cup of tea." They are going to pubs where people want to bloody thump them. The whole time they feel they are up against a society that doesn't have any respect. We all want respect in our own field. They want us when they want us and deride us when they don't.

PC in a large Midlands urban force, age 32, eight years service.

Every pressure group in the country is against the police – because all political parties have put us forward as a sort of ball to play with. The only losers are us really. OK, we've had a pay increase, but we've had to take riots, public disorder, people beating policemen up very, very often now.

I think that the government cannot allow the morale of police to go down because of the pay level. Because we are "the boys in blue" we are "Maggie's boys". But we are not all Tory voters. It's unbelievable, that. People just don't believe that some policemen vote Labour. I think there's a lot of bobbies that would go on strike now if the pay went down, I know I would be quite prepared to. Yet when I joined eight years ago, my vision of the police was good and clean. I wouldn't have dreamt of striking. But now I look at society and how it deals with me, and I think: "Why should I bother about them? They don't give a shit about me."

I've been in situations in the street when I've been in a violent confrontation in plainclothes and in uniform, where the public's slugging me. Somebody's just mugged somebody and you are arresting them, and you're the one who's getting slagged off by the public! There was two young lads had a fight in the street and one had a terrible eye splattered with blood. Me and my partner separated them. That's when the public noticed us and it was, "Look what the police have done to them." Then you've got a volatile crowd. You say, "Hang on a second, they are the ones who – blah, blah, blah," and it's: "You fucking bastards!" Now why the hell should I bother about them people? They don't give a shit about us.

Superintendent in a northern force, age 44, twenty-five years service, and a graduate.

I have a dual thing about the future. I have to temper my rosy retrospective view about my early years by remembering the people who said when I joined twenty-five years ago that they were glad they weren't joining then because things had so much changed for the worse. The 1968 Theft Act had just come in and the men were moaning about "How are they going to live with it?" And then the breathalyzer, it was the same thing: "How are we going to manage?" but we did. Now we're in the first flush of PACE, and all the new technology which so daunts us, but I don't suppose they pose any problems for the PCs who've joined since PACE who don't know policing without it. Tape recorders would have been unthinkable a few years ago, everyone would have been aghast, but now they're welcoming them because they can see the advantages of them. Complaints used to worry us sick; any of the older officers remember what an upsetting thing it was to get a complaint because they were rare. Nowadays young PCs just take them in their stride.

In some ways I'm pessimistic about how things are going. On the other hand, in many ways the service is coming out of the dark ages managerially and technologically. The first flush of Special Course graduates from the police college has produced some real successes who are flying high in many forces. And people are realizing through the trial and error of Policing by Objectives that there is more to policing than just arresting people. There are serious efforts made for career development. In my day, you joined and looked forward to thirty years as a PC, maybe aspiring to the CID or Traffic. Now there are fantastic opportunities for people with potential.

On the other hand, there's also a strong feeling in the ranks about the Thin Blue Line, being put under unfair pressure, especially by the government. Ever since the miners' strike and the prison officers' strike, whenever the tab has to be picked up by government, they put us in a position which many of us don't want to be in. They use us as strikebreakers instead of the civil law which is available to them.

One result of that has been the growing emphasis on public order training and technology. Even a few years ago it was rare to see a couple of officers together for very long except on a march or a demonstration. Now every force has its own elite response group, highly trained in firearms and aggressive tactics. There's a whole wing of police that now lives and breathes that style of policing.

It does affect the rest of police culture, even if we don't do it ourselves. The macho canteen culture was always there, long before the public order problems. But I wonder how much it's really there and how much people just feel they have to say those racist, sexist things. You know how hard it is to stand up and declare yourself religious, and yet many people profess a religious faith. I think it's just as hard to stand up and say "I abhor racism" in a van or canteen, but underneath they do.

But you have to say there are two types of bobbies, those that want to think and those that don't. Even for those that do, the pressure on them in the relief just to keep schtum and go along with the lads is probably just as big a restraint on new ideas as poor management.

You know, everyone always tells me how they remember being cuffed around the ear by their local bobby for stealing an apple, and how much they miss the good old days when that happened because there was always a local bobby around to keep everyone in line. Well, the streets of this city would be littered with apples, it would be a forest of trees, not just an orchard, for all the people that have said that to me. But I have never met a single bobby who remembers stopping someone for stealing an apple. Not one. So I tell the public that the good old days really never happened. There was no Dixon of Dock Green, they never had a local bobby on their street corner twenty-four hours a day. It's a myth that keeps them warm, I suppose. The truth is, the only way we could put a man on every street is to drown the country with coppers, and no one would like that. We do it from time to time in small areas for a short time, and then crime is affected by us. But the rest of the time it's out of the question. The trouble is, people would rather have their myth than know the truth.

RUC Sergeant, age 43, fourteen years service. Now in Belfast.

Obviously, when you get married and have children your priorities to a large extent are switched towards your family. That causes me a lot of concern, if I was dead and they were trying to soldier on. The children are now getting to an age where they watch the news and they are very apprehensive. They want to see me home at night, they're going about locking doors. They become themselves so very security conscious, though I try to shelter them from things as much as I can.

We moved from Portadown recently, where a lot of Loyalist fury has been spent on the police because of the parades issue and the Anglo-Irish Agreement. Policemen forced out of their homes, petrol bombs, that type of thing. My young fellow, he was nine at the time, he found it difficult to sleep, crying at night. He still does sometimes.

When some of the chaps from England refer to their problems, policing problems, public order, burglaries and such things, put in that perspective they seem to me to be rather light problems. I am not trying to make light of them, it just seems their worries aren't all that grave by comparison.

I joined before the troubles started in 1967. I don't think I would have been so keen to join if I had known that it would affect my life in so many ways.

MORAL

To conclude: these interviews are both true and false.

They reflect a true disillusionment shared by many officers, some of whom have left, some of whom are on the verge of leaving. Their departure is doubly sad for both the police service and for us. Not only does it mean the loss of their valuable experience and training, but also it renders the service ever more vulnerable to trouble from bad influences or, simple inexperience.

They are false in that there are many thousands of officers who remain committed to policing values despite their cynicism. In other words, although they feel these things very deeply, they go out each day and night and try to react to every situation as it requires them to. Their ability to do this is under threat from all the various strains that have been laid out in this book. It is dedicated to all those officers still willing to keep trying. But we must not take their willingness for granted as we do now.

R.G.

March 1989

Selected Reading and Reference

Books

Alderson, John *Law and Disorder* (Hamish Hamilton, 1984).

Benn, Melissa and Worpole, Ken *Death in the City* (Canary Press, 1986).

Benyon, John and Bourn, Colin *The Police: Powers, Procedures and Proprieties* (Pergamon Press, 1986).

Blair, Ian *Investigating Rape: A New Approach for the Police* (The Police Foundation/Croom Helm, 1985).

Brown, Andrew *Watching the Detectives* (Hodder & Stoughton, 1988).

Christian, Louise *Policing by Coercion: PACE* (GLC/Pluto Press 1988).

Geary, Roger *Policing Industrial Disputes: 1893 to 1985* (Cambridge University Press, 1985).

Hain, Peter (ed.) *Policing the Police* Vol. 2. (John Calder, 1980).

Hampton, William *Democracy and Community* (Oxford, 1970).

Holdaway, Simon *Inside the British Police: A force at Work* (Blackwell, 1983).

Judge, Tony *A Man Apart* (Barker, 1972).

Kettle, Martin *Uprising: the Police, the People, and the Riots in Britain's Cities* (Pan, 1987).

Kinsay, Lea, and Young, Jock *What Is to Be Done About Law and Order?* (Penguin, 1984).

Kinsey, Lea and Young, Jock *Losing the Fight Against Crime* (Basil Blackwell, 1986).

Knight, Stephen *The Brotherhood* (Grafton, 1984).

Mark, Robert *In the Office of Constable* (Collins, 1978).

McNee, David *McNee's Law* (Collins, 1983).

Punch, Maurice *Conduct Unbecoming: Police Deviance and Central* (Tavistock, 1985).

Reiner, Robert *The Blue-Coated Worker* (Cambridge University Press, 1978).

Reiner, Robert *The Politics of the Police* (Wheatsheaf, 1985).

Rhea, Nicholas *Constable Along the Lane* (Hale, 1986).

Small, Stephen *A Group of Young Black People* (Policy Studies Institute, 1983).

Smith, David, J., and Gray, Jeremy *Police and People in London: the PSI Report* (Policy Studies Institute, Gower 1985).

Stalker, John *Stalker* (Harrap, 1988).

Waddington, P. A. J. *Arming an Unarmed Police: Policy and Practice in the Metropolitan Police* (Police Foundation, 1988).

Weatheritt, Mollie *Innovations in Policing* (Police Foundation/Croom Helm, 1986).

Whitaker, Ben *The Police in Society* (Sinclair Browne, 1979).

Official Reports

Arrangements in England and Wales (Bath Social Policy Papers).

Benyon, John *A Tale of Failure: Race and Policing* (Centre for Research in Ethnic Relations, 1986).

Gifford, Lord *The Broadwater Farm Inquiry 1986.*

Manolias, Mary and Hyatt-Williams, Arthur *Post-Shooting Experiences in Firearms Officers* (JWP on Organizational Health and Welfare).

Morgan, Rod *Setting the PACE:* Police Community Consultation.

Oliver, Ian *The Metropolitan Police Approach to the Prosecution of Juvenile Offenders* (Peel Press, 1978).

Police Complaints Authority: Annual Reports: 1986/87/88 (Triannual Report, 1988).

The Principles of Policing and Guidance for Professional Behaviour (Metropolitan Police, 1985).

Race, Crime and Arrests (Home Office Research Study No.58).

Report of a Working Party on the Establishment of an Independent Element in the Procedure for Complaints Against the Police (HMSO Command 8193, 1981).

Reports of Her Majesty's Chief Inspector of Constabulary: 1981–87 (HMSO).

Reports of the Commissioner of Police of the Metropolis: 1981–88 (HMSO).

Royal Commission on Criminal Procedure 1981 (HMSO Command 8092).

Royal Commission on the Police 1962 (HMSO Command 1728).

RUC Chief Constable's Annual Report (1984–87).

The Scarman Report on the Causes of the Brixton Disorders 1981.

Sloan, Kenneth *Public Order and the Police* (Police Review).

Stress in the Public Sector (Health Education Authority).

Southgate, Peter *New Directions in Police Training* (Home Office/HMSO).

Waddington, P. A. J. *The Effects of the Police Manpower Depletion During the NUM Strike 1984–85* (Police Foundation, 1985).

Periodicals

Police (monthly, 1979–89) the Journal of the Police Federation.

Police Review (weekly 1979–89) An excellent synthesis of police thinking and news.

Policing (quarterly) Thoughtful analysis of policing issues.

Index